# THE EARLY MEDIEVAL MONASTIC SITE AT DACRE, CUMBRIA

Rachel M Newman, Christine Howard Davis, and Roger H Leech

With Contributions by
Marion Archibald, Cathy Brooks, Simone Bullion, Peter Hill, Ross Jellicoe, Mike McCarthy, Adrian Olivier, Patrick Ottaway, Adam Parsons, Elizabeth Pirie, Helen Quartermaine, and Dominic Tweddle

Illustrations by
Peter Lee, Adam Parsons, and Ken Robinson

2022

LANCASTER IMPRINTS 30

*Published by*
Oxford Archaeology North
Mill 3
Moor Lane Mills
Moor Lane
Lancaster
LA1 1QD
(*Phone:* 01524 541000)
(*website:* www.oxfordarchaeology.com)


*Distributed by*
Oxbow Books Ltd
10 Hythe Bridge Street
Oxford
OX1 2EW
(*Phone:* 01865 241249; *Fax:* 01865 794449)


*Printed by*
Print2Demand, 17 Burgess Road, Hastings, East Sussex, TN35 4NR

The appendices are available on the Oxford Archaeology (OA) Library at:
https://eprints.oxfordarchaeology.com/6183/

ISBN 978-1-907686-37-5
ISSN 345-5205

*Series editor*
Rachel Newman
*Indexer*
Marie Rowland
*Design, layout, and formatting*
Adam Parsons

Front cover:   *Detail of the 'lion' on the ninth-century Northumbrian cross fragment; gilded early medieval strap-end*

Rear Cover:   *Top: the northern churchyard under excavation; top left, an iron hinge for a chest; middle left, the drain in the southern churchyard; bottom left, the stylus from the drain*

LANCASTER IMPRINTS   Lancaster Imprints is the publication series of Oxford Archaeology North. The series covers work on major excavations and surveys of all periods undertaken by the organisation and associated bodies.

# Contents

# List of Illustrations

## Plates

### Tables

# Abbreviations

| | |
|---|---|
| HA | *Historia Abbatum* |
| HE | *Historia Ecclesiastica Gentis Anglorum* |
| HSC | *Historia Sancti Cuthberti* |
| VSC | *Vita Sancti Cuthberti* |

# Contributors

†Marion Archibald
formerly of the British Museum

Cathy Brooks
formerly of Carlisle Archaeological Unit

Simone Bullion
formerly of Lancaster University

†Peter Hill

Chris Howard-Davis
formerly Oxford Archaeology North

Ross Jellicoe
formerly of Lancaster University

Roger Leech
formerly of the Cumbria and Lancashire Archaeological Unit

Mike McCarthy
formerly of Carlisle Archaeological Unit

Rachel Newman
Oxford Archaeology North, Mill 3, Moor Lane Mills, Moor Lane, Lancaster LA1 1QD

Adrian Olivier
formerly of the Lancaster University Archaeological Unit

Patrick Ottaway
PJO Archaeology, 6 Riseborough House, Rawcliffe Lane, York, YO30 6NQ

Adam Parsons
Oxford Archaeology North, Mill 3, Moor Lane Mills, Moor Lane, Lancaster LA1 1QD
†Elizabeth Pirie

Helen Quartermaine
formerly of the Lancaster University Archaeological Unit

Dominic Tweddle
formerly of York Archaeological Trust

Andrew White
formerly of Lancaster City Museum

# Summary

St Andrew's Church, Dacre (NY 460 266), is one of those rare early medieval sites in being associated with a documentary reference verifying its existence and character. In the *Historia Ecclesiastica Gentis Anglorum*, completed in 731, the Venerable Bede records a miracle taking place in a monastery built by the River *'Dacore'* and taking its name from the same. There, a monk was cured of blindness by a miracle enacted by the hair of the dead St Cuthbert, which was clearly being stored at the site as a relic. The provenance of this information was also of the first order, as Bede had heard it from the Abbot of Dacre himself, one Thrydred. The site then disappears into the mists of time until the twelfth century, when William of Malmesbury claimed that at least part of the events surrounding the meeting in 927 between King Æthelstan, the first of the Wessex line to call himself *Rex Anglorum* (King of the English), and the kings of the nascent polity of the Scots, Welsh, and the Lords of Bamburgh, the rump of the once-great Northumbrian kingdom, took place at Dacre, where the son of Constantine, King of Scots, was baptised 'at the sacred font'. In the D recension of the *Anglo-Saxon Chronicle*, this is recorded as having taken place *aet Aemotum*, 'at the Eamont', the river that flows about a mile (1.6 km) to the east of Dacre, from Ullswater, past Penrith and the Roman fort of Brougham, before its confluence with the River Eden.

Physical evidence to support this provenance came from the finding of very high-quality early medieval sculptural fragments in and around the church in the nineteenth- and early twentieth centuries, one fragment of a cross-shaft of early ninth-century date being unusual in having human figures climbing amongst the vinescroll on the main face, as well as an exotic beast, a 'lion', amongst the foliage. This clearly forms part of the great tradition of Northumbrian stone sculpture. The other, slightly later, tenth-century slab, when found built into the east wall of the chancel of the medieval church in 1875, was thought to depict the events recorded by William of Malmesbury, and is thus called the Dacre Stone. The iconography, depicted in the Anglo-Scandinavian style of that period in Northumbria, has been reinterpreted as depicting not just Adam and Eve, with the apple tree and serpent, but also the sacrifice of Isaac, rather than the baptism of the king's son, but nevertheless, the sophistication of this is marked. In addition, a drain emerging from the southern boundary of the medieval churchyard was excavated in the 1920s, which was thought to be part of this early monastic site.

The opportunity to examine such an important site came in 1982, when permission was granted to build a house in the plot of land immediately to the west of the churchyard. It was also noticed that there were earthworks to the north and east of a modern northern extension to the churchyard, which seemed to have been affected by this. Excavations therefore took place in the Orchard to the west of the churchyard, and in the northern churchyard extension, the latter between 1982 and 1985, when the drain in the southern churchyard was also re-excavated.

The northern churchyard proved to be the site of an extensive early cemetery, containing over 200 graves, though the leached condition of the soils meant that bone survival was minimal. Many of these graves, however, contained iron chest fittings, of a type recognised at a growing number of Northumbrian burial sites of the seventh- to ninth centuries. These seemed to have been focused on something, presumably a church, to the south, on the approximate position of the medieval parish church. Unusually, there was clear evidence of a western boundary to this cemetery, beyond which were at least two buildings, one a rectangular post-built structure of a type increasingly associated with early medieval Northumbria. The other was more unusual, with an apparently rounded eastern end, the only part within the excavation. This was associated with two hearthstones, one a reused millstone, and a wealth of early medieval material, including pins, buckles, and strap-ends, spindle whorls, and loomweights, and vessel and window glass.

Early ditches were excavated in the south of the churchyard, and to the west, in the Orchard, which seemed to have been followed when the medieval churchyard was established. In the southern churchyard, this ditch was overlain by the substantial stone drain, first excavated in the 1920s, which proved to have been constructed of reused Roman stones, perhaps from a bridge or mill. This seemed to have served two foci to the north, and could be traced in the field to the south, curving in a south-easterly direction through further earthworks. In the Orchard, the primary ditch was also sealed by a stone structure, apparently the north-western corner of a building, now wholly and tantalisingly lost beneath the churchyard.

It is likely that the centre of monastic activity was within the medieval churchyard, as has been recorded at the monastic sites of Wearmouth and Jarrow in the North East, but whilst the monastery had clearly been established by 731, when the *Historia Ecclesiastica* was completed, there was no obvious evidence for when it ceased to exist. The datable artefacts fit well within an eighth- to ninth-century context, yet the Dacre Stone, with its sophisticated iconography, is clearly later than this *floruit*, seemingly of tenth-century date. The cemetery showed signs of erosion, in that the graves were shallow, as though it had fallen out of use before the medieval churchyard was established. This was seen physically in the form of a bank and ditch that had cut through the early cemetery, only some 6 m to the north of the medieval church, the bank sealing many of the shallow graves. Subsequently, in the earlier thirteenth century, a wall was constructed on the crest of the bank, and this stood as the northern churchyard boundary until about 1950.

A very similar stretch of wall in the Orchard to the west was probably part of the same feature. Built against its interior face was a small building, probably of thirteenth- or fourteenth-century date, which would explain the peculiar shape of the churchyard at that point. It is tempting to see this as connected with the church, perhaps to house the parish priest.

Perhaps ironically, the earthworks that led to the excavations in the northern churchyard did not prove to be early medieval in date, but were instead evidence of a medieval farmstead immediately beyond the churchyard, apparently accessed from a hollow-way, visible in the field to the east. This consisted of at least three buildings, all apparently of timber. That to the east was probably the domestic accommodation, as the south gable had been rebuilt to incorporate a fireplace, while that to the west was probably a barn, and the northernmost structure, with a stone floor and drain, was probably to house animals. This seems to have fallen out of use by the fifteenth century, when the village either shrank or moved to its present site to the west of the churchyard. Dacre then remained as it does today, a small village away from the main routeways, both ancient and modern, with an important hidden history of the part it played in the development of the modern country.

# Résumé

L'église St Andrew, Dacre (NY 460 266), est l'un de ces rares sites du début du Moyen Âge à être associé à une source documentaire attestant son existence et son caractère. Dans l'*Historia Ecclesiastica Gentis Anglorum*, achevée en 731, Bède le Vénérable rapporte qu'un miracle a eu lieu dans un monastère construit au bord de la rivière Dacre et dont il en prend le nom. Là, un moine aurait été guéri de la cécité grâce aux cheveux du défunt St Cuthbert, clairement conservés sur le site comme une relique. La source de cette information était également de première main, car Bède l'avait entendue de l'abbé de Dacre lui-même, un certain Thrydred. Le site disparaît ensuite dans la brume des temps jusqu'au XIIème siècle, lorsque Guillaume de Malmesbury affirme qu'une partie des événements entourant la rencontre en 927 entre le roi Æthelstan, premier de la lignée du Wessex à s'appeler *Rex Anglorum* (roi des Anglais), les rois des nations naissantes écossaise et galloise, et les seigneurs de Bamburgh, les restes du jadis puissant royaume de Northumbria, eu lieu à Dacre. A la suite de cette rencontre le fils de Constantin, roi d'Écosse, a été baptisé « dans les fonts baptismaux sacrés ». Dans la révision D des *Anglo-Saxon Chronicles*, cela est enregistré comme ayant eu lieu *aet Aemotum*, « à l'Eamont », la rivière qui coule à environ un mile (1,6 km) à l'est de Dacre, depuis Ullswater, passant par Penrith et le fort romain de Brougham, avant sa confluence avec la rivière Eden.

Les preuves physiques qui supportent cette source documentaire proviennent de la découverte au XIXème et début du XXème siècle dans et autour de l'église de fragments sculpturaux de très haute qualité du début du Moyen Âge. Parmi eux un insolite fragment de croix du début du IXème siècle, montrant des figures humaines grimpant parmi des branches de vigne sur la face principale, ainsi qu'une bête exotique, un « lion », dans le feuillage. Ce style fait clairement partie de la grande tradition de la sculpture sur pierre northumbrienne. Une autre sculpture, plus tardive, est une dalle du Xème siècle retrouvée en 1875 dans le mur est du chancel médiéval, a été interprété lors de sa découverte comme représentant les événements rapportés par Guillaume de Malmesbury, et est donc appelée la Pierre de Dacre. L'iconographie, du style anglo-scandinave de cette période en Northumbrie, a été réinterprétée comme non seulement Adam et Ève, avec le pommier et le serpent, mais aussi le sacrifice d'Isaac, plutôt que le baptême du fils du roi Constantin ; néanmoins, la sophistication du travail reste remarquée. Par ailleurs, un drain émergeant de la limite sud du cimetière médiéval a été fouillé dans les années 1920, faisant probablement partie du site monastique primitif.

L'occasion d'examiner un site aussi important se présente en 1982 lors de l'obtention d'un permis de construire d'une maison sur un terrain adjacent à l'ouest du cimetière. Il a également été noté que des terrassements au nord et à l'est de l'extension moderne nord du cimetière semblaient avoir été affecté par ce permis de construire. Des fouilles ont donc eu lieu dans le verger à l'ouest du cimetière et dans l'extension nord du cimetière, cette dernière entre 1982 et 1985, lorsque le drain dans le cimetière sud a été de nouveau fouillé.

Le cimetière nord s'est avéré être le site d'un vaste cimetière primitif contenant plus de 200 tombes, mais l'état perméable des sols signifiait que la survie des os était minime. Beaucoup de ces tombes, cependant, contenaient des ferrures de cercueil en fer d'un style en croissance dans les sites funéraires de Northumbrie aux VIIème/IXème siècles. Ces tombes semblent être concentré à un endroit précis, sans doute une église, au sud, sur la location approximative de l'église paroissiale médiévale. Etrangement, on retrouve des indices clairs d'une limite ouest à ce cimetière, au-delà de laquelle se trouvaient au moins deux bâtiments, dont une structure à poteaux rectangulaire d'un type de plus en plus associé à la Northumbrie du début du Moyen Âge. L'autre structure était plus inhabituelle, avec une seule extrémité faisant part de la fouille d'apparence semi-circulaire. Cette partie a été associé à deux foyers en pierre, dont l'un était une meule réutilisée, et une richesse de matériaux du début du Moyen Âge, y compris des épingles, des boucles et des extrémités de sangle, des verticilles de fuseau et des poids de métier à tisser, et des récipients en verre et des vitres de fenêtre.

Les premiers fossés ont été creusés au sud du cimetière et à l'ouest dans le verger, ces derniers semblent avoir succéder à l'établissement du cimetière médiéval. Dans le cimetière sud, ce fossé a été recouvert par l'imposant drain en pierre, fouillé pour la première fois dans les années 1920, et s'avère avoir été construit en pierres romaines, réutilisées peut-être à partir d'un pont ou d'un moulin. Ce drain semble se diviser en deux en direction du nord, et peut être suivi dans le champ au sud, courbant en direction du sud-est à travers d'autres terrassement. Dans le verger, le fossé primitif était également scellé par une structure en pierre : le coin nord-ouest d'un bâtiment maintenant entièrement perdu sous le cimetière.

Il est probable que le centre de l'activité monastique se trouvait dans le cimetière médiéval, semblable a ceux enregistré sur les sites de Wearmouth et de Jarrow dans le nord-est, mais alors que le monastère avait clairement été établi en 731, lorsque *l'Historia Ecclesiastica* a été achevée, il n'y avait aucune preuve flagrante du moment où il a cessé d'exister. Les artefacts datables s'inscrivent bien dans un contexte du VIII$^{ème}$ au IX$^{ème}$ siècle, mais la pierre de Dacre, avec son iconographie sophistiquée, est clairement postérieur, supposément du X$^{ème}$ siècle. Le cimetière montrait des signes d'érosion, en attestent les tombes peu profondes, comme s'il était tombé en désuétude avant la création du cimetière médiéval. Cela se manifeste par la présence d'un talus et d'un fossé traversant le cimetière primitif, à seulement 6 m au nord de l'église médiévale, le talus scellant de nombreuses tombes superficielles. Par la suite, au début du XIII$^{ème}$ siècle, un mur a été construit sur la crête du talus, marquant ainsi la limite nord du cimetière jusqu'en 1950 environ.

Un tronçon de mur très similaire à l'ouest dans le verger faisait probablement partie de la même structure. Un petit bâtiment était construit contre sa face intérieure, probablement du XIII$^{ème}$ ou XIV$^{ème}$ siècle, ce qui expliquerait la forme particulière du cimetière à cette période. Il est tentant de le voir lié à l'église, peut-être comme logement pour le curé de la paroisse.

Peut-être ironiquement, les travaux de terrassement qui ont conduit aux fouilles dans le cimetière nord ne se sont pas avérés être du début du Moyen Âge, mais marquaient plutôt la présence d'une ferme médiévale immédiatement au-delà du cimetière, sans doute accessible par un chemin creux, visible dans le champ à l'est. Cette ferme comprenait au moins trois bâtiments, tous apparemment en bois. Celui à l'est était probablement le logement domestique, car le pignon sud avait été reconstruit pour incorporer une cheminée, tandis que celui à l'ouest était probablement une grange, et la structure la plus septentrionale, avec un sol en pierre et un drain, servait probablement à abriter des animaux. Le complexe semble être tombé en désuétude au XV$^{ème}$ siècle, lorsque le village a rétréci ou s'est déplacé de son site actuel vers l'ouest du cimetière. Dacre est depuis resté comme aujourd'hui, un petit village à l'écart des routes principales, à la fois ancienne et moderne, avec une histoire cachée mais significative quant au rôle qu'elle a joué dans le développement du pays moderne.

# Zusammenfassung

Die St Andrews Kirche in Dacre (NY 460 266) ist einer dieser seltenen frühmittelalterlichen Fundplätze von denen wir auch schriftliche Kenntnisse aus mittelalterlichen Urkunden haben, welche ihren frühmittelalterlichen Bestand und Teil ihres Werdegangs bestätigen können. In Bedes *Historia Ecclesiastica Gentis Anglorum* aus dem Jahre AD731 wird zum Beispiel von einem Wunder berichtet das in einem Kloster geschah welches am Flusse ‚Dacre' lag und den gleichen Namen trug. In diesem Kloster wurde einer der Mönche mit Hilfe eines Haares des Heiligen Cuthbert von seiner Blindheit geheilt. Dieses Haar war ohne Frage ein Reliquies die zu dieser Zeit im Kloster von Dacre aufbewahrt wurde. Der Bericht über dieses Wunder kam aus erster Hand: Bede hatte die Neuigkeit vom Abt von Dacre – ein Mann namens Thrydred - selbst gehört. In den Jahren nach der Beschreibung dieses Wunders verschwinden Berichte über das Kloster von Dacre jedoch in den Nebeln der Zeit – bis ins 12. Jahrhundert, als William von Malmesbury von Ereignissen erzählt, die mit dem Zusammentreffen von König Æthelstan, dem ersten Herrscher des Hauses Wessex, der sich *Rex Anglorum* (König der Engländer) nannte, den damaligen Anführern der noch in der Entstehung begriffenen schottischen und walisischen Königreiche und den Lords von Bamburgh, den Überbleibseln des einst grossen Königreiches von Northumbria zusammenhingen. Das Treffen fand im Jahr AD927 statt und hatte die Taufe von Constantine, dem König der Schotten zum Anlass. Diese fand an der „Heiligen Quelle" statt. In der „D" Ausgabe der Angelsachsen-Chronik (*Anglo-Saxon Chronicles*) wird der genaue Ort als *aet Aemotum*, 'am Eamont', beschrieben. Der Eamont ist ein Fluß welcher etwa 1.6km östlich von Dacre verläuft und seine Quelle in Ullswater hat. Er fließt an Penrith und dem römischen Kastell Brougham vorbei bevor er in den Eden mündet.

Archäologisch läßt sich die Existenz eines solchen Klosters in Form von frühmittelalterlichen Steinsculpturfragmenten nachweisen. Die Steinmetzarbeiten sind figürlich von extrem hoher Qualität und wurden in und um die moderne Kirche im 19. und frühen 20. Jahrhundert gefunden. Eines dieser Fragmente ist sehr ungewöhnlich: die auf dem Querbalken eines Steinkreuzes dargestellten menschlichen Figuren klettern aufwärts um eine Weinranke. Teil dieser Darstellung ist außerdem eine fremdländisch aussehende Kreatur, vielleicht ein „Löwe". Es steht ausser Frage dass die auf diesem Fragment ausgeführte Arbeit aus der langen Tradition Northumbrischer Steinmetzarbeiten stammt. Die andere Skulptur kann in einen etwas späteren Zeitraum datiert werden (10. Jahrhundert). Diese wurde 1875 in der Ostmauer des Altarraums der mittelalterlichen Kirche entdeckt. Zu jener Zeit wurde angenommen, dass die Darstellung auf diesem Stein figürlich darstellt, was William von Malmesbury beschrieben hatte: deshalb wurde diese Skulpur als „der Stein von Dacre", Dacre Stone, bekannt. Die Ikonographie, die  im damaligen anglo-skandinavischen Stil Northumbrias in den Stein gehauen wurde, konnte neu interpretiert werden: danach ist das Motiv nicht nur Adam und Eva, der Baum der Erkenntnis und die Schlange, sondern auch das Opfer Isaaks. Diese Interpretation ist wahrscheinlicher als die der Taufe des Königssohns und das hohe Niveau der Steinmetzarbeit steht außer Frage. Außerdem wurden in den 1920er Jahren bei der Grabung eines Ablaufes oder einer Ablaßleitung, welche am südlichen Ende des mittelalterlichen Kirchgrunds stadtfand, mögliche Fundamente des frühmittelalterlichen Klosters gefunden.

Die Gelegenheit, diese wichtige frühmittelalterliche Fundstelle genauer zu untersuchen hatten wir 1981, als das Bauamt die Erlaubnis für den Bau eines Hauses erteilte, das direkt an der westlichen Grenze des Kirchhofs gebaut werden sollte. Bei der anfänglichen Baubegleitung wurden als Erdwälle oder Schanzen gedeutete Befunde nördlich und östlich der modernen Erweiterung des Kirchhofs festgestellt. Aus diesem Grunde wurden Grabungen in einem Obstgarten westlich des Kirchhofs und in der nördlichen Erweiterung des Hofs durchgeführt. Die letztere fand zwischen 1982-1985 statt, zeitgleich mit einer weiteren Untersuchung des Ablaufs/der Ablaßleitung im südlichen Teil des Kirchhofs.

Auf der nördlichen Seite des Kirchhofs befand sich einst ein großflächig angelegter frühmittelalterlicher Friedhof mit über 200 Gräbern. Leider konnten im ausgelaugten Boden keine Knochen und Skelettreste überdauern und die Knochenfunde sind extrem begrenzt. Eine große Anzahl der Gräber enthielten jedoch eiserne Kisten- oder Sargbeschläge von einem Typ, den man heute vermehrt in Northumbrischen Friedhöfen des 7.-9.Jahrhunderts findet. Alle Gräber folgten einer bestimmten Ausrichtung, vermutlich nach der Kirche, die sich südlich, an etwa der gleichen Stelle wie die spätere mittelalterlichen Kirche befand. Ungewöhnlicherweise gab es klare Hinweise auf die westliche Grenze des Friedhofes; jenseits dieser Grenze können wenigstens zwei Gebäude vermutet werden: eines davon ist ein rechteckiger Pfostenbau, gebaut in einer Art, die immer mehr mit frühmittelalterlicher Northumbrischer Bauweise in Verbindung gebracht wird. Der andere Bau war ungewöhnlicher, mit wenigstens einer offensichtlich abgerundeten Seite – leider die einzige Seite, die der Grabungsschnitt miteinschloß. Die Befunde innerhalb der Gebäude waren unter anderem zwei Herde und einen wiederverwendeten Mühlstein; des Weiteren förderte die Grabung eine große Anzahl von frühmittelalterlichen Funden zu Tage, z. B. Gewandnadeln, Gürtelschließen und –beschäge, Spinnwirtel, Webgewichte, Glasgefäße und Fensterglas.

In den frühen Zeitraum datierende Gräben konnten sowohl im südlichen Teil des Kirchhofs als auch im Westen, im Obstgarten, gesichert werden; beim letzteren Befund zeigt die Lage der Gräben deutlich dass sich die Anlage des mittelalterlichen Kirchhofs nach ihnen gerichtet hatte. Im südlichen Kirchhof wurde der Graben von einem nicht unbeträchtlichen Steinablauf überlagert welcher bereits in den 1920s gegraben worden war. Für diesen Ablauf wurde Stein aus einem ehemals römischen Mauerwerk genommen: der Stein wurde vermutlich von einer benachbarten Mühle oder Brücke abgetragen und hier wiederverwendet. Der Entwässerungsablauf selbst schien mit zwei Fundstellen im Norden zusammenzuhängen und sein Verlauf konnte bis in ein Feld südlich des Kirchhofs weiterverfolgt werden. Hier wandte sich sein Verlauf nach Südosten durch weitere Erdwälle hindurch. Im Obstgarten war der erstmalige Graben durch einen Bau aus Stein versiegelt, vermutlich die nordwestliche Ecke eines Gebäudes dessen Fundamente heute leider fast vollkommen und unerreichbar unter dem Kirchhof verborgen sind.

Es ist sehr wahrscheinlich dass der Mittelpunkt des Klosterlebens sich im mittelalterlichen Kirchhof abspielte, so, wie wir es auch von anderen frühmittelalterlichen Klostern kennen, z.B. Wearmouth and Jarrow. Auch hier haben wir mittelalterliche Urkunden und Schriften die bestätigen dass das Kloster AD731 gegründet wurde (als die *Historia Ecclesiastica* fertiggestellt wurde), aber wir haben keinerlei Hinweise auf seinen Niedergang oder seine Auflösung. Die Funde aus Dacre datieren alle in das 8. und 9. Jahrhundert, aber der „Stein von Dacre" mit seiner komplexen Ikonographie und eleganter Ausührung ist ganz offensichtlich ein späteres Stück aus dem 10. Jahrhundert. Der Friedhof zeigt deutlich Anzeichen von Erosion; keines der Gräber hatte mehr seine ursprüngliche Tiefe und es kann angenommen werden, dass der Friedhof nicht mehr in Benutzung war als der mittelalterliche Kirchhof eingezäunt wurde. Dies konnte durch Befunde bestätigt werden: eine Wall-und-Graben-Anlage durchzogen den frühmittelalterlichen Friedhof, ca. 6m nördlich der mittelalterlichen Kirche, mit dem Wall direkt über einer Anzahl der flachen Gräber angelegt. Einige Jahre später, im frühen 13. Jahrhundert, wurde eine Mauer auf dem Wall gebaut und diese Wall-und-Mauer-Anlage diente als nördliche Grenze des Kirchhofs bis ca. 1950.

Ein ähnlicher Wall im Obstgarten westlich des Kirchhofs war höchstwahrscheinlich Teil derselben Anlage. Direkt an ihrer Innenseite hatte man – vermutlich im 13. oder 14. Jahrhundert – ein kleines Gebäude errichtet, welches die eigenartige Krümmung der Kirchhofsgrenze an dieser Stelle erklären würde. Es liegt nahe, dass dieses Gebäude eine enge Verbindung mit der Kirche hatte – vielleicht war es das Wohnhaus des Gemeindepfarrers.

Ironischerweise waren die Schanzen, welche letztendlich zu den Grabungen im nördlichen Teil des Kirchhofs führten gar keine frühmittelalterlichen Erdwälle. Stattdessen handelte es sich hier um die Grenzen eines mittelalterlichen Gehöftes, welches direkt an den Kirchhof grenzte. Dieser Hof konnte offenbar über einen Hohlweg erreicht werden, welchen man heute noch in einem Feld östlich des damaligen Hofes sehen kann. Der Hof bestand aus mindestens drei Holzbauten. Das östlichste war vermutlich das Bauernhaus mit Schlaf- und Kochstellen; der Umbau des Südgiebels schloß eine Feuerstelle mit ein. Das westliche Gebäude war vermutlich eine Scheue und der Bau im Nordosten, mit einem Steinfußboden und Abflüssen, diente vermutlich als Stall. Der Hof hatte bis in das 15. Jahrhundert Bestand: entweder schrumpfte die Einwohner- und Gebäudezahl danach oder der Dorfkern wurde an seine heutige Stelle westlich des Kirchhofes verlegt. Danach verblieb Dacre genau wie wir es heute vorfinden: ein kleines Dorf, abgelegen von alten sowie als auch neuen Hauptstrassen, aber mit einer ungeahnt wichtigen, gut verstecken Geschichte von Dacres bedeutender Rolle in der Entstehung unseres modernen Staates.

# Acknowledgements

The excavations at Dacre were undertaken by the Cumbria and Lancashire Archaeological Unit, now Oxford Archaeology North. Dr R H Leech initiated the project and directed the excavations of 1982 and 1983, the 1984 and 1985 seasons and the subsequent post-excavation programme being directed by Rachel Newman. The genesis of this volume has been long and complicated, with many longeurs, but throughout members of the Parochial Church Council have kept faith and continued to treasure this important site of Christian worship. The work has, from the start, been largely funded by Historic England, in the form of, firstly, the Department of the Environment, then English Heritage, with grants also from the Lake District Special Planning Board (now the Lake District National Park Authority), the British Academy, the Society of Antiquaries of London, and the Cumberland and Westmorland Antiquarian and Archaeological Society.

First and foremost, the authors are indebted to Helen Quartermaine, who acted as Finds Supervisor during the 1984 and 1985 excavations and subsequently undertook a large amount of the post-excavation processing, compilation of the full excavation archive, and much of the in-house finds work; also to Christine Howard-Davis, whose editorial control over , and updating of, the finds reports is much valued, as was her advice, support, and information on the finds in general; to John Williams, Director of the organisation from 1984 to 1989, and to Adrian Olivier, for his constant support throughout the project. Especial thanks are due to Philip Howard, Louise Hird, Michael McCarthy, and Cathy Brooks, Andrew White, the late Elizabeth Pirie, Marion Archibald, Dominic Tweddle, Patrick Ottaway, the late Henry Cleere, the late Peter Hill, Ross Jellicoe, Simone Bullion, and James Rackham, and Louisa Gidney, for writing the specialist reports, and to John Hunter of Bradford University, Trevor Cowie of the National Museum of Antiquities, Edinburgh, and Lesley Webster of the British Museum for commenting on individual pieces of pre-Conquest glass. We also thank Jenny Jones, Vanessa Fell, and G Smythe for the X-raying and conserving of finds. Peter Lee deserves particular gratitude for his skilful publication drawings, as does Ken Robinson, who drew the location maps and also produced most of the archive drawings. Adam Parsons has drawn all these together and selected and made them suitable for publication in the twenty-first century. John Williams gave constantly good advice on the layout of this report and also commented on early drafts with great dedication; we are also most grateful to Rosemary Cramp and Angus Winchester, with whom aspects of the site were discussed and who read elements of the text in detail. In addition, we thank Professor Cramp for giving unreserved permission to use images from *The British Academy Corpus of Anglo-Saxon Stone Sculpture: 2, Cumberland, Westmorland, and Lancashire-North-of-the-Sands* (1988).

Mention must be made of all those who took part in the excavations, as site workers, university trainees, and volunteers, especially the late Alan James, and special credit is due to Martin Brann, Robert Middleton, Piet Aldridge, Victoria Brandon, and Heather Dawson, who acted as Site Supervisors, and particularly to Pamela Leech, who was Finds Supervisor in 1982 and 1983. Ken Robinson, in 1983, and Malcolm Harrison, in 1984 and 1985, were responsible for the machine removal of material and subsequent backfilling.

For Historic England and its earlier incarnations, Bill Startin instigated the project, when Inspector for the area, and his successors as inspectors, David Fraser, Gerry Friell, and Andrew Davison, continued to support the project through its long gestation; particular thanks are owed to the late Geoff Wainwright, who supported the project during his time as Chief Archaeologist. Barney Sloane is especially thanked for unlocking funding for the final phase of the project to bring it to fruition, and Tony Wilmott, Mark Bowden, and Helen Keeley provided advice and quality assurance during the post-excavation programme, the latter in particular being thanked for her support.

Thanks are due to Mr and Mrs William Petty, the owners of the Orchard (Site 1), to the Chancellor of the Diocese of Carlisle, for granting the faculties allowing the excavation of consecrated ground, the Churchwardens for much practical help, the Parochial Church Council, and, Peter Wood, for his help and support, and most particularly, the then Vicar of Dacre, the late Reverend Kenneth H Smith, and his family, for their constant support, enthusiasm, and immense kindness. The Lake District Special Planning Board, through Andrew Lowe, offered both financial and also much practical support. The residents of the village and parish of Dacre showed great patience, when confronted by the mountainous spoil-heap and the correspondingly large hole in their churchyard, and thanks should be offered to them and to the late Colonel and Mrs P Baily for providing accommodation. Finally, we would like to express our warmest thanks and gratitude to the late Mr and Dr E H A Stretton of Dacre Castle, for their unfailing help, hospitality, kindness, and enthusiasm towards both the excavation and the excavators throughout the project, without whom the whole experience would not have been nearly so pleasurable.

*Figure 1: Site Location*

# 1

# INTRODUCTION

It has generally been presumed by scholars in the last 200 years that the church of St Andrew, Dacre (NY 460 266), near Penrith in Cumbria (Fig 1), lies above the site of an early medieval monastery (*eg* Collingwood 1912; *p 10*). The opportunity to test this hypothesis with modern archaeological techniques arose in 1981, when permission was granted to build a house on the vacant orchard site immediately to the west of the present churchyard. During a visit to the site in May 1981, earthworks were identified in the field to the north and east of a modern churchyard extension north of the church, which clearly curtailed these earthworks. No reference to them could be found on nineteenth-century maps, the earliest dating to at least 1808 (CA Q/RE/1/46), which implied that they represented features of at least eighteenth-century date, but probably earlier.

Burial in the churchyard extension had begun at the west in the early 1950s and, by 1981, had advanced to a line approximately parallel to the western end of the church, clearly threatening archaeological deposits connected with the earthworks. Accordingly, following the granting of a faculty by the Chancellor of the Diocese of Carlisle, an initial season of trial excavations was carried out in 1982 to evaluate the potential of both the Orchard and the northern churchyard extension for further archaeological work. This and all subsequent seasons were funded mainly by English Heritage (formerly the Department of the Environment; now Historic England), with grants also from the Lake District Special Planning Board (now the Lake District National Park Authority), the British Academy, and the Cumberland and Westmorland Antiquarian and Archaeological Society.

In 1985, a large stone-lined drain in a southern extension to the churchyard (*p 16*; Pl 1) was relocated and excavated (Site 3), to discover whether it belonged to a period of similar date to the features in the northern churchyard (Site 2). This work was funded by grants from the Society of Antiquaries of London, the Lake District Special Planning Board (now the Lake District National Park Authority),

and the Cumberland and Westmorland Antiquarian and Archaeological Society.

## Archaeological and Historical Background

### Location
The village of Dacre is situated some four miles (6.4 km) to the south-west of Penrith, mainly on a terrace on the steep northern side of the valley of the

DACRE CHURCHYARD, CUMBERLAND, August, 1929.

*Plate 1: The drain excavated in the 1920s in the southern churchyard*

1

*Figure 2: Dacre village (Map data © Google, Getmapping plc, Infoterra Ltd, and Bluesky Maxar Technologies, 2020)*

Dacre Beck (Fig 2). It lies within a triangular block of land, created by the River Eamont and Ullswater to the east and south, and the A66 to the north, at the very north-eastern corner of the Lake District, historically the south-east edge of Cumberland. This is close to an historically important crossroads, where what is today the A66, the road from the North East over Stainmore, then on to Keswick, crosses what is now the A6, the main north-south route to the west of the Pennines. The A66 still follows the high land to the north of the valley. The church of St Andrew stands at the north-eastern edge of the village, in what is now a cul-de-sac, but footpaths linking it to the neighbouring settlements of Stainton and Aldby indicate that it was once on a through route.

The northern side of the valley of the Dacre Beck is formed by sandstone of the Skiddaw Group, intercalated with conglomerates of the Mell Fell group (Fig 3), formed approximately 400 million years ago (BGS 2019). These are overlain by thick deposits of Quaternary Till, boulder clay, and alluvial sands and gravels, formed up to two million years ago (Jarvis *et al* 1984; BGS 2019). This stony mixed subsoil made the excavation of the lower archaeological levels of the site difficult, as the undisturbed subsoil changed abruptly horizontally and was vertically layered, so that it was frequently hard to tell where the disturbed, archaeological, levels ceased and the undisturbed subsoil began.

Little is known of the origins of the settlement at Dacre. There are numerous antiquarian reports of the finding of cist burials in the area (*eg* Collingwood 1923; 1926), and two major henges, Mayburgh and King Arthur's Round Table (Dymond 1891; Burl 1976), lie some five miles (8 km) to the east. These are thought to have been major meeting places in the Neolithic period and Bronze Age. Small hillforts, such as that at Dunmallard to the south-east (Clifton Ward 1878, 248), are, however, rare in the vicinity (Hoaen and Loney 2004). Several major Roman roads bisected the area and it seems clear that at least the trans-Pennine road across Stainmore (Road 82, Margary 1957, 434-5; the line of which is largely followed by the present A66, although not in the section immediately to the north of Dacre) was an important routeway before the Romans utilised it. The nearest identified Roman settlements, both forts, were on the trans-Pennine road, at Troutbeck to the west and Brougham to the east (Shotter 2004), but virtually nothing is known of rural civilian settlement in this part of Cumbria during the period.

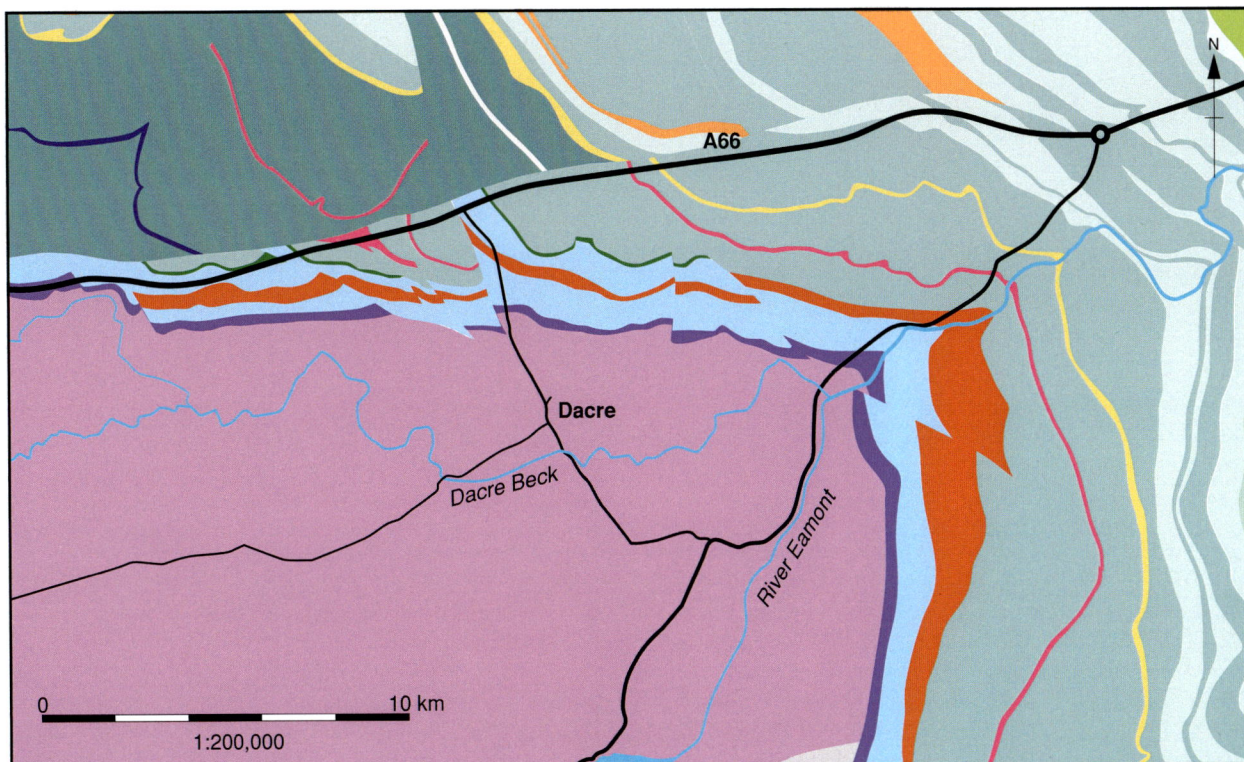

Great limestone member
Limestone member
Alston formation- mudstone, siltstone, and sandstone
Wintertarn sandstone member
Village limestone formation

Limestone member
Ashfell limestone formation- mudstone
Stainmore formation
Ashfell sandstone
Knipe Scar limestone formation

Mell Fell conglomerate
Marsett sandstone
Shale member
Fourth shale member
Birker Fell Andesite

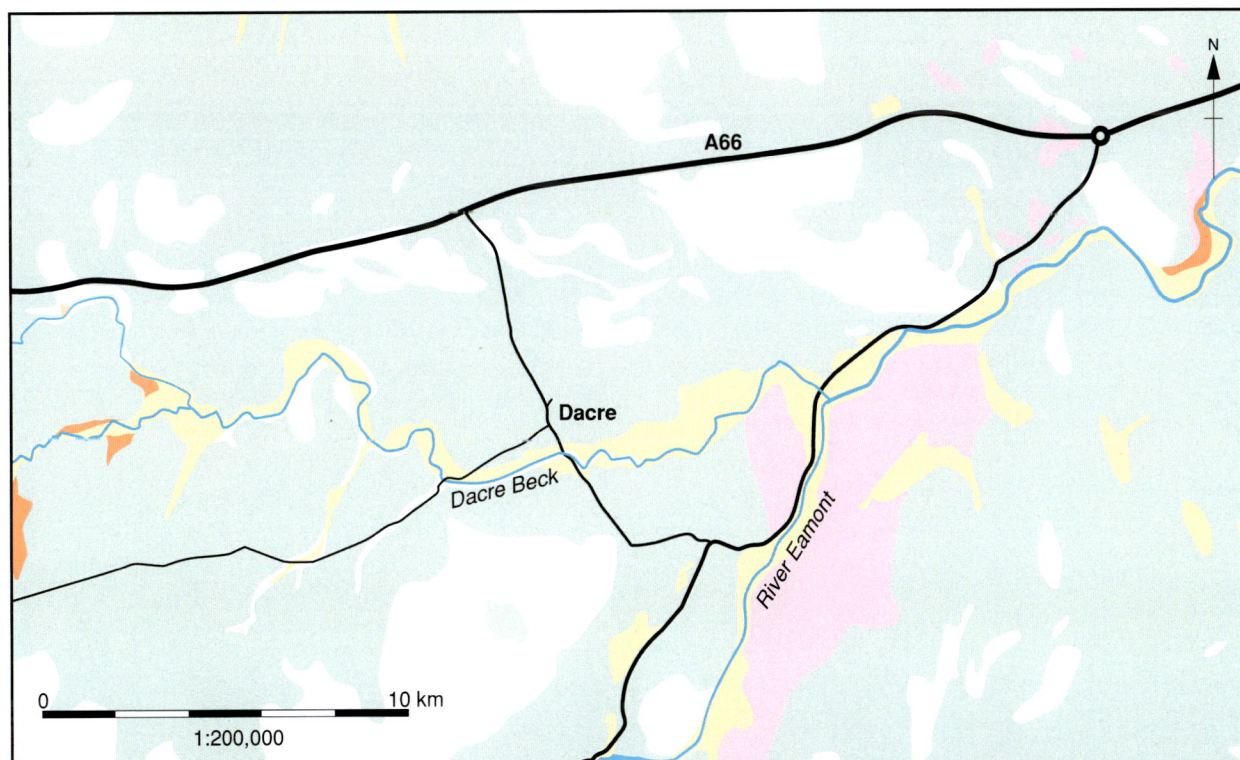

Till, Devensian
Alluvium, clay, silt, sand, and gravel
Glaciofluvial deposits, Devensian- sand and gravel
River terrace deposits

*Figure 3: The solid and superficial geology of Dacre and the surrounding area*

3

## The early medieval period in the north

The time between the ending of Roman rule in Britain at the beginning of the fifth century and the Norman Conquest, in 1092 in northern Cumbria (Swanton 2000), was a period during which massive social and cultural changes took place. Once known as 'the Dark Ages', it is now seen as vibrant, when cultural exchange with the Mediterranean world was re-established and the first great works of literature were written in Old English (Whitelock 1974, 206) and Old Welsh (Skene 1868). It was also a time of change politically, when the seemingly monolithic Roman Empire was divided and elements seceded, to be replaced by small, highly volatile, territorial units, which then increasingly merged into larger kingdoms, such as the Anglian kingdom of Northumbria (Fig 4), in the seventh century (Rollason 2003; terminology following Bede).

There does not seem to have been an immediate or sudden collapse, however, since there is a growing body of evidence that, at least in Romanised settlements, such as the frontier forts (*eg* Wilmott 1997), or towns such as Carlisle (Newman 2011), the 'Roman' way of life continued into the fifth century, and perhaps a little beyond. This accords well with the few documentary sources about the period, such as the writings of St Patrick, which make it clear that he came from a Romanised lifestyle somewhere in the west of Britain (Bieler 1952; the area of the Severn estuary has been suggested, but arguments have also been made for Carlisle and the Hadrian's Wall hinterland; Thomas 1981).

By the sixth century, the few textual sources would suggest rapid change, with ruling families enjoying short-lived successes, resulting in constantly shifting political boundaries (Charles-Edwards 2013; Rollason 2003). To the west of the Pennines, the kingdom most frequently mentioned in these sources was known as Rheged, the golden age of which was, according to medieval Welsh literature, in the late sixth century during the reign of Urien (Williams 1968; Pennar 1988; Kirby 1962, 79-80). Exactly how far its remit ran is, however, a matter for debate (McCarthy 2002), although its heartland has often been equated with the lands around the Solway Firth, perhaps centred on the *civitas Carvetiorum* at Carlisle (Higham 1986). The death of Urien in 593 at the siege of Bamburgh seems to have led to the kingdom's decline, although there continued to be references to other members of the royal family into the seventh century (Higham 1993, 99).

Information about the origins and growth of the kingdom of Northumbria is heavily dependent on the works of the Venerable Bede, a monk at the renowned monastery of Jarrow, near the mouth of

*Figure 4: Northumbria and the early kingdoms of Britain*

the Tyne (Colgrave and Mynors 1969). He seems to have been born in the early 670s and was placed in the sister monastery of Monkwearmouth as a child, before moving to Jarrow at its consecration in 685, where he remained for the rest of his life, dying in 735 (*ibid*). He therefore lived through much of the period he writes about, or knew people who had witnessed the great events of the time. His great work, the *Historia Ecclesiatica Gentis Anglorum* (*ibid*) was written in the early eighth century, and is frequently referred to as the first great historical work about the English (*eg* Ifor Evans 1940), although its purpose is exactly what its title tells us it is: a history of the conversion to Christianity of the English people, specifically the Northumbrians. His influence lived on after him, although the level of information about Northumbria from the later eighth century onwards plummets, as much because the sources do not survive, rather than that they were never written (Rollason 2003).

The Anglian polities that became Northumbria seem to have come into existence by the later sixth century, although there is evidence for British antecedents (*ibid*). These were Deira, to the south of the River Tees, and Bernicia to the north, which came together under a single over-king in the early seventh century to form Northumbria. The ruling dynasty switched between those of Deira and Bernicia, although the kingship was held by the Idings of Bernicia from the 630s to the end of the century (*ibid*). Whilst the ethnic mix of these kingdoms is a matter for debate (Higham 1992a), over time the culture became Anglian, with Old English being the language of the rulers, still visible in the number of place-names of Old English derivation (*eg* Armstrong *et al* 1950).

Northumbria was territorially aggressive from the beginning, quickly extending its power across what is now the north of England and southern Scotland. Under the leadership of Æthelfrith (592-616), who was remembered as a tyrant as late as the early eighth century (Charles-Edwards 2003, 36), the kingdom expanded at the expense of British peoples to the north, west, and south-west, although its earlier aggression may be indicated by the Battle of Arthuret in 573 (Miller 1975). This aggression culminated in victory at the Battle of Chester (variously dated 605/6, 613 in early sources, but often cited as 615/16; see Lewis and Thacker 2003), signalling this extension west of the Pennines, and it is perhaps notable that the Mersey, the traditional southern boundary of Northumbria, can be translated as 'boundary river' (Higham 1992b, 21).

At its height, Northumbria seems to have consisted of most of lowland Scotland, excepting only the lands of the British kingdom of *Alt Clud*, and all of what is now northern England. According to Bede (Colgrave and Mynors 1969, bk 2, ch 5), the three great kings who came after Æthelfrith, Edwin, Oswald, and Oswiu, ruled 'over the inhabitants of Britain, English and Britons alike, except for Kent only'. He also mentions activity in the Isle of Man and Ireland (*op cit*, bk 4, ch 26).

Exactly when the area now known as Cumbria was incorporated into Northumbria is unclear, although it could have been as part of this westwards campaign. It is, however, also possible that the control was established through more peaceful means, as, according to the *Historia Brittonum*, traditionally attributed to Nennius (Giles 1848), a marriage took place between one Rieinmellt, a daughter of the house of Rheged, to Oswiu, a younger son of Æthelfrith (Rollason 2003, 88). If this were true, then she had been replaced by a daughter of the Deiran royal family by the time that Oswiu became king in 642, although there is some evidence to suggest that he had produced children before this latter union (*ibid*).

Northumbria in the mid-seventh century, as recorded by Bede, was enjoying a Golden Age.

Relative stability politically, and the Christian values by then espoused, led to a flowering of culture, witnessed by the number of illustrated manuscripts, many still surviving, that originated in the scriptoria of renowned monasteries such as Lindisfarne, and Wearmouth and Jarrow. The corpus of the stone sculpture that has been found in association with church sites across the north of England is perhaps the most visible product of this (*eg* Cramp 1984; Bailey and Cramp 1988; Lang 2002; Bailey 2010).

It seems that this apparent stability decayed in the eighth century, although to what extent this has been accentuated by the record being maintained only by terse annalistic entries following the death of Bede in 735 is a matter of debate (Rollason 2003, 197). These annals seem to indicate growing political instability and factionalism, reaching a peak in the mid-ninth century, with rival kings vying with each other for dominance (*op cit*, 9; Ferguson 2010, 135; Earle and Plummer 1892). In addition, the increasingly intense pressure that Northumbria was put under by Viking incursions from the end of the eighth century (Fig 5) eventually led to its collapse at the hands of the 'Great Heathen Host' of 865/6, which took York and killed the rival claimants to the throne, installing a puppet of its own (Roesdahl 1991, 234-7). This incursion was different from what had gone before, as it seems the aim was conquest, rather than raiding (Downham 2007). During this period, the kingdoms of East Anglia and Mercia were also effectively destroyed (Rollason 2003, 212, 235).

In 874, after the Host had over-wintered at Repton, it split, and a faction under Halfdan moved north into Northumbria. The other element, under Guthrum, turned southwards to attack Wessex (Earle and Plummer 1892), the one remaining kingdom of the Anglo-Saxon heptarchy (Roesdahl 1991). Halfdan's host over-wintered on the Tyne in 875, before 'subduing' the land, and in 876, he 'divided the lands of the Northumbrians' (Earle and Plummer 1892, A recension (the Parker Chronicle)) amongst his followers. His death, in 877 in Ireland, led to a diminution of Viking power and influence, to the extent that a small Anglian polity seems to have been established by the end of the ninth century, seemingly centred on Bamburgh (Rollason 2003, 213). There is evidence of the settlement in the Wirral of Vikings expelled from Dublin in 902 (Edmonds 2009), and it is likely that there would have been some relocation after the last Viking king of York was killed in 954 (Swanton 2000; Downham 2007, 121-2, 182).

The reaction to the near collapse of the Anglo-Saxon kingdoms under the onslaught of the Great Heathen Host culminated in the development of the kingdom

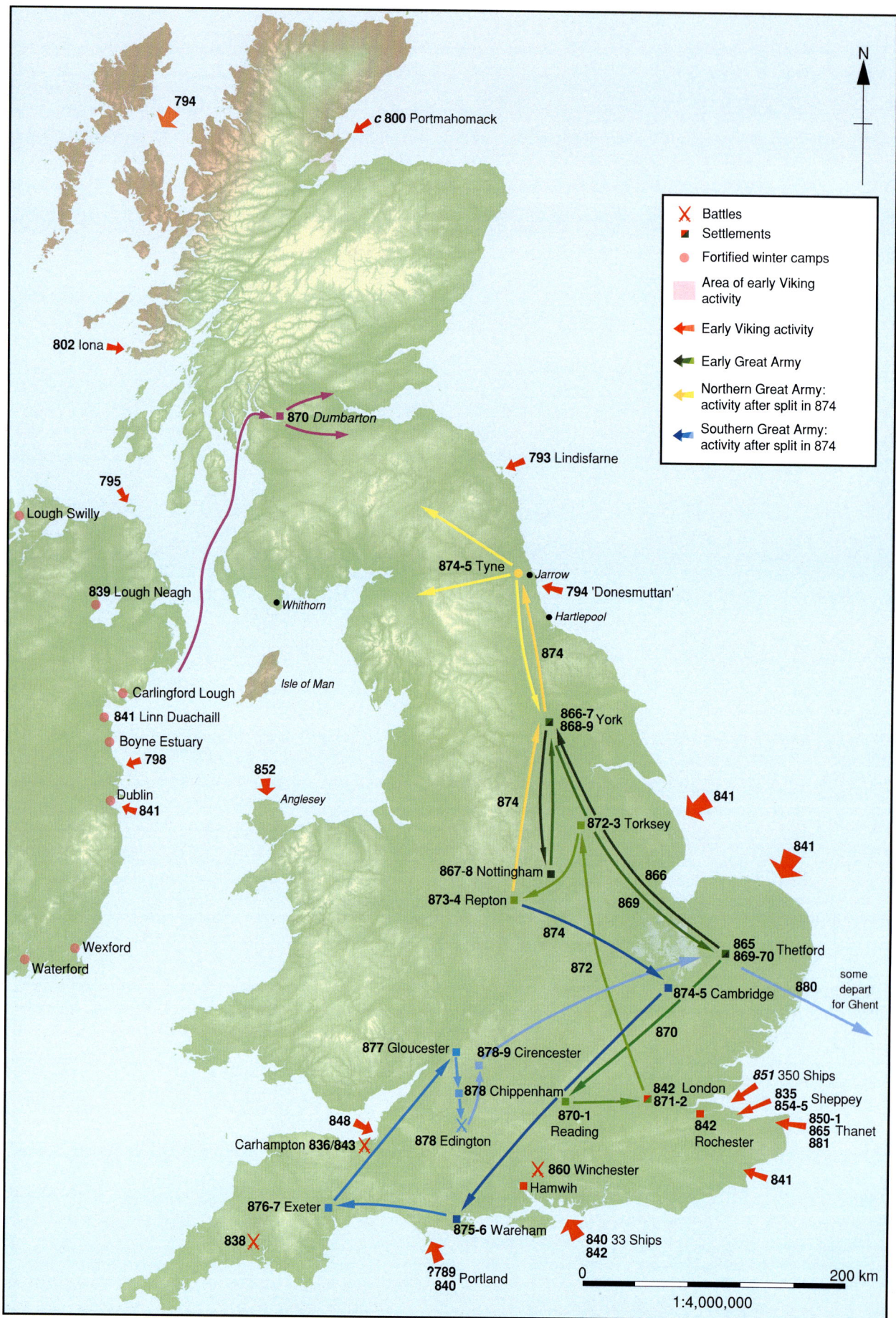

## Legend

X Battles
■ Settlements
● Fortified winter camps
Area of early Viking activity
→ Early Viking activity
→ Early Great Army
→ Northern Great Army: activity after split in 874
→ Southern Great Army: activity after split in 874

## Map labels

794
*c* 800 Portmahomack
793 Lindisfarne
802 Iona
795
870 *Dumbarton*
839 Lough Neagh
*Whithorn*
874-5 Tyne
*Jarrow*
794 'Donesmuttan'
*Hartlepool*
874
Carlingford Lough
841 Linn Duachaill
*Isle of Man*
866-7 York
868-9
Boyne Estuary
798
852
*Anglesey*
874
841
Dublin
841
841
872-3 Torksey
867-8 Nottingham
866
873-4 Repton
869
Wexford
Waterford
874
865 Thetford
869-70
872
some depart for Ghent
874-5 Cambridge
880
877 Gloucester
878-9 Cirencester
870
878 Chippenham
*851* 350 Ships
842 London
835 Sheppey
848
871-2
854-5
Carhampton 836/843 X
878 Edington
870-1 Reading
842 Rochester
850-1
865 Thanet
881
X 860 Winchester
841
876-7 Exeter
Hamwih
838 X
875-6 Wareham
840 33 Ships
842
?789 Portland
840
0                    200 km
1:4,000,000

*Figure 5: Britain and eastern Ireland in the ninth century*

of England as a unified political unit by the end of the tenth century (Stafford 1989; Ferguson 2010, 216-17). Alfred of Wessex defeated Guthrum at the decisive battle at Edington in 878, and took London in 883, leading shortly after to the establishment in the Midlands of what was later known as the Danelaw (Roesdahl 1991, 237). He had also established *burhs*, fortified proto-towns, throughout the south of England as a response to the threat created by the Host's presence, enabling close control, administration, and defence of the surrounding countryside (Williams 2008, 199). This policy was extended northwards by his son and successor, Edward the Elder, and his daughter, Æthelflaed, Lady of the Mercians, in the first two decades of the tenth century, as their armies gradually won back control of the Midlands (Rollason 2003, 257-8), with a *burh* being established in Chester in *c* 907 (Carrington 1994). It has also been suggested that the borough at Penwortham, on the river Ribble near Preston in Lancashire, named as such in Domesday Book (Morgan 1978), was also founded around this time, as a bulwark against Viking activity using the Ribble as a routeway to York (Higham 2004).

This policy of expansion was continued by Edward's son and successor, Æthelstan, who engaged increasingly directly with the Viking Kingdom of York (Rollason 2003, 265). It seems that, though he removed the king in York in 927, the Vikings continued to pose a sufficient threat for the northern and western kings, along with the Lord of Bamburgh, to meet with Æthelstan in that year (*p 11*; Earle and Plummer 1892, D recension), when he took tribute from them. During the next decade, however, it seems that these kings came to believe that the greater threat came from Æthelstan and his claims to be *Rex Anglorum* (king of the English), as they allied themselves with the Vikings, culminating in their defeat at the battle of Brunanburh in 937 (*op cit*, A recension).

Throughout the rest of the tenth and eleventh centuries, the growing power of England, and that of the Kingdom of the Scots, to the north, meant that the old Kingdom of Northumbria was caught between these two expanding polities (Kirby 1962; Sawyer 1978; Woolf 2007). The lands west of the Pennines remained outside the full control of the English crown throughout this time, however, and did not fall under the over-lordship of the king of England until William II marched north and took Carlisle in 1092 (Kapelle 1979).

## Cumbria in the seventh to ninth centuries
To what extent the political take-over by Northumbria led to English settlement west of the Pennines is unknown, although the number of place-names of Old English derivation in Cumbria (Armstrong *et al* 1950) implies a strong influence during the post-Roman period. How this could have come about is debated, although several models can be put forward (Rollason 2003, 65-6): conquest by incomers leading to the destruction or degradation of the existing British population, with the resulting kingdom of Northumbria owing little to its Roman or sub-Roman past; controlled cession of political power from the small British kingdoms to Anglo-Saxons, producing a change in the ruling elite, but not the organisation of the wider population; or perhaps a more subtle change, creating a new 'Northumbrian' identity without much change in ethnicity (Oosthuizen 2019).

Few settlement sites from this time are known (Fig 6), their recognition being almost wholly dependent on radiocarbon dating (Newman 2006, 97). Many of the radiocarbon date ranges cover the period from the seventh to ninth centuries, such as that from Stainton, to the north of Carlisle, where the radiocarbon dates from a settlement have been modelled, suggesting that it existed broadly from *cal AD 710-880* to *cal AD 780-950* (Brown *et al* in prep). This site produced five rectangular post-built structures, similar to those found south of Penrith, at Whinfell, and in particular Shap, which also produced fragments of three loomweights of early medieval form (Heawood and Howard-Davis 2002).

Close to Penrith, the site of Fremington (Oliver *et al* 1996) produced four sunken-featured buildings (Pl 2) of a type typical in the south-east of England of the Anglo-Saxon migration, known as *grubenhauser* (Hamerow 1993), as well as the corner of what seemed to be a rectangular post-built structure. A kiln was also found, containing over 200 sherds of crude, hand-made pottery, from at least five vessels. These were straight-sided and thick-walled, although there were hints that a bowl form might also have been made (Oliver *et al* 1996, 149-50). Such vessels are difficult to date, perhaps the closest parallels being the so-called 'native' pottery from Yeavering (Hope-Taylor 1977, class 1(A)), but the number of early medieval artefacts from the site, and the character of the buildings on it, would indicate that the pottery is also early medieval (Oliver *et al* 1996, 150). Documentary sources (for instance, Bede's *Historia Ecclesiastica* (Colgrave and Mynors 1969) and the *Anglo-Saxon Chronicles* (*eg* Swanton 2000)) indicate that this influence came primarily from the kingdom of Northumbria rather than from the South.

Clear physical evidence for a period of Northumbrian domination in Cumbria is largely limited to the relatively few stone crosses and other markers

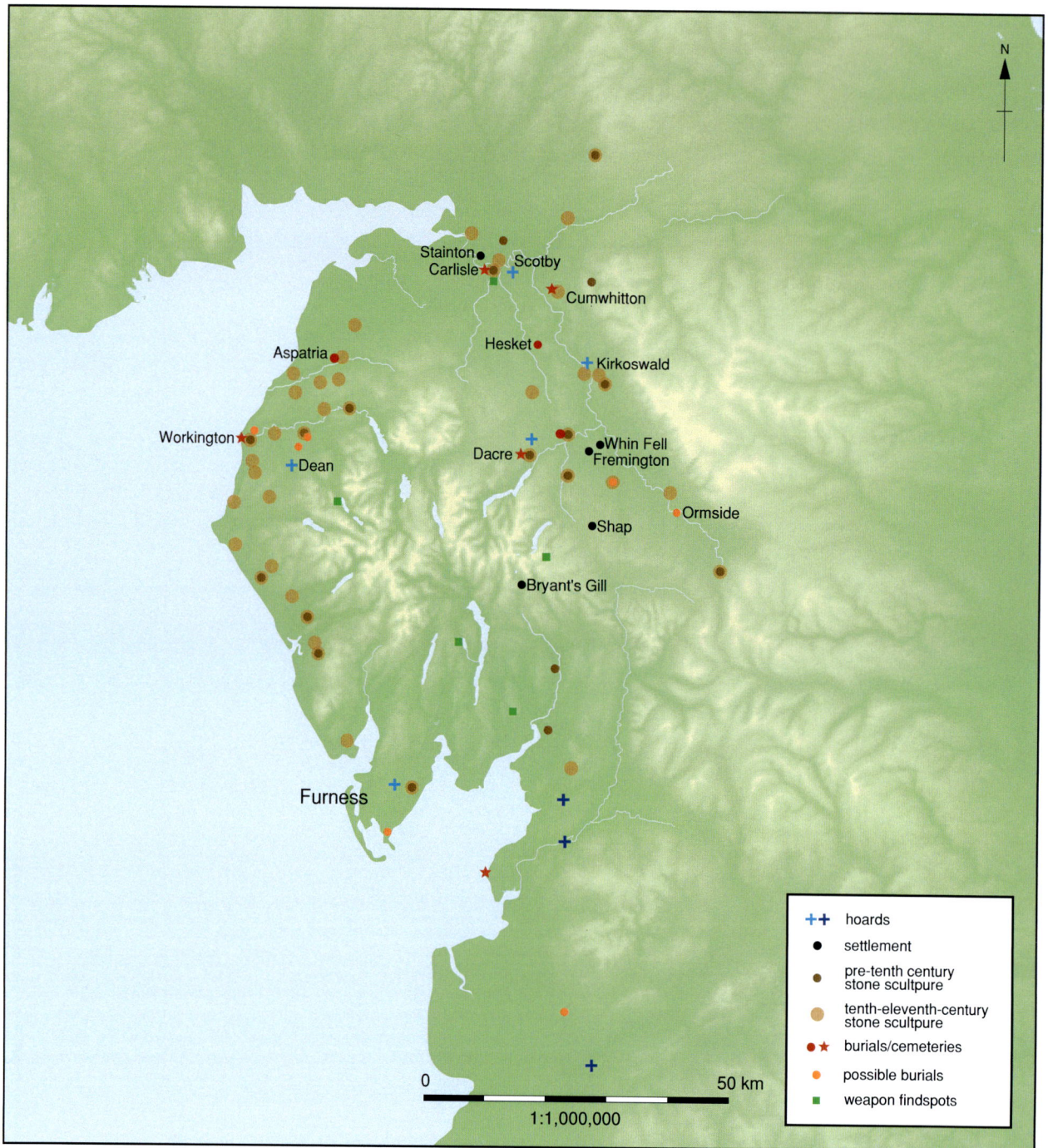

*Figure 6: Early medieval sites and sculpture in Cumbria*

that can be dated to before the tenth century (Pl 3), mainly found in the Eden valley and the western coastal strip (Bailey and Cramp 1988). This evidence for Christian worship has been supplemented by two key modern excavations of burials, where the soil conditions have not been inimical to the survival of the skeletons, at the west end of the Cathedral at Carlisle (McCarthy 2014), and at St Michael's Church, Workington (Zant and Parsons 2019). At both sites, radiocarbon dating of bones has confirmed the early medieval date of the cemeteries, at St Michael's demonstrating that there were two clear phases of burial: in the

seventh to ninth centuries (Pl 4), and the first half of the eleventh century. The later, tightly dated, phase there could be distinguished spatially and also in the use of stone cists for some of the interments (*ibid*), its date seemingly more in accord with the few dates from Carlisle Cathedral (Batt 2014, table 3).

The evidence for a continuing Northumbrian influence to the west of the Pennines in the eighth and ninth centuries is largely dependent on the iconography of the stone crosses, and the lack of evidence for change in the dated archaeological

*Plate 2: One of the sunken-featured structures at Fremington*

sites. At that time, the first loyalty of an individual would have been to their kin, and beyond that to an agreed leader; the idea that a kingdom was a fixed territory would thus not have been conceivable at this period. Evidence for the organisation of land tenure and estates, from contemporary poetry, later historical records, and archaeology, together suggest that the practice of clientage was widespread throughout Britain (Yorke 2006, 67), though power would have frequently changed hands, for when a leader failed to provide safety, material wealth, preferment, or land, their power would have eroded, and may have been challenged or even lost (Higham 1986, 287).

The collapse of Northumbria in the mid-ninth century resulted in 200 years or more of political fluidity in the North West, as alliances shifted

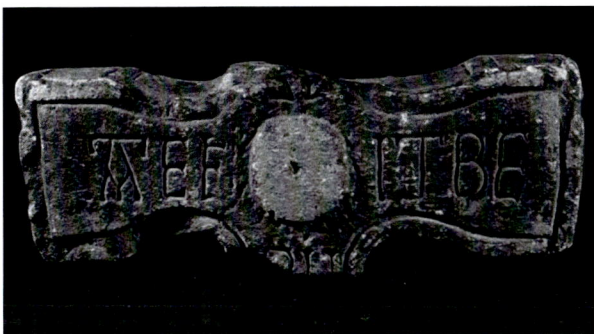

*Plate 3: The inscribed eighth-century cross fragment from Carlisle*

*Plate 4: One of the graves containing early coffin fittings at St Michael's Church, Workington*

9

*Plate 5: Furnished grave in the Viking-age cemetery at Cumwhitton*

and different polities expanded and contracted (*pp 5-7*). A matter of continuing debate is the role played by the Kingdom of Strathclyde, seemingly the reconfigured *Alt Clud*, after its centre, Dumbarton Rock, was sacked by a Viking force in 870 (Woolf 2007). There are a few documentary references, particularly to kings of Strathclyde/Cumbria, to suggest an extension southwards of this British kingdom, perhaps involving a re-emergence of British culture (Higham 1986, 317-18; Phythian-Adams 1996; Rollason 2003, 251-5; Downham 2007, 160-1; Edmonds 2015; Elsworth 2018). The extent to which Cumbria was independent in these years has also been debated (*ibid*).

The extent to which people of Viking descent held political power in Cumbria from the later ninth century to the eleventh is also unknown. It is, however, significant that the known sites of graves: the early tenth-century pagan burials at Aspatria (Rooke 1792); Hesket-in-Forest (Hodgson 1832); Cumwhitton (Pl 5; Paterson *et al* 2014); and Ormside (Edwards 1998); together with the wealthy Christian burials at Carlisle Cathedral (McCarthy 2014) and St Michael's Church, Workington (Zant and Parsons 2019), cluster in the Eden valley and on the west coast (Fig 6). These also coincide broadly with the areas where stone sculpture with Scandinavian iconography is found (Bailey and Cramp 1988), usually taken to indicate where relatively newly converted people with a Scandinavian heritage,

or at least tastes, were in a position either to build new, or donate to existing, churches (Bailey 1980). This perhaps suggests that people with 'Viking' cultural tastes were holding estates of some size in these areas, although their relationship with Strathclyde is again a matter of debate (Edmonds 2015).

## Documentary and archaeological history of Dacre

The earliest reference that appears to refer to Dacre occurs within Bede's *Historia Ecclesiastica Gentis Anglorum* (completed *c* 731). In this, he wrote of a miracle, which had taken place some three years before, in a monastery constructed near the river *Dacore* (*Est autem factum in monasterio, quod iuxta amnem Dacore constructum ab eo cognomen accepit* (Colgrave and Mynors 1969, bk 4, ch 32)). This monastery was clearly functioning at the time of writing, since Bede stated that one Thrydred was currently the abbot and that he had heard of the miracle from the monk upon whom it had been performed. Bede never stated where '*Dacore*' was, although it has been assumed that the monastery was under the authority of the Northumbrian church (Phythian-Adams 1996, 64-5). No other source makes any reference to a monastery at '*Dacore*', and, although another settlement named Dacre survives near Ripon, North Yorkshire, it is not an ancient ecclesiastical parish, and contains no evidence of an early church site. There is, of course, the possibility of other settlements once called by this name, which have either failed or have had their names changed,

*Figure 7: The confluence of the rivers Eamont and Eden, with possible sites for the meeting of the kings in 927*

in the manner that *Streoneshalh* became Whitby (Smith 1969). Both the surviving settlements have taken their names from nearby streams, the name deriving from the Celtic 'trickling stream' (Armstrong *et al* 1950, 10).

The Worcester recension (D) of the *Anglo-Saxon Chronicles* (Earle and Plummer 1892) is the only version to record the acceptance of the submission of Hywel, king of the West Welsh, Constantine, king of Scots, Owain (probably misnamed king of Gwent in the *Anglo-Saxon Chronicle*, but presumably the same as Eugenius (Owain) king of the Cumbrians, mentioned by William of Malmesbury; Giles 1876), and Ealdred Ealdulfing of Bamburgh, to Æthelstan, king of the expanding kingdom of the English in 927 (*p 7*; though dated to 926 in the D recension of the *Anglo-Saxon Chronicles*; Earle and Plummer 1892). This chronicle stated that the submission was accepted at Eamont (*on (th)aere stowe (th)e genemned is aet Eamotum. on .iiii. idus Iulii.* (*op cit*, 107)), where the kings swore to renounce idolatry. It is not apparent, though, whether 'Eamont' referred to a specific settlement or simply to an area (Fig 7).

The Worcester Chronicle (the D recension), as its name implies, is believed to have been written at Worcester, but it clearly used information from Northumbria, presumably in the form of a chronicle or annals, as a major source, although this northern work does not survive (Garmonsway 1975, xxxvii). William of Malmesbury, writing in the early twelfth century, recorded in his *Gesta Regum Anglorum* that the submission took place at '*Dacor*', and that, furthermore, the son of Constantine was baptised, with Æthelstan acting as godfather:

*Fugit tunc Analafus filius Sihctrici Hiberniam, et Godefridus frater ejus Scotiam; subsecuti sunt e vestigo regales missi ad Constantinum regem Scottorum, et Eugeniem regem Cumbrorum, transfugam cum denunciatione belli repetentes. Nec fuit animus barbaris ut contra mutirent, quin potius sine retractione, ad locum qui Dacor vocatur venientes, se cum suis regnis Anglorum regi dedidere. In cuis pacti gratia filium Constantini baptizari jussum, ipse de sacro fonte suscepit (Hardy 1840, 212-13).*

*Anlaf, the son of Sihtric, then fled into Ireland, and his brother Guthferth into Scotland. Messengers from the king [Æthelstan] immediately followed to Constantine, king of the Scots, and Eugenius, King of the Cumbrians, claiming the fugitive under a threat of war. The barbarians had no idea of resistance, but without delay coming to a place called Dacor, they surrendered themselves and their kingdoms to the sovereign of England. Out of regard to this treaty, the king himself stood for the son of Constantine, who was ordered to be baptised, at the sacred font (Giles 1876, 132-3).*

It would seem too great a coincidence if '*Dacor*' was not the Dacre near Penrith, given that the meeting is obviously the same as that noted in the D recension of the *Anglo-Saxon Chronicles*. It would appear that William, the librarian of the monastery at Malmesbury, also had access to documentation which has subsequently been lost, since a monk from South-west England would be unlikely to have detailed geographical knowledge of eastern Cumbria; like Bede, he is respected amongst the

*Plate 6: The Eamont, with Mayburgh henge (left), and King Arthur's Round Table (right; Map data © Google, CNES/ Airbus, Getmapping plc, Infoterra Ltd, and Bluesky, Maxar Technologies 2020)*

early scholars as a rigorous historian, using only reputable sources (Hollister 2001).

The modern village of Dacre is situated a little over a mile (1.6 km) from the confluence of the Dacre Beck with the River Eamont, and it is possible that it could have been the place of meeting referred to by the Worcester recension. Other possible candidates, however, could be the henges of Mayburgh and King Arthur's Round Table at Eamont Bridge (Pl 6) or the settlement at Penrith, which has produced stone sculpture of tenth-century date (Bailey 1980, 27). It seems likely that the area lay at the northern extreme of, or immediately beyond, Æthelstan's kingdom, since such meetings commonly occurred at boundaries (Pantos 2003). The reference in William's *History* to 'the sacred font' in association with Dacre appears to suggest that he knew of it as a religious centre, although this might very well have been taken from Bede, whose works William revered; indeed, in writing

the *Gesta Regum Anglorum* he sought to emulate him (Giles 1876, viii).

The present church does not contain any obviously pre-Norman elements. The earliest part is the tower, which contains twelfth-century architecture (Pevsner 1967), while the chancel is largely late Romanesque in style, although some earlier voussoirs, with diagonal carving, some built into the later clerestory, may come from a relatively early chancel arch (*pers obs*). The nave contains elements of twelfth- to fifteenth-century date. However, support for the hypothesis that the church at Dacre was founded on a pre-Conquest site came in the late nineteenth century with the discovery of two pieces of sculpture.

The first was found during the rebuilding of the east wall of the chancel in 1875 (Mathews 1891, 226), and it had clearly been cut down from its original cross shape; the 'back' had also been crudely chipped.

*Plate 7: The tenth-century Dacre Stone*

*Plate 8: The ninth-century cross fragment with inhabited vinescroll at Dacre*

Known as the Dacre Stone (Pl 7), this would appear to be the shaft of a cross of tenth-century date, decorated in an Anglo-Scandinavian style, and is one of the very few overtly Christian carvings of the period in Cumbria from a clearly pre-existing church site, where it may have been inspired by paintings from the earlier buildings (Bailey 1977, 61; Bailey and Cramp 1988, Dacre 2). This stone, on its discovery, was believed to give credence to William of Malmesbury's claim that the meeting in 927 took place, at least in part, at Dacre, since at that time it was thought that the central figures represented the baptism of the son of Constantine (Mathews 1891, 227). This has subsequently been reinterpreted as depicting the sacrifice of Isaac (Bailey 1977).

The second and earlier fragment of a cross-shaft (Pl 8) was found in *c* 1900 'in deep clay' during the digging of a service trench to a cottage close to the church (Collingwood 1912, 157). Its iconography and style clearly link it to Northumbrian sculpture of eighth-ninth-century date (Bailey and Cramp 1988, 91), although it is very unusual in its details, perhaps reflecting an orientalising influence, seen, for example, at Breedon (Leicestershire) and Otley (West Yorkshire), the combination of human figures and fantastic beasts also being seen at Hoddom (Dumfries and Galloway; Bailey and Cramp 1988, Dacre 1). One side of this fragment was worn and

the stone had obviously been reused, perhaps in a pavement or floor, at some period between the destruction of the cross and its discovery.

A stone-lined drain, thought initially to be a passage, was discovered in the extension that had been created in the nineteenth century along the south side of the original medieval churchyard. This was opened in the late 1920s and proved to be formed of massive blocks of stone, worked in two distinct patterns (Hudleston 1932, 76). It also became clear that the drain was actually the outlet of two channels (Pl 9), which had flowed downhill from points close to the church. Further excavations on this alignment to the south of the track beyond the churchyard merely produced the remains of an open ditch (*op cit*, 75-6). No finds were recorded.

The association of this feature with a church site producing pre-Norman sculpture led to the assumption that this Dacre was indeed the site of the monastery referred to by Bede (Colgrave and Mynors 1969, HE, bk 4, ch 32). It was noted that a large stone-lined drain had been excavated in association with early medieval structures at Whitby (Peers and Radford 1943, 31) and Hudleston inferred that the present church had been constructed over an earlier structure, with the buildings served by these drains lying beneath

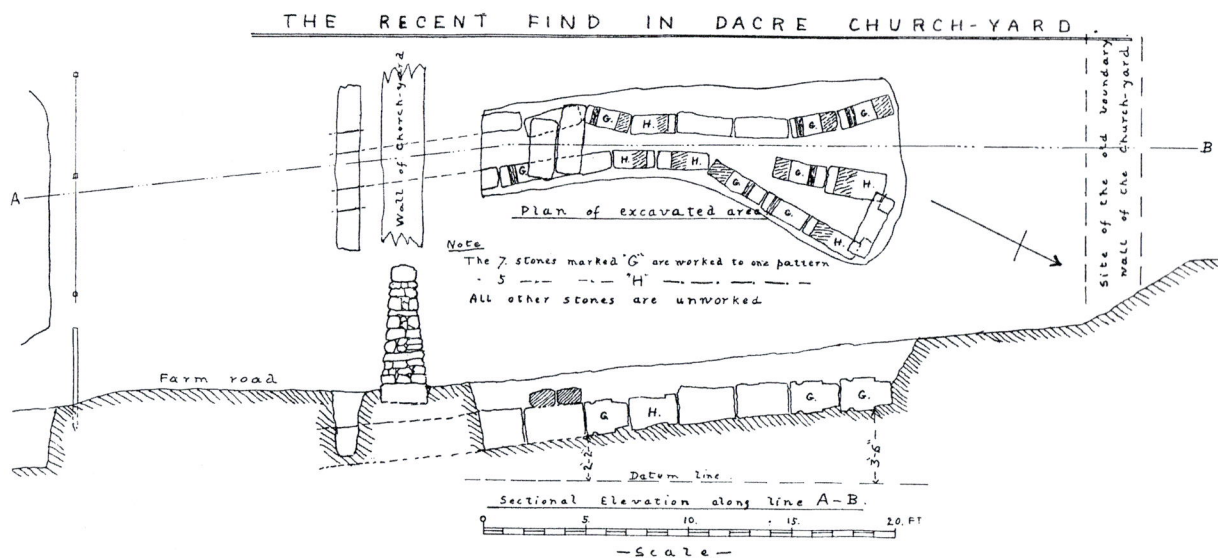

*Plate 9: The plan of the drain in the southern churchyard (Hudleston 1932)*

*Plate 10: The Dacre Bear to the north-east of the church*

the medieval churchyard to the south of the church (Hudleston 1932, 76-7).

The churchyard contains a further unusual feature: the presence of four upright stone figures, one roughly at each corner of the church (Pl 10), although they are not aligned with the present church. Three of the figures resemble bears (Pl 11), while the fourth, at the north-east corner, has some similarities with a lion. The two figures on the southern side of the church appear to have gripping beasts on their backs, but all are worn to a greater or lesser extent. They were first recorded in 1704, during Bishop Nicolson's visitation: 'At each corner of the

churchyard... there stands a Bear and Ragged Staff, cut in Stone' (Ferguson 1877, 128). Nothing is known of their origin, but many have speculated, including, since each of the figures is different, suggesting that they tell a story (Ferguson 1890a).

## Methodologies

A trench, to examine the archaeological potential of the Orchard, was sited immediately outside the western churchyard in 1982 (Fig 8). The northern part of this was extended east-west, to investigate

*Plate 11: The Dacre Bear to the south-west of the church*

in the southern part of the site, the major area of activity being confined to the north, particularly the north-eastern corner closest to the churchyard. This north-eastern part proved to have features which seemed to have been sealed by layers of thirteenth- and fourteenth-century date and it was therefore decided to investigate the site further.

To the north of the church, within the churchyard extension, earthworks identified in the field to the north and east appeared to continue into the consecrated area, although there was no surface evidence, presumably because the new churchyard had been improved when consecrated. The site sloped from north to south, with the hint of a natural terrace, aligned east-west, parallel to the Dacre Beck, about half-way down. Two trial trenches, aligned north-south, were dug in 1982 to establish the archaeological potential of the area, particularly of the earthworks, in which a sequence of activity stretching from some time before the thirteenth century was recorded. This identification led to excavations, undertaken in three seasons in the summers of 1983-5, which examined the entire area available within this extension, some 1100 square metres, although, because spoil had to be contained within the site, the entire area was never open at once. An extensive geophysical survey was also undertaken in 1982 of the field to the north and east of the churchyard.

the widest possible extent within the Orchard's confines and, in 1983, further examination of the hillwash deposits took place to the south, in a narrow trench laid east-west. The initial trench demonstrated that little activity had taken place

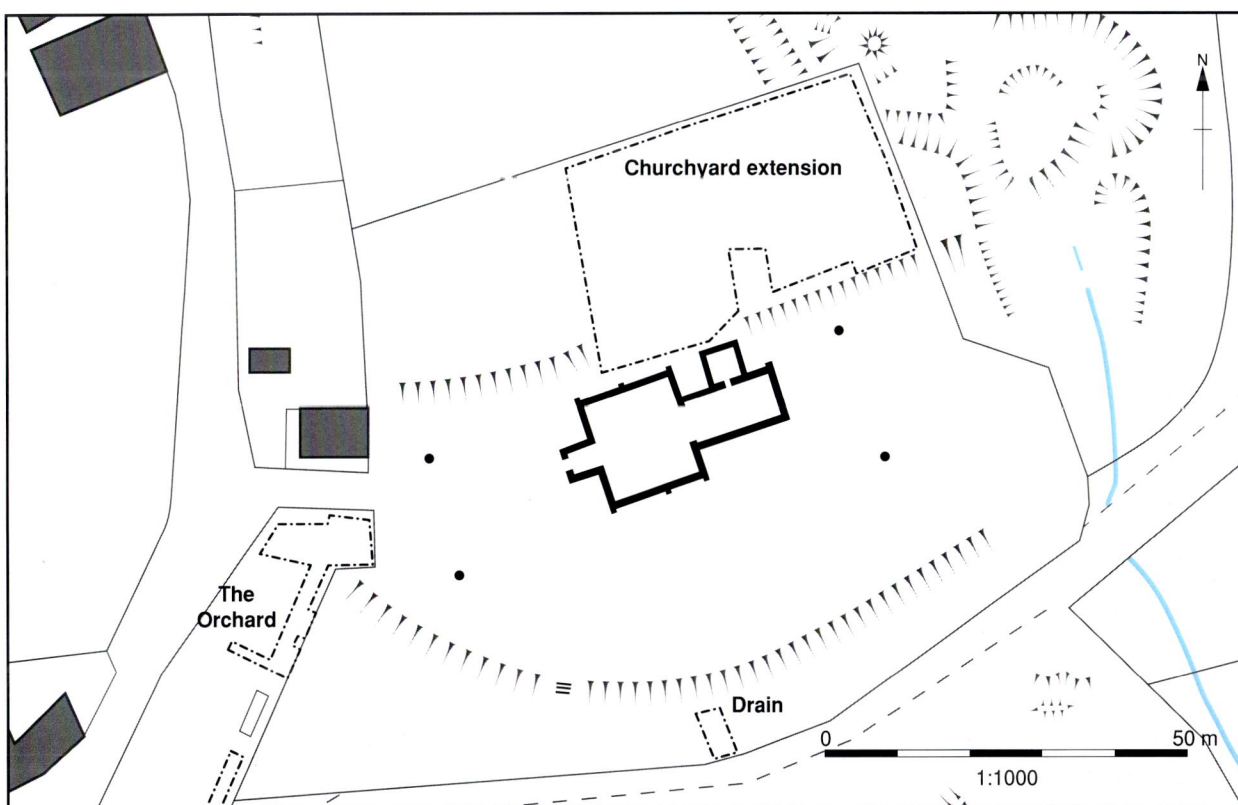

*Figure 8: The principal areas of investigation*

15

A small trench excavated in 1985 re-examined the large stone drain that had been discovered in *c* 1929 (*p 13*), presumably during grave digging, in the southern extension to the medieval churchyard. The *c* 1929 work had been reported briefly (Hudleston 1932) but few details seem to have been recorded. The drain was relocated during survey work in 1982, appearing as a parchmark both inside the churchyard and in the field to the south. Because of the position of the known graves surrounding the drain, an irregularly shaped trench, roughly a parallelogram, was excavated.

The initial aim of the re-excavation was to assess the significance of the supposed drain in the light of the results of the excavation to the north of the church, particularly since it had been assumed by Hudleston, although he gave no corroborating evidence, that the drain was pre-Norman (Hudleston 1932, 75-6). Much more of interest was discovered, although the limited area available for excavation, and the amount of disturbance from the excavation of *c* 1929, made the results somewhat speculative. The lack of well-dated finds prevented a very detailed chronology being established and, for the most part, the phasing of the site was based on stratigraphical evidence alone.

Thus three separate sites were excavated at Dacre: Site 1 to the west, in the old orchard; Site 2 to the north of the medieval churchyard; and Site 3 to the south. Since these were disparate areas, each was phased separately. Phasing was further complicated in each site by the lack of stratigraphy linking the various parts, so that it was frequently difficult to relate one element to another. Finds and particularly pottery have necessarily played an important part in dating the later phases, although a high incidence of potentially residual artefacts and, in places, possibly intrusive material have added to the complexity. The horizontal nature of much of the stratigraphy also created problems, in that it was difficult to relate individual features from isolated areas, since many of the features lacked corroborative dating evidence.

Each site posed its own problems, but in every case difficulties arose when dealing with features cut into the subsoil, since the underlying geology comprised mixed post-glacial deposits of stones and sand, which in places appeared to be stratified. In Site 2 in particular, a sandy, sometimes mottled soil sealed the pure sand element of the subsoil (*713, 1391, 537*); this also seemed to be of subsoil type, but clearly had been disturbed by human activity. All the earliest features and some of the early medieval graves (*Ch 2*) appeared to have been cut from this level, although the actual point from which they had been cut may have been masked by leaching. This leaching of the site made the recognition of the graves

particularly difficult, as not only had it led to the almost total destruction of the skeletons within the graves (*Ch 2*), but frequently the cuts only showed up during drying, as extremely subtle variations of texture and colour. In the dry summers of 1982-4, regular artificial wettings were essential.

Throughout the excavation, an adaptation of the former Central Excavation Unit recording system was used to process both contexts and finds. Although the excavation encompassed three physically separate sites, a single running sequence of numbers was issued for contexts, and another for finds, rather than the allocation of blocks of numbers for each site. To facilitate the recognition of potentially aceramic contexts of post-Roman and pre-Norman date, most of the medieval pottery was three-dimensionally recorded, and groups or sometimes even individual sherds were given object record numbers. Other usual bulk finds, such as animal bones, were also relatively uncommon at Dacre, so object record numbers were issued for small groups of objects of the same material. This sometimes led to the allocation of more than one object record number for bulk finds from any one context, particularly when the context was excavated over more than one season.

During the 1984 and 1985 seasons, the majority of the finds records were input on to a battery-operated lap-held Epson HX-20 computer on site, and these and all other finds records were subsequently edited in the office on an ACT Sirius microcomputer. The context records were also input at the end of each season. All lists and catalogues for the archive and this publication have been machine-generated, using the English Heritage-developed Delilah suite of programs.

The layer lists, containing basic context descriptions, information on phasing, and lists of finds by context, also provide details of layer combinations and form part of the archive. Conflation of layers has taken place during analysis at two levels: firstly when the layers have been found to be the same; and secondly as a convenient short-hand, particularly in the construction of the matrix (contained within the archive), when individual features have all been found to be sealed by, and to cut, the same layers. The primary number, or cut number for a negative feature, is referred to in the text.

The finds from all three sites were recorded by material, as individual objects or in small, related groups within a given context. Within the archive catalogues, objects are listed by site, context number, broad phase, and object record number, in that order of precedence. This system has been followed in the full catalogues, which are to be found in the archive, but only the objects of direct relevance to the interpretation of the site are discussed in the main text.

The bulk of the analytical phase of the project was undertaken during the 1980s and early 1990s, after which a long hiatus occurred, before the draft text was edited and made fit for publication. During the intervening time, methodologies have moved on rapidly, so inevitably this report is to a great extent an object of its time. This is particularly the case for radiocarbon dating, as the site was excavated before the development of Accelerator Mass Spectrometry (AMS), and no samples proved large enough for conventional techniques. The site has therefore been phased stratigraphically, with date ranges applied using the material assemblages associated with each. Similarly, the lack of human and animal bone has curtailed scientific analysis, and there was little in the way of charred plant remains. The discursive elements of the volume have, however, benefited from up-to-date research, taking into account the growing number of early medieval sites in northern England and Scotland, either with documentary references to monasteries, or traditional associations with early saints, that have been excavated during the last 50 years.

## The Structure of the Volume

The information contained in this volume has been divided between the printed text ('hard copy'), with the medieval pottery fabric series and the ironwork catalogue placed online as appendices, with other catalogues archived. Both the hard copy and online appendices should be used for a detailed analysis of the site. Extensive cross-referencing of all aspects of the site should allow the easy re-examination of the stratigraphy and reconstruction of finds groups.

The activity on the site essentially falls into two parts: early and later medieval, with most of the areas excavated seeing little activity in the post-medieval period. Thus, the volume has been designed to reflect this, with *Chapters 2* and *3* describing the early medieval activity and the finds relating to this, and *Chapters 4* and *5* relating to the medieval and later activity. *Chapter 6* discusses the site in its broader context, primarily concentrating on the early medieval phase.

## The Archive

The excavation produced a substantial number of artefacts, ranging from a few of prehistoric and Roman date, through an important early medieval assemblage, and both medieval and post-medieval material. The detailed information, comprising site records, printouts of early computerised material, both black and white and colour photographs, and plans and sections, has been collated and indexed, together with the electronic and paper material generated by the processing and analysis of the data. As much of this work was undertaken in the early years of electronic processing, many of the programs used are no longer current, and thus paper copies have been made. The archive also includes conservation records and x-rays, as well as details of other analyses. Together these form the full archive, comprising all finds, and digital and paper site and analytical records, which will be deposited in the Tullie House Museum and Art Gallery, Carlisle.

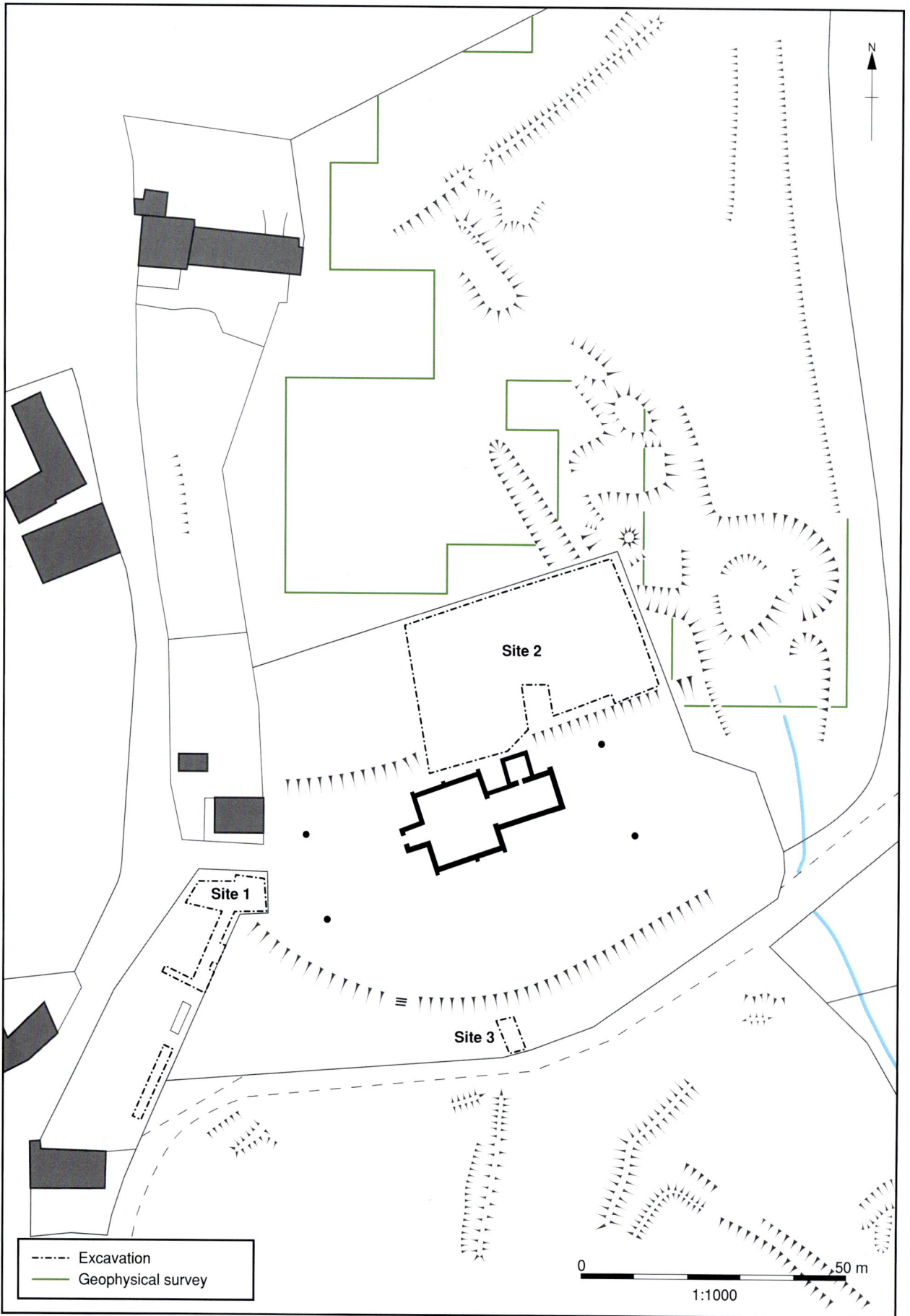

*Figure 9: Locations of the three sites excavated*

# 2

# THE EARLY MEDIEVAL ACTIVITY

Activity that clearly pre-dated the foundation of the medieval parish churchyard was found in all three sites. This included potential small-scale prehistoric occupation, at least in the vicinity, and the possibility of some Romano-British settlement in the area. The bulk of the contexts related to activity on the wider site, probably from the seventh century to around the time of the Norman Conquest (in this part of Cumbria, in 1092; Swanton 2000). Given that the activity in the three sites (the Orchard, Site 1; the northern churchyard, Site 2: and the southern churchyard, Site 3; Fig 9) can rarely be closely equated, the sites have been described individually.

## The Northern Churchyard (Site 2)

The area to the north of the medieval church sloped from north to south and was dominated by a scarp slope about midway, extending east-west across the site, though lessening in size to the east (Pl 12). This formed the lip of a terrace, the upper element being cut by the present churchyard wall, and the southern terrace containing much of the early medieval activity, as well as the present, medieval, church.

## Earliest activity

The earliest features to the north of the medieval church were isolated from each other, but they all cut or lay immediately above the subsoil and were notable for a lack of associated finds. Thus only a generalised date for each can be given.

In the west of the site, feature 569 (Fig 10) appeared to cut a water-created gully in the substratum at the lip of the natural terrace. Irregular cut 929, through layer 537 on the lower terrace (p 21), appeared to form a rough semi-circle, although it may actually have represented two sides of a north-south linear

*Plate 12: Looking north-west across the northern churchyard*

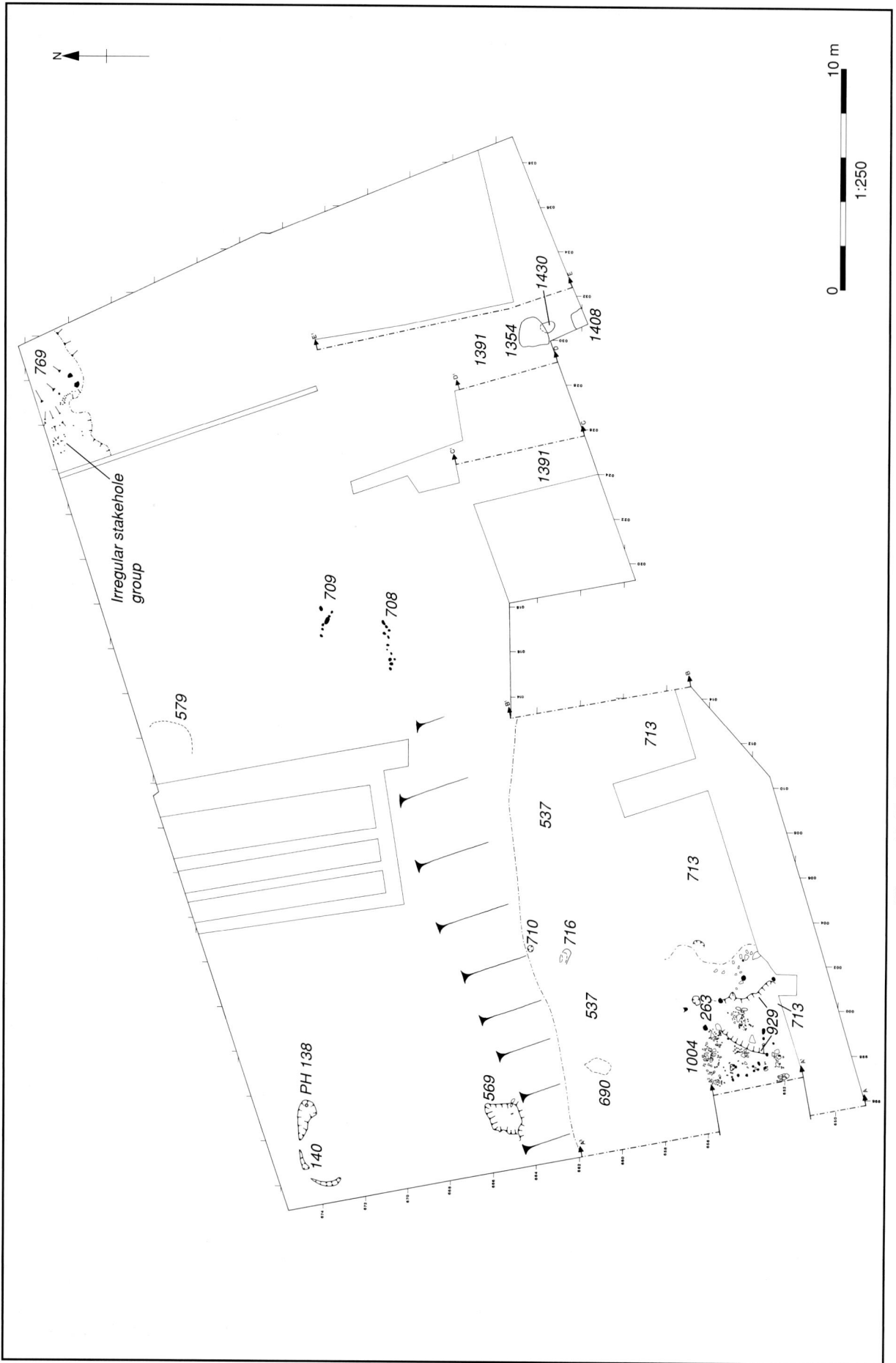

*Figure 10: Earliest activity in the northern churchyard*

Irregular stakehole group

769

579

PH 138

140

709

708

569

710

716

537

537

690

1004

263

929

713

713

713

1391

1354

1391

1430

1408

N

10 m

1:250

0

20

feature. In the same area, stone spread *1004* contained a significant element of worked red sandstone, which appeared to have been rubble from a stone structure. The proximity of the undisturbed subsoil may, however, indicate that it lay in a disturbed area, and these features may actually represent initial activity on the site, particularly since this was in the area of a later, though seemingly early medieval, timber building (*p 33*).

Two lines of stakeholes (*708, 709*) to the east, on the upper terrace, seemed to form a rough semi-circle or oval, with a diameter of approximately 3 m; these were clearly cut by early medieval graves, while an irregular mass of stakeholes in the north-east corner of the site cut a layer of sand (*769*). It is potentially feasible that both groups may have belonged to roundhouses, although the distance between *708* and *709*, at only 3 m, would have made this a very small structure; equally, either could have been caused by vegetation or animal activity. A roughly circular area of small stones (*579*) lay on a slight rise in the subsoil in the far north of the site, which may have been natural, although it was very regular. No finds were associated with any of these features.

Gully *140*, on the upper terrace in the north-western corner of the site, was narrow and steep-sided, forming a rough, discontinuous semi-circle. It was cut at its eastern end by posthole *138* (*p 37*), which contained a piece of handmade pottery, as well as medieval pottery (*Ch 3, p 49*). Although gully *140* contained no finds, the presence of the unusual pottery in the posthole suggests that this was an early feature. Most of the lithics from the site were found on the upper terrace, particularly close to this feature. This is perhaps reminiscent of part of a drip gully from a roundhouse, which could again have had a diameter of *c* 3 m, although, equally, it could have been formed by burrowing animals.

A small patch of clay (*690*), which contained a single small chip of samian ware, lay below mixed layer *537* immediately beneath the scarp slope of the terrace in the west of the site, whilst layers *713* and *1391*, immediately above the subsoil on the lower terrace, were cut by early medieval graves. Mottled layer *537*, which sealed *713*, had obviously been disturbed by later activity, including the early graves. Lens *994*, at the base of *537*, was less stony and mottled, and partially covered stone spread *1004* (*above*).

Several other early features, also lacking dating evidence, appeared to be stratigraphically higher. All may in fact have belonged to the early cemetery level (*below*), but they could not be definitely associated. These included numerous stakeholes, clustered in the south-west of the site, which were sealed by a stone spread (*263, p 35*), though apparently later than cut *929*. These seemed to form a rough semi-circle, with a diameter again of approximately 3 m. The stakeholes formed a double row around the west side, but became more erratically spaced to the north, south, and east. There did not seem to have been any association with the cemetery, the western extent of which was immediately to the east (*p 23*).

Posthole *710* and an irregular crescent-shaped cut (*716*) were isolated features at the western edge of the cemetery (*below*), and two large, rounded cuts (*1354, 1408*) were identified between the lowest of the graves. Cuts *1354* and *1408* were fairly similar in shape and size, being sub-rounded and 1.38 x 1.34 x 0.20 m and 0.59 x 0.99 x 0.16 m, respectively; these were perhaps tree-holes, although whether they were early in date remains uncertain. A further cut (*1430*), possibly a posthole, was associated.

## The early medieval cemetery

A cemetery containing more than 234 graves occupied the central part of the site, and spread over both terraces. It covered an area of at least 33 x 24 m, but its full extent is not known, although the graves rapidly decreased in density to east and west and appeared to cease within the excavated area. The northern and southern boundaries lay outside the excavation, although the graves seemed to be less dense towards the north-east. It seems likely, from the concentration at the southern edge of the excavated area, that the focus of the cemetery was in that direction, perhaps under, or slightly to the east of, the present church. Its size, and the number of graves cutting others (approximately half of those excavated), suggest a long period of use; on four occasions, a sequence of four graves was identified.

There is some evidence to suggest that the cemetery was enclosed (Fig 11). A shallow ditch (*160*), 1.22 m wide and only 0.1 m deep, extended into the north-west of the site on the upper terrace for some 13 m. It was aligned north-west to south-east, its southern, butt end curving into the cemetery, and was cut by grave *319*. It may in fact have been a much earlier feature, but its juxtaposition with the graves suggests that it could have been associated. Two short lengths of heavily disturbed linear features (*1106, 915*) to the south, on the lower terrace, had been truncated by the boundary ditch that seems to have been the first definition of the medieval churchyard (*215; Ch 4, pp 91-3*). These seemed to have belonged to two different features, rather than a single ditch, although both appeared to be aligned north-south. Ditch *1106*, to the west of the graves, was sealed by wall *644* (*pp 23-4*), and may have been its predecessor as a boundary, whereas ditch *915*, which lay due south of ditch *160*, had been cut by graves *888, 898*, and *858*. On the eastern side of

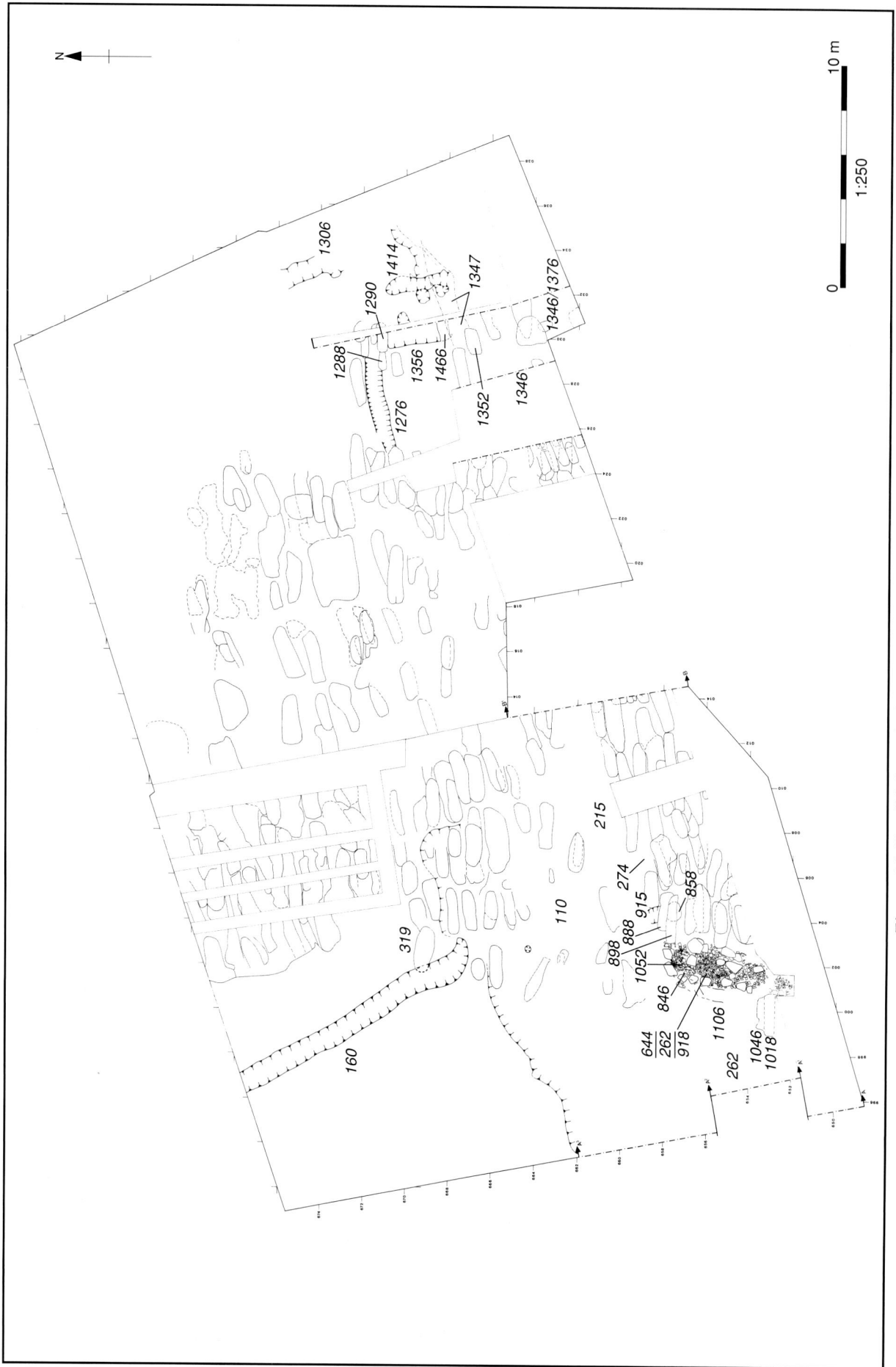

Figure 11: Possible boundaries to the early medieval cemetery

the cemetery, three short lengths of shallow ditches, aligned roughly north-south, were identified. Ditch *1356* had been cut by graves to both north (*1290*) and south (*1466*), whereas both ditches *1414* and *1306* were to the east of the graves. The latter two were very indistinct, but *1414* possibly terminated in a butt end to the north.

Wall *644* marked the western boundary of the main area of graves, with only graves *1018* and *1046* beyond it, although these may have been later, since they were situated immediately to the north of identifiably medieval and modern burials. Only a single course of stone remained of the wall, presumably forming its foundations. These were laid directly on the ground, no cut being visible in the surrounding layers. It had an angular stone facing with a core of cobbles, although the facing stones were somewhat intermittent and may have been reused from some other source, as several seemed to have dressed faces turned in towards the centre of the wall. It was aligned almost exactly north-south, being 5.5 m long by 1.20 m wide, and had been cut by the first churchyard boundary ditch (*215*), as well as by later graves in the medieval and modern churchyard (Pl 13). There was no evidence of any other stone features that could have been connected with *644*. At the point where it was cut by boundary ditch *215*, there was limited evidence that it was turning eastwards, perhaps indicating the position of an entrance into the cemetery (Pl 14). There was, however, nothing to suggest it had continued to the north, either on the lower terrace or, indeed, the upper terrace.

*Plate 13: Wall 644, looking north*

Layer *262*, to the west of the graves, seemed to belong to this phase also, appearing to slump into the hollow created by cut *929* (*p 19*). Large amounts of cobbles were spread across its upper surface, presumably from the decay of wall *644*, although the layer was partially covered by that feature also. It sealed a layer of decayed red sandstone (*918*), containing three pieces of quartz, which might point, as the stratigraphy does, to this being associated with the cemetery (*Ch 3*). It had in

*Plate 14: Wall 644, looking west, showing the possible turn (right)*

turn been cut by feature *1052* (0.42 x 0.14 x 0.11 m), which may have been the base of a posthole. This in turn was sealed by a localised patch of burning (*846*) mixed with clay, partially covered by the undisturbed core of wall *644*. No obvious purpose could be seen for either *1052* or *846*, and neither contained any finds, but the latter certainly would appear stratigraphically to have belonged with the cemetery.

The incidence of all these features immediately to the east and west of the cemetery area, and identified at the same level, suggests that they may have been connected, presumably forming a boundary, although they cannot belong to a single feature. If they are to be regarded as defining the cemetery, this would add weight to the theory that this had a long period of use and expanded from its original dimensions, although the possibility that it was sub-divided into different areas, perhaps for different sectors of the population, cannot be disregarded. Clearly, the inner ditches on both the east and west sides did not belong to its final phase, since they had been cut by graves, and, indeed, they might even have been prehistoric in origin. Burial did not take place immediately adjacent to ditches *1306* and *1414* in the east, nor next to the northern sector of ditch *160*, which perhaps indicates that the cemetery was not 'full' when it was abandoned.

Wall *644* was obviously late in the sequence, which may partially explain why it was so different from the other features, but its presumed proximity to the focal point of the cemetery may also provide a reason. If it can be assumed that a church in approximately the same position as the present building formed its focus, at least in its last period of use, wall *644* may have provided a more substantial boundary at the western, public, end of the structure.

A further ditch (*1276*) may once have marked the northern extent of the cemetery in the east of the site, or a sub-division, perhaps for privileged burial,

within it. It was identified to the north of ditch *1356*, and had been cut by early medieval graves (*eg 1288*, *1290*), which had effectively destroyed the relationship between the two ditches.

Layer *274*, in the west of the site, was cut by graves. A few large stones near its surface possibly derived from the decay of wall *644* to the west, yet the quantity of teeth and coffin fittings attests to its function as a cemetery level. A lead run (*Ch 3, p 75*) and a small scrap of window glass (*Ch 3*) may have come from an ecclesiastical structure nearby. It was separated from layer *110* to the north by the later churchyard boundary ditch (*215; Ch 4, pp 91-3*). Layers *1346* and *1376* to the east were also cut by graves. Layer *1376* was only found to the south of medieval churchyard boundary ditch *215*, below layer *1346*, where it seemed to seal the earliest features in this part of the site (*eg* cut *1408, p 21*). Layer *1346* also sealed layer *1347*, which was cut by grave *1352*. The large quantity of gravel within *1347* gave the impression that it might have formed part of a semi-metalled surface.

Although it was generally impossible to identify the exact point from which any grave had been dug, none was recognised cutting the hillwash that covered the entire site (*32, Ch 4, pp 93-4*). If indeed no graves did in fact cut this hillwash, they seem to have been truncated, since none, as excavated, was more than 0.50 m deep. The lack of any markers for the graves may also have been a result of this apparent erosion, although it is certainly possible that the entire cemetery could have been unmarked. The truncation may simply have been the result of the movement of soil down the slope, which had clearly been a fairly constant process, or possibly there had been subsequent removal of soil in the area of the early cemetery, particularly after the medieval churchyard had come into being.

Graves were clearly sealed by the northern medieval churchyard boundary bank (Fig 12; *151, Ch 4, p 91*),

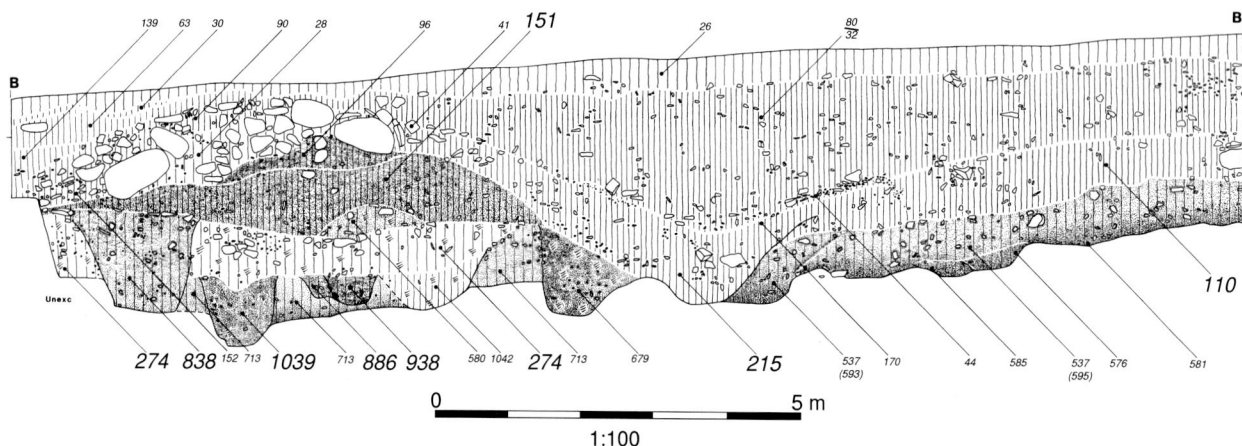

*Figure 12: Section through the hillwash building up against the later medieval churchyard boundary, sealing early medieval graves*

24

*Plate 15: The graves on the upper terrace in the centre of the excavation*

where the grave cuts as excavated were less than 1 m deep, which suggests that up to 1 m of soil had been removed from the cemetery area between the last burial and the formation of the later churchyard to the south. The fact that the medieval churchyard boundary bank and ditch (*Ch 4*) cut through the earlier cemetery suggests that there had been a period of abandonment, and the exact location of the consecrated ground had been lost, or ignored, when the medieval churchyard was consecrated, although, significantly, the tradition of a Christian cemetery on the site had not.

The graves were recognised only as rectangular cuts, frequently irregular in outline (Pl 15), although most had rounded east and west ends. There was no evidence that any had been marked in a manner that left any trace in the archaeological record. This irregularity appeared to reflect the shape assumed after the collapse of coffins, rather than the shape of the original cut. This was seen in grave *389*, immediately below the terrace scarp, in the west of the cemetery, where the collapsed subsoil sealed part of the side of a decayed coffin; Pl 16).

*Plate 16: The decayed side of a coffin in grave 389*

The sizes of the excavated cuts varied considerably, but complete examples ranged from approximately 1.50 m to 2.20 m in length, with only a few larger, and they were predominantly 0.40-0.70 m in width. This suggests that the cemetery largely contained adults. In most parts of the site, some attempt had been made to organise the graves in orderly lines, where the heads and feet matched almost exactly (Pl 17). In many places, these lines were closely packed, some clearly intercutting (Pl 18). The density of graves varied markedly across the cemetery although they were most densely packed in the south, below the medieval churchyard boundary, and on the upper terrace in the western part of the cemetery; there were notably fewer, and a less dense concentration, in the north-east (Pl 19).

Even the 'best preserved' skeletons survived only as the shadows of jaws, still *in situ*, with a stain marking the upper vertebrae and clavicles. In most cases, however, the only skeletal remains were the enamel shells of teeth (Pl 20), the decay having been the result of the severe leaching of the site, the acid soils being inimical to bone survival. However, enough evidence survived to establish that the bodies had been laid supine and, where

identifiable, the head was at the west end of the grave. Two beads only were found within grave cuts (*1262, 568; Ch 3, p 83*), in the east of the site, which implies that the burials did not contain grave goods. Large numbers of quartz pebbles were, however, noted within the layers associated with the graves and, on at least one occasion, in the fill of one (*199*, grave *200*), a phenomenon identified in other early Christian cemeteries (*eg* the Hirsel (Cramp 2014) and Whithorn (Baker 1988, 30; Hill 1997)). Given the cumulative weight of evidence, there is every reason to suppose that these burials were Christian.

Grave *389* was the only one to contain the decayed remains of wooden planks that had formed the sides and top of a collapsed coffin (*above*), although other graves, particularly those beneath the later churchyard boundary bank (*151, Ch 4, p 91*), contained stains which seemed to indicate the positions of coffins (*eg 964*, against wall *644*). Large numbers of coffin fittings were, however, recovered (Pl 21; *Ch 3*). During 1985, these were three-dimensionally plotted, producing matched pairs within individual graves (*eg* in fill *909*, grave *910*, to the east, again below the medieval churchyard boundary).

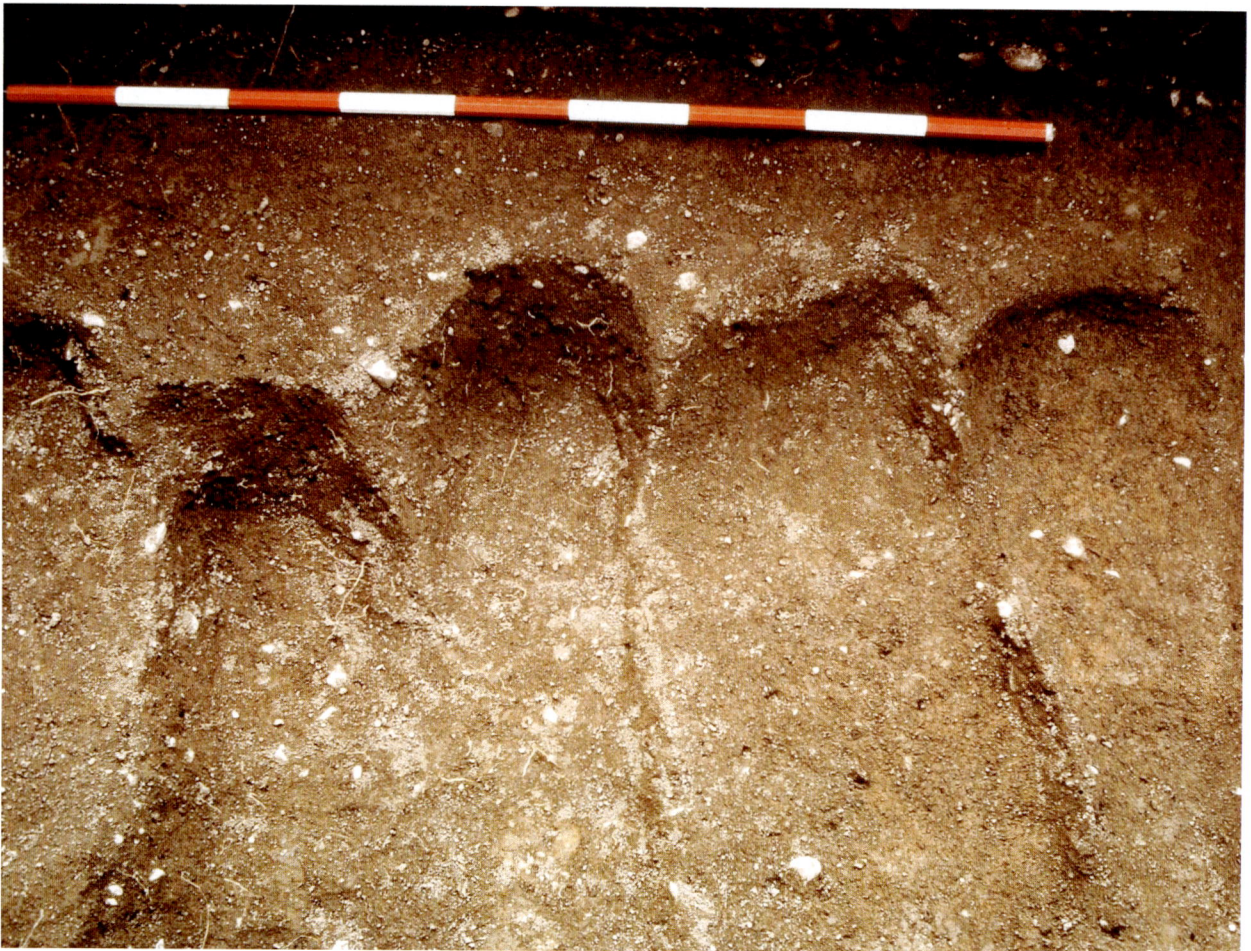

*Plate 17: A neat row of graves*

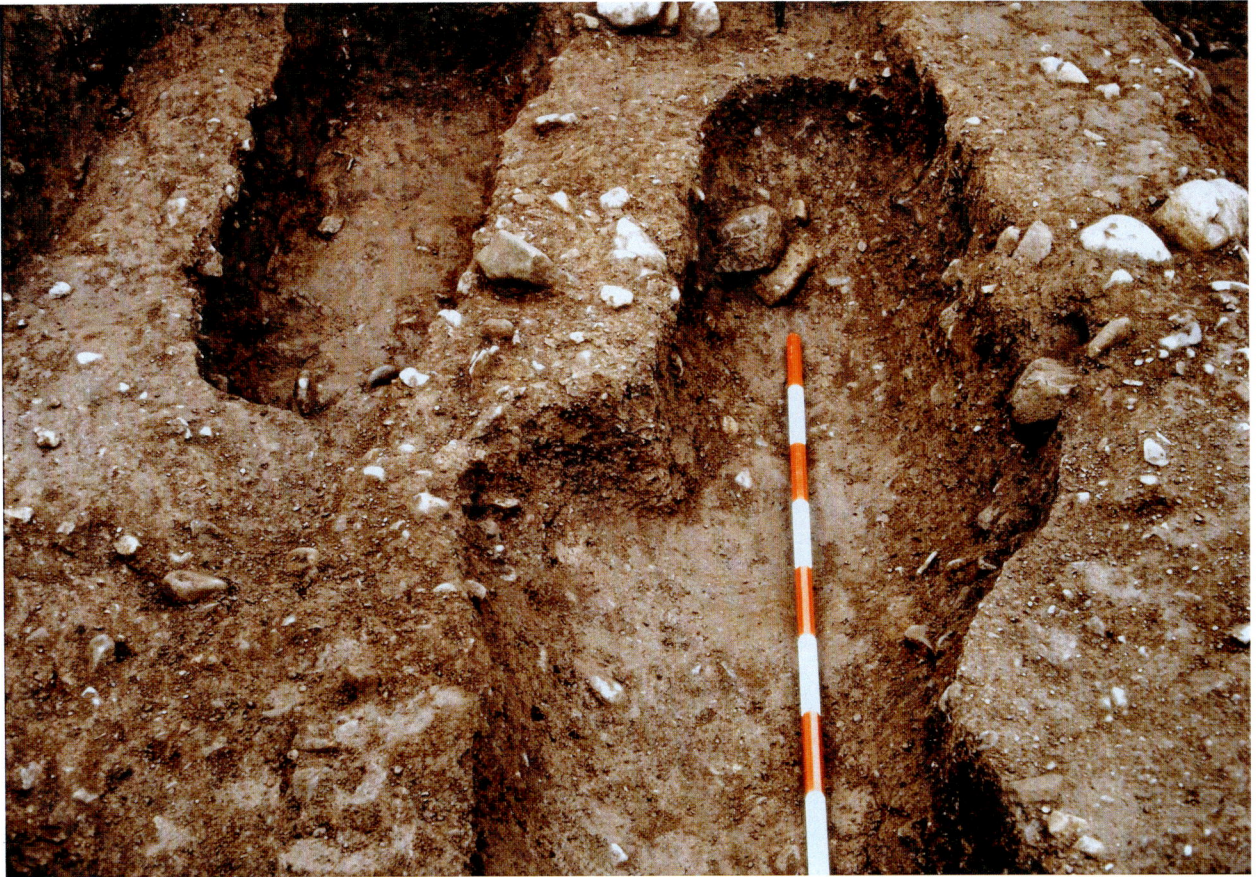

*Plate 18: Intercutting graves in the west of the cemetery*

*Plate 19: Looking north across the eastern extremity of the cemetery*

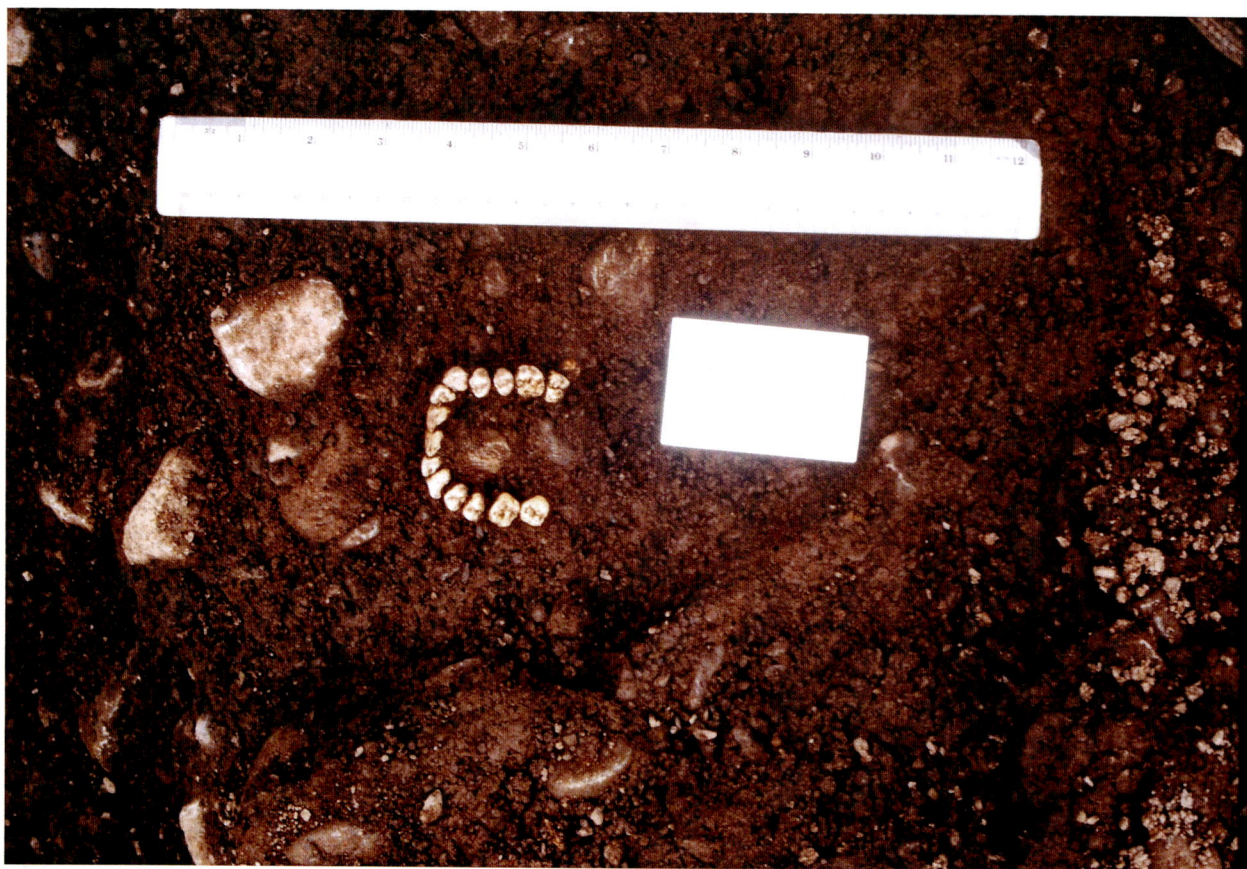

*Plate 20: The rare survival of* in situ *teeth in one of the graves*

There is some evidence for a progressive shift in the alignment of the graves, although all were aligned approximately east-west along the slope (Fig 13). Stratigraphically and, as far as the results were valid, statistically, the most accurately oriented (east-west) graves, and those with obtuse (greater than 90°-from north) alignments, were almost always early in the sequence in the southern part of the cemetery. Given that this was the area where the graves seemed to be grouping towards a focus, it may be assumed that the earliest burials would have been there. To the north, there was a greater incidence of acutely angled graves, which tended to group around the orientation of the present chancel (77° from north), and this perhaps implies an earlier church beneath the standing structure. Indeed, these graves seemed to be stratigraphically later than the accurately oriented graves below the later churchyard boundary (*151, pp 24-5*). The information recoverable from an analysis of the graves would indicate that the orientation of burials shifted on at least two occasions during the use of the cemetery, and certainly the construction of wall *644* seems to have had some effect on grave alignment.

*Plate 21: An intact articulated hinge component from a coffin*

Little pottery appeared to be associated with the graves, but what there was, where identifiable, could be divided into Roman and medieval. Grave *1424*, in the extreme south of the site, contained a scrap of abraded samian ware, and two more abraded pieces were found in grave *1366*, a short distance to the north-east. A sherd of Romano-British greyware was found in each of graves *268* and *299*, in the mass of graves on the upper terrace. Two twelfth-to fourteenth-century sherds and an unidentified

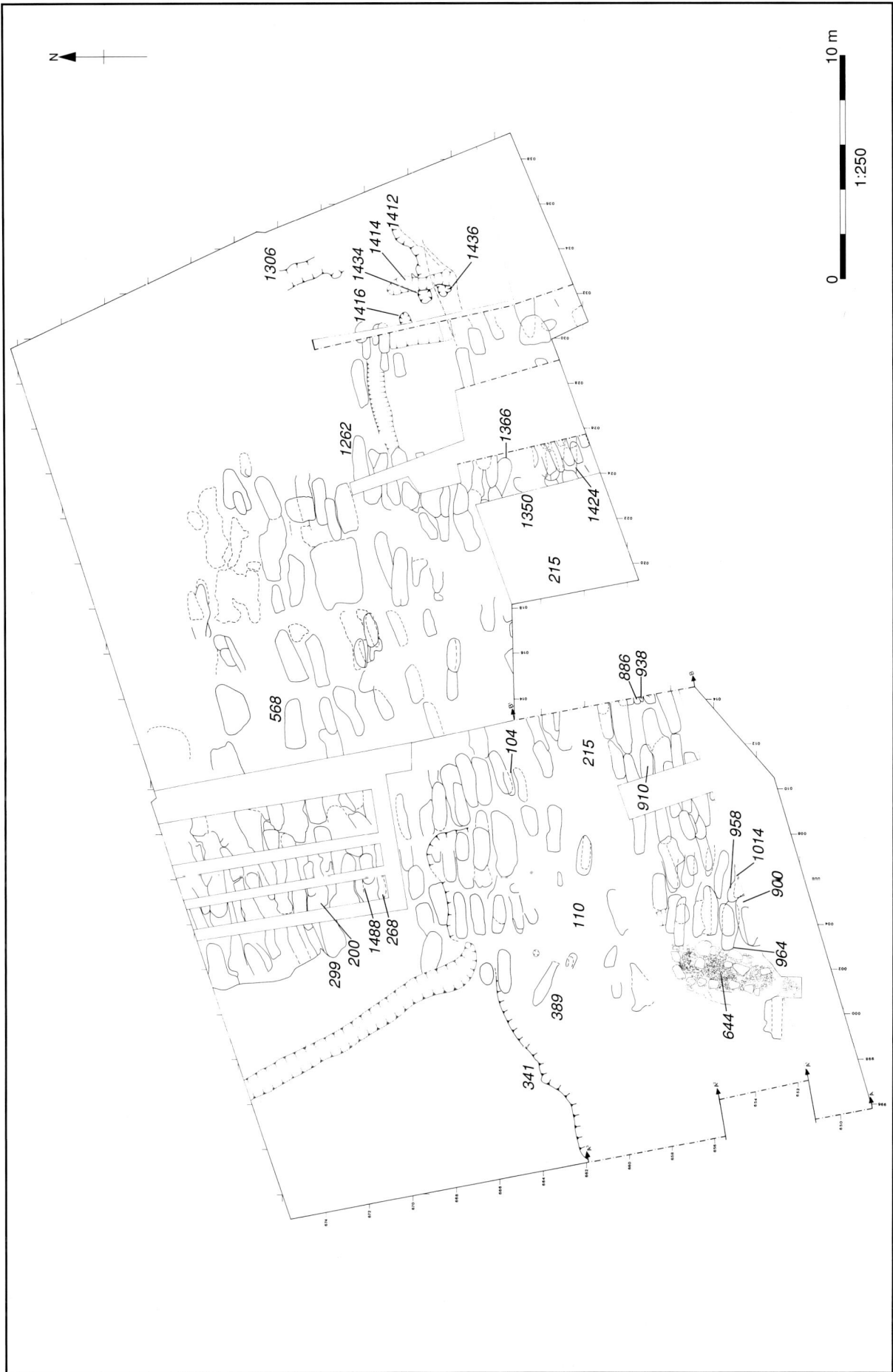

Figure 13: The early medieval cemetery

fragment were found in the upper fill (*103*) of grave *104*, and a further twelfth-fourteenth-century sherd was also found near the top of grave *1488*, both again on the upper terrace. The fact that the medieval pottery was identified near the top of the two graves indicates that it was intrusive, although grave *104* was the latest stratigraphically in the cemetery. Similarly, the wear on each of the sherds of Roman pottery perhaps indicates its residuality.

Ditch *1306*, in the far east of the site, was the only boundary feature to contain finds: two sherds of thirteenth- to fourteenth-century pottery in the upper part of the fill. Again, while this pottery perhaps suggests that this was a later feature, it does not fit well into subsequent activity, and it was beneath a medieval croft (*Ch 4*), which had been constructed almost immediately above it, with only a slight build-up of soil between. This would imply considerable erosion between the two phases of activity, as suggested by the evidence from below churchyard bank *151* (*pp 24-5*). Seven sherds of twelfth- to fourteenth-century pottery were also found near the top of layer *110*, on the upper

terrace (Fig 11). This may actually have accumulated at the base of hillwash *32* (*Ch 4, pp 93-4*), for the definition between these layers was indicated only by a gradual increase in the sandiness of the soil, and the horizon 'boundary' may have been slightly lower than identified on site. Only a single grave, *104*, was identified as cutting the upper part of *110*, and it is possible that this was later than the bulk of the early cemetery, perhaps belonging to, though lying outside, the medieval churchyard. Nevertheless, the minimal amount of pottery within the graves as a group points towards the cemetery belonging to an aceramic period, presumably before the twelfth century, particularly as the element excavated was effectively deconsecrated by the construction of the medieval churchyard boundary (*Ch 4, p 91*).

Several features were excavated amongst the early graves that did not fit readily with a cemetery while it was in use (Fig 14). Posthole *886* was cut by posthole *938* in the south of the excavation, close to the east end of the medieval church, although both cut cemetery level *713* and appeared to have been sealed by layer *274*. Rounded cut *958* to the west, aligned sharply

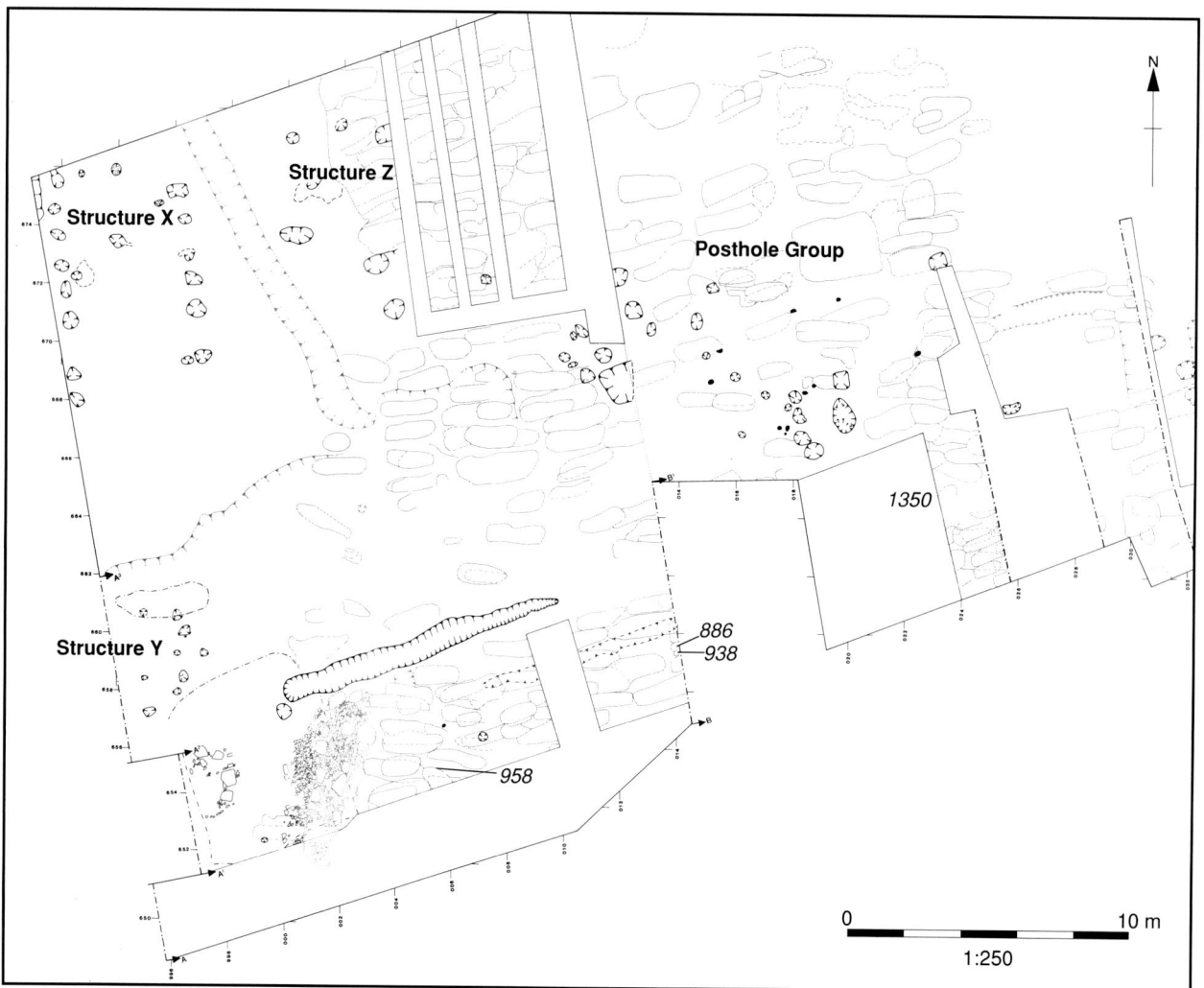

*Figure 14: Structures around the cemetery*

north-west/south-east and 0.80 m long by 0.60 m wide, also appeared to have been sealed by *274* and was cut by grave *900*, yet seemed to cut graves *964* and *1014*. This would suggest that it had been dug during the time the cemetery was in use, although its function was not obvious. Feature *1350*, again aligned more sharply, there north-east/south-west, cut layer *1346* in the area of dense burials near the east end of the medieval church, and had in turn been cut by medieval boundary ditch *215* (*Ch 4, pp 91-3*). It may have been a grave, although if this were the case, the outline had become very distorted.

Three postholes were sealed by layer *1235* (*Ch 4, p 94*) to the east of the cemetery. Posthole *1434* was cut by cemetery boundary *1414*, whilst *1436* seemed in turn to cut *1414*. The third, *1416*, some 0.70 m to the north-west, was not associated with any other feature. All were very much larger than the postholes associated with the medieval croft (*Ch 4*) and were also stratigraphically earlier, although they had no obvious function in association with the cemetery, since none was clearly connected with a grave, and their relationship with the cemetery boundary was not clear.

The edge of the natural east-west terrace across the central part of the site had been enhanced by an artificial cut (*341*, in the west of the site, and *1412*, in the south-eastern corner), which was overlaid by upper cemetery level *110* and layer *1235*. In the east, *1412* appeared only as a shallow cut, sloping towards the south, although it cut eastern cemetery boundary *1414*, yet in the west, where the natural slope was greater, cut *341* was only distinct at the base of the slope. The stratigraphy would suggest that this cutting back may have taken place at the end of the cemetery's use, but its purpose remains uncertain. Structure Y (*p 33*) was certainly situated within this cutting back into the terrace edge. Layer *1411*, within the hollow created by cut *1412*, would appear to have been the earliest hillwash on the site. No finds were associated with any of these features.

## The structures around the cemetery

Several structures were found around the perimeter of the early cemetery (Fig 14). Two buildings in the west did not relate directly to the graves but could have been contemporary with them, although other postholes were obviously later than the cemetery, and may, in fact, be medieval in origin (*Ch 4*). All seemed to have been sealed by hillwash *32* (*Ch 4, pp 93-4*) and were identified only at the level of the subsoil. No good dating evidence or occupational debris was associated with any structure, although each was clearly later than the earliest features.

### Structure X

A rectangular posthole structure (X) on the upper terrace was aligned north/south, with overall dimensions of at least 8.50 x 5 m. The 14 postholes forming the sides (eight in the western alignment and six in the eastern; Pl 22) were relatively regularly spaced at *c* 0.5 m intervals, although a wider gap of *c* 1-1.4 m between the postholes at

*Plate 22: Structure X, looking south*

the southern end of each alignment (*176* and *227* on the west, and *225* and *240* on the east; Fig 15) perhaps signifies a cross-passage between two opposed entrances. The remains of the postholes at the southern end were much shallower (less than 0.2 m), seemingly implying that this structure may have suffered from the same erosional forces as the early medieval cemetery. There was no clear evidence for a gable post at either end.

Several further postholes were recorded in the same area as this structure, though not related specifically to either wall. Posthole *238* (0.48 x 0.20 m by 0.13 m deep), adjacent to posthole *240* at the southern end of the eastern side, may have been associated with the putative entrance, or may simply be evidence of refurbishment. Very small posthole *136* (0.28 x 0.24 x 0.21 m), along the possible line of the northern gable, may represent some trace of the north wall, although the fact that it was smaller than most of the other postholes could suggest that it was part of an internal division. This would mean, however, that the building extended beyond the churchyard into the field to the north. The proximity of posthole *136* to posthole *127*, though, which was anomalous in the structure and contained medieval material, may point to a

later date for it. Postholes *168* and *143* were not parts of the main wall lines and may in fact have belonged to earlier activity, conceivably being associated with gully *140* (*p 21*), although *143* may also indicate some sub-division of the building.

Feature *134*, immediately to the north-west of Structure X and extending only a short distance (0.2 m) into the excavation, appeared to be square or rectangular (2.16 m long by 0.35 m deep), aligned north/south, and contained four deeper holes in the base. It may in fact have been part of a pit, similar to others in the area thought to be medieval in origin (*eg 113* and *164*; Ch 4, *p 101*), but it contained no finds and its purpose remains uncertain.

A rectangular timber structure (Z), aligned north/south, may also have existed on the upper terrace, some 4 m to the east of Structure X and approximately parallel to it. Four postholes (*196*, *223*, *301*, *1500*) seemed to form a roughly rectangular pattern, enclosing an area of 6 x 3.50 m. In addition, postholes *213*, *308*, and *1506* were also in the area but did not form absolutely straight sides, although posthole *1506*, lying slightly outside the line of the structure, may have been part of a north wall. Similarly, it is conceivable that *213* could have

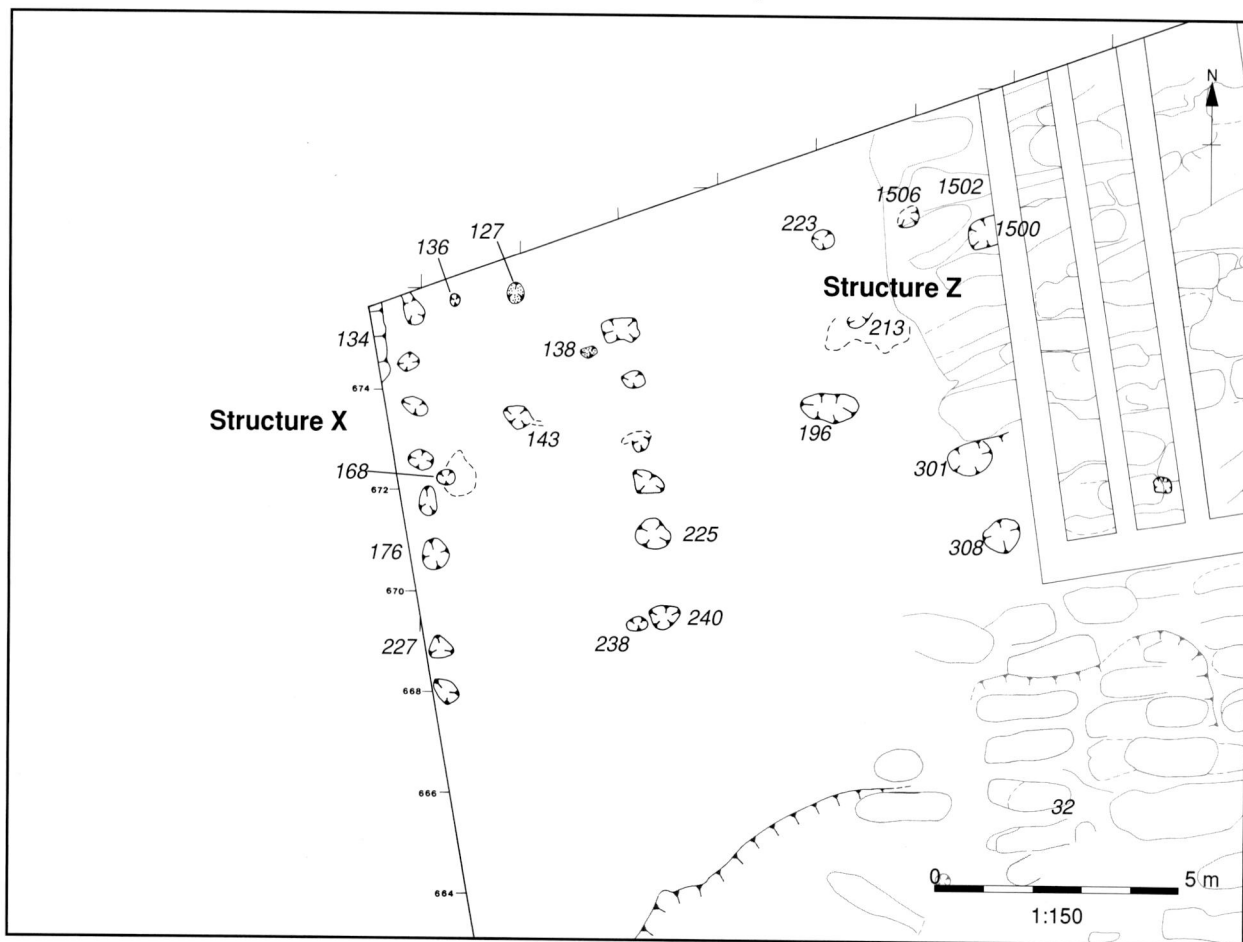

*Figure 15: Structures X and Z*

32

been part of a west wall, and *308* could be seen as an extension to an east wall. Posthole *1506* was the only one to cut a grave (*1502*), which suggests that at least this part of the early cemetery had become disused by the time this putative structure had been constructed.

A group of postholes forming no clearly recognisable pattern cut the central cemetery area (Fig 14). At least some of them may have related to later activity (for example, the medieval croft; *Ch 4*), although none contained datable evidence. In contrast to the structures forming the croft, however, no finds were associated with them.

**Structure Y**
Although Structure Y was only partially exposed, since much was below the active churchyard to the west, the excavated part appeared to have been curved, and the evidence is consistent with either a sub-rectangular or sub-circular building (Pl 23). The seven irregularly spaced postholes forming a broad arc suggested an approximate width of 3.5 m for the structure (Fig 16), although these varied in size from 0.2 m to 0.5 m, and 0.1-0.5 m deep, so may not all have been contemporary. Two further small postholes (*350*, *363*) were recorded in the interior of the structure, and an apparent stakehole (*332*) was found immediately to the south of posthole *330*, one of those forming the eastern end of the

building. Their precise function remains uncertain, presumably being associated with internal fittings, although no occupation was directly associated.

There was some evidence for the structure having been rebuilt at some point, as three postholes were found outside the main wall line, and an internal occupation layer associated with two hearths overlay the original wall line. The postholes (*556*, *558*, *718*) seemed to describe a similar arc to the earlier structure, yet also defined the extent of apparent occupation layer *172*, which clearly sealed the earlier postholes. They were again irregularly spaced and varied in size from 0.29 m to 0.52 m, although they were fairly uniform in depth (0.14-0.22 m). Layer *172* was rich in charcoal and contained significant amounts of pre-Norman material: an abraded sherd of samian ware; a largely intact ceramic bun-shaped loomweight; nine small fragments of coloured window glass; and a narrow piece of lead sheet (*Ch 3*).

Hearths *208* and *186* seem to have been used consecutively, since although they were placed side by side, hearth *208* had clearly been disturbed by the setting around hearth *186* (Pl 24). Hearth *208* comprised an irregularly shaped flat slab of red sandstone (0.68 m in diameter), although the irregularity had at least partly been caused by the decay of the stone, as a result of repeated heating; its

*Plate 23: The postholes forming Structure Y, close to the bank and ditch of the later churchyard boundary*

*Figure 16: Structure Y*

*Plate 24: Building Y, with the millstone reused as hearth 186*

34

original shape may have been rounded. Hearth *186* was formed by a reused small top stone from a mill (0.90 m in diameter; *Ch 3, pp 80-1*), the grinding side uppermost, and was in a better state of preservation, although the heat of the fire had caused the stone to crack, close to the edge of the central socket. It had been kept in place by upright chock-stones, which had largely decayed.

The south-western corner of the northern churchyard, in the area occupied by Structure Y, and to the immediate south, contained a significant quantity of debris, including the remains of hearths. Whilst most related to secondary ironworking, appreciable amounts were indicative of smelting, in the form of bloomery slag (Fig 17). Although this cannot be firmly linked to Structure Y itself, it would suggest both primary ironworking in the vicinity, as well as blacksmithing. Another concentration was seen to the east of the cemetery, sealed by the later medieval croft (*Ch 4, p 92*).

## Later cemetery features

The cemetery wall (*644*) to the south-east of Structure Y may have decayed at the time that the later incarnation of the structure was standing. A spread of cobbles (*688*; Fig 18), identical to the stones forming the core of the wall, lay to the west, as did a group of large angular stones (*686*), which resembled the facings of *644* in both size and shape. These suggest that the wall collapsed outwards, away from the cemetery, and was left in a dilapidated state.

The ruins of wall *644* and the area to the west were overlain by layer *273*, which separated the apparent collapse of the wall from a further layer (*263*), which consisted of a mixture of cobbles and broken pieces of red sandstone, possibly representing a surface of some sort (Pl 25). Layer *263* was found immediately below the earliest medieval churchyard boundary (bank *151, Ch 4, p 91*) and seemed to have been cut by the associated ditch (*215*) to the north. There was no

*Figure 17: Metalworking debris on the site*

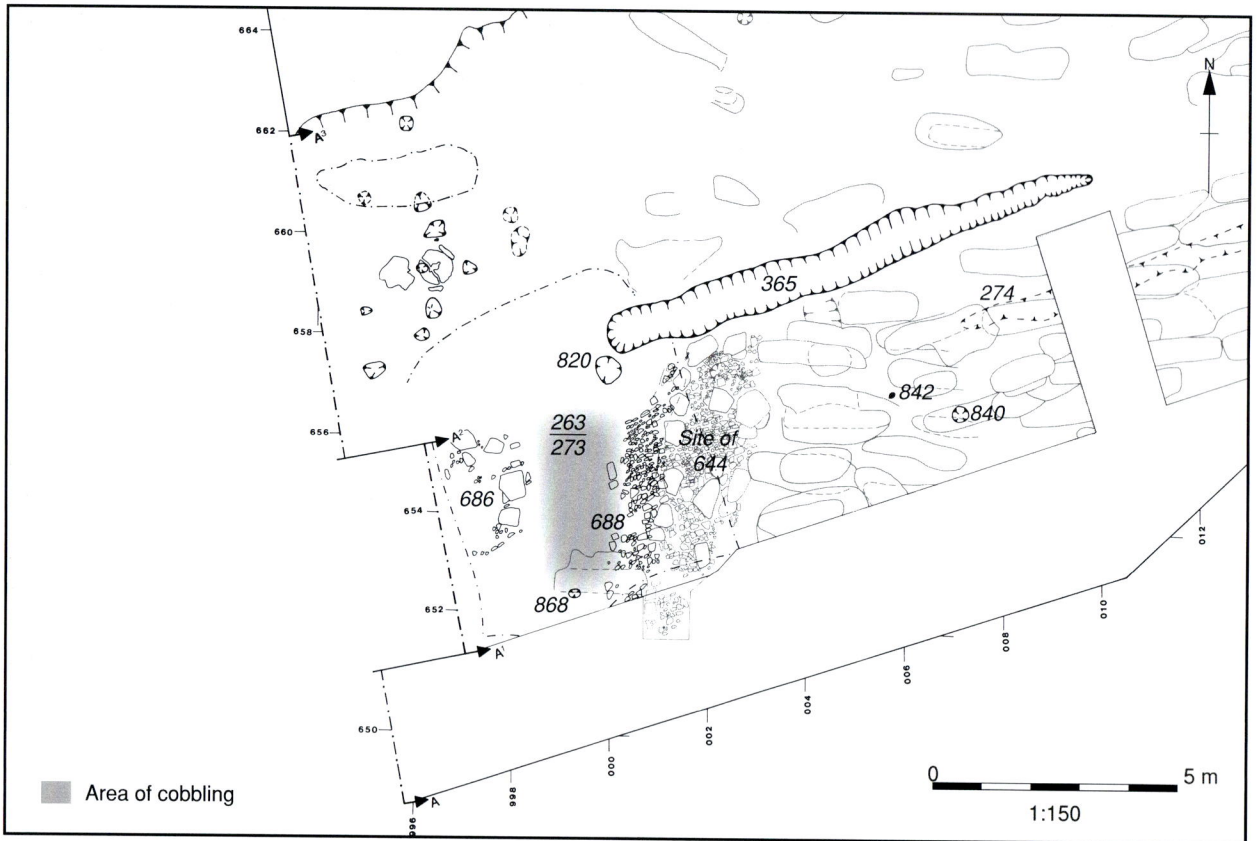

*Figure 18: Later features*

*Plate 25: Possible metalled surface 688*

obvious activity to the east of 263, above the cemetery, but this area seems to have suffered severely from erosion before the medieval churchyard was created.

Postholes 820 and 868 seemed to be associated with layer 263 in this south-western part of the site, although 868 may have been slightly earlier. Indeed, they could be seen as forming one side of it, and they followed the same alignment as wall 644 to the east, posthole 820 having been cut by the later churchyard boundary ditch (215; Ch 4, pp 91-3). Two other isolated postholes (840, 842) lay amongst the densest grouping of graves to the east, but it is likely, given the analogous situation in other parts of the site, that these features post-dated the cemetery, since they appeared to cut cemetery level 274, rather than being potential evidence of the graves having been marked.

A small ditch (365, 19.90 m long and 1.60 m wide) may have been dug during this time of dilapidation, although it was on the same east-west alignment as the later, medieval churchyard boundary ditch (215, Ch 4, pp 91-3), and it could simply represent a section of that later ditch that had been dug to a deeper level (it was only 0.24 m deep). It contained a large amount of rubble, decreasing in density towards the east, being concentrated at the point where wall 644 ended abruptly at the lip of the ditch, so it was likely to be the collapse of this. Although ditch 365 was in close proximity to this early cemetery boundary, the fact that rubble, presumably from the decay of 644, filled it makes it unlikely that they were contemporary. Ditch 365 therefore perhaps formed the earliest formal boundary for the medieval churchyard.

**Dating**
The dating of this activity is problematical and it cannot be certain that all the features were contemporary with each other. Structure X on the upper terrace is perhaps the least secure, as two postholes in the area (127, 138; Fig 15), albeit not directly connected with the main walls, contained thirteenth- to fourteenth-century pottery. This could potentially date the whole construction, particularly as rectangular structures of a similar size clearly belonged to the medieval croft to the south-east (Ch 4). These two postholes, however, could have been associated with a pit (113; Ch 4, p 101), cutting the north-eastern corner of the structure, which was clearly medieval in origin. A layer (321), sealing Structure Y, contained a fragment of vessel glass with early medieval parallels (Ch 3, pp 84-5), but also a single sherd of twelfth- to thirteenth-century pottery, although human teeth from this layer may indicate the disturbance of the early cemetery during its deposition. Another layer (247), apparently in the same stratigraphic position as layer 172, associated

with the later phase of Structure Y, produced a sherd of Roman pottery but also a tiny chip of blue window glass which could conceivably be later medieval (Ch 3, pp 48-5). The copper-alloy garment hook (Ch 3, pp 53-4) was also found in the vicinity. The amount of pre-Norman material from the layers around and above Structure Y, particularly the pins from within and beneath the medieval boundary bank (151/96) and ditch (215; Ch 4), and the fragments of window glass and loomweight from layer 172, would seem to indicate a date in the eighth- to eleventh century for this building.

Layer 273 contained two sherds of Roman coarseware and a single sherd of twelfth- to thirteenth-century pottery, whereas 263 contained a single sherd of thirteenth-fourteenth-century pottery. This small quantity of medieval pottery is similar in date to that found in much greater quantities in overlying layers (see Ch 4), although the fact that it was stratigraphically earlier perhaps indicates that surface 263 was eleventh- or twelfth-century in date.

## The Orchard (Site 1)

The Orchard also sloped quite steeply from north to south, with the wide upper part on the same terrace as the majority of the medieval church and modern churchyard (Fig 19). Both the early and later medieval activity was concentrated in this upper area, with deep deposits of hillwash forming the main feature of the rest of the site.

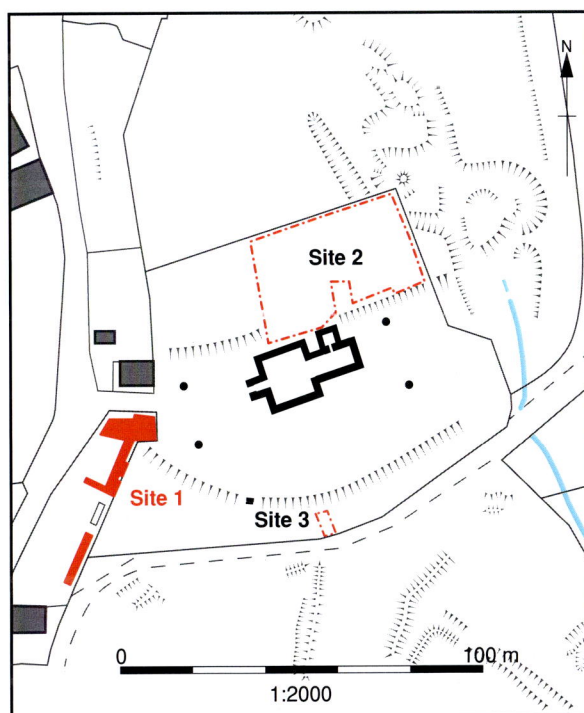

*Figure 19: The location of the Orchard (Site 1)*

## The early boundary

The earliest activity in the north of the Orchard comprised a wide U-shaped ditch (*67*; Fig 20), 2.10 m wide and 0.50 m deep, which cut the gravel substratum and curved in an arc from east to north (Pl 26). It was sealed by a wall (*17, below*), that emerged from under the present churchyard boundary, and had clearly silted up over a period of time. The upper fill contained debris of later phases: stones from possible medieval churchyard boundary wall *18* (*Ch 4, p 112*); and also six sherds of medieval pottery of fourteenth- to sixteenth-century date. The arc it drew seemed to extend westwards the sweep of a bank visible within the churchyard to the east, which apparently formed an early southern boundary of the consecrated ground. Excavations in the southern churchyard in 1985 (*Site 3, p 41*) found traces of a ditch (*1260*) in a similar primary position, which clearly pre-dated this bank, and it is possible that these two ditches were elements of the same feature. The primary position in the archaeological sequence of ditch *67*, and the lack of ceramic evidence from the lower part of the fill, perhaps lend support for an early, possibly pre-Norman, date for the ditch.

Two other features (*114* and *124*) of uncertain function, which cut the natural subsoil in the far north-eastern part of the site, lay below clearly medieval activity. These were both quite irregular in outline, aligned broadly north/south, and quite large, measuring 2.70 x 0.88 x 0.80 m and 1.50 x 1.20 x 0.25-0.40 m respectively. The gravelly fills did not contain finds, though there were noticeable amounts of charcoal, and it is possible that either could have been a natural formation, such as a tree throw.

The deep primary hillwash (*59*), which was interleaved with lenses of clay (*61*) and gravel (*60*), is likely to have started to form early in the sequence of human activity. Four large stones (*97*) lay above hillwash *59* at the southern extreme of the trench, and beneath a series of walls, the latest of which formed the present churchyard boundary. These seemed to be *in situ*, rather than tumble from the decay of the adjacent boundary, so were likely to have been the foundations for the earliest of the walls forming the western side of the churchyard.

## Structure overlying the early boundary

A well-built wall (*17*) of yellow sandstone sealed the eastern part of ditch *67*, the material very unlike any other structure on the site. It was apparently dry-bonded and constructed of small, irregularly sized blocks in an imitation of ashlar, although only the northern and western faces, which met at an acute angle, were visible, since the wall lay almost entirely beneath the present western wall of the churchyard (Pl 27). A large amount of yellow sandstone was found below the churchyard wall to the south, but

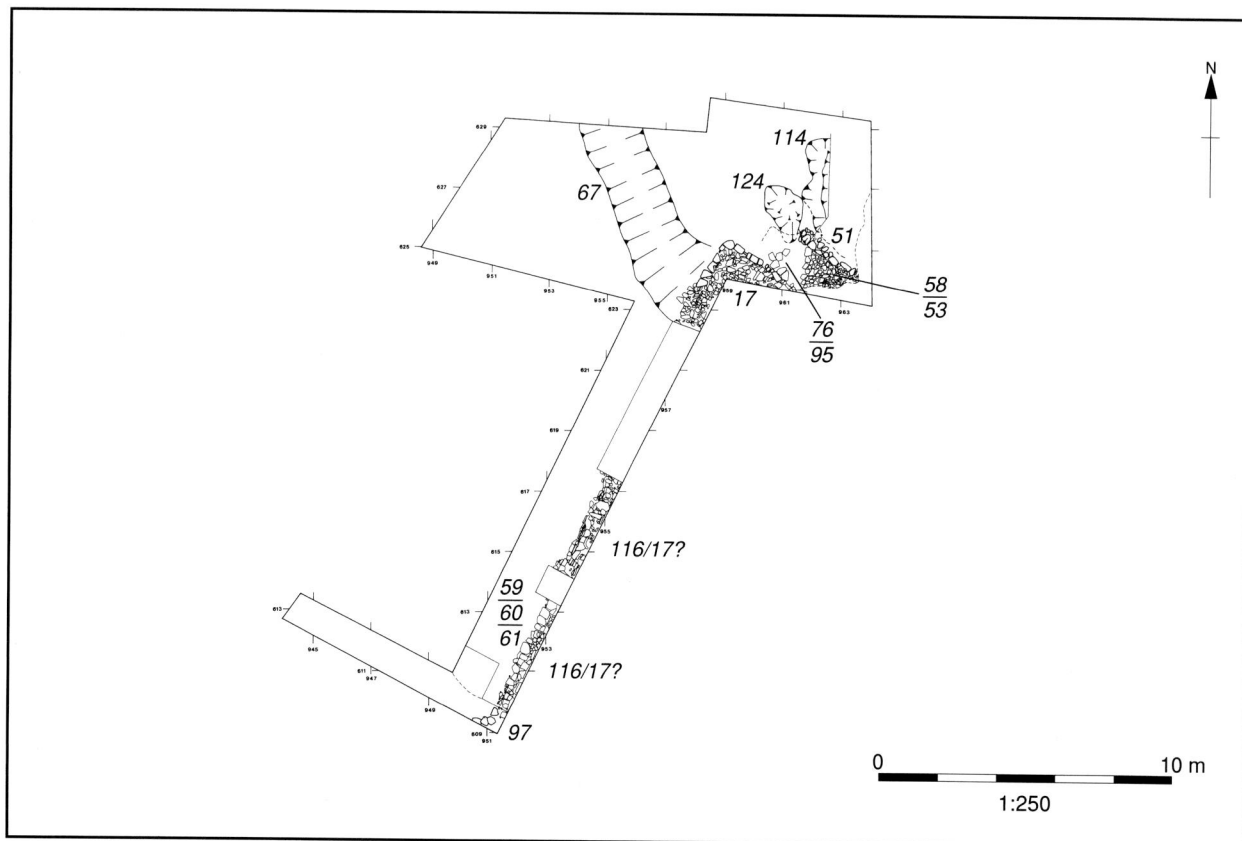

*Figure 20: The early features in the Orchard*

38

*Plate 26: The early ditch (67) in the Orchard*

*Plate 27: Wall 17 in the Orchard*

*Plate 28: Surface 53, with kerb 51*

the construction was rougher and it is not certain that it was part of wall *17*. Indeed, this southern section may have been later than the rest of *17*, perhaps an early churchyard boundary, incorporating the yellow sandstone as reused material.

The superior quality of the stonework at the return between the north and west faces suggested that the wall there formed part of a structure now almost completely hidden below the present churchyard. It would seem that wall *17*, or at least the better-constructed portions of it, pre-dated the formulation of the medieval churchyard, it being subsequently incorporated into the later boundary (*Ch 4, p 112*).

Wall *116* continued the line of wall *17* to the south, differing from it in that it was less well made and contained less yellow sandstone. The relationship between the walls could not be ascertained, though *116* may represent a rebuild of *17*, although it is possible that it formed part of a separate wall, connected with the use of the land as an orchard, which reused some material from wall *17* once it had decayed.

A stony layer (*76*) containing fragments of charcoal, to the north of wall *17*, seemed to butt against it, and it may have been created as a foundation for surface *53* (*below*). Its stratigraphical position implied an early date, yet finds from this layer were mixed, varying from a pre-Norman strap-end (*Ch 3, p 53*), which

suggests early medieval activity in the vicinity, to a sherd of thirteenth/fourteenth-century pottery. It is likely that this indicates some contamination, since the area to the north of wall *17* appeared to have been disturbed by gardening activity (*Ch 4, p 114*), although it remains a possibility that the earlier finds were residual. A darker area (*95*) at the base of layer *76*, which may have been an intrusion, also contained two sherds of thirteenth/fourteenth-century pottery.

A surface (*53*) of river-worn cobbles with some angular stones, close to the present churchyard wall in the north-east corner of the site (Pl 28), had been carefully laid above layer *76*, and appeared to have been parallel to wall *17*. Although the direct relationship had been destroyed by a modern intrusion, it was probably related to the structure of which this wall was a part, perhaps acting as a path, some 1.30 m wide. Surface *53* had been entirely covered by clay *58*, which might perhaps have been a base for a further surface, of which no trace remained, since it coincided with *53* exactly. If this were the case, the proposed path would seem to have had an extended lifespan. The possibility of this being a resurfacing is, however, negated somewhat by the lack of evidence for wear on *53*.

Both surface *53* and clay *58* were retained by a kerb of upright stones (*51*) on the north, which ended abruptly immediately to the west of surface *53*, as

40

though it had been cut away. The stones forming this kerb were largely glacial erratics, with some carboniferous sandstone interspersed, creating a face to the south, against the surface, though with a more irregular northern side. It seems to have been disturbed, since a fragment of clay pipe was found amongst the stones.

## The Southern Churchyard (Site 3)

The small trench in the southern churchyard was excavated on the terrace beneath that containing the medieval church and the bulk of the churchyard, in an area that had been consecrated in the later nineteenth century (Fig 21). The excavation was focused on the drain known to exist there, excavated in the later 1920s (Hudleston 1932), and a very small area around it, constrained to the south by the present churchyard wall, and by known graves to the east, west, and north.

### Earliest activity

The earliest activity on the site was a deep, steep-sided, V-shaped ditch (*1260*; Fig 22), 1 m wide by 0.80 m deep, which was aligned east-west and cut the clay substratum. Despite the differences in width and depth, this could have been the same feature as ditch *67* to the north-west (in the Orchard, *p 38*), since both followed the same alignment as the bank visible in the churchyard. This bank was probably the medieval churchyard boundary, yet it might

have followed the line of ditch *1260*, since it was clearly stratigraphically later. The differences in shape and dimensions between ditches *1260* and *67* may well have been dictated by the varying subsoil each was cut through, since it would have been impossible to create a steep ditch within the stony subsoil underlying the Orchard, and the wider, U-shaped cut seen there would have resulted, while ditch *1260* had silted up whilst retaining its steep profile, being cut through a very sticky bluish clay. The primary clay fill (*1259*; Fig 23) contained a very stony deposit (*1152*) at the northern lip, which had probably come from layer *1299*, to the north, which was also extremely stony, in marked contrast to the clay layers excavated to the south. There was no evidence that ditch *1260* cut layer *1299*, though *1299* had clearly not been produced by upcast from the ditch, but it seems that it may have formed a bank along the north side of the ditch, presumably made of material from elsewhere on the site. Thus fill *1152* would seem to have been slippage from this presumed bank.

The relative positions of ditch *1260* and layer *1299* would suggest that the area enclosed was to the north, under the present churchyard. There was, however, no trace of a bank associated with ditch *67* in the Orchard, although it must be admitted that the area, where this would have been, contained the most concentrated later activity (*Ch 4*). No datable material was recovered from the ditch, and only a small scrap of lead (*Ch 3*) and a heavily patinated flint flake were found within *1299*; however, the absence

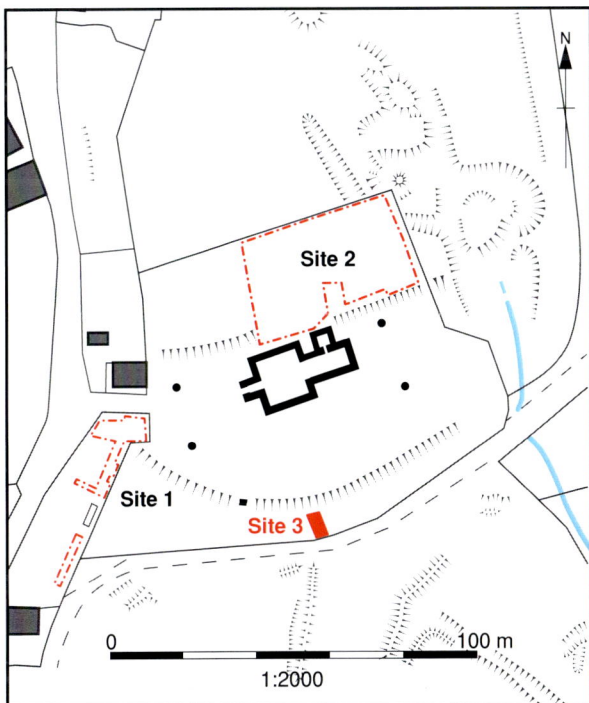

*Figure 21: The location of the southern churchyard (Site 3)*

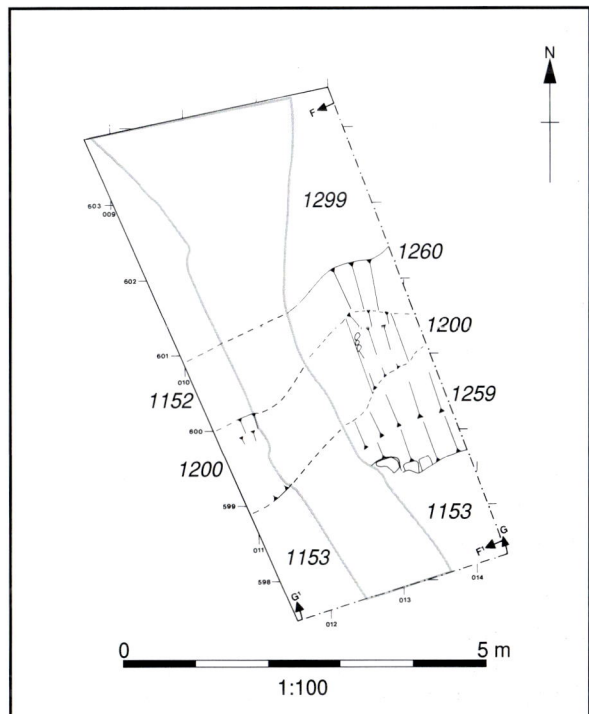

*Figure 22: The early ditch in the southern churchyard*

41

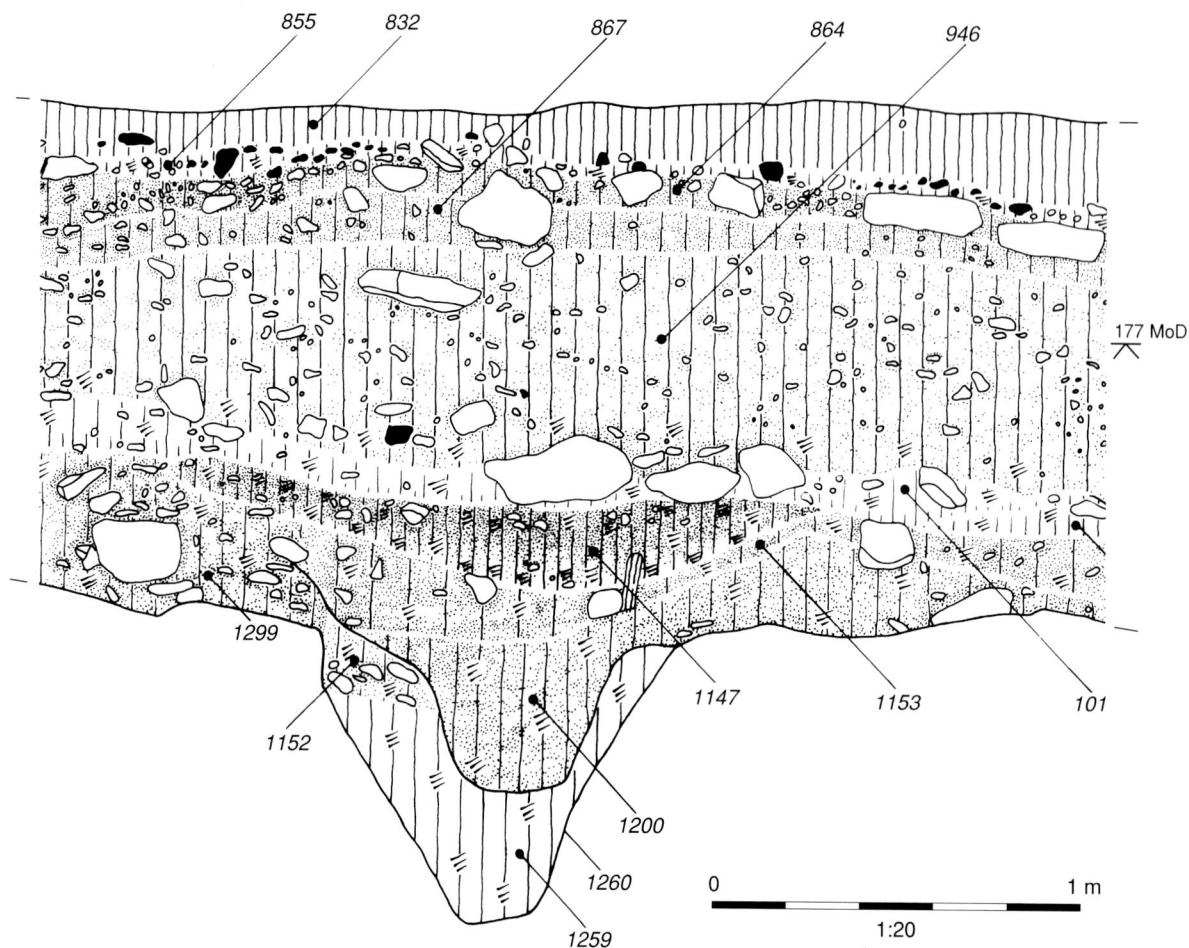

*Figure 23: Section through the early ditch in the southern churchyard*

of any ceramic evidence does point to an early date for the feature, as does the stratigraphical evidence.

Ditch *1260* seems to have been recut in the form of *1200*, for the latter's edges appeared too steep to have been otherwise created, and its clayey, almost stoneless, fill was very different from fill *1259* of ditch *1260*. The precise reason for the recutting, however, remains obscure, but presumably reflects the continued use of the feature.

The recut seems to have silted up from the south, as the same material both filled *1200* and extended to the southern limit of the excavation. Layer *1153* above this also extended to the south; this was similar to layers immediately above and, with its flat upper surface, could represent the beginning of a levelling process. A few unworked pieces of wood and a struck lithic (perhaps a knife; *Ch 3; p 48*) came from the fills of *1200* but no pottery was recovered. This is perhaps significant, as all clearly medieval layers in this site contained at least some sherds.

The layers above the ditch formed a very distinct group within the site, although they can be sub-divided into individual features. These provided

evidence of human activity, although they were only present to the south of possible bank *1299*, which continued to be visible.

The lowest layer (*1147*) was very similar to ditch fill *1200*, though separated from it by sandier deposit *1153*. The upper part was notable for the amount of wood surviving, where identifiable, of oak (J Huntley *pers comm*). Most of it was unworked and seemingly randomly deposited, but at least two fragments of planking, a wedge-shaped piece, and also a rounded stake were recovered, which perhaps related to features to the south of the excavation. If this did represent some sort of surface, it is not clear whether it lay inside or outside a structure.

A single squared wooden post (*1233*; Fig 24), again of oak (J Huntley *pers comm*), was found at the base of layer *1147*, cutting into the upper layers of ditch fill (*1199, 1153*), although it did not seem to be *in situ*. A single posthole (*1344*) further to the south, which also seemed to cut layer *1153*, appeared to be stratigraphically earlier than a fence (*1167*), which was obviously associated with layer *1147*, although it was only seen in the southern edge of the excavation. Fence *1167* (Fig 25) was constructed

42

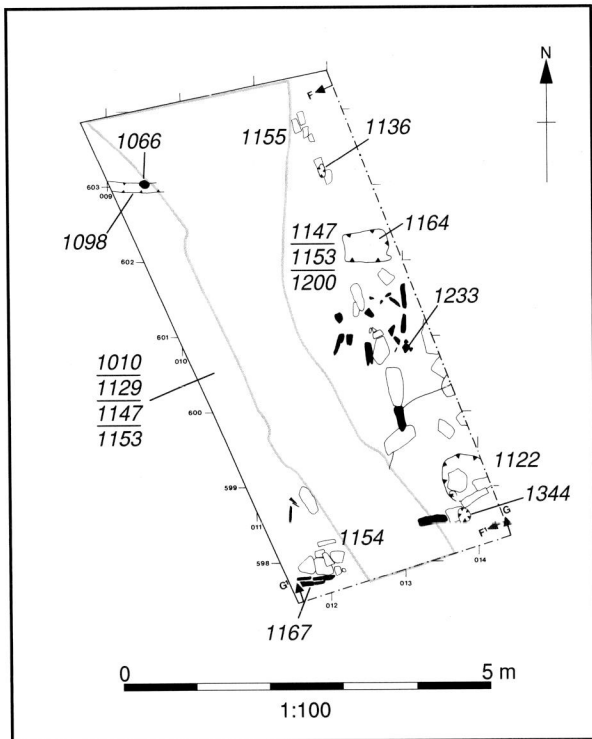

*Figure 24: Early features in the southern churchyard*

1167, at the base of layer 1147, but their function, if any, remains obscure.

A broken north-south line of large stones (1155), aligned approximately north-south and some 9 m long by a single stone in width, in the north-eastern corner of the site, had apparently sunk into the top of layer 1147, unless this had continued to build up around the stones. A parallel group of stones was seen in the eastern section of the excavation, associated with layer 1129 (below), although it could not be established whether they were related. In other circumstances the formation could have been produced by ploughing, but the waterlogged condition of the layers below makes this highly unlikely. It could possibly have been associated with some sort of structure, although it seemed too insubstantial to have been the base of a wall.

Dark greyish silty-clay layer 1129 was identified above most of the earliest features. A large amount of unworked wood fragments, which had survived in the waterlogged conditions in the southern part of the site, formed a band at the top of the layer, and may again have constituted some kind of flooring. The uppermost layer in this sequence (1010), a compact and quite stony reddish sandy clay, was not waterlogged and contained a large quantity of charcoal. Two areas of burning within 1010, each capped by a clay lens, appear to have been hearths, although they were probably not contemporary with each other. There was no

of narrow interwoven branches, which seemed too insubstantial for a structural wall, but the possibility that a building lay to the south of the excavated area cannot be dismissed. Indeed, a wattle and daub wall could have provided at least some of the waterlogged mixed clay spreads to the north. A dump of large boulders (1154) lay against the north side of fence

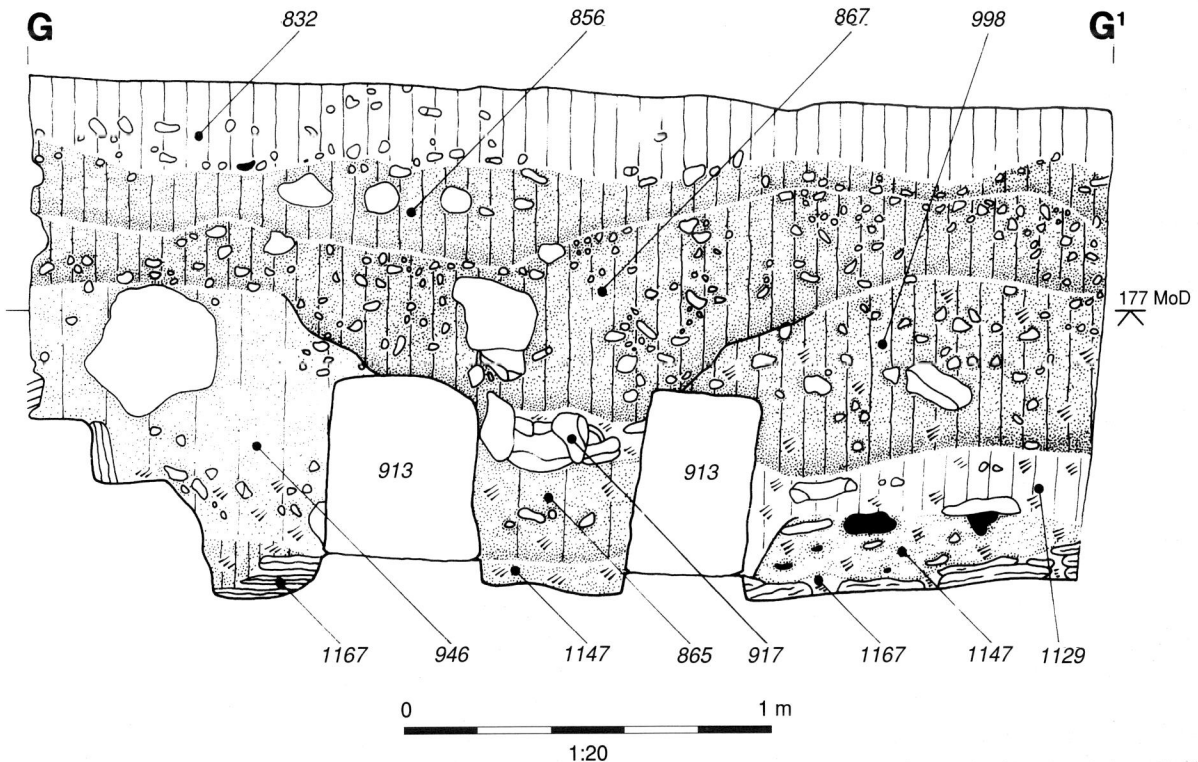

*Figure 25: The southern section in the southern churchyard*

43

indication whether they were situated within a structure or in the open air, or whether they were domestic or industrial.

The finds from this activity are restricted to a piece of scrap lead and a fragment of glass bangle (*Ch 3; p 75; p 49*) from layer *1010*. The absence of pottery and the stratigraphical position, below drain *913* (*below*), suggests that the activity was pre-Norman.

Five features of uncertain phase, all in the northern part of the trench, seemed to have been related on stratigraphical grounds; none contained any dating evidence. Feature *1164*, a shallow rectangular cut in the east of the site (0.66 x 0.43 x 0.07 m), closely mirrored the underlying cut for infilled ditch *1260*, but there is no apparent reason why the ditch should have been known about in succeeding phases. A shallow sub-circular feature (*1122*; 0.75 x 0.60 x 0.19 m) to the south contained a large flat piece of a light-coloured soft wood, fitting into the base, although whether this wood had been dumped or was in its original position was not clear, given the restricted area that could be examined. A short length of a narrow gully (*1098*; 0.42 x 0.35 x 0.24 m) in the north of the site, filled with relatively large flat stones, only appeared to the west of drain *913*. It seemed to have pre-dated the drain, although it could possibly have been associated with it. Two small, shallow, and isolated postholes in the north of the site, *1136* and *1066*, the latter cutting gully *1098*, may also belong to this phase of activity.

## The drain

A massive stone-built drain (*913*; Fig 26) presumably led water from the area in which the parish church now stands, downhill to a tributary of the Dacre Beck. Two channels, merging into a single outflow (Pl 29), appeared to issue from beneath the bank to the north of the excavation (seemingly the earlier, medieval churchyard boundary) and the outflow remained visible as a cropmark in the field to the south of the site, where it seemed to curve eastwards (rather than continuing southwards, as Hudleston (1932) presumed). Only a length of some 7 m was available for excavation, however, and most of this had been opened in *c* 1929; an area of only 0.50 m² survived intact, immediately to the north of the present churchyard wall. Twenty stones, forming the sides of the drain, were examined and all bar one was clearly a massive, reused block.

The stones were rectangular, averaging 0.75 x 0.35 x 0.55 m, and were roughly dressed (Fig 27), probably with a pick or punch, although the relative smoothness of some of the surfaces might indicate the use of a chisel or axe. Each contained a lewis hole. The workmanship was generally careless (P Hill *pers comm*), the lewis holes being roughly cut, and the dressing of the sinkings on the joints was similarly treated.

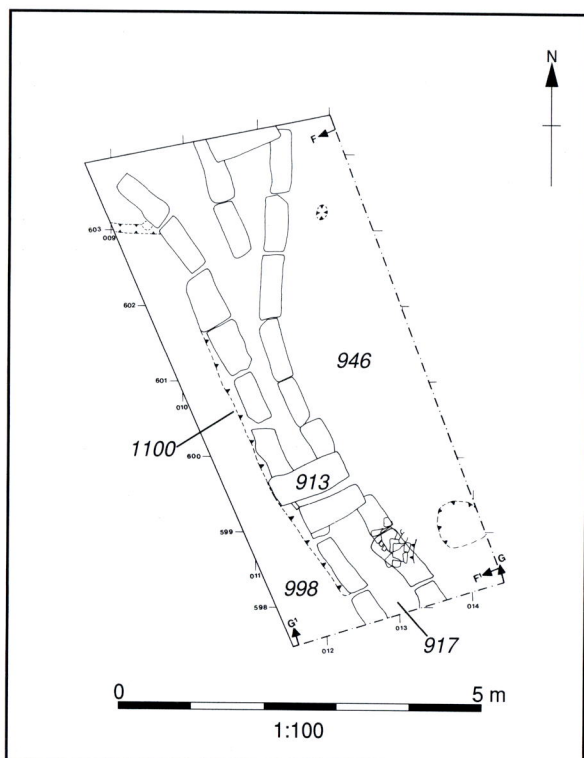

*Figure 26: Drain* 913

*Plate 29: Drain* 913

44

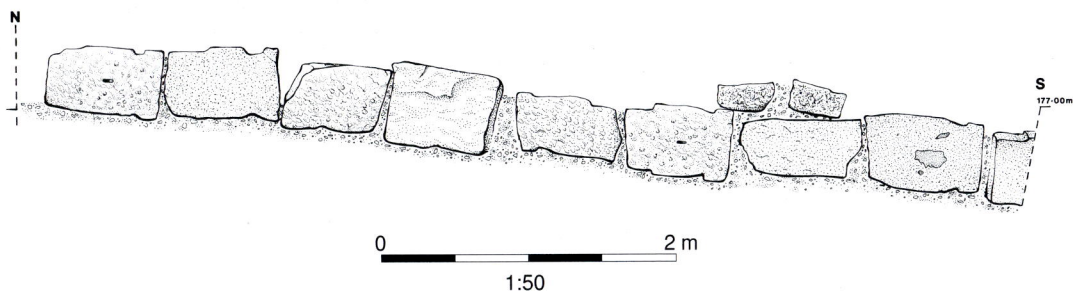

*Figure 27: The western elevation of drain 913*

Each of the tooled stones had one broad side smoothly cut and one roughly pecked, and the lewis hole was always in the centre of the pecked side (Pl 30). The stones had been cut in two distinct profiles, but there were strong similarities, since both types had a recess worked on both joints, behind the face. The first type was shaped like a thick T, producing a long wedge shape (Pl 31); the other had a narrow groove on both narrow edges at one end and a wider groove at the other, creating a roughly semi-circular recess. In both cases this could have served some restraining purpose, either receiving an iron or wooden rod, or being run in with lead. The opposite end of the stones probably originally ran back into a wall, and was checked out on each joint from the back of the stone for about a third of its length. This may again have been seating for either timber or stone, although it was so carelessly worked that it is difficult to see them fulfilling such a function, but it demonstrates that the stones had a former purpose and had been reused in the drain (P Hill *pers comm*). A single stone was marked with a crude X, perhaps a mason's mark.

Both types seem to have been laid flat originally. Quantities of mortar were found on some of the stones, which seem more likely to have related to their primary use, rather than having acted as a sealing agent for the drain. The presence of the lewis holes helps to establish the intended original orientation, if it can be assumed that they were contemporary with the dressing. They must have been laid side-by-side or one on top of the other, with the smooth side acting as the bedding plain, the lewis hole on the upper side. It is difficult to identify the original function of such oddly shaped stones, though it seems likely that they were intended to resist thrust, most probably from water pressure, and thus may originally have formed part of a civil-engineering structure (P Hill *pers comm*). The variation in the quality of the dressing may indicate at least one stage of redressing and reuse, when perhaps they were laid in several courses, rather than in a single layer.

Three flat rectangular capping stones, averaging 1 x 0.45 x 0.20 m, survived *in situ*, two together in the centre and one over the eastern channel to the north. These were the only capping stones to have been recorded in *c* 1929, so it can be presumed that any other capping had been removed before that date.

A slight cut (*1100*; Fig 26), only visible at the base of the stones on the western side of the drain, penetrated

*Plate 30: The 'groove edged' block type, with lewis hole*

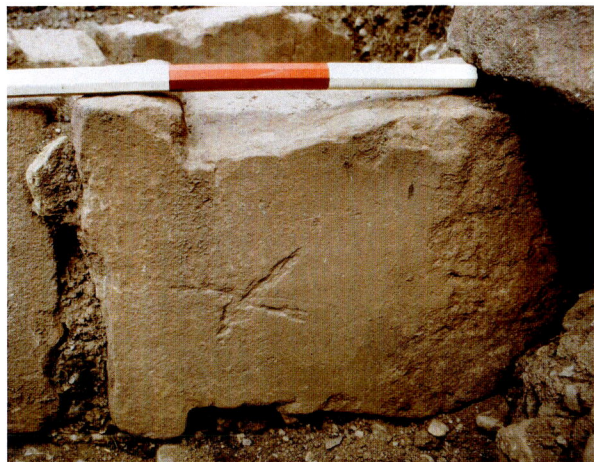

*Plate 31: The 'thick T'-shaped blocks, this with a possible mason's mark*

45

underlying layer *1010*, but was not visible either to the north, or on the eastern side of the stones. This seems to have been a small bedding trench for the stones to keep them upright when they were first put in place. It may, however, simply represent a slight instability in the underlying layers, which caused the stones to settle.

It is not likely that drain *913* had been a free-standing structure, but had been sunk into the ground. In the absence, however, of any evidence for a cut into the surrounding layers within the narrow confines of the excavation, it must be assumed that the stones were placed within a wide trench, the edges of which were beyond the excavated area, and the layers surrounding it, reddish friable gravelly silt *946* to the east, and dark yellowish gravelly silt *998* to the west, were backfill into this. Close examination of these layers revealed apparent tip lines from north to south.

The stones appear to have been Roman in origin and may have been used in a large, engineered structure, such as a mill or bridge (P Hill *pers comm*), which in this area would almost certainly have been of military construction. No such structures are known away from military sites, although the Dacre Beck is large enough to power a mill, and the River Eamont is less than a mile (1.5 km) to the east, which might well have been bridged and certainly could power quite a substantial mill. Alternatively, such massive masonry could have been used in official buildings connected with a fort. The nearest known Roman site at which such buildings could be expected is at Brougham, some six miles (9.6 km) to the north-east. Unless some other, at present unsuspected, site closer to Dacre provided the stone, the manhandling of such enormous blocks over this sort of distance would have taken a huge amount of organisation and the availability of man-power on a large scale, even if the Eamont was used as a routeway.

It seems clear that *913* was a large, well-constructed drain, but although it appeared to emanate from under what is assumed to have been an early churchyard boundary, it does not seem to have related directly to the churchyard itself, clearly suggesting that *913* pre-dated its formal construction. Indeed, even if the churchyard was severely waterlogged (and there is no reason to think that it ever was), it is unlikely that so much effort would have been put into constructing so substantial a drain simply to bury corpses in dry ground: the only possible reason for a drain in a relatively dry churchyard would have been to serve structures standing within the area.

The presence of this drain at Dacre would suggest buildings of considerable importance in the area of the present churchyard, for it seems likely that the best stone would have been reserved for the most prominent buildings, and the water and drainage systems would have used materials of a lesser quality. The two channels indicate that it may have formed part of a foul-water system, presumably serving two buildings or more to the north, the projected direction of the two channels indicating that there was not a close relationship with the position of the present church, since the projection of the eastern arm would lead to a point somewhere close to the junction between the present nave and chancel, and that of the western arm would suggest activity in the west of the present churchyard (*Ch 4*). A potential parallel with the situation at Jarrow may be indicated, where a range of two buildings was excavated to the south of the early churches, themselves on the footprint of the present parish church (*Ch 6*; Cramp 2005).

The artefactual evidence for the dating of the drain is sparse, but telling, since early medieval metalwork was found within the backfill of the *c* 1929 excavation, although a very few sherds of medieval pottery were contained within layers *946* and *998*, on either side of the drain stones. Layer *998* contained a single small sherd of apparently fourteenth-century pottery, whilst layer *946* contained a few finds, including four small sherds of thirteenth/fourteenth-century pottery, two from on or near the surface of the layer. Part of a medieval ceramic roofing tile was also found at a somewhat lower level. The presence of these five sherds of thirteenth/fourteenth-century pottery is perhaps hard to reconcile with the logical arguments for dating the drain considerably earlier, but it seems likely that they were intrusive, resulting from the movement of material through the activity of animals, or adjacent grave digging. Indeed, the two sherds of thirteenth-fourteenth-century pottery from the surface of layer *946* may point to the date at which some of the capping stones were robbed, and the pottery may thus suggest that the context in which the drain originally stood had been tampered with subsequently.

Almost the whole of the available interior of drain *913* had been cleared in *c* 1929, but in places a thin skim of possibly primary silting survived (*865*), in the form of a brown gravelly clay. A single small sherd of twelfth/thirteenth-century pottery was found near the base of this, although its presence might have been a result of disturbance from the *c* 1929 excavation, or perhaps suggests when the drain had been abandoned. The only intact backfill that had escaped the excavations of *c* 1929, at the southern extremity of the site, was a mass of medium and large river cobbles (*917*), closely packed in a matrix of sticky yellow clay, that had clearly been placed deliberately.

# 3

# MATERIAL CULTURE: PREHISTORIC, ROMAN, AND EARLY MEDIEVAL ARTEFACTS

## Introduction

*C Howard-Davis*

The excavations produced a substantial assemblage of finds from all three sites, ranging in date from the prehistoric period to almost the present day. Their discussion has been divided chronologically (*Chs 3* and *5*), although there are several pertinent comments which apply to finds of all dates from the sites. Perhaps the most important of these is the high level of disturbance and, in consequence, residuality, which has meant that very few of the artefacts dated earlier than the Norman Conquest are in their original place of deposition, and much of the medieval material has been redeposited. The material has been disturbed in part by continued activity within the bounds of the site, but in addition, many have been brought onto the northern site in particular from further north during periods of erosion, the redeposition being found in layers of hillwash.

The soil conditions at Dacre, like those over much of Cumbria, are highly inimical to the survival of bone unless it is burned. This is particularly pertinent to the

Plate 32: Hand-made pottery

excavation of the cemetery (*Ch 2*), but it also means that animal bone, including worked-bone artefacts, is almost entirely absent from the assemblage.

Most of the finds were reported on over 30 years ago, and the state of knowledge with regard to the early and later medieval periods in Cumbria, and the North West more generally, has changed significantly in that time. On the whole, however, the original conclusions stand, and extra references to local and regional comparanda have only been made in areas where significant advances have been made.

## Prehistoric Artefacts?

### Pottery

*H Quartermaine*

A single body sherd in a largely undiagnostic hand-made fabric (Pl 32) was recovered from a posthole (*137*; OR 419) in the north-west quadrant of the northern churchyard. This was in the area of what seemed to be an early structure (X), although it also contained medieval pottery (*Ch 2, pp 31-2*). The thick greyish fabric is tempered with large limestone grits, and there is possible decoration in the form of an incised horizontal line, although this could equally represent the imprint of grass or straw, made whilst the clay was still soft.

The original identification was that it formed part of the lower body of a substantial prehistoric vessel, its very coarse nature perhaps suggesting a late Bronze Age date. However, similar, very coarse pottery was subsequently found at the early medieval site at Fremington, near Brougham (Howard-Davis 1996a), only 11.4 km to the east of Dacre. This would suggest that a tradition of coarse hand-made early medieval pottery with similarities to Bronze Age vessels existed in the North, as also seen at Yeavering in Northumberland (Hope-Taylor 1977), and that this fragment was actually made in the seventh- or eighth century AD.

## The lithics

*C Howard-Davis*

A small group of 34 possible prehistoric lithics was collected. Of these, one appears to be a natural fragment of volcanic tuff, and all the others are flint. Nineteen of the fragments are debitage, in brown and grey flint of varying quality; all are relatively small and several of them bear a heavy white patina, while one fragment is burnt. Three have edge damage of the kind that might be associated with *ad hoc* use, but it is equally likely to be the result of trampling.

Nine of the pieces are clearly tools, or broken parts of tools. One is irregular in shape but has steep retouch at one end, giving it a superficial resemblance to a scraper, while two others are small scrapers, and another two appear to be fragments of piercing tools or awls; a further object is a knife. The presence of such tool types suggests a domestic nature for the assemblage, and might place their deposition in the late Neolithic period or early Bronze Age.

The fragmentary nature of the tools and their scatter across the site suggests that their presence is not indicative of any immediate prehistoric occupation. The most likely suggestion is that there was, perhaps, a small, and probably transient, settlement in the wider vicinity, and that erosion of the neighbouring hill-slopes has carried material towards the site.

## Roman Artefacts

## Pottery

*H Quartermaine (samian ware); L Hird (coarseware)*

A small amount of Roman pottery was recovered, mainly from the northern churchyard, which, with the addition of a second-century bow-brooch (*below*), two melon beads (*p 51*), and a fragment of glass bangle (*p 51*), may indicate some low-level activity in the locality. Nothing amongst this pottery would seem out of place in the second- or early third century AD, but extreme abrasion, alongside its distribution throughout the stratigraphic sequence, makes it clear that little, if any, was in its original place of deposition.

There were nine severely abraded fragments of samian ware, one from the Orchard and the remainder from the northern churchyard. Whilst their extremely poor condition precluded analysis, the consistent presence of samian ware on early medieval monastic sites, in proportions greater than is normal on Roman sites (Bidwell 2006a, 325), is intriguing, and hints at deliberate use in such a context.

There are, in addition, nine coarseware sherds, probably from nine individual Romano-British vessels, deriving from jars, mostly in reduced greywares. The single fragment of fine orange oxidised ware was from the Orchard, found on early stone surface 53 (*Ch 2, p 40*). A small fragment from medieval surface 45 (associated with the croft in the northern churchyard; *Ch 4, p 107*) was from a mortarium of Mancetter-Hartshill origin.

## Metalwork

*A C H Olivier*

A single poorly preserved trumpet brooch (**1**; Fig 28) was unstratified (*162*). Regarded as a Roman introduction, trumpet brooches may possibly have been in production in southern Britain as early as AD 30-50 (Simpson 1979, n70; Crummy 1983, 14), although this is not the case in the North. The form was certainly fully developed by AD 75 (Mackreth 1986, 64) and was still in use during the first half of the second century AD. In this particular case, the replacement of the more usual spring, mounted in a lug, by a simple hinge, set in a sleeve, suggests that this variant might, perhaps, be relatively late in the development of the form (Bayley and Butcher 2004, 161). A similar brooch was found in excavations at Jarrow (Cramp *et al* 2006, 230, CA1), where the suggestion was made that it was amongst scrap metal brought to the monastic site for recycling.

1     Badly corroded trumpet brooch; the original surface is almost entirely absent and consequently little surface detail survives. The lower portion of the bow is narrow and V-shaped in cross-section, with a raised central spine. The moulding below the crest of the bow comprises a narrow central disc (with a milled edge) set between opposed cusps of acanthus leaves. Very faint traces of an additional transverse moulding survive above (and below?) this central ornament. All these mouldings are carried round the bow. The expanded trumpet-head is relatively flat, and decorated at its circumference with a shallow groove. The hinged pin is attached to the bow by means of an axial bar seated in a sleeve (cast in one with the bow) on the underside of the head. A head-loop, now missing, was formed by the continuation of this axial bar forward of the trumpet-head. The waist of the loop is held in place by a cast collar, the ends of which are bent round to clip the wire of the loop. The upper surface of this collar is ornamented by two grooves, forming a slight, central ridge, having faint traces of milled decoration.
L: 53 mm
Site 2, *162*, Unstratified, OR 1593

## Glass objects

*H Quartermaine*

There are three items of glass that may be dated to the Roman period, none of them from vessels. Like the bow brooch, it is possible that they were brought to the site at a much later date, for reuse, as such beads are a relatively common find in early medieval cemeteries (White 1987; 1988), or for recycling, although they could provide cumulative evidence of nearby Roman activity.

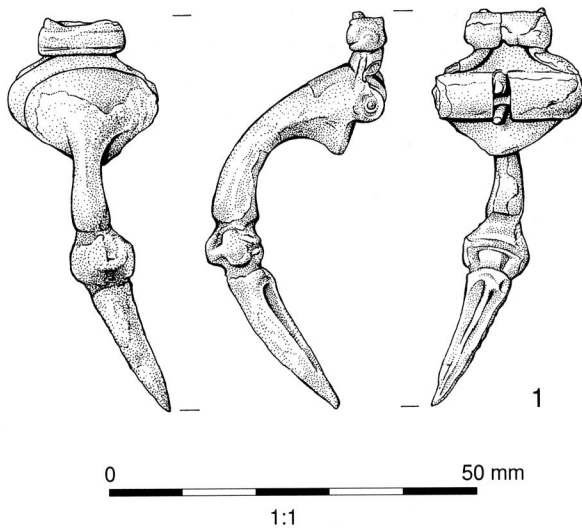

Figure 28: The trumpet brooch

Two are melon beads, one (**2**; Fig 29), of turquoise frit, being associated with the early medieval cemetery (*665*), while the other (**3**), of dark blue translucent glass, is presumably residual in late hillwash (*27*). Frit melon beads seem to have been manufactured and used in Britain from the late Iron Age onwards and continued in use, with little change, into the early medieval period (Guido 1978), being perhaps, by then, valued for their colour and size. Certainly, the inclusion of singleton Roman beads in Anglo-Saxon necklaces seems to have been common (Brugmann 2004, 29). The abraded condition of bead **2** might suggest that it had been in use long before its deposition, and that, like the trumpet brooch (**1**, *p 50*), its origins lay in a nearby, but as yet undiscovered, Roman rural settlement.

Translucent blue-glass melon beads like **3** are more restricted in date, common only in the first and second centuries AD (Guido 1978, 100). Having probably been introduced at the Roman Conquest, evidence suggests that they were subsequently made in Britain (Johns 1996, 101). They reappeared in the post-Roman period (Guido 1978, 100), but late examples are less well-made and can generally be distinguished with relative ease (*ibid*). As melon beads are often found in post-Roman contexts (White 1988, 111), and examples are known throughout the period, from sixth-century graves at Catterick (Wilson *et al* 1996), eighth-century levels at Whitby (Peers and Radford 1943, fig 22, 72 and 73), and from Viking-age burials in Cumbria (Paterson *et al* 2014, 82) and on the Isle of Man (Megaw 1937, 237, pl 117a, no 4), it remains possible that both beads were reused, and should be considered with the early medieval beads from the site.

A small fragment of opaque turquoise glass (**4**), from occupation pre-dating the drain (*1011; Ch 2*)

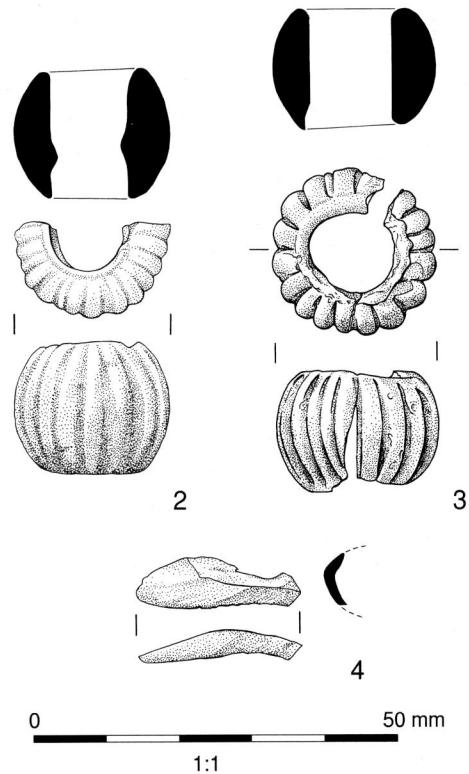

Figure 29: Roman-type melon beads and part of a glass bangle

in the southern churchyard, is most likely to be part of a plano-convex-sectioned glass bangle of a type common throughout the Roman period (Kilbride-Jones 1938). It seems evident that fragments of such bangles were either sought for recycling during the early medieval period, or that the wearing of such armlets continued well into those centuries. Like melon beads, bangle fragments are occasional finds at a number of early medieval sites (White 1988) and examples are known from other northern sites, for example Whitby (Peers and Radford 1943, fig 22, 72 and 73). In addition, there are several fragments from Whithorn (Price 1997), as well as fragments from both Wearmouth and Jarrow (Cramp 2006a, fig 31.4.1), where they were thought to be personal possessions rather than recycling (*op cit*, 258), and one from excavations close to the early Minster in Ripon (Price 1996). In addition, glass bangles are frequently found on Irish sites, such as numerous examples from Lagore Crannog (Hencken 1950, 145-7).

2      Very abraded turquoise frit melon bead.
       Ht: 20 mm; Diam: 22 m; Diam (perf): 12 mm
       Site 2, *665*, cemetery level, Early medieval, OR 1441

3      Deep blue translucent glass melon bead, now in two pieces.
       Ht: 18 m; Diam: 24 mm; Diam (perf): 12 mm
       Site 2, *27*, hillwash, Medieval/Post-medieval, OR 1105

4      Bangle fragment in opaque turquoise glass.
       L: 23 mm
       Site 3, *1011*, occupation pre-dating drain, Early medieval
       OR 1821

# The Early Medieval Artefacts

## The pottery
*M McCarthy and C Brooks*

Only two tiny fragments of early medieval pottery (Fabric 13; *Appendix 1*) were recovered, both from medieval hillwash *121* in the northern churchyard, apart from the cruder pottery with similarities to that from Fremington, that could equally be prehistoric in date (*p 49*). The sherds are dark grey and fine-tempered, with a reddish core, and are burnished on both surfaces. They have been identified as possible middle Saxon imports (A Mainman *pers comm*) and resemble what has been called Class 14 or Class 15 at Hamwic (Hodges 1981, 21-8), types which are believed to originate in northern France or the Low Countries, though no production site is known. Similar wares are known from other English sites, including Ipswich (C Coutts *pers comm*) and York (Mainman 1990), where they appear in middle Saxon contexts. The finds from Dacre are too small to indicate form, but spouted, handled pitchers are typical for this ware (*ibid*). The sherds are remarkable in representing the most northerly known examples of this fabric.

Apart from this, no pre-Norman potting tradition can be identified with any certainty in Cumbria (McCarthy and Brooks 1992, 22), although there is a putative clamp kiln from Fremington, where coarse vessels, probably of seventh- to eighth-century date, were found (Newman 2007; Howard-Davis 1996a, 150). It is, however, quite possible that this lack merely reflects the almost total absence of archaeological work close to the centres of pre-Norman estates in the region. At Cockermouth, for instance, excavations have mostly been away from the early settlement core (*cf* Leech and Gregory 2012), in the post-Conquest town, whilst at Penrith, Kendal, and Egremont, no large-scale excavations have been undertaken on sites which, from their location, might have been expected to yield early wares (McCarthy and Brooks 1992).

## The Northumbrian coins
*E Pirie*

One *sceatta* and five *stycas* (or Northumbrian pennies, *pace* Naismith 2017, 115) were recovered, all from the northern churchyard. All were produced in a period from the reign of Eadberht (AD 738-57) to that of Æthelred II (*c* AD 844-9/50). The *stycas* were in fairly good condition, but the *sceatta* was fragmented. Stratigraphic evidence indicates that no coin was found in its primary place of deposition.

*Sceattas*, small silver coins from the kingdom of Northumbria, were struck, by anonymous moneyers, in the mid-late eighth century (Booth 1984). They first appeared during the reign of Eadberht and are the earliest substantial series of English coins to proclaim their royal origin and control in an unambiguous manner. Their issue was aimed to regularise the currency of Northumbria under a central control, and to restore confidence in the coinage in a period of debasement and chaos (*op cit*, 71). This coinage was later superseded by the issue of stycas, which are characterised by the registration of moneyers' names.

Elizabeth Pirie (1996) divided Northumbrian stycas into three general types: Period I, which are silver and early copper-alloy issues, dating from *c* 790-835; Period Ia, which are silver issues and date to *c* 790-830; and Period II, which are later copper-alloy issues of *c* 837-55. Period I coins, particularly those of Period Ia, survive comparatively rarely, in contrast to those from Period II, which seem to have resulted from a much more intensive production, with moneyers coining for both kings and archbishops (*ibid*). This coinage seems to have collapsed early in the reign of Osberht, by about 855. There is a single Period Ia *styca* (**1**) from Dacre, all the others (**3-6**) being of Period II type (Pl 33). Whilst this division has been superseded and simplified (Naismith 2017, ch 5), the dating of the individual coins stands.

1      EANRED *c* AD 810-*c* 841
      *Styca*
      Moneyer: Hvaetred [? early in reign]
      Obv: + EANREDREX, round central cross
      Rev: + HVAETRED, round central cross
      The piece is of low weight but almost as new; it could well have been lost almost at once, that is, *c* 820.
      Wt: 0.73 g (11.2 gr); die-axis: 90°
      Site 2, *1235*, upper cemetery level, Early Medieval, OR 2008

2      EADBERHT *c* AD 738-57
      *Sceatta*
      Obv: + EOTBERHTVS, evangelistic cross in border of pellets (now worn)
      Rev: obscure
      The evangelistic cross in a border of pellets only appears on coins of Booth's Class F (Booth 1984, 77) but the S of the inscription is a proper S and not the inverted L variety

*Plate 33: Northumbrian coinage from Dacre*

which is more common on Eadberht's *sceattas*. The reverse on such coins is the animal facing right; there is invariably a triquetra below the body and sometimes a cross below the tail. Only a few of the Class F specimens noted in Booth's corpus are without provenance. The range of sites is mostly eastern: Whitby; Sancton; and Hayton in Yorkshire; Caistor-on-the-Wolds and Epworth in Lincolnshire (*op cit*, 79). F11 from Malham is the nearest known example to Dacre (*ibid*).
Wt: 0.35 g; die-axis: indeterminate
Site 2, *310*, rubble spread, Eleventh/twelfth century, OR 1077

3      Archbishop VIGMVND *c* AD 837-54
*Styca*
Moneyer: Edilveard Obv: + VIGMVNDA[REP], round central cross
Rev: + EDIL [V] EARD, round central cross
The spelling of the title as AREP (not IREP) serves to indicate that this issue may be assigned to the last years of Eanred's reign, *c* 837−*c* 41. The condition of the coin suggests that it was lost during the reign of Æthelred II or of Osberht.
Wt: 0.41 g (6.1 gr), worn and chipped; die-axis: 90°
Site 2, *1328*, layer, Medieval, OR 2335

4      ÆTHELRED: second reign (traditionally *c* AD 844-8)
*Styca*
Moneyer: Eanvvlf
Obv: + EDILREDREX (retrograde, letters reversed), round central evangelistic cross
Rev: + EANVVLF (tops of letters to the middle of the coin), round central cross
As a moneyer, Eanvvlf is known to have worked, with Monne, for Osberht (from *c* 849/50 until the coinage collapsed, *c* 855). The two are also known to have shared this obverse in the name of Æthelred II. The die is at least aberrant, if not altogether irregular. One cannot be quite decisive in saying whether the coin is a genuine, but late and degraded, issue for Æthelred himself, or whether it is a forgery from the reign of Osberht.
Wt: 0.73 g (11.35 gr); die-axis: 30°
Site 2, *89*, hillwash, Late medieval/Post-medieval, OR 269

5      ÆTHELRED II *c* AD 844-49/50
*Styca*
Moneyer: (ostensibly) Monne
Obv: AEDIL.RED, retrograde, round central cross with pellets in the angles
Rev: M.O.NN+E, retrograde with letters inverted, round central cross
The coin is an irregular issue reflecting the official coinage of Æthelred II. There was a break in the normal pattern of such coinage at the end of Æthelred's first reign and during Redvvlf's usurpation; this may well have been the flashpoint which triggered off an epidemic of imitation. This piece belongs to a massive die-linked chain of about 400 examples, which must have been spread out over Æthelred's second reign; the coin's condition is good (for a copy), and it need not have been in circulation long before it was lost.
Wt: 0.86 g (13.2 gr); die-axis: 135°
Site 2, *162*, Unstratified, OR 2350

6      *Styca*
This is a complete freak which defies conventional description of obverse and reverse; the only thing one can be certain of is that the fabric is that of a *styca*. The piece would seem to have been struck several times: at least double-struck by the same die or over-struck by one pair of dies on another. It is an intriguing possibility that

the obverse dies of **4** (*above*) might have been involved, as the ghosts of comparable initial and central crosses can be seen, the latter now well off-centre. Dating is difficult, but there is nothing to suggest it is very different from that of **4**, *c* 848-55.
Wt: 0.51 g; die-axis: indeterminate
Site 2, *162*, Unstratified, OR 365

## Fine metalwork
*D Tweddle with C Howard-Davis*
Several pieces of fine metalwork have been identified as of pre-Conquest date; one is a brooch; two are finger-rings; three are strap-ends; one is a hooked tag; and five are pins. There are also a single stylus, three unidentified mounts, and two sheet fragments.

### Dress and personal adornment
A single brooch (**1**; Fig 30) was recovered from rubble spread *101* (*Ch 4*), along the north side of the earliest churchyard boundary bank in the northern churchyard. It was identified as a strip or safety-pin brooch, a type only relatively recently recognised as of Anglo-Saxon origin (White 1988; discussed in detail by Weetch 2014, type 31B). A group of 32 copper-alloy, silver, and iron brooches of this kind were found at Flixborough, and remain the largest known group (Rogers *et al* 2009, 1, fig 1.1). Made in one piece, the form allows little scope for variation, with most having a flat, lozenge-shaped bow, decoration of which is confined to ring-and-dot, or simple incised geometric, motifs (possibly crude interlace), as seen on this example.

These brooches tend to be somewhat flimsy and, when found in grave deposits, tend to lie at the hip, raising the possibility that they fastened under-garments (White 1988, 41). Although few examples can be confidently dated, a seventh- to early ninth-century date range has been suggested (Weetch 2014, type 31B); the stratified examples from Flixborough all came from reasonably secure late eighth/early ninth- to late ninth/early tenth-century contexts (Rogers *et al* 2009, 3), and such a date-range would not be out of place at Dacre.

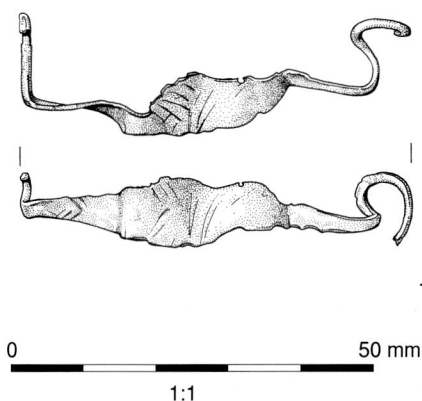

1

0                 50 mm

1:1

*Figure 30: Strip or safety-pin brooch*

1    Strip or safety-pin brooch. The flat bow is lozenge-shaped, assuming a D-shaped section at both ends, which extend as wire to form the spring and the catch. The catch survives almost intact, but the spring has been opened out and distorted, and the pin is missing. The upper side of the bow is decorated with an incised herringbone, or perhaps debased interlace, pattern.
L: 58.8 mm; W: 9.6 mm; Th: 0.8 mm; Diam (wire): 1.9 mm
Site 2, *101*, churchyard boundary bank, Eleventh/twelfth century, OR 421

Two small buckles (*Ch 5, p 124*; **1** and **2**) were originally identified as belonging to an early medieval tradition, having some similarities to those in the late Roman classification proposed by Hawkes and Dunning (1961), albeit lacking the characteristic zoomorphic decoration seen on most of these, and the fact that they were found within the first medieval churchyard boundary, along with many other early medieval artefacts. However, their form, with an offset pin bar, is now more commonly understood to begin in the later twelfth century and continue through to the fourteenth century (PAS 2016a).

A plain strap-end, (**2**; Fig 31), from rubble *310* in the west of the northern churchyard (*Ch 4, p 97*), which overlay the early cemetery, is not particularly chronologically diagnostic. However, its close resemblance to plain strap-ends with crudely notched or scalloped upper edges, demonstrably made at Flixborough, and assigned a broadly ninth-century date (for instance, Thomas 2009a, 10, fig 1.4, no 74), and occasionally found elsewhere in eighth-eleventh-century contexts (*op cit*, 9), suggests that this might belong to the same period.

Object **3**, from an early layer (*76*; *Ch 2*; *p 40*) in the Orchard, is probably the earliest of the three strap-ends from the site. It has a distinctive ring terminal enclosing an openwork equal-armed Y. The strap fitted into a split in the upper end of a slightly expanded extension, decorated on the front face with a chip-carved eight-strand interlace plait, and was held in place by a single rivet close to the upper

edge. The form is hard to parallel, but it might have been intended for use as a strap fitting (PAS 2014a, DUR-738FF5; 2014b, LVPL-1B78B7), though viewed in isolation, the terminal, although smaller, quite closely resembles spoked distributor rings seen in some later Viking-age belt sets, intended for the suspension of a scabbard or other items (Pritchard 1991, 148). However, such distributors usually do not have fixed buckle plates, and also have the holes between the spokes orientated towards the straps, whereas the buckle plate and decorative shoulders obstruct two of the apertures on this example, making it useless for such a function. In its general shape, it perhaps resembles an example from Ogbourne St George, Wiltshire (Thomas 2000, no 1327), which is regarded as generally Anglo-Scandinavian in type.

The gilt copper alloy from which the strap-end is made suggests an eighth-century date, since gold was the material to which the eighth-century metalworker aspired (Wilson 1964, 9-10), although, as it was rarely available, gilded copper alloy was a commonplace substitute, as seen in the three openwork book mounts from Whitby (*op cit*, 192-3, pls XXXVIII-IX), and the pin set from the River Witham in Lincolnshire (*op cit*, 132-4, pl XVIII). The chip-carved decoration also supports this dating, being a standard decorative technique used on almost all high-quality pieces of gilt copper-alloy metalwork in the eighth century, as is the delicate fine-meshed interlace (Thomas 2009a). The technique went out of use during the ninth century, with the increasing popularity of silver as a material for high-quality objects, and the relative decline in the use of copper alloy.

The third strap-end (**4**), from an early medieval layer in the east of the northern churchyard (*Ch 2*), is much easier to place, as it has the form and decoration typical of an extensive ninth-century series (Thomas 2000, type A). It has slightly convex sides, and tapers towards an animal-head terminal at the lower end; apart from the terminal, the

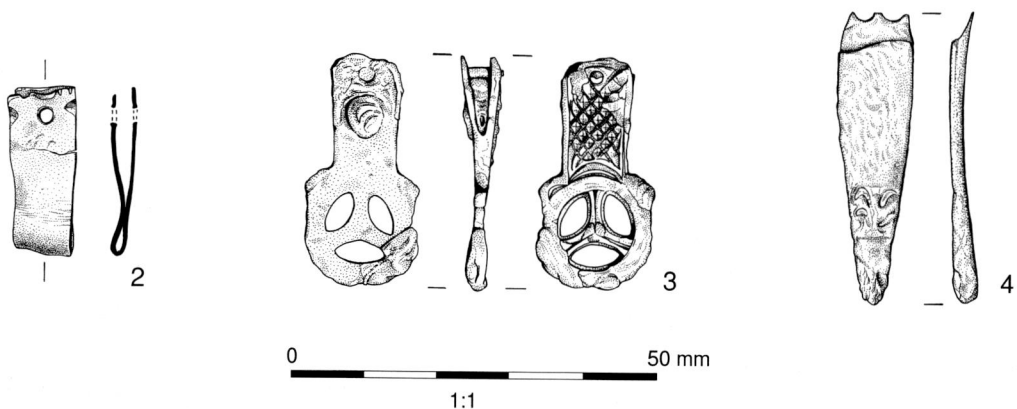

Figure 31: Copper-alloy strap-ends

outer face is apparently undecorated, as is the rear. Large numbers of strap-ends of this general type are known from early medieval England, and they are fairly evenly distributed south-east of a line from the Bristol Channel to Whitby in North Yorkshire (Thomas 2009a, 8), with lesser numbers of northern and western outliers following a more coastal distribution, but not exclusively so (*ibid*), since Dacre is well inland. A significant group of six examples was found on Winderwath Common, Asby, south of Appleby (Edwards 2002, where other local examples are summarised), and the number known from Scotland has now increased significantly (Blackwell 2018).

Copper-alloy examples seem to copy more prestigious objects in silver, inlaid with niello, and often have similar zoomorphic decoration on the front face, as is the case with the series from York (Waterman 1959, 76-7, fig 10, 1-5) and Whitby (Peers and Radford 1943, 55-8, fig 11). Similar decoration appears also on a mould fragment from Crown and Anchor Lane, Carlisle (Taylor and Webster 1984; Webster, in Padley 2010, 221-2, fig 113), which must have been used for casting copper-alloy strap-ends, rather than for producing silver ones, which were worked cold. There are, however, also examples with much simpler ornament, such as the enamelled cross-hatching on examples from Fishergate, York (Rogers 1993, fig 652, nos 5317, 5321); in other examples, the front face is undecorated as in object **4**, for example, from Cheddar, in Somerset (Rahtz 1979, 284, fig 95.95), and Southampton (Addyman and Hill 1969, 70, fig 27.4). The Trewhiddle-style decoration employed on the more luxurious silver examples, and copied on some of the copper-alloy specimens, together with the association of some examples with coin-dated hoards, serves to confirm the dating of the main series of these strap-ends in the ninth century.

2    Buckle plate or strap-end. It is made from a single strip, expanding slightly towards the square ends. This is bent in half, and has a single rivet hole on both sides at the open end. There is a triangular nick in the edge of the plate on the front face, above and below the rivet hole, and there are further nicks on the squared end.
L: 22.4 mm; W: 9.6 mm; Th: 3.3 mm
Site 2, *310*, rubble spread, Eleventh/twelfth century, OR 1144

3    Copper-alloy strap-end, partially gilded. It has a square upper end and tapers slightly towards a circular terminal, which encloses an openwork inverted Y with concave sides. There is a boss at the junction of the arms, and each element has a median incision. There are protuberances on the shoulders of the circle, abutting its point of junction with the body of the strap-end. The front face of the body is decorated with a chip-carved eight-strand plait. The mineralised remains of the strap have been inserted into a split in the upper end and are held in place by a single copper-alloy rivet. The domed head of a second rivet is

centrally placed on the ungilded reverse, but this does not appear to penetrate the front face.
L: 31 mm; W: 16.1 mm; Th: 5.9 mm
Site 1, *76*, layer, Earliest activity, OR 279

4    Copper-alloy strap-end, heavily worn and curved lengthwise. The curved long edges taper towards an animal-head terminal, which has comma-shaped ears, and the eyes are well-defined. The main field is undecorated. The strap fitted into a split cut in the upper end and was held in place by two rivets. The front of the split end is broken away completely and the rear is partially broken away; only the lower half of the pair of rivet holes survives.
L: 39 mm; W: 10.5 mm; Th: 3.7 mm
Site 2, *1041*, layer, Medieval?, OR 2117

Object **5**, from close to the edge of early medieval layer *357* (*Ch 2; p 37*), is a hooked tag or garment hook (Fig 32). This would originally have been attached (probably sewn) to a garment, where it would probably have served the same purpose as a modern hook-and-eye, or was possibly used as a fastener for purses (Owen-Crocker 2004, 155). As is usual, this example had been cut from sheet metal, and has punched ring-and-dot motifs encircling the two fixing holes, and a third, purely decorative motif, set asymmetrically. Such items occur commonly in the pre-Conquest period, having a distribution pattern broadly similar to that of strap-end **4** (Thomas 2009b, 17). In the North West, a single example has been found at Carlisle Cathedral (Keevil 1989, fig 2 no 1; Paterson and Tweddle 2014, 211, illus 15), and one also came from the early medieval settlement at Fremington, near Brougham, although this was from the ploughsoil (Howard-Davis 1996b, fig 6.22 no 6), several also being known from Scotland (Blackwell 2018).

They appear in a variety of forms and materials, with the earliest seeming to belong in the seventh century (Rogers 1993, 1359), continuing in use well into the eleventh century. They can be made of copper alloy, sometimes gilded, as is the case with the example from York (Waterman 1959, 80, fig 10, 11), or of gilded silver, such as an example from Lincolnshire (Leahy and Coutts 1987, 10, pl 3). Hooked tags fall into two groups, those with triangular plates and those with round or

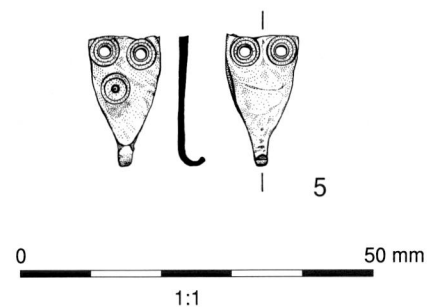

*Figure 32: Garment hook*

sub-round plates, of which triangular plates are generally thought to have appeared earlier (Read 2008; Thomas 2009b, 17), in the seventh to eighth century, with sub-rounded plates following in the late eighth century. In the ninth century, garment hooks were more often made of silver, reflecting the general shift to the use of silver as a material for high-quality metalwork (Wilson 1964, 9-10).

There are examples from a number of late pre-Conquest sites, including 16-22 Coppergate, York (Roesdahl *et al* 1981, YD20), North Elmham Park (Wade-Martins 1980, 10-12), and Flaxengate, Lincoln (Roesdahl *et al* 1981, G3-4), where there is abundant evidence for their manufacture. Thus, although the Dacre example could be as late as the tenth- or the eleventh century, an earlier, eighth- or ninth-century date seems more likely.

5      Copper-alloy garment hook. It has a triangular plate developing into a down-turned hook at the apex. Two nicks, one in each side, separate the hook from the plate. The hook has a D-shaped section and is decorated with rows of horizontal incisions on each side of the mid-line. The plate has two perforations near the square base, each encircled by a pair of concentric rings. Just to the left of the centre of the plate is a stamped dot surrounded by concentric rings. On the underside, the perforations are also surrounded by pairs of concentric rings.
L: 17.9 mm; W: 10.7 mm; Th: 1.8 mm
Site 2, *357*, layer/fill, Early medieval?, OR 1037

In addition, there are five pins (**6-10**), which might have been used as dress or hair pins, and two finger-rings (**11-12**), both in precious metals. The most elaborate of the pins is **6** (Fig 33), from medieval churchyard boundary ditch fill *317* (*Ch 4*). This has a triangular head, decorated, on one side, with highly conventionalised plant ornament, and separated from the broken shank by a collar.

There is a single close, albeit more substantial, parallel from Wicken Bonhunt, in north-west Essex, where it is dated to the ninth century (Ross 1991, 249). In the case of the Dacre object, however, the thick and fleshy nature of the conventionalised foliage, which is reminiscent of acanthus, would perhaps suggest a later date in the tenth- or eleventh century. In the detailed typological discussion of the development of early medieval pins (*ibid*), the Wicken Bonhunt example was regarded as a unique type (*op cit*, 250, fig 5.28.a) and no other close parallels have been encountered. Such pins were, however, probably more widely used in the pre-Conquest period (see, for instance, St Augustine's Abbey, Canterbury, Kent; Radford 1940, 507). There is also a silver pin with a decorative sub-triangular head riveted to an iron shank from Flixborough (Rogers 2009, fig 1.29, no 681), which, whilst not an exact parallel, is in a similar vein.

Pin **7,** from the first medieval churchyard boundary bank (*358; Ch 4*), has a narrow, baluster-shaped head with a polyhedral middle element, the use of which motif probably serves to place it in the eighth century, or just into the ninth. In this period, pins with polyhedral heads are ubiquitous; examples are known, for example, from Whitby, North Yorkshire (Peers and Radford 1943, 63-4, figs 13-14), from numerous sites in York (Waterman 1959, 78-9, fig 11, 7-12; Mainman and Rogers 2000), and Southampton (Addyman and Hill 1969, 68, fig 26.8). Most, however, have large heads decorated with ring-and-dot motifs, but occasionally the heads are smaller, like this example, being only a little broader than the shank. There are, for example, pins of this type from Meols (Bu'lock 1960, fig 3; Griffiths *et al* 2007) and Whitby (Peers and Radford 1943, fig 14). Whitby has also produced a pin with a baluster head similar to that from Dacre, but with a bulbous, not polyhedral, middle element (*ibid*); perhaps the Dacre pin represents a conflation of these two types. The narrow baluster head has now been recognised, in York, as a discrete type (Mainman and Rogers 2000, type 3, 2577), found in Anglian levels at Fishergate, where it is dated to the first half of the ninth century, and also at Coppergate, and it was therefore possibly a variant on a pre-Viking-age Irish type.

Object **8** is probably also a pin head, from layer *1235* in the east of the northern churchyard, overlying the early medieval cemetery. It now resembles a droplet with a biconical profile, but it is likely that there was originally a shank which has broken away, and then the stump corroded to a point. There are good parallels for this type of rather rounded biconical head from Anglian sites in Cumbria, such as the post-Roman deposits of the Carlisle Millennium excavations (Howard-Davis 2009, 732) and Blackfriars Street, Carlisle (Graham-Campbell 1990). Elsewhere in northern England, there are notable examples from Whitby Abbey, where there are at least two examples (Peers and Radford 1943), and from Fishergate, York (Mainman and Rogers 2000). These parallels would suggest a date for the Dacre example in the eighth-, or the first half of the ninth, century.

The precise date and function of **9**, from stone spread *310* (*Ch 4, pp 97-8*), in the west of the northern churchyard, is more difficult to determine. It has the shape and form of a dress pin, but the considerable thickness of the shank, averaging 3-4 mm in diameter, and the slight expansion towards the lower end might seem to preclude such a usage. There are, however, pins with a similar diameter from early medieval levels at Blackfriars Street in Carlisle (Graham-Campbell 1990, fig 165.5). There are also types of pre-Conquest dress pin, most notably the ringed

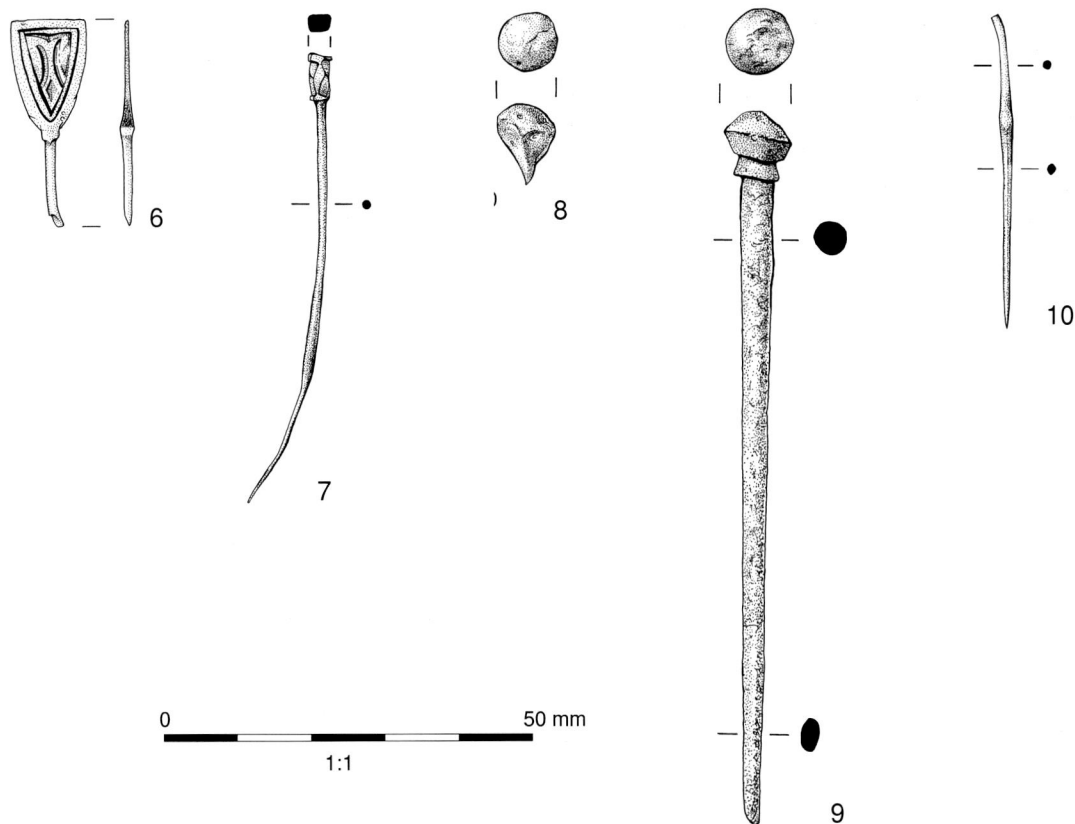

*Figure 33: Pins*

pins, first made in Dublin (Fanning 1994), which have shanks of a similar diameter, again swelling towards the lower end, examples of this form being known from Meols (Bu'lock 1960, fig 5; Griffiths *et al* 2007) and York (Waterman 1959, 79, figs 11, 13-14; Tweddle 1986, 229, fig 101). Like the ringed pins, this example may have had a specialised function. The angular, biconical form of the head, with an expanding collar below, is not easy to parallel, but it may be a coarser version of the rounded biconical head, which is often encountered, as on **8**, and, indeed, this type often has a collar below the head, as on examples from Carlisle and Whitby (Howard-Davis 2009, 732; Peers and Radford 1943, fig 14). Clearly, pin **9** more closely resembles this pin type than any other pre- or post-Conquest variety.

Object **10**, from the lower level of the bank forming the first medieval churchyard boundary (*359; Ch 4*), is the lower part of a pin shank, with the head broken away. It can tentatively be placed in the pre-Conquest period only because of the swelling of the lower part of the shank, which is a feature characteristic of many pre-Conquest pins, but not commonly encountered in later periods (PAS 2016b).

6　　Triangular or styliform pin head with slightly convex sides. A short projection of square section develops from the apex, which continues into a shank of circular section. This is broken at the lower end. The front face of the head is decorated with two concentric incised frames containing conventionalised plant ornament.
L: 27.9 mm; W: 10.5 mm; Th: 0.7 mm; Diam (shank): 1.9 mm
Site 2, *317*, fill of early churchyard boundary ditch, Eleventh/twelfth century, OR 1396

9　　Baluster-headed pin. It has a narrow-diameter faceted baluster-shaped head between two beads. The shank is mostly of uniform diameter, but swells about two-thirds of the way down from the head before tapering abruptly to a point.
L: 59.7 mm; W: 2.9 mm; Th: 2.5 mm; Diam (shank): 1.9 mm
Site 2, *358*, first churchyard boundary bank, Eleventh/twelfth century, OR 1059

8　　Globular pin head. The shank is broken away or was never formed properly.
L: 10.6 mm; Diam (head): 7.7 mm
Site 2, *1235*, layer overlying early medieval cemetery, Medieval?, OR 2502

9　　Biconical-headed pin. The biconical head expands again before being shouldered. The shank is broken at the lower end, which is slightly flattened.
L: 84.6 mm; Diam (head): 9.1 mm; Diam (shank): 4.9 mm
Site 2, *310*, rubble spread, Eleventh/twelfth century, OR 986

10　　Pin shank. It is roughly broken at the upper end, which is of circular section. About a third of the way from the break, the shank swells and assumes a square section before tapering to a point. On one face, an incised line parallels each edge.
L: 41.9 mm; Diam: 2.05 mm
Site 2, *359*, first churchyard boundary bank, Eleventh/twelfth century, OR 1062

There are also two finger-rings, one of silver and one of gold, both effectively unstratified (*162*). The silver example (**11**; Fig 34) is of a highly unusual form, having a flattened pyramidal bezel, with conventionalised foliage on both shoulders, drawn with punched dots, which are inlaid with niello. It is very reminiscent of the medieval stirrup-ring, a form which appeared in the twelfth century, and was at its most popular in the thirteenth (Egan and Pritchard 2002), but that is most often set with a small gem at the apex, which is not the case here. There are, however, some interesting medieval parallels, for instance, a silver-gilt stirrup-ring with similar decoration, inlaid with niello (PAS 2005, SUR-085774).

Whilst the form of this ring is effectively unparalleled in early medieval metalwork, the use of silver and niello might point to a date in the ninth century, a period when, for rich metalwork of the Trewhiddle style, the use of silver inlaid with niello was the norm (Wilson 1964, 23-7). The division of the decoration into small triangular fields is again typical of the Trewhiddle style, seen, for example, on horn mounts from the Trewhiddle hoard itself (*op cit*, 184-9, pls 36-7), as is the lavish use of punched dots (*ibid*). The use of similar conventionalised foliage within small sub-triangular fields is paralleled both in the Wensley and Gilling swords (Watkins 1986, 93-9, figs 3-5, pl 9), although there without the use of punched dots.

The gold finger-ring from Dacre (**12**), from the backfill of the early medieval drain in the southern churchyard, is again not easy to place. It is made from finely beaded wire, tapering towards the ends, which are overlapped and joined. The pattern of wear suggests that, despite its small size, it is a finger-ring and not a beaded collar or setting for another decorative object, as is often seen in early medieval goldwork (see, for instance, PAS 2016c, NARC-BD1E51; 2016d, LIN-1E8803). A similar-sized ring made from beaded wire (PAS 2012, KENT-65F288), although of uncertain provenance, has been dated provisionally to the tenth- or eleventh century.

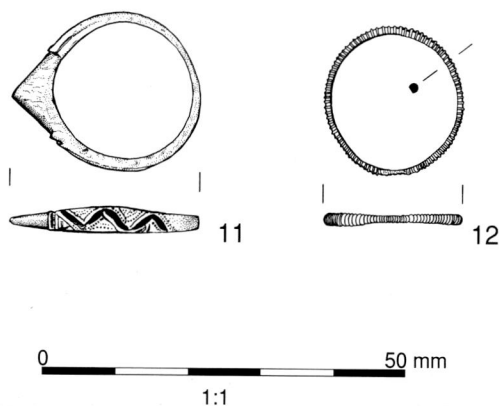

*Figure 34: Finger-rings*

Although rather differently constructed, it seems probable that this piece should be grouped with the twisted gold finger-rings of the Viking Age. These vary in size from the massive, as at Soberton, Hampshire; Chester (Roesdahl *et al* 1981, E20); and Hungate, York (*op cit*, YD28), to the delicate, as from the site of the New Examination Schools, Oxford (Hinton 1974, no 24, 48, pl XII). Although made from twisted rather than beaded wire, they are similar in size to the Dacre example, and equally skilfully joined at the rear. It must be admitted, however, that alternative dates are possible, particularly as the majority of pre-Conquest metalwork which employs beaded filigree is of eighth- or ninth-century date.

11    Silver finger-ring. The bezel takes the form of a flattened pyramid. There are shoulders at the junction with the hoop, which is of rectangular section. To each side of the bezel, the hoop is decorated with five triangular fields defined by punched oblique lines forming zig-zags. Each of the triangular fields thus created is filled with conventionalised foliate ornament drawn with punched dots. Remains of a black inlay (niello?) survive in some of the oblique lines.
Diam (including bezel): 26 mm; Diam (without bezel): 21.6 mm; Th: 3.7 mm
Site 2, *162*, Unstratified, OR 440

12    Gold finger-ring made from a single beaded wire lapped and joined at the rear. The beading is worn smooth on the inside.
Diam: 20.2 mm; Diam (wire): 1.8 mm
Site 3, *162*, Unstratified, OR 1745

**Other objects**
There are only six pre-Conquest objects which do not fall into the category of dress or personal adornment: a stylus (**13**); a possible horn mount (**14**); an escutcheon (**15**); and two fragments. The stylus (**13**; Fig 35), from the backfill (*835*) of the excavation within the early medieval drain in the 1920s (*Ch 1, p 13*), has a round-sectioned shank with an expanded, undecorated eraser, squared at the upper end, which falls into Pestell's Class I (Pestell 2009, 125). The triangular or V-shaped eraser probably identifies this as a pre-Conquest object, as later styli normally have a T-shaped eraser. Parallels are known from Jarrow (Cramp *et al* 2006), Whitby (Peers and Radford 1943, 64-5, fig 15), and St Augustine's Abbey, Canterbury (Radford 1940, 507). In addition, there are iron specimens from Parliament Street (Tweddle 1986, 192, fig 90), and 16-22 Coppergate, York (*ibid*). All of them have a V-shaped eraser, although the detailing and decoration varies.

None of these provides a particularly close parallel to the Dacre example, although one of the Whitby styli comes close, differing mainly in the use of mouldings encircling the shank (Peers and Radford 1943, fig 15.6), which are absent at Dacre.

In general terms, it was thought that styli were linked closely with the literacy concentrated in monastic institutions, but in recent years, reported finds from metal detecting, and particularly from the excavations at Flixborough, make it clear that they were relatively common items, in rather more general use (Pestell 2009).

Object **14** is extremely unusual in having a frilled or serrated lower edge; it tapers slightly towards one end, and there is a perforation. The object most closely resembles a small mount from Flixborough with a similar scalloped edge, taper, and perforations, although there it was made of iron. The Flixborough example is identified as a mount, and paralleled with an unpublished example from the Hamwic excavations, both of similar early date to Dacre (Ottaway *et al* 2009, 166). The only other identified objects which have features closely resembling these are the horn mounts from the Trewhiddle hoard (Wilson 1964, 184-9, pls 36-7), which, like the Dacre example, have a frilled or serrated lower edge and taper towards the ends. Two of these even have a perforation in exactly the same position as that on the Dacre mount. It has been suggested that the Trewhiddle mounts came from drinking horns, the derivation of the frilled or serrated lower edges being in the pendant triangular fields, or vandykes, displayed around the rims of pagan Anglo-Saxon pieces, such as the drinking horns from Sutton Hoo and Taplow (*op cit*, 57).

Its lack of decoration makes it difficult to date the Dacre example precisely. Perhaps, given the scarcity of horn mounts of this period, it should be placed in the ninth century, close in date to the Trewhiddle hoard, deposited in *c* 871, and the mount from Burghead, Morayshire, which is also close in date to the Trewhiddle examples, although it was probably from a blast horn rather than a drinking horn (Graham-Campbell 1973, 43-51, fig 19, pl 15).

The precise function of object **15** is even more difficult to determine. It is convex-sided, with a rounded upper end and a taper towards the lower end, and is curved in section. Additionally, it has a moulded projection on the lower end and two rivets on the vertical axis. The rivets suggest it was perhaps a mount or escutcheon, and it is possible to envisage it being mounted on either a wooden or metal vessel. The Dacre mount bears a generic resemblance to the hanging-bowl mounts from Whitby (Peers and Radford 1943, 9, 11), although there are no close parallels. A pre-Conquest date is suggested by the potentially early context from which it is derived, coming from the material apparently removed from the interior of the early medieval drain in the southern churchyard.

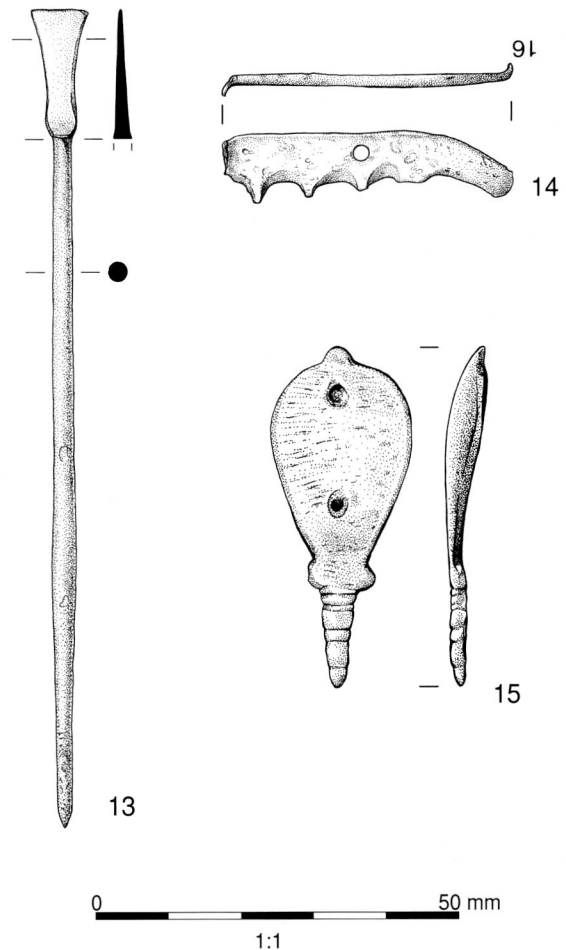

*Figure 35: Stylus and escutcheons*

13      Stylus. The square-ended eraser tapers before becoming parallel-sided. The stem is of circular section and is parallel-sided, only tapering towards the point from about two-thirds of the way along its length.
L: 108.9 mm; W: 8.1 mm; Diam (shank): 3.3 mm
Site 3, *835*, backfill of drain, Early medieval, OR 1588

14      Mount. It tapers towards one end and has a straight upper edge. The lower edge forms a series of small pendant vandykes with concave edges. The right-hand end is rounded, the left-hand end roughly broken.
L: 39.6 mm; W: 9 mm; Th: 2.2 mm
Site 2, *162*, Unstratified, OR 2434

15      Escutcheon. It has a semi-circular upper end, with an axial extension, and tapers toward the lower end, where it develops into a slightly tapering projection of D-shaped section decorated with three transverse mouldings, each flanked by a pair of concavities. Just above this extension, a small semi-circular lug projects to each side. There are two iron rivets on the vertical axis of the escutcheon, which curves longitudinally and horizontally. The front face has a slightly chamfered edge and is apparently silvered.
L: 44.9 mm; W: 18.8 mm; Th: 2.6 mm
Site 3, *162/833*, Unstratified/1920s excavation backfill, Early medieval, OR 1611

In conclusion, it can be suggested that the presence of fine metalwork of this quality clearly indicates that the richest phase of occupation at the site fell within the pre-Conquest period, with the majority of finds being manufactured in the eighth- and ninth centuries. Its quality indicates activity associated with a fairly high status, either of the establishment, some of its occupants, or its visitors, and it should be noted that most of the finds could be placed equally well in either a secular or an ecclesiastical context. The personal nature of the finds, items of dress and adornment, must preclude the notion that they represent gifts to a monastery by wealthy patrons or *ex voto* dedications (except perhaps the finger-rings), as indeed does their distribution, which suggests casual loss rather than deliberate deposition. Only one object, the stylus, can be regarded, conventionally, to be of unambiguous ecclesiastical usage, although this has now been challenged (Loveluck 2007), but if it is not a casual loss, it may point to the existence at Dacre of a scriptorium. Thus it seems more likely that they reflect the personal wealth or status of some members of, or visitors to, the community.

The pre-Conquest material is therefore of importance not only for the quality and rarity of individual finds, but also because they form one of the largest groups of metalwork of this date from north-west England, an area which is generally under-represented in the surviving corpus of such objects. This alone may account for the fact that few good parallels can be drawn with material from other parts of the country.

Most of the undated objects consist largely of featureless pieces of sheet or scrap. They do, however, include a small ingot of square section with rounded ends (**16**; Fig 36) from the topsoil (*26*) in the northern churchyard, and an unstratified copper-alloy run-off (**17**), which, taken together, indicate that there has, at some stage, been copper-alloy working on the site. It is particularly unfortunate that both are effectively unstratified, as the ingot bears a strong resemblance to tenth-eleventh-century examples

in precious metals (see, for instance, Kruse 1986, pl 1, for Viking-age ingots found locally). Given the richness of the pre-Conquest metalwork, as opposed to the rather meagre collection of medieval and post-medieval finds (*Ch 5*), it is tempting to link these objects with the pre-Conquest settlement on the site, but this must remain speculation.

16      Copper-alloy ingot. It is of square section, slightly chamfered along the upper edges, and rounded at each end.
L: 27.2 mm; W: 4.9 mm; Th: 4.7 mm
Site 2, *26*, Topsoil, OR 1768

17      Copper-alloy droplet or run-off.
L: 19 mm; W: 14 mm; Th: 7 mm
Site 2, *162*, Unstratified, OR 378

# Ironwork
*Patrick Ottaway*
Only selected items of early medieval ironwork (see *Appendix 2* for a complete catalogue) were subjected to conservation cleaning. Therefore, many of the illustrated objects were drawn from X-rays only.

## Tools and implements
Of the 22 tools or other implement fragments from the site, only one knife, **15**, could possibly be dated, by its form, to the early medieval period. A second object, a wool-comb tooth (**2**), came from the fill of a posthole in Structure X (*123*; posthole *128*; *Ch 2, pp 31-3*), and its presence would accord well with the finds of lead and stone spindle whorls and loomweights from this period (*p 73; pp 77-8*).

## Structural ironwork and fittings
*Nails, bolts, and staples*
There are over 350 nails in the assemblage. All but a few are hand-made, with shanks of rectangular cross-section and roughly rounded heads, features which are impossible to date. Sixty-four nails came from the early medieval levels in the northern churchyard, and are therefore probably eighth- to tenth-century in date. This is a period for which there are relatively few published nails, although they are not uncommon finds on sites; for example, over 1400 nails came from mid-ninth- to late tenth-century contexts at 16-22 Coppergate, York (Ottaway 1992a, 608-11). Thirty-one of the Dacre nails were found in 18 of the graves. Grave *604* contained five (*Appendix 2*), the other graves one or two, but although many nails originally associated with graves may have been disturbed, it is not conclusive that the coffins were nailed together. Most of the early nails are incomplete, but one is unusually long, at 120 mm; the rest are, or were, about 40-75 mm long and so are comparable to the vast majority of nails from 16-22 Coppergate. One small nail (**71**), from an eleventh/twelfth-century level, has a tin-plated head.

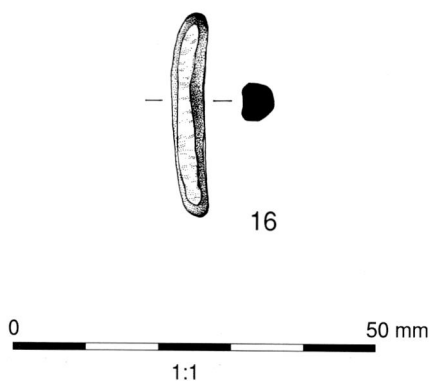

16

0                 50 mm

1:1

*Figure 36: Copper-alloy ingot*

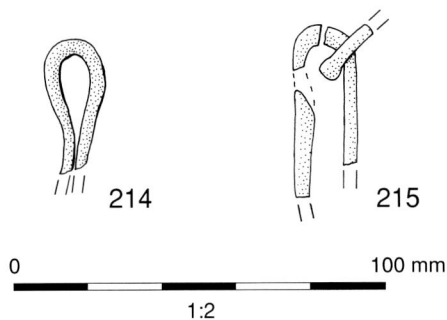

*Figure 37: Iron staples*

Several staples were found (Fig 37), three of which are U-shaped examples from early medieval graves. These may originally have been used to attach a hasp, handle, or other fitting to the coffins.

*Chest or coffin fittings*
The excavations have produced a remarkable collection of iron hinge straps and other chest or, more likely, coffin fittings. Only 14 of the early medieval graves produced stratified examples, but although the remainder were poorly stratified or residual, the character of the vast majority of them suggests a pre-Norman date. It is likely, therefore, that they derived from graves and had become disturbed subsequent to burial. Thus, it seems reasonable to discuss them as a single group.

There are some 50 hinge straps, all of which employed the same simple method of articulation. One strap (component A) was curved over at the head to form a loop, which was linked to a hole at the head of the second strap (component B). Component A straps would usually have been fitted to the lid of a chest, or coffin, and component B straps to its rear (*Ch 6*). There are several forms of each component.

In its commonest form (component A), the main body of the strap narrows from the head to the base, where it either curves over into a short, pointed projection, which was hammered into the chest lid (**221a**, **242**, **254**, **281**, **293**, **306**; Fig 38) or comes to a rounded pierced terminal, through which a nail would have held it in place (**275**, **277a**, **287a**, **307** (Fig 39), **310a**, and possibly **290**; Fig 40). These straps are also pierced for a nail near the head. Objects **251**, **264**, **279a**, **315**, **317a**, and **326b** are incomplete straps (Fig 41), the bodies of which narrow but lack bases. An unusual feature of **277**, **281**, and **307**, which sets them apart from the other straps in this group, is their triangular cross-section (Fig 39).

Variant forms include that of **294** (Fig 41), which has slightly convex sides along its entire length,

and is at its widest about a third of its length from the head, where it is pierced. It was curved over at the base. Object **313** narrows towards the base, where it is pierced, but instead of having a terminal is simply rounded off. The base of **331** is missing, but it had parallel sides.

Another group of straps can be defined by the distinct convexity of their sides below the head (**234a**, **258**, **285**, **328**; Fig 42). They are at their widest a little below the head, where they are pierced twice, with holes arranged transversely, rather than axially, as is more common. The base of **285** is missing but can be seen to have curved over; the base form of the others cannot be determined. Objects **299** and **321** are similar but triangular in cross-section. The base of **299** is missing but **321** has a rounded pierced terminal. Object **321** is also unusual because the two surviving nails are plated with non-ferrous metal.

Examples of component B hinge straps may be divided into two groups according to how the hole at the head, by which the component A strap was linked to it, was formed. In the largest group, the hole was formed by drawing out the head of the strap, curving it around, and welding the tip back on to the side of the strap. The commonest form in this group is comparable to the commonest form of component A straps, in that the main body narrows from the head to the base, where it is either pointed and curved over for fixing into the coffin back (**221b** (Fig 38), **253**, **322**, **325**, **326a** (Fig 43), and probably **323** and **332**, although their bases are incomplete), or formed into a rounded pierced terminal (**287b** (Fig 39), **291**, **314**; Fig 43). These straps also have a nail hole near the head.

Object **295** is slightly different, in that although it narrows towards the base, where it was curved over, there is an unusual, localised widening around a nail hole near the head. Object **279b** is a strap which narrows, but its base is missing (Fig 41). Object **273** is a strap with a drawn-out and welded loop and parallel sides, while objects **234b** (Fig 42), **243**, and **259** are similar (Fig 43), but their loops have been carefully formed so that the head of the strap and base are symmetrically rounded. Object **310b** has straight parallel sides before narrowing near the base (Fig 40), which is missing, and objects **227**, **247** (Fig 44), and **329** are incomplete straps with drawn-out loops, but their form cannot otherwise be determined.

The second group of component B straps has holes punched into the head of the strap. Object **270** has slightly convex sides and narrows towards the base, which was probably curved over; it also has

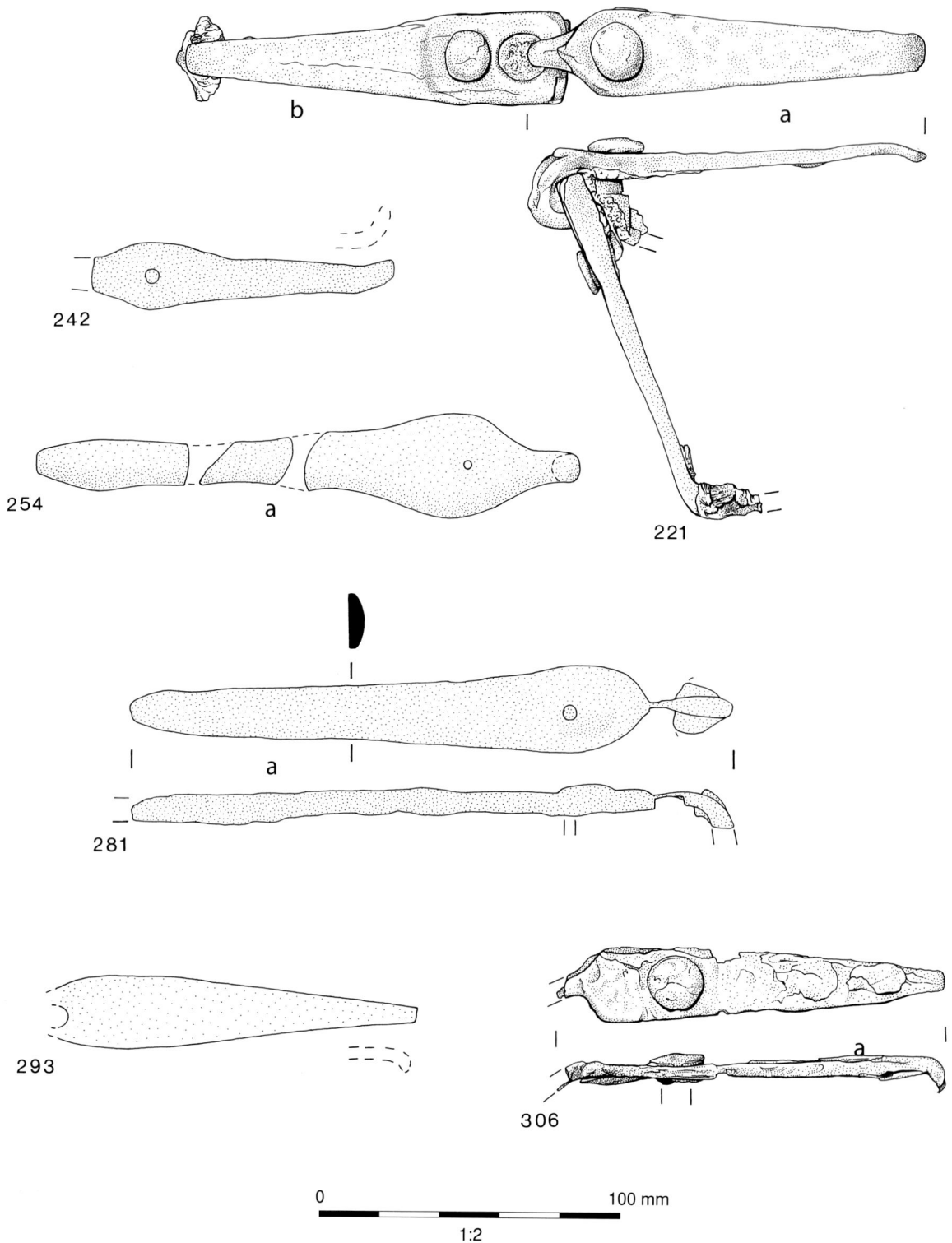

*Figure 38: Component A hinge straps, with a pointed projection*

the slight triangular cross-section noted on three of the component A straps. Another strap (**253**; Fig 43) narrows from the head towards the base, where it was probably curved over. Object **277b** (Fig 39) has an almost flat top and narrows towards the base, where it has a rounded pierced terminal; it is also unusually thick (10 mm), while object **253** has rounded upper corners and is pierced for a nail near the head. Object **304** (Fig 44) is probably a component B hinge strap, but its head is missing, while object **317b** is the head end of a strap, but the form of the hole cannot be determined. Objects **238**, **276**, and **280** are the lower ends of either component A or B hinge straps which have been curved over at the base, while object **230** was probably an incomplete hinge strap, which is broken at each end.

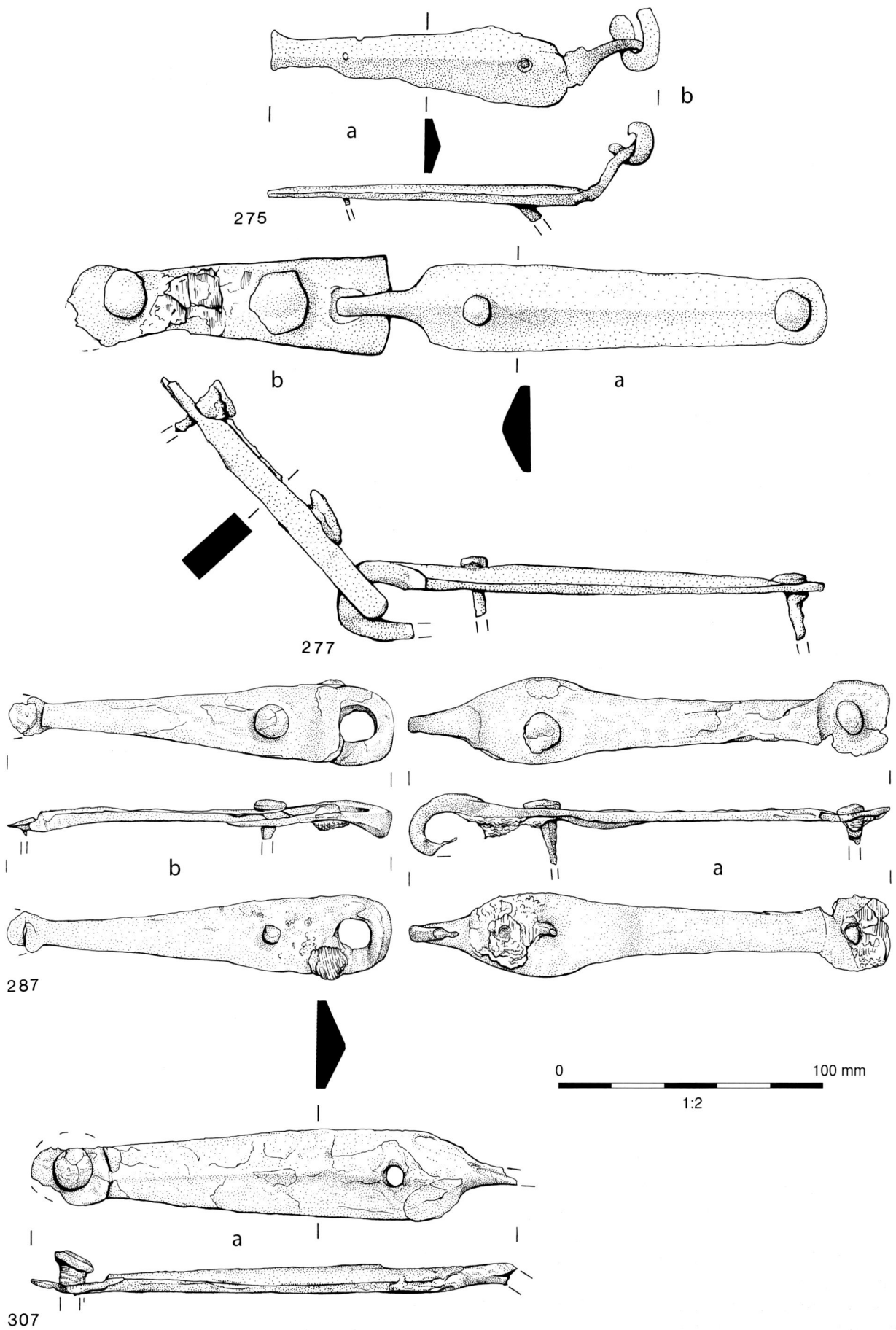

*Figure 39: Component A hinge straps, with a rounded pierced terminal, 1*

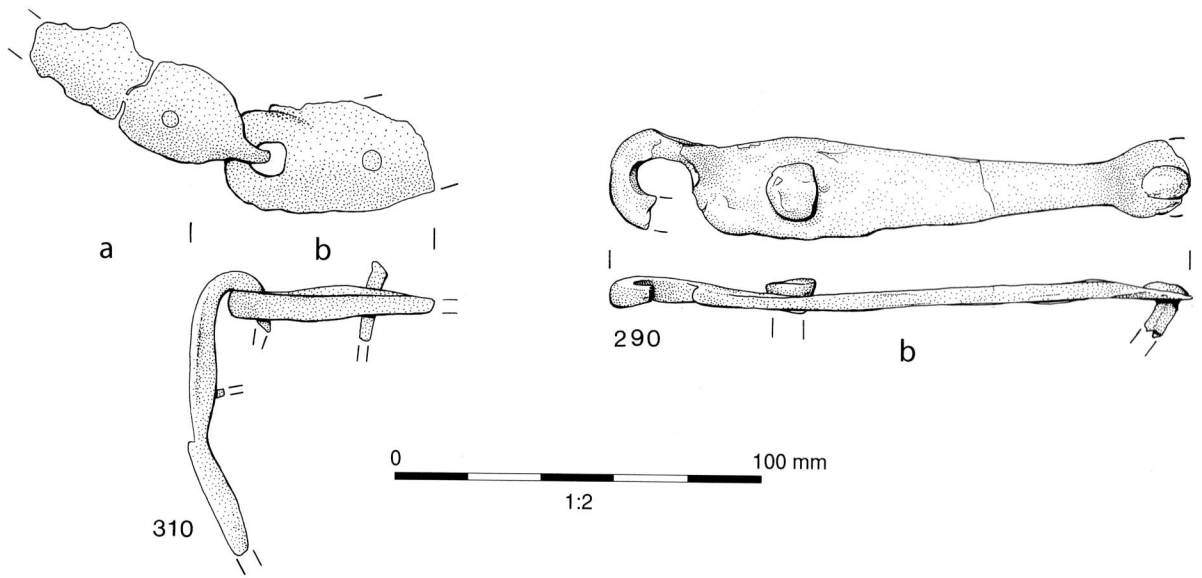

*Figure 40: Component A hinge straps, with a rounded pierced terminal, 2*

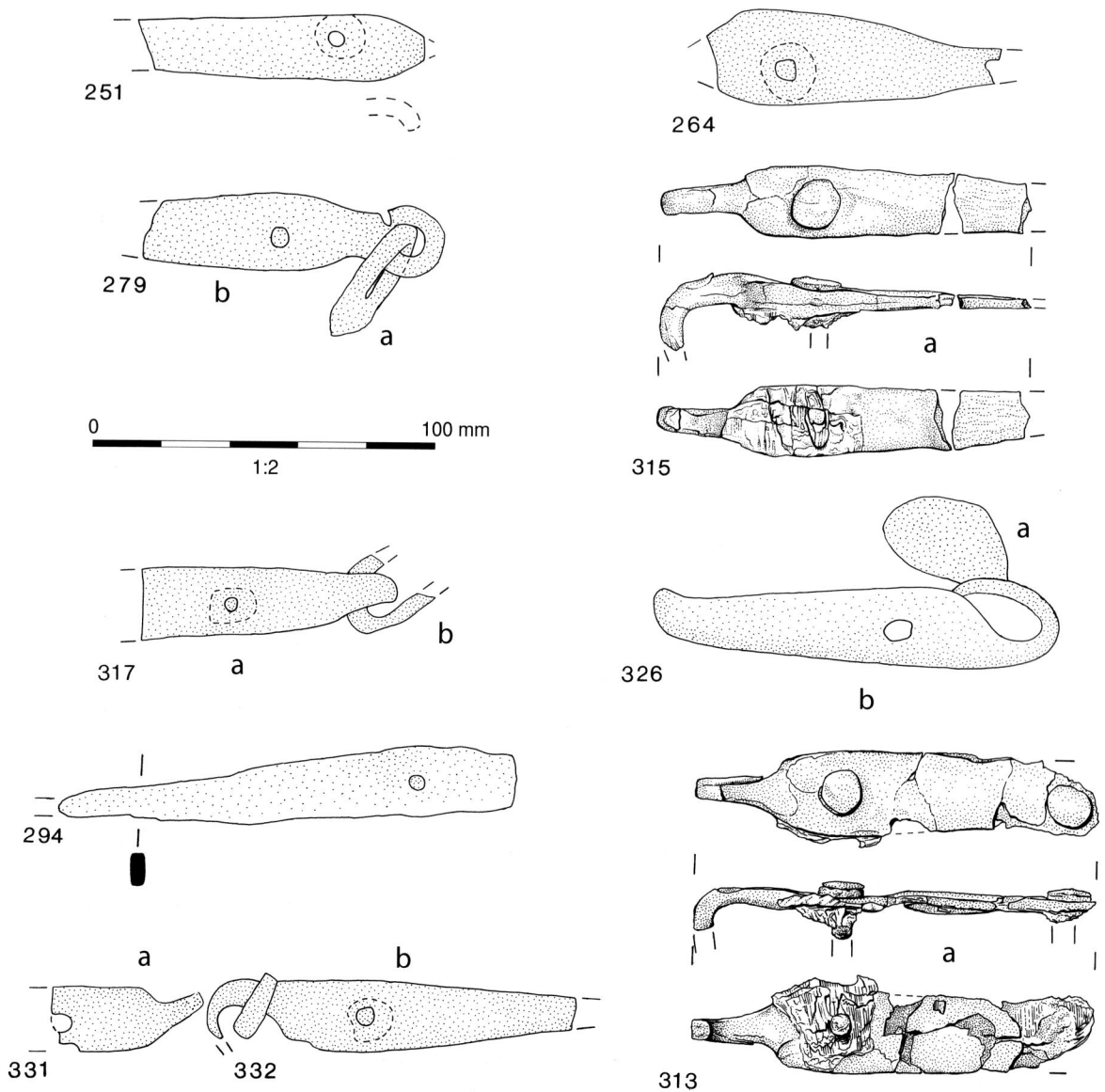

*Figure 41: Incomplete iron hinge straps and variant forms*

62

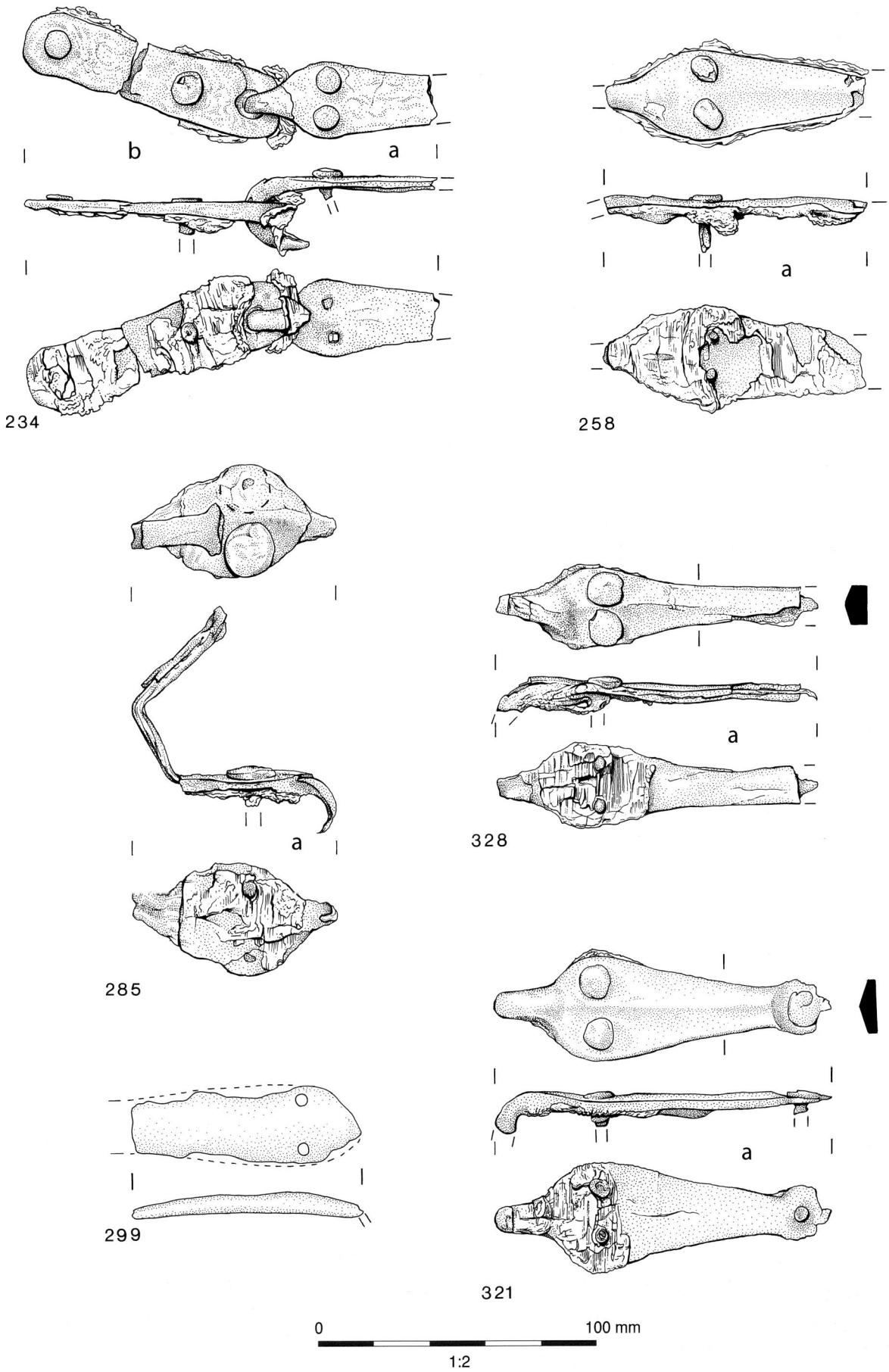

234

b    a

258

a

285

a

328

a

299

321

a

0                                      100 mm

1:2

*Figure 42: Iron hinge straps with convex sides*

63

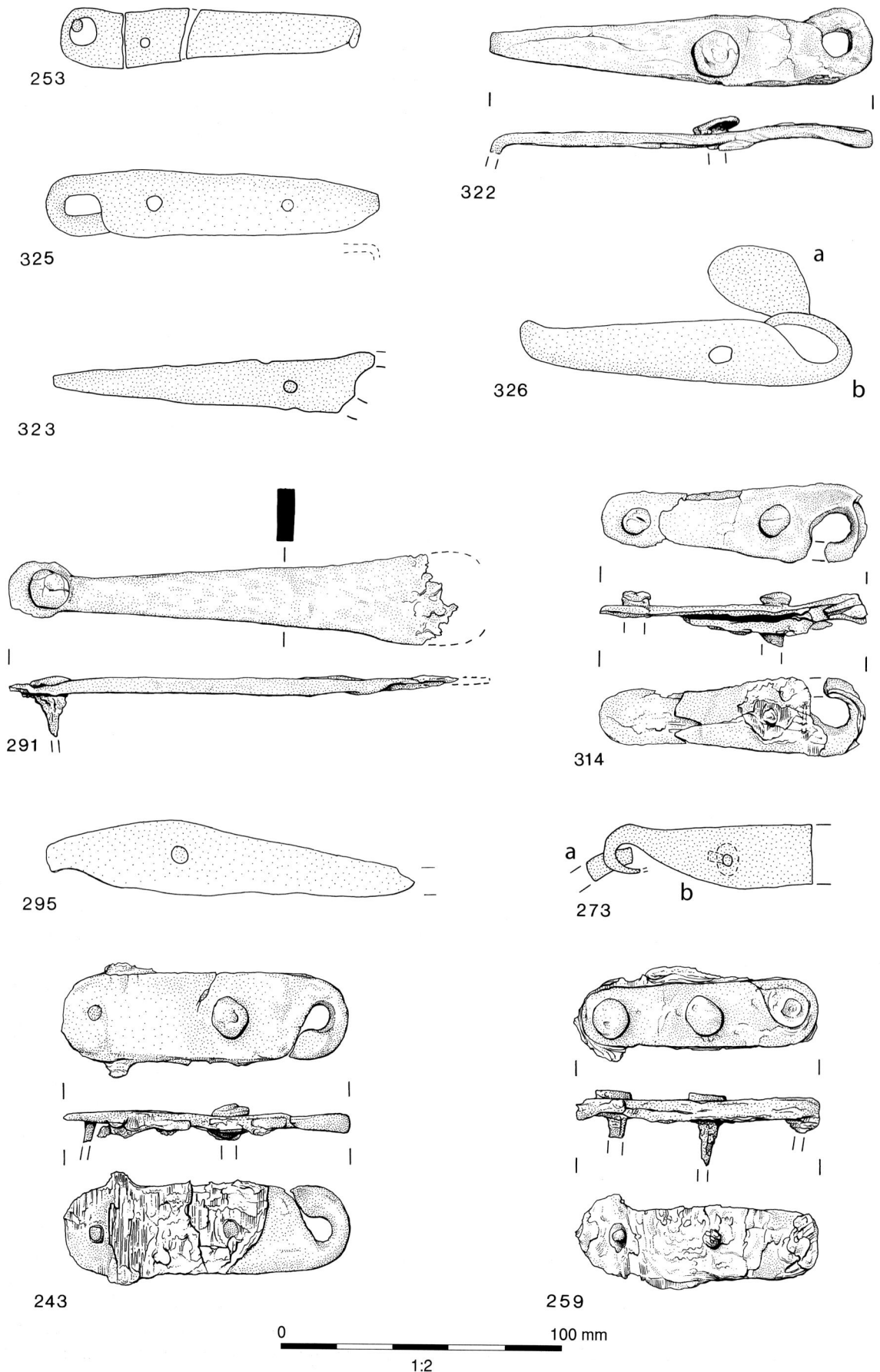

253

325

323

322

326 a b

291

295

314

273 a b

243

259

0 100 mm
1:2

*Figure 43: Component B hinge straps, with drawn-out loops*

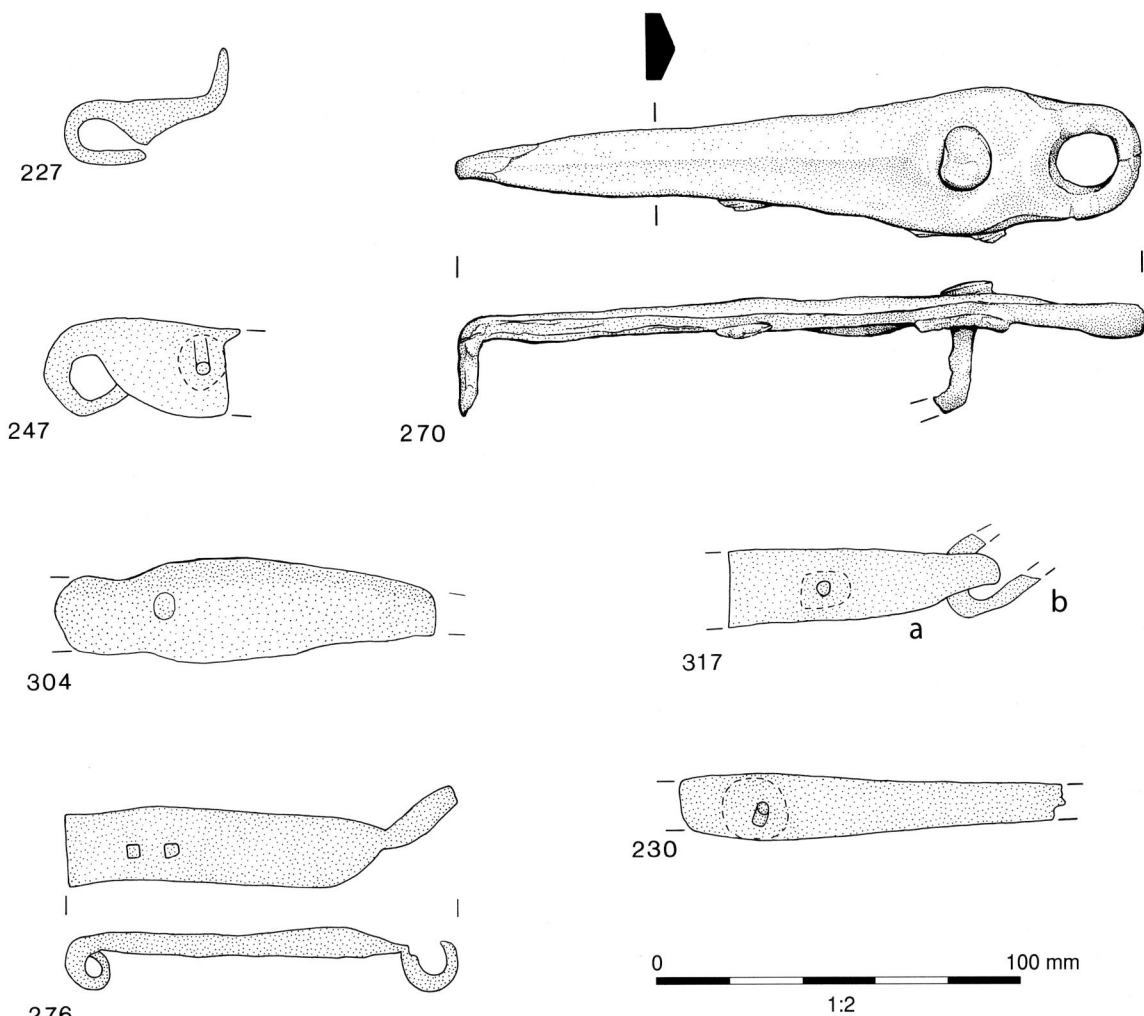

*Figure 44: Component B hinge straps, with drawn-out and punched terminals*

It is likely that most of the Dacre coffins were jointed rather than nailed together, but a few were probably strengthened at the corners by L-shaped brackets. There is evidence for four forms. In one, the widest part of the bracket is at the corner and the arms narrow towards rounded pierced terminals (**303, 309**, and **311**; Fig 45). The surviving arm of **266** narrows but has a simple rounded end rather than a distinct terminal; **225** and **246** may be arms from similar brackets. Object **297** is the arm of a second type of bracket, which had parallel sides and a rounded pierced terminal; **231, 233, 245, 248, 250, 261, 262, 269, 298**, and **308** are probably broken arms of brackets with this form. Objects **222, 223, 224, 237, 240, 249, 265, 267, 271, 272, 278, 300, 301**, and **318** are probably the broken arms of a third form, which were parallel-sided, with simple rounded ends. Object **278** seems to be one of these parallel-sided straps which has a drawn-out and welded loop at one end and is broken at the other. This also contains the remains of a staple in the loop, suggesting this may have been a cruder method of attaching it, or that it has been some form of hinge strap or hasp similar to **335** (*below*).

There are several other pierced straps from the site (*eg* **228, 232, 244, 255, 256, 263, 282, 289, 296, 327**; Fig 46) which are now incomplete or fragmentary, and so their original function cannot be determined, although the majority were probably part of hinge straps or corner brackets similar to the more complete examples. Of greater interest, however, is a single example of a fourth type, **239**, which is a complete short strap, pierced and rounded at each end, with slightly concave sides. It was possibly some form of additional strengthening or binding strap. Object **286** has straight parallel sides, two nail holes, and at the head end has been widened before the hole has been punched in it.

The head of hasp **335** is pierced for attachment to a lid, and at the base it has been formed into a small, pierced plate, which would have fitted into a vertical opening in the face of a chest, engaging with the arm of a lock bolt comparable to those found on the site. Originally, the hasp was probably L-shaped and was therefore attached to a box with a flat lid. It came from the base of the hillwash overlying the cemetery and thus was not directly associated with a grave.

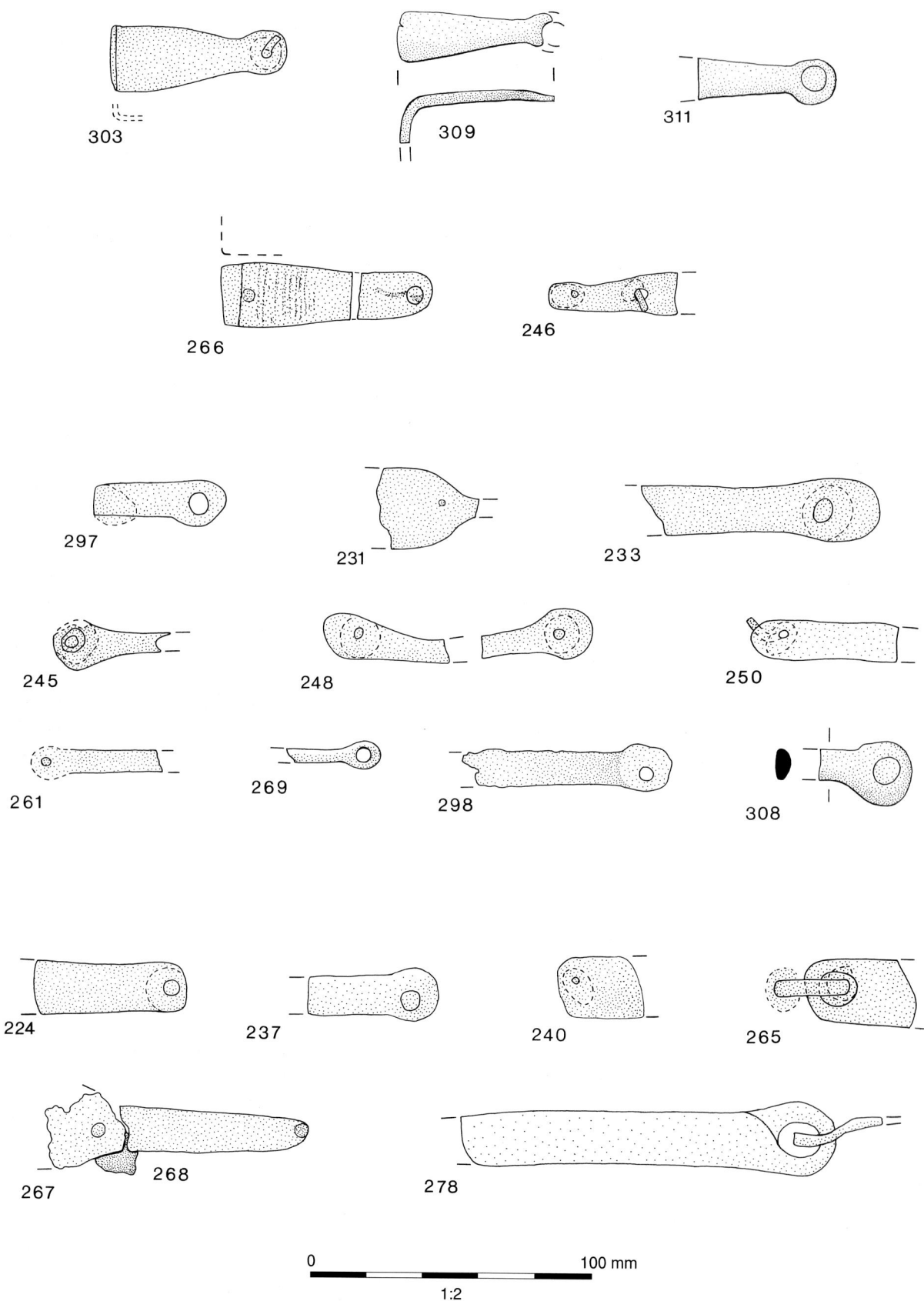

*Figure 45: Iron corner brackets*

Object **339** may be a hinge strap, but the hole at the intact end appears too small to allow easy articulation; another possibility is that it was a stapled hasp, and was attached to the front of a box lid by a staple, the remains of which appear to have survived. A second staple would have been fixed to the base of the hasp

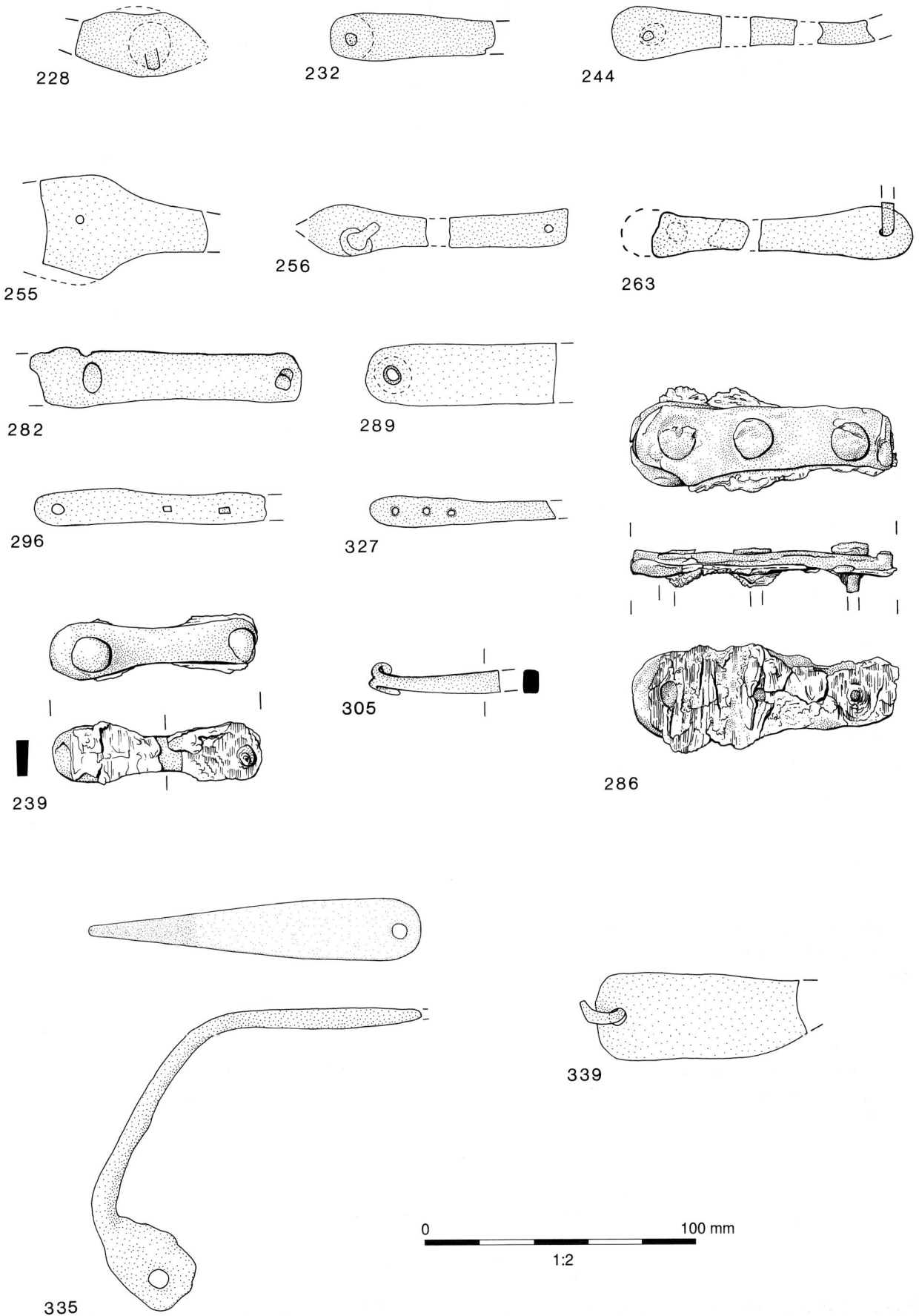

228
232
244
255
256
263
282
289
296
327
305
239
286
335
339

0          100 mm
1:2

*Figure 46: Iron straps*

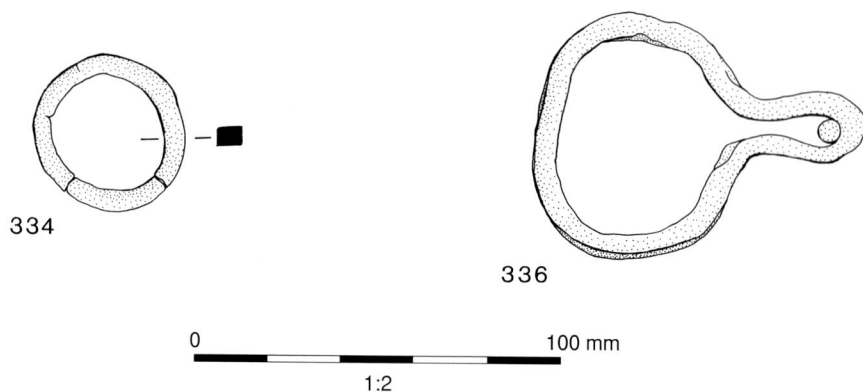

334

336

0    100 mm

1:2

*Figure 47: Iron fittings*

in such a way that it could pass through an opening in the front of the chest and engage with the lock.

*Other fittings*

Object **340** is a hinge pivot, while objects **337-8** are two large, crudely formed U-eyed hinges, probably from a door (though these may equally be medieval; *Ch 5, pp 127-9*). Objects **334** (Fig 47) and **342** are rings, **334** (40 mm in diameter) coming from grave *190*, while object **336** is a small, looped handle, in which a fragment of the staple that attached it to a box or chest survives.

*Locks and keys*

There are five lock bolts and one probable fragment (**343, 345, 347-9**; Fig 48) suitable for securing the lids of large chests, of which all are probably of the same date as the cemetery, although only two are from early medieval contexts, and only one, **345**, from a grave (*888*). Each bolt consists of a central plate with a projecting arm at each end. The bolts were held in place by small, looped staples, which survive on all of them, except **343**. When in the locked position, the leaf spring (one end of which was nailed on to the inner face of the chest) pressed against the curved-over end of the central plate and one of the projecting arms engaged the hasp, thus holding the lid closed (Fig 49). To unlock it, a key with a T-shaped bit was inserted through a horizontal keyhole in the chest, passed through the slot in the centre of the lock, and twisted through 90° so that the prongs engaged in the holes on each side of the slot. There are grooves in the face of **345** which presumably helped guide the key to the holes. Alternatively, if, as in the case of **348**, the lock had no central slot, a key with an L-shaped bit was passed through the keyhole and under the bolt before engaging in the holes. Once engaged, the key was pulled back slightly to release the spring, and the bolt could then be slid along to free the hasp. Object **350** is probably the bit of a slide key.

**Coffin reconstruction**

Since relatively few of the coffin fittings can be ascribed to specific graves, and since no grave appeared to

contain anything like a full complement of fittings, it is not possible to reconstruct any individual coffin. A few general comments on the probable form of the coffins may, however, be offered.

Abundant mineralised wood remains survive on the fittings, and analysis suggests that the coffins were constructed from boards rather than dug-out tree trunks, an alternative method of making chests in the medieval period (Geddes 1984, 297). No grave is recorded as containing more than five nails, so coffins were probably jointed rather than nailed together, but had fittings such as hinge straps and corner brackets nailed onto them. This accords with contemporary practice, judging by a number of surviving chests of ninth- to tenth-century date, including two of those in the ninth-century Oseberg Ship (Grieg 1927, 121-3, figs 65-7) and the tenth-century Mästermyr tool chest (Arwidsson and Berg 1983). It may also be noted that jointed wooden coffins of the period, without iron fittings, have been found at Barton-on-Humber, Humberside (Rodwell and Rodwell 1982, 301-2; Youngs *et al* 1983, 185), but coffins which were nailed together are also known, at, for example, Castle Green, Hereford (Shoesmith 1980, 27-35).

The lids were probably flat and fitted to the body of the coffin by two pairs of hinge straps (*p 59*). The presence of a lock bolt in grave *888*, and the discovery of one or two hasps and four or five other lock bolts on the site indicates that the lid might, on occasions, have been fastened down. Since there seems, at first sight, no practical reason for locking a coffin, the presence of a lock in grave *888*, and in other contexts of locks which possibly came from coffins, suggests that domestic chests were on occasions reused in a burial context. A useful way of resolving this question would have been to examine the skeletal remains, had they survived (*p 86-7*), since any evidence for unusual constriction of a body in order to fit it into a coffin might suggest the receptacle was not originally intended for burial. This was apparently the case

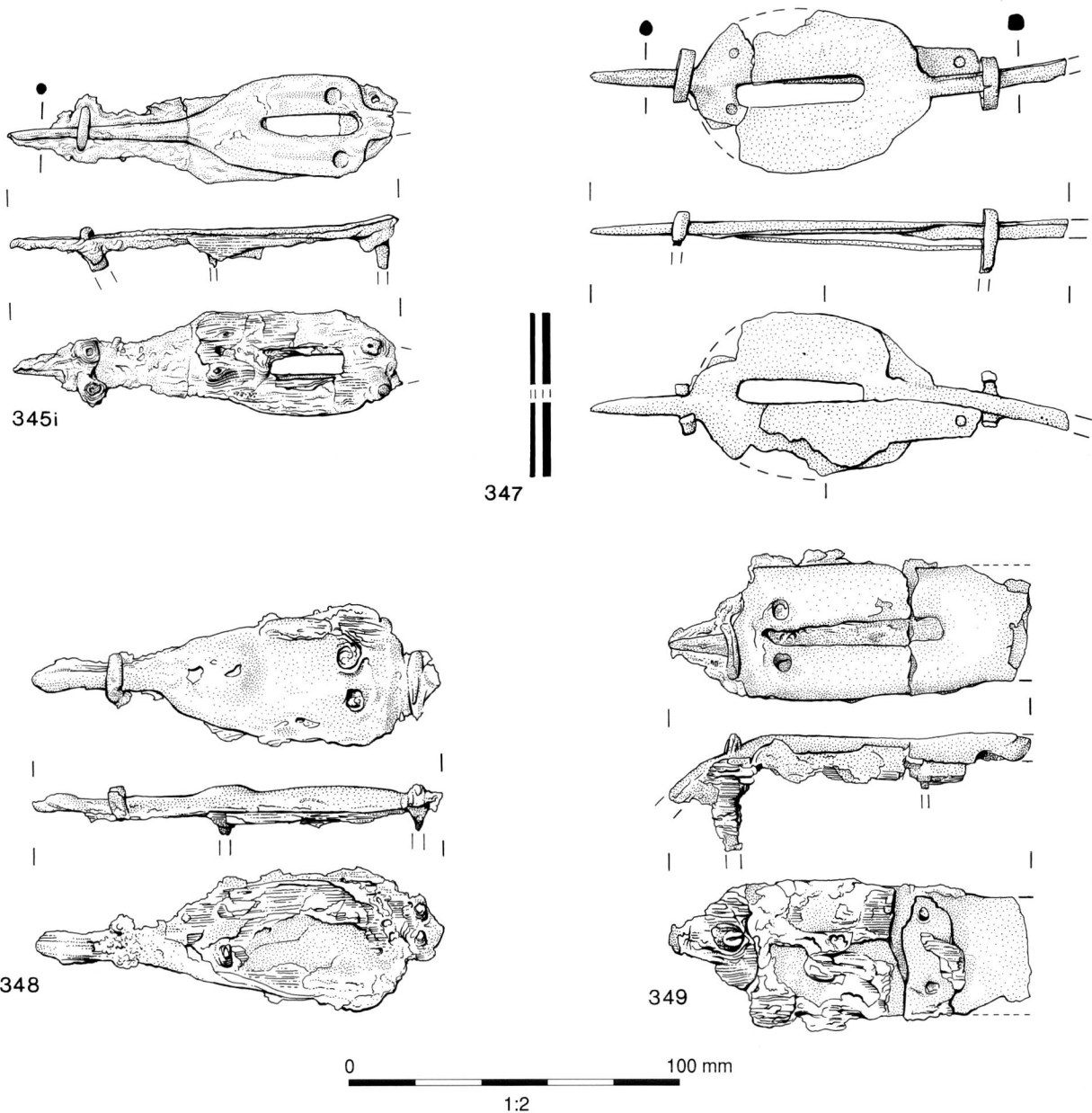

345i

347

348

349

0                                          100 mm

1:2

*Figure 48: Iron locks*

in the early Viking-age burial in a locked chest at Førlev, Denmark (Brøndsted 1936, 191-2, fig 102).

**Dating**

The dating of the iron fittings from Dacre is of considerable importance for establishing the date and context of the cemetery itself, since few other artefacts can be directly or indirectly associated with the graves. Although a pre-Norman date is indicated by stratigraphic evidence and is confirmed by the general character of much of the ironwork, placing the material within a narrower timeframe presents problems.

Several excavations elsewhere (Table 1), however, allow some informed suggestions to be made on the basis of both the form of the fittings and

the burial rite, inasmuch as it involved the use of iron-bound coffins. These include a group of pre-Conquest cemeteries in which burials in coffins with iron fittings have been found: Hereford (Shoesmith 1980), Monkwearmouth, in the graves contemporary with the early medieval monastic buildings (Cramp 1969; Clogg 2006); Repton, Derbyshire (Biddle and Kjølbye-Biddle 1992; Ottaway nd a); Ailcy Hill, Ripon (Hall and Whyman 1996; Ottaway 1996), Thwing, East Riding of Yorkshire (Manby 1986; Ottaway nd b), York Minster (Phillips 1985, 44-6; Kjølbye-Biddle 1995), Carlisle Cathedral (McCarthy 2014), and St Michael's Church, Workington (Zant and Parsons 2019). In addition, there is a single burial within a locked coffin from the Anglian cemetery at Garton Slack, North Yorkshire (Mortimer 1905, 254).

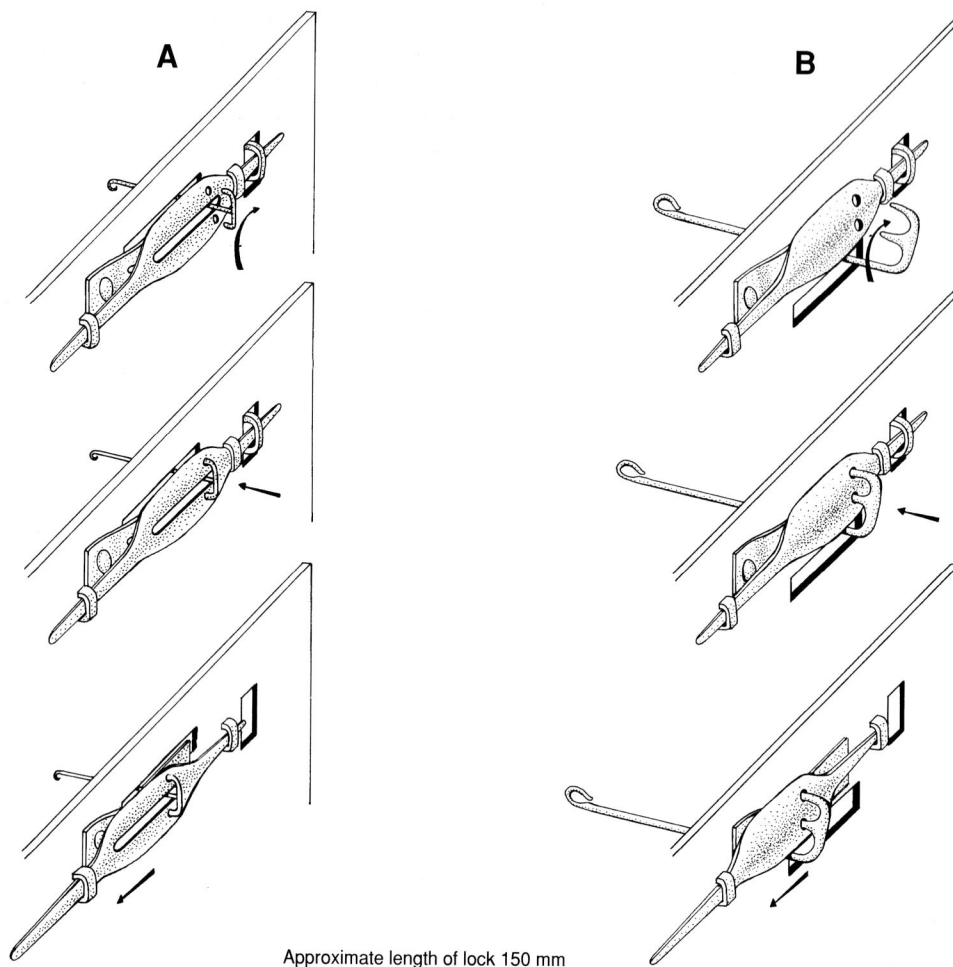

*Figure 49: Reconstruction of the two principal types of lock at Dacre*

| Site | No | Reference |
|------|-----|-----------|
| Ainderby Steeple, N Yorks | 5 | Rogers 2004a |
| Carlisle Cathedral, Cumbria | 1 or more | Ottaway 2014 |
| Dacre, Cumbria | 4 or 5 | Ottaway 1986 |
| Flixborough, Lincs | 1 certain, probably more | Ottaway 2007 |
| Garton Slack, E Riding of Yorks | 1 | Mortimer 1905 |
| Hayton, E Riding of Yorks | 1 | Ottaway 2015 |
| Hereford | 1 or 2 | Shoesmith 1980 |
| Melton, E Riding of Yorks | 1 | Ottaway nd c |
| Monkwearmouth, Co Durham | At least 1 | Clogg 2006 |
| Newcastle upon Tyne | 1-2 | Ottaway 2010 |
| Norton on Derwent, N Yorks | 2 | Rogers 2004b |
| Pontefract, W Yorks | 2 | unpublished |
| Repton, Derbys | 15 | Ottaway nd a |
| Ripon, N Yorks | At least 5 | Ottaway 1996 |
| Spofforth, N Yorks | 8 | Ottaway 2006 |
| Thwing, E Riding Yorks | Up to 26 | Ottaway nd b |
| Winchester | 1 | Goodall 1990 |
| York Minster | 6 | Kjølbye-Biddle 1995 |
| St Michael's Church, Cumbria | At least 2 | Zant and Parsons 2019 |

*Table 1: Cemeteries with evidence for iron-bound chests used as coffins*

The Garton Slack burial cannot be independently dated, but it comes from a cemetery of unfurnished inhumations adjacent to, but distinctly separated from, a cemetery of furnished inhumations. The implication may be that the furnished inhumations belong to the later years of paganism, while the unfurnished burials belong to the earliest years of Christianity in east Yorkshire, perhaps in the later seventh- or early eighth century. The Monkwearmouth, Ripon, and Thwing graves probably date from the eighth- or first half of the ninth century, while the Hereford and Repton graves with iron fittings are probably late ninth- to tenth century (Shoesmith 1980, 25).

The simple linked hinge is not in itself an indicator of pre-Norman date, although after the Conquest chest hinges made from two components which articulated about a central pin began to replace the linked form. Linked hinges similar to those from Dacre have been found in all these cemeteries, but also in other pre-Conquest contexts in Britain, including on a door from the ninth-century mill at Tamworth (Ottaway 1992b), and in Anglo-Scandinavian (mid-ninth- to mid-eleventh century) contexts at 16-22 Coppergate, York (Ottaway 1992a, 637-9). Viking-age examples from Scandinavia occurred on chests in the Oseberg Ship, Norway (Grieg 1927, 121-3, figs 65-7), on the chest from Førlev, Denmark (Brøndsted 1936, 191-2, fig 102), a coffin from Fyrkat, Denmark (Roesdahl 1977, fig 191), and on the Mästermyr tool chest (Arwidsson and Berg 1983).

The form of the straps may be a more significant indicator of a pre-Conquest date; parallels can be readily found in the period, but rarely in material from later contexts. Component A straps, which narrow to a point at the base, where they are curved over, occur not only in British cemeteries (above) but elsewhere in Europe on, for example, the Førlev chest (Brøndsted 1936, 191-2, fig 102), an eighth-ninth-century coffin from Dunum, Friesland (Schmid 1970, abb 8.3b), and the coffin from Fyrkat (Roesdahl 1977, fig 191). The form with a rounded pierced terminal is also common in the British cemeteries, except for Monkwearmouth, where it does not appear. Parallel-sided straps are known from the other cemeteries, again with the exception of Monkwearmouth. Other straps from Dacre are, however, not easy to parallel closely; those with distinctly convex sides over much of their length, and a pair of holes arranged transversely at their widest point, are unusual, although similarly paired holes can be seen on a strap from Ripon (Ottaway 1996, 101).

Component B straps, whose heads have been drawn out and then curved over to make a loop, are very characteristic of the pre-Conquest period. The form

is common in all the cemeteries (above) and may be seen on a pair of late seventh-eighth-century date from Yeavering, Northumberland (Hope-Taylor 1977, fig 90, 4-5), the hinge strap from Tamworth (Ottaway 1992b), and straps from 16-22 Coppergate, York (Ottaway 1992a, 624-5). Straps which narrow towards a pointed curved-over base, or to a rounded terminal, again occur widely in the other cemeteries, and Scandinavian examples of the former include those from Førlev and Fyrkat (Brønsted 1936, 191-2, fig 102; Roesdahl 1977, fig 191). The Yeavering straps are parallel-sided and so are similar to **234b** and **256** (*pp 59, 65*).

Hinge holes formed by punching the head of the strap are less common in the pre-Conquest period, although there are several examples from Monkwearmouth (Clogg 2006) and Repton. Dacre strap **277b** (*p 60*), which has a flat top and narrows towards the base, can only be paralleled at Monkwearmouth.

Intact corner brackets were scarce at Dacre, although there were probably several forms (*p 65*). Those where the arms narrow from the corner towards distinct rounded terminals are paralleled on the Garton Slack coffin (Mortimer 1905, pl 91), and another example occurred in a tenth-eleventh-century context at Castle Green, Hereford (Shoesmith 1980, 37-8, fig 32, 9). Brackets with parallel-sided arms and rounded pierced terminals occur in numbers in the Repton and Ripon cemeteries (Ottaway nd a; 1996), and examples with simple rounded ends at Hereford (Shoesmith 1980, 37-8, fig 32, 3, 11-2) and Repton again.

The hasp (**335**, *p 65*) from Dacre cannot be paralleled exactly. Hasps (for locks) do, however, occur on coffins from Repton, Ripon, Thwing, and York Minster, and a late ninth-century grave (no 74) in the Cathedral Green cemetery at Winchester (Goodall 1990, 1016-17).

The lock with a sprung sliding bolt of the form that occurs at Dacre (*p 68*) appears to originate in the Roman period (Manning 1985, O66; Ottaway 1992a, 662). Amongst the earliest post-Roman examples is a group of eight, six of which have the axial central slot, from the sixth- to seventh-century cemetery at Buckland, Dover (Evison 1987, 100-1, figs 17, 21, 30, 33, 34, 39, 51, 124). Several of the locks employing this form of bolt, both with and without an axial central slot, came from contexts dated, at least provisionally, to between the eighth and tenth centuries. There was an example on the Garton Slack coffin (Mortimer 1905, pl 91), several have been found in the Ripon (Ottaway 1996, 106-9) and Thwing (Ottaway nd b) cemeteries, and they also occur on coffins from York Minster (Kjølbye-Biddle 1995). Three were found at 16-22

Coppergate, York, two in tenth-century contexts, and one with a central slot, in an eleventh- to twelfth-century context, but likely to be residual (Ottaway 1992a, 660-2). No bolts of this type are known from medieval sites without pre-Conquest occupation. Continental examples appear to be scarce but they include one on the Førlev chest (Brønsted 1936) and several, with central slots, from the Dunum cemetery (Schmid 1970, abb 8.3d).

In conclusion, the evidence of comparable material suggests a probable date for the burials at Dacre with iron coffin fittings, if not the cemetery as a whole, between the eighth- and late tenth centuries. Further work on the comparable collections may allow this dating to be refined, if it proves possible to give certain stylistic features of the hinges and locks a more restricted date range (*Ch 6, p 144*).

### Burial rite

Further suggestions for dating the ironwork may perhaps be made on the basis of the burial rite itself (see also the review by Elizabeth Craig-Atkins (2012)). The use of iron fittings, other than nails, on coffins can be traced back to the Roman period. Hinge straps were, for example, found in two graves from Cirencester (Viner and Leech 1982, 88-9 fig 36) and corner brackets in graves from Lankhills, Winchester (Clarke 1979, 336-41 figs 43-5). When inhumation again succeeded cremation in the late sixth or seventh century, it is known that coffins with hinges, corner brackets, and other straps were occasionally used, but the graves at Dacre and the other early medieval cemeteries may be distinguished by the substantial nature of their fittings, and by the occurrence of locks and hasps, suggesting the reuse of domestic chests.

While, however, this latter practice may have occurred throughout the period, the specific use of locked coffins may be a rite with a relatively short life. Given the probable date (eighth- to ninth-century) of the Garton Slack (Mortimer 1905), Ripon (Hall and Whyman 1996, 122-4), Thwing (Manby 1986), and Dunum cemeteries (Schmid 1970), and of the burials in locked coffins from Winchester Cathedral Green and York Minster (late ninth to tenth century; Goodall 1990, 1016-17; Kjølbye-Biddle 1995), a date in the eighth, ninth, or early tenth century is most likely for the Dacre burials with iron fittings.

### Dress fittings

Object **354** (Fig 50), from layer *1203* in the eastern part of the site, is probably the shank of a ringed pin, presumably of pre-Conquest date, although it is not plated with non-ferrous metal, as would normally be the case (*eg* Ottaway 1992a; Goodall 1980). Object **355**, from late hillwash (*36*), is the neck and goad of an iron prick spur, which is plated with non-ferrous

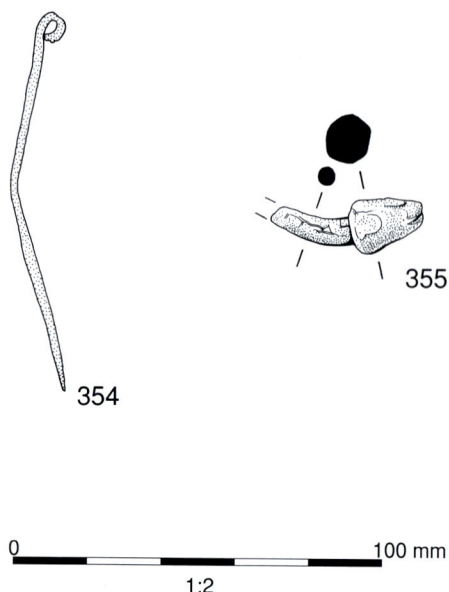

*Figure 50: Miscellaneous iron objects*

metal. The goad has a rectangular cross-section and is tapered to a point, so is likely to be tenth- or eleventh century in date.

An unusual small object (**351**; Pl 34) was associated with the earliest activity in the Orchard (*76; Ch 2, p 40*), which superficially appears to be the same shape as a strap-end, although iron would not be a normal material for such an object. It is convex-sided, and has a rounded upper end and a taper towards

*Plate 34: Iron fitting or escutcheon*

the lower, with a curved section. The fact that it is broken at either end, however, suggests that it was perhaps actually part of a larger mount or escutcheon.

351 Escutcheon, roughly broken at the upper end, it tapers toward the lower end, which is broken away. The long edges are asymmetrically convex, and form a slight shoulder just below the upper end.
L: 30.5 mm; W: 12.7 mm; Th: 4.2 mm
Site 1, *76*, layer, Earliest activity, OR 279

354 Shank of ringed pin, bent in the centre.
L: 100 mm
Site 2, *1203*, layer, Medieval, OR 1979

355 Neck and goad of a prick spur. The goad has a rectangular cross-section and tapers to a point; it is plated with non-ferrous metal.
L: 43 mm; W: 12 mm
Site 2, *36*, hillwash, Post-medieval, OR 1203

## Lead

*by H Quartermaine*

Few of the 205 fragments of lead can be confidently attributed to the early medieval period, either on the grounds of form or their stratigraphic position. The three spindle whorls are, however, of early medieval type, although all are effectively unstratified. The use of lead spindle whorls at this date was not usual, but there is evidence that some were being produced and used at Coppergate (Roesdahl *et al* 1981, 119; Walton Rogers 1997, 1743). Lead whorls are also known from Hereford, at least one coming from a tenth-century context (Shoesmith 1985, 13, fig 8.2).

Spindle whorl **1** (Fig 51) is the lightest of the three whorls. Its upper surface is decorated with three concentric beads, the innermost forming a raised flange around the perforation. Albeit much cruder in execution, it bears similarities to the decorative

schemes employed on some Anglo-Scandinavian disc brooches, but those are not pierced, and they are also larger than the Dacre piece (for instance, Roesdahl *et al* 1981, 106, YD16). It does, however, also bear a marked similarity to an unprovenanced spindle whorl (*op cit*, 119). The other two whorls were similar in weight and type, being slightly bun-shaped and undecorated.

1 Flat discoid spindle whorl or possibly a crude disc brooch, decorated with concentric rings on one side only.
Diam: 23 mm; Diam (perf): 6 mm; Th: 1.5-2 mm; Wt: 6 g
Site 2, *162*, Unstratified, OR 1021

2 Annular spindle whorl, with a flat base and slightly convex upper surface, on which two opposing grooves can be seen spreading from the central perforation.
Diam (base): 25 mm; Diam (perf): 9 mm; Th: 8 mm; Wt: 33.22 g
Site 2, *71*, hillwash, Post-medieval, OR 325

3 Annular spindle whorl, with a flat base and convex upper surface.
Diam: 25 mm; Diam (perf): 9 mm; Th: 8 mm; Wt: 32 g
Site 2, *162*, Unstratified, OR 1421c

Object **4** (Pl 35), again unstratified, is a crudely shaped lump, with a rounded bottom and oval cross-section. It has been made by pouring hot lead into an indentation into a stone or plaster, some of which still adheres to the external surface. The flat top shows signs, around the edge, of the surface-tension lip from it being poured. Lead has been used as a means of attaching iron into masonry (known as caulking) since antiquity (Field and Legge 2017), though no trace of iron was found in this example. The rectangular indentation is 24 mm wide and at least 7 mm thick, on one side of the lump, 25 mm from the top of the object. This was clearly created by the use of a tool such as a crow- or pry-bar to prise the lead from the hole it was poured into.

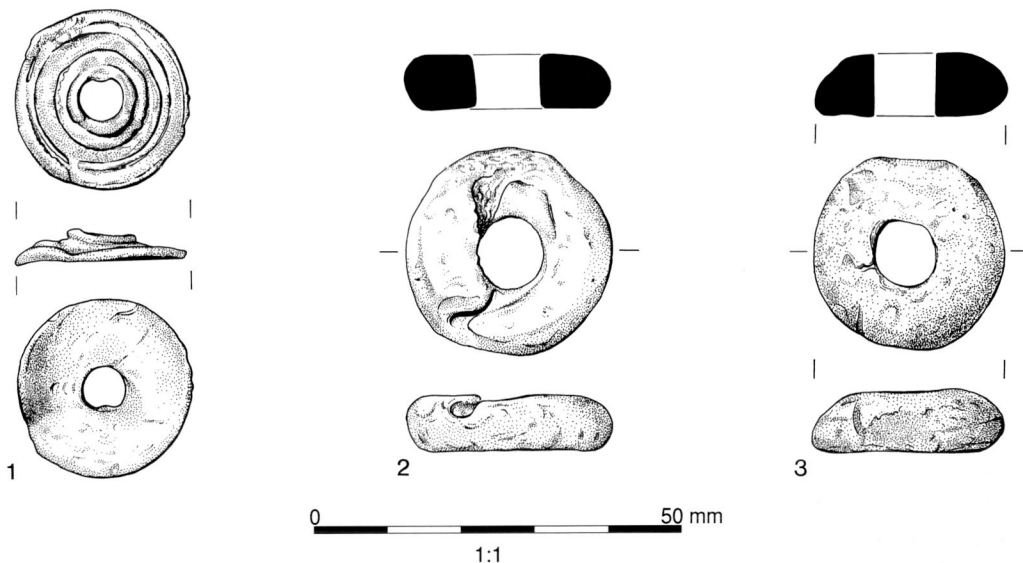

0            50 mm

1:1

*Figure 51: Lead spindle whorls*

4 Irregular lump, with a deep indentation caused by its removal from its original position.
L: 41 mm; W: 41 mm; Th: 46 mm; Wt: 603 g
Site 2, *162*, Unstratified, OR 1752c

Eleven rolls of thin sheet (**5-14**; Fig 52) were found, almost exclusively in the southern part of the northern churchyard. They were not attributable to any particular phase, although the earliest appearance (**5**) is associated with the pre-Conquest cemetery, and a second example (**6**) is from layer *633*, which accumulated immediately above the early cemetery (*Ch 2*). Others are from medieval or later material, or were unstratified.

They appear to have been made by wrapping a small rectangle of thin sheet around a central core, perhaps rope, cord, or bundled netting. Similar objects have been found in a monastic context at Jarrow (Cramp 2006b, pl 12). Several others, however, are known from the medieval site at Winding Street, Hastings, where they are described as fishing net or line weights, on the basis of their association with fish hooks and the proximity of the coast (Devenish 1979, 129 and 130, fig 3.5.a). Indeed, Ullswater and the River Eamont lie within two miles (3 km) of the site at Dacre, with the Dacre Beck only a few hundred metres to the south of the site, and it would seem likely that fishing supplemented the monastic diet. It is, however, probable that such objects served numerous less specific purposes, for example, weighting cords and heavy fabric (such as wall-hangings or ceremonial robes), acting as seals, and, as now, closing the bottoms of net bags. It is often forgotten that nets are not exclusively associated with fishing, but also make excellent storage containers, providing convenient airy storage for perishables and, when empty, occupying little space. Fragment **15**, a neatly cut tablet from the southern churchyard, is the only piece from a pre-Conquest context (layer *1011*, pre-dating the early medieval drain; *Ch 2*).

5 Rolled weight.
L: 33 mm; Wt: 21.99 g
Site 2, *713*, layer, cemetery level, Early Medieval, OR 1756

6 Unrolled weight.
L: 26 mm; Wt: 9.50 g
Site 2, *633*, Layer sealing early cemetery, Early Medieval, OR 1427

7 Rolled weight.
L: 29 mm; Wt: 15.28 g
Site 2, *583*, hillwash, Medieval, OR 1447

8 Rolled weight.
L: 39 mm; Wt: 24.44 g
Site 2, *139*, churchyard layer, Medieval/post-medieval, OR 625

9 Rolled weight.
L: 29 mm; Wt: 7.15 g
Site 2, *28*, churchyard wall, Medieval, OR 1082

10 Probable rolled weight, now unrolled and distorted, with all the edges torn. There is a small round hole near one edge that might be a deliberate piercing.
L: 20 mm; Wt: 6 g
Site 2, *162*, Unstratified, OR 622a

11 Two rolled weights.
i) L: 41 mm; Wt: 28.30 g
ii) L: 27 mm; Wt: 10.27 g
Site 2, *162*, Unstratified, OR 1421b

12 Rolled weight.
L: 34 mm; Wt: 27.07 g
Site 2, *162*, Unstratified, OR 1633e

*Plate 35: Irregular lead lump*

13    Rolled weight.
      L: 29 mm; Wt: 9.44 g
      Site 2, *162*, Unstratified, OR 1752d

14    Rolled weight.
      L: 34 mm; Wt: 23.35 g
      Site 2, *162*, Unstratified, OR 1773

15    Off-cut? Squared but undecorated.
      L: 32 mm; W: 21 mm; Th: 3 mm
      Site 3, *1011*, Earliest activity, OR 1794

**Solidified drips and scrap**

It is possible that the large number of solidified drips may include some partially melted window kame, suggested by the general shape and dimensions of some of the fragments. Few of these drips and scraps were stratified, although two from the northern churchyard (*eg* **71**; Fig 52) and three from the southern churchyard were found in pre-Conquest contexts.

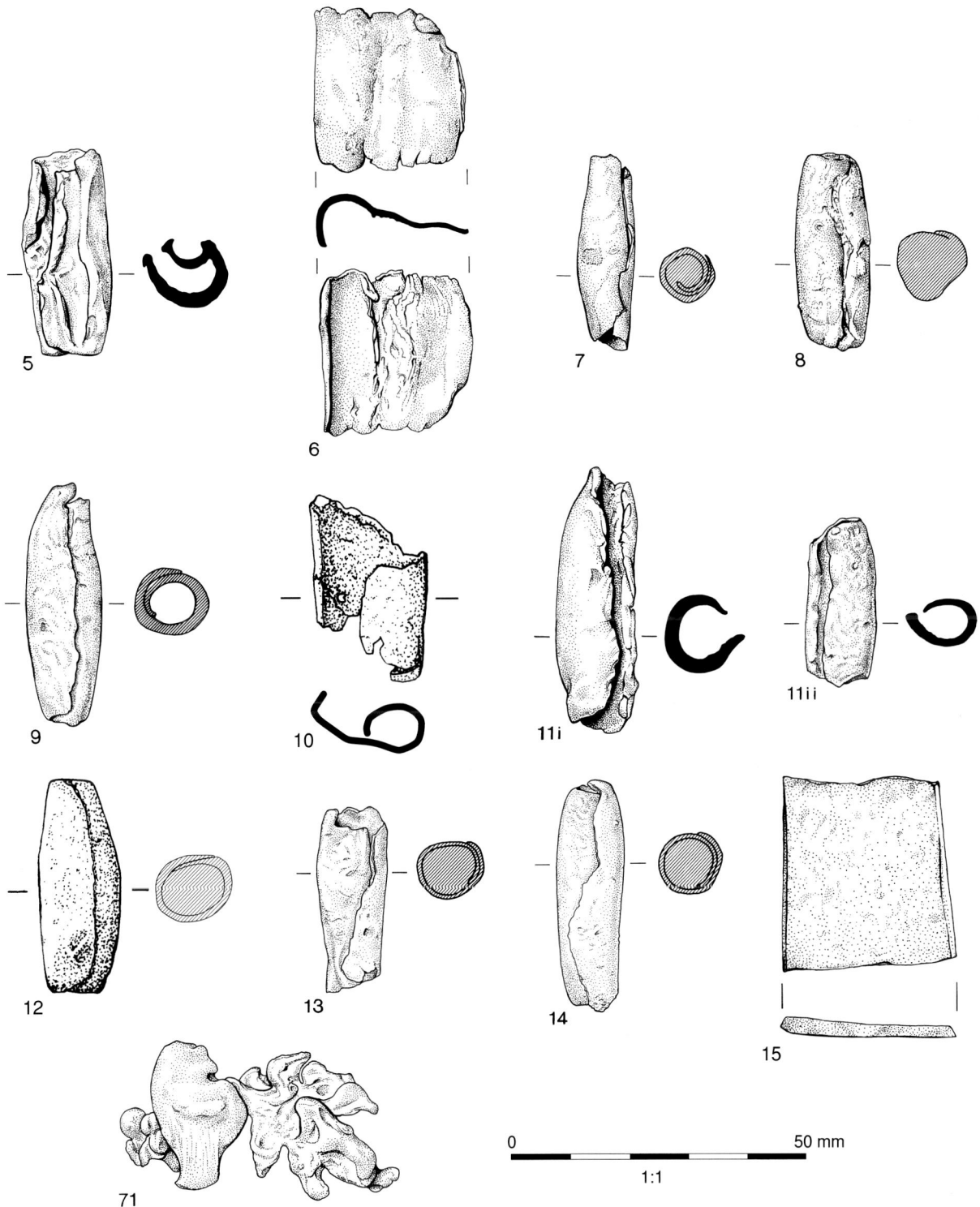

*Figure 52: Rolled weights and other lead objects*

75

## Stone

### The cross fragment
*by R Trench-Jellicoe*

A fragment from the central section of a pre-Conquest cross (Fig 53), carved from a medium-grained micaceous red sandstone, was unstratified in the Orchard. The crossing in the head and base of the shaft are missing at either end of the fragment, and the surface is 75-95% worn and abraded, although part of the outline remains, surviving in a poor condition and heavily weathered. The condition of the carving indicates that it suffered extensive

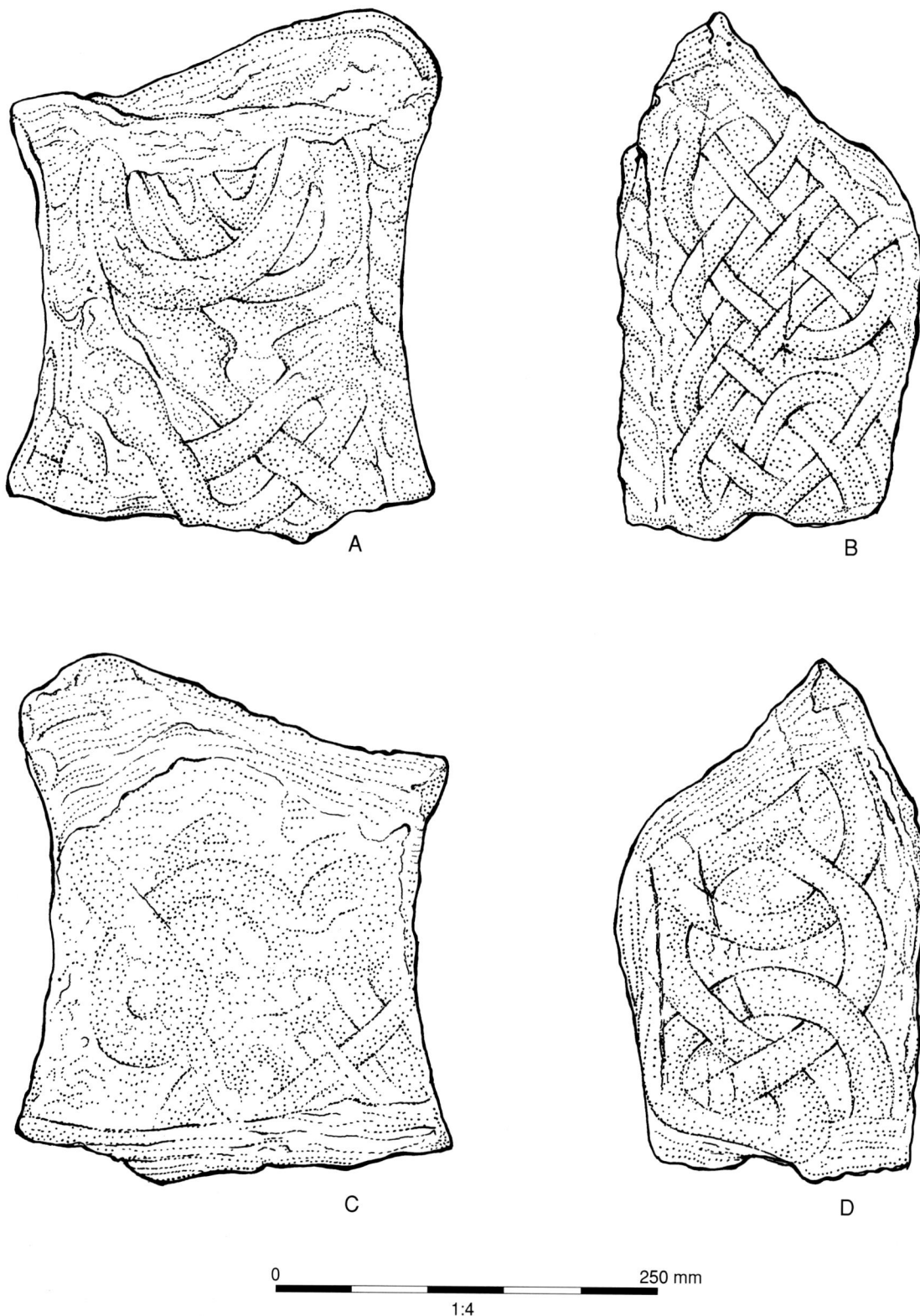

*Figure 53: The carved stone cross fragment*

weathering whilst standing, presumably pointing to a relatively long life in the open air, and the monument has clearly been reused after the cross had been broken up, probably as building stone.

1    *Face A*: the right edge is bordered with a cable moulding, while the other carries the damaged and worn remains of another. Asymmetrically positioned, two pointed leaves lie in the middle of the field; that near the edge is viewed frontally, the other being in profile. They decorate the terminals of crossed stems (13 mm wide), which interweave with other abraded elements beyond. The element filling the space left by the asymmetrical positioning of the leaves is filled with a bulbous terminal close to the left edge, which is in higher relief than the remainder of the surviving carving. This expands as it approaches the edge of the fragment. Another strand appears nearby, and this, like the leaf stems, interweaves with other elements. Beyond the leaf points, two looped strands (12-15 mm wide) interweave but are lost over the edge of the fragment. The whole perhaps represents an inhabited, tangled scroll (Cramp 1984, fig 10).

*Face B*: the left edge shares the cable moulding of Face A, the right border being lost. The decorated width of irregular interwoven strands (10 mm wide) depicts a lattice pattern, but with a return break towards one edge.

*Face C*: neither border survives, and the face is extensively abraded, although some hole points survive and there are ghosts of curving interwoven strands, apparently of two different widths, which interweave in an irregular pattern.

*Face D*: this appears to comprise an almost complete register of a half pattern similar to type 21Diii (*op cit*), represented by a mirror versions of RA656 (Allen and Anderson 1903, II, no 656), which occurs in three instances in Scotland. The strands are 14 mm wide. Insufficient survives of the pattern to confirm the potential identification of this motif as a ring-lock twist (Cramp 1984, type 27Civ).
L: 380 mm; W: 255 mm; Th: 140 mm
Site 1, *258*, Unstratified, OR 223

The fragment has narrow curving edges and is perhaps an example of cross-head type B10 (*op cit*, fig 3), though it apparently lacked a ring. The looped strands on A suggest that this was the end nearest the crossing, and that the loops were part of a Stafford knot (*op cit*, type 23Eiii), the strands of which perhaps extended to fill the neck of each arm, surrounding a roundel or boss at the crossing. The vegetal decoration interweaves with a bulbous expanded element, which may represent the upper part of an enmeshed beast, perhaps similar to that on Irton 1C (Bailey and Cramp 1988, illus 361), although it more probably depicts another damaged leaf. Both types of leaf can be paralleled at Irton 1B, and one also occurs at Kirkby Stephen (*op cit*, 363-4, 394).

The disposition of the various elements suggests that this is the lower arm of the cross, and that there may

have been no formal division between the shaft and cross head. The asymmetrical layout of the scroll, and slight irregularities of the interlace, with breaks in the scheme (more typical of Anglo-Scandinavian work), shares some affinities with the lower panel of Irton 1C, dated to the ninth century by Bailey and Cramp (*op cit*, illus 360), although this dating could be questioned (stylistically, there are elements that could belong to the later tenth or eleventh century; *pers obs*). It also suggests the design and perhaps the carving of the piece is not amongst the first rank of workmanship.

The Dacre fragment would seem to stand chronologically in the middle of the three monuments found there (*Ch 1, pp 12-13*). In particular, it is carved in a moulded relief technique and continues the tradition of the inhabited vinescroll on Dacre 1A/C (early ninth century; *op cit*, 90-1) and has the rectangular profile of Anglian monuments. This is in sharp contrast to the typically Anglo-Scandinavian flat-slab section of Dacre 2 (tenth to eleventh century; *op cit*, 91-2).

## Other stone artefacts
*by C Howard-Davis*
There were, in all, 23 objects of worked stone, few of which can be assigned a firm date. Those thought to be of jet or a similar black substance, however, appear to be exclusively from pre-Conquest contexts.

*Spindle whorls*
Three spindle whorls were recognised, and it is likely that they are all early. Whorl **1** (Fig 54) is a flattened hemispherical disc, decorated with turned grooves, conforming to Penelope Walton-Rogers' type A1 (1997, 1738, fig 806). Whilst effectively unstratified, the carefully turned sub-conical whorl is of a form that appears frequently in early medieval contexts, and numerous examples are known (see, for instance, Parliament Street, York (Tweddle 1986, 231) or more generally in York, where they are regarded as typically of eighth- to tenth-century date (Walton Rogers 1997)). They appear most commonly in chalk and limestone, which are easily turned, but this example is in a locally available tuff. It is very similar in appearance to two shale examples found in an early medieval context at Bryant's Gill, Kentmere (Philpott 1990, 55), and it would not be unreasonable to suggest a similar date.

Whorl **2**, from the first medieval churchyard boundary bank (*378; Ch 4*), is discoid, with a carefully bevelled, beaded outer edge, conforming broadly to Walton-Rogers' type B (1997, fig 807). These are less easily dated with any precision, but at Beverley (Foreman 1991) they appear as early as the eighth century, but were found mainly in eleventh- and

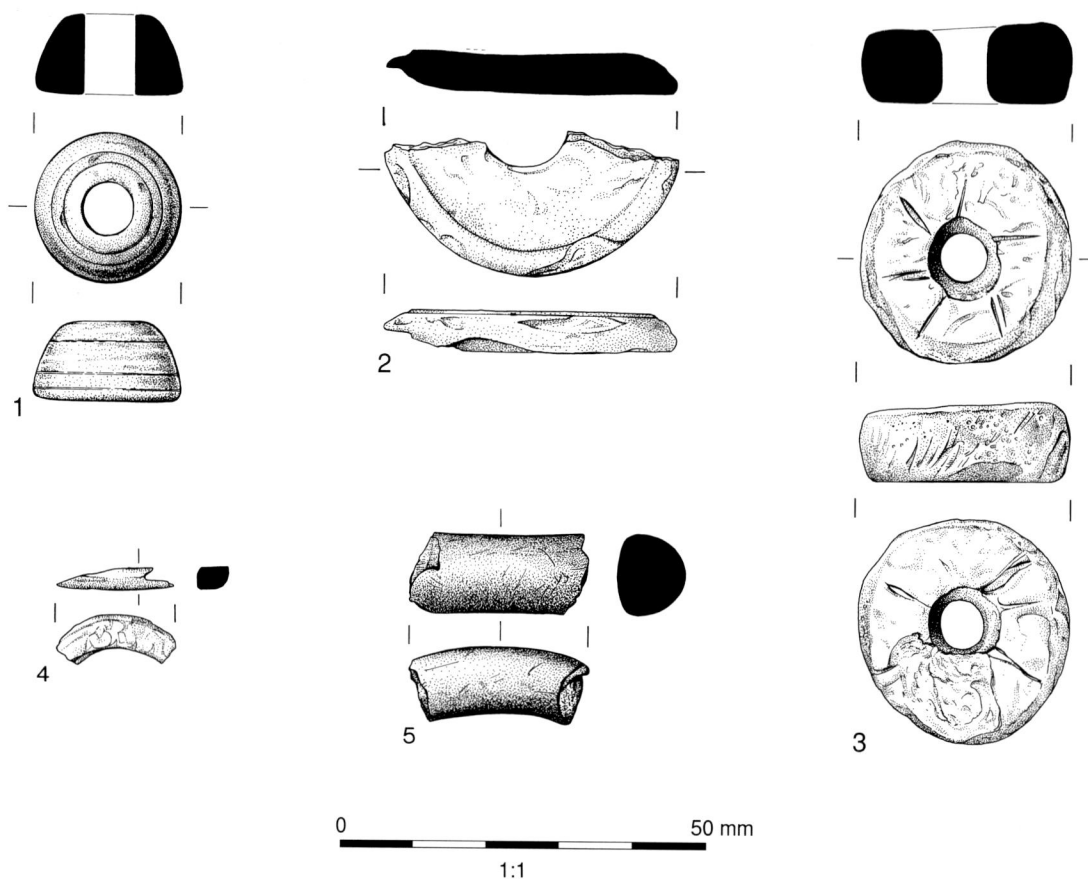

*Figure 54: Stone objects*

twelfth-century contexts. Object **3**, from topsoil *26* in the northern churchyard, is a roughly made type B whorl in a black 'jet-like' substance, which would seem at first glance to be `home-made'. It is now becoming clear that such artefacts were often hand-carved rather than turned, especially in Scotland (Hunter 2008), which might account for its appearance. It is, however, closely paralleled by one in shale from the early medieval levels at Portchester (Cunliffe 1976, fig 141, 81) and the crudely incised radial decoration is matched on a late Anglo-Saxon siltstone example from Northampton (Oakley and Hall 1979, 288, SW13). In addition, there is a chalk example with similar radial decoration from York (Walton-Rogers 1997, fig 8-08, no 6560). The use of jet or 'jet-like' material for spindle whorls is not common, although two are known from Whithorn (Hunter 1997) and another from St Michael's, Workington (Paterson *et al* 2019, fig 28).

1     Flattened hemispherical spindle whorl, made from fine-grained green-grey tuff, probably of local origin. It has incised or turned horizontal concentric circles as decoration. The whole whorl, except for the base, is highly polished. The base is decorated with a single incised line.
Diam (base): 18.5 mm; Diam (top): 13 mm; Th: 11 mm; Diam (perf): 7 mm; Wt: 5 g
Site 2, *162*, Unstratified, OR 1568

2     Discoid spindle whorl made from Carboniferous fine-grained sedimentary rock, which is probably of local origin. Only 45% of the whorl remains. It is burnished, and bevelled on the upper perimeter.
Diam: 22 mm; Th: 5 mm; Diam (perf): 10 mm; Wt 5.85 g
Site 2, *378*, churchyard boundary bank, Eleventh/twelfth century, OR 1254

3     Discoid 'jet' spindle whorl. An irregular radial pattern is crudely incised on the flat surfaces. The perforation is drilled, whilst the edges are worked but unpolished.
Diam: 20 mm; Th: 10 mm; Diam (perf): 10 mm; Wt 7.4 g
Site 2, *26*, Topsoil, OR 402

*Other jet artefacts*

Two other jet or jet-like artefacts were noted, in addition to spindle whorl **3**. Object **4**, from a lower level of the medieval churchyard boundary bank (*355; Ch 4, p 91*), is a badly damaged fragment of a small-diameter ring, probably for a finger, and **5**, from the topsoil, is part of a larger-diameter bangle. The plano-convex section of both objects is reminiscent of Roman glass, jet, and shale bangles (see especially Kilbride-Jones 1938; Lawson 1976, fig 4.20b) and, like the small glass-bangle fragment (Glass **4**, *p 49*), it is difficult to establish a date for their original deposition. They were certainly most common during the Roman period, but also appear on early medieval sites, for example in the nearby Viking-age burials at Cumwhitton, where a bangle and a ring, in a jet-like oil-shale, were found in grave 2 (Paterson *et al* 2014). Dating is further complicated by the tendency of early medieval groups to seek out, value, reuse, and even copy Roman objects, and this must be considered as a factor in attempting to date such simple artefacts.

Although oil shales are more widely distributed, most jet on British archaeological sites originated from Whitby in North Yorkshire (Allason-Jones 1996), and it is quite likely that much of it passed through York, where a thriving late Roman jet-working industry seems to have persisted into the early medieval period (Tweddle 1986, 186). It would therefore not be unreasonable to suggest some loose trading link, probably via Stainmore, with York and the Yorkshire Coast, and the presence on the site of a small fragment of unworked jet might reinforce this supposition.

4    A fragment of highly polished jet, the profile broken, although it may have been D-shaped. It is perhaps the remains of a small bangle or ring.
     Diam (inner): 20 mm; Th: 4 mm
     Site 2, *355*, churchyard boundary bank, Eleventh/twelfth century, OR 1158

5    Plain armlet or bangle of jet, with a D-shaped profile.
     Diam (inner): 60 mm; W: 10 mm; Th: 9 mm
     Site 2, *26*, Topsoil, OR 1257

*Whetstones*
Nine whetstones or whetstone fragments were identified, the majority from hillwash or late contexts. They are, like many stone artefacts, difficult to date. There seems to have been an extensive and long-lived trade in suitable stone (Moore and Oakley 1979, 282-3), but none of those from Dacre can be ascribed to the best-known sources, such as Norwegian ragstone or Purple Phyllite (D T Moore *pers comm*). It seems more likely that they represent suitable stone collected on an *ad hoc* basis from the local drift, since they are all made from rock indigenous to the Lake District and southern Scotland, including the Borrowdale Volcanic series.

The shape of a whetstone is to a large degree governed by its function, and it is perhaps ill-advised to search widely for parallels; **8** and **12** (Fig 55), both from hillwash deposits (*1235* and *121*), are, however, parts of small, perforated whetstones of the kind worn at the belt. Parallels, both in form and stone-type, are known from pre-Conquest contexts in York (Waterman 1959, 98; Tweddle 1986, 184, fig 87; Mainman and Rogers 2000, figs 1007-9) and Whitby (Peers and Radford 1943, 68-9). Whilst chatelaine sets are a persistent

type, it is perhaps relevant to note their frequent appearance in early Anglo-Saxon (pagan) graves, reaching their greatest complexity and frequency in the seventh century AD (Cook and Dacre 1985).

6    Fine sandstone whetstone; either unfinished or crudely fashioned. One end may be worked as a thumbstop, although it seems an *ad hoc* implement.
     L: 79 mm; W (max): 27 mm; Th (max): 20 mm
     Site 2, *665*, cemetery level, Early medieval, OR 1472

7    Fine-grained grey sedimentary whetstone (Fig 55), probably a greywacke of local origin. It is well burnished with a shaped thumbstop or worn by use.
     L: 114 mm; W: 27 mm (max); Th: 13 mm
     Site 2, *323*, fill of churchyard boundary ditch *215*, Medieval, OR 1143

8    Fragment of an Old Red Sandstone whetstone, smoothly worked and with a drilled perforation (Fig 55).
     L: 46 mm; W: 24 mm; Th: 14 mm; Diam (perf): 7 mm
     Site 2, *1235*, lowest hillwash, Early medieval/medieval, OR 2219

9    Fragment of fine-grained sedimentary (probably of local origin) whetstone, with a squared profile.
     L: 17 mm; W: 11 mm; Th: 9 mm
     Site 2, *137*, fill of posthole *138*, Medieval?, OR 930

10   Fragment of fine-grained sedimentary whetstone. Finely worked, with a rectangular profile.
     L: 16 mm; W: 10 mm; Th: 7 mm
     Site 2, *121*, hillwash, Early medieval/medieval, OR 404

11   Fragment of waterworn Red Sandstone whetstone, worked, with a curved upper end.
     L: 87 mm; W: 19 mm; Th: 13 mm
     Site 2, *121*, hillwash, Early medieval/medieval, OR 454

12   Local fine-grained sedimentary rock (Fig 55), fragment only. Perforated.
     L: 40 mm; W: 9 mm; Th: 4 mm
     Site 2, *121*, hillwash, Early medieval/medieval, OR 936

13   Fine-grained sedimentary (possibly a greywacke of local origin) whetstone (Fig 55). Trapezoidal in shape.
     L: 90 mm; W (max): 19 mm; Th (max): 15 mm
     Site 2, *89*, hillwash, Late medieval/post-medieval, OR 322

14   Waterworn fine-grained tuff, which has fractured conchoidally. It may have been used as a polishing tool or whetstone.
     L: 104 mm
     Site 2, *162*, Unstratified, OR 1569

Several of the examples from Dacre are quite worn (**8**, **9**, and **13**) and the wear patterns they exhibit are indicative of their use for sharpening blades rather than points, presumably, in the case of **8** and **13**, small personal knives rather than tools or weapons.

*Miscellaneous*
There were also some rough stone discs, too large for counters, tokens, or tallies, but perhaps lids for small-mouthed vessels. One, from the northern churchyard, came from an early medieval layer.

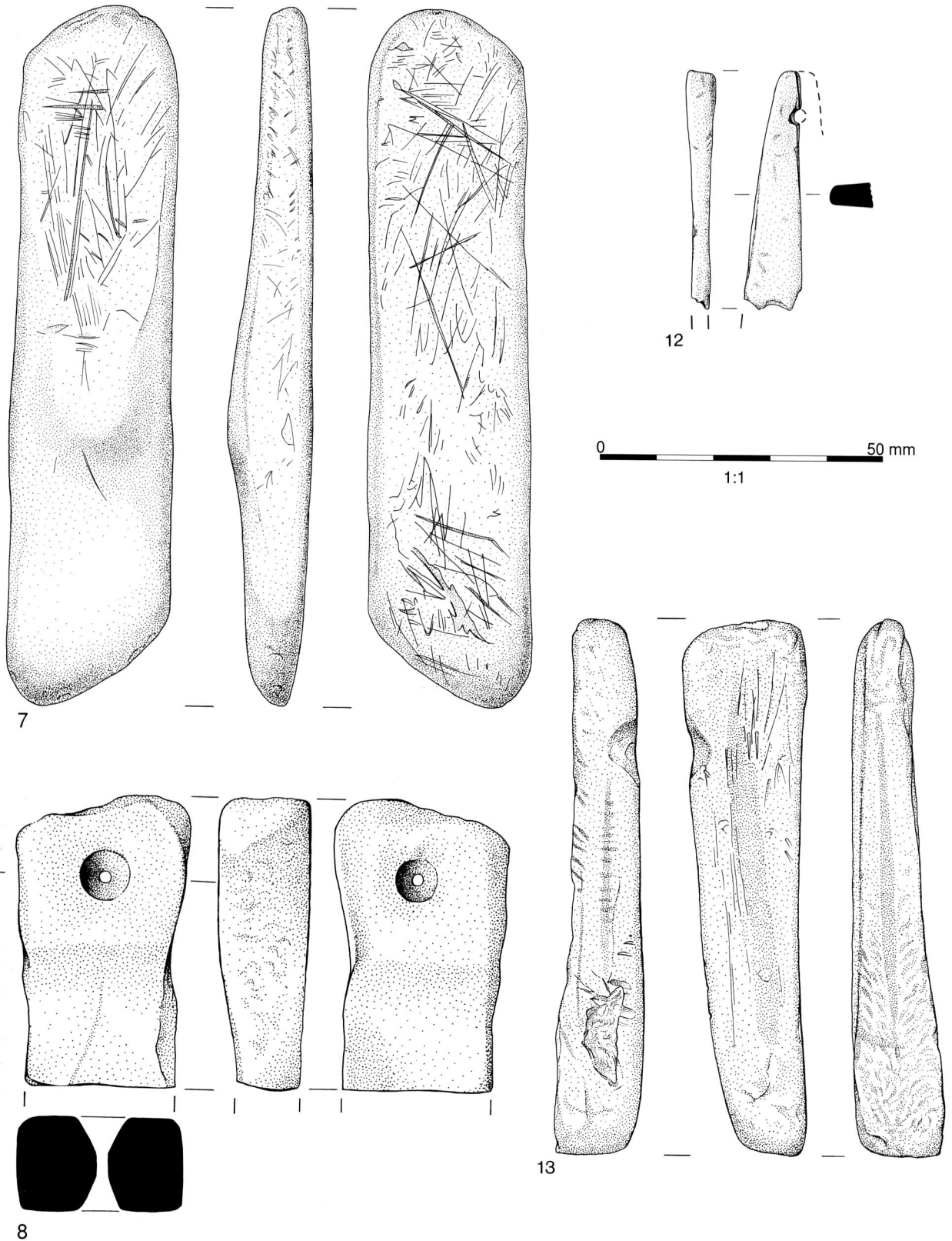

*Figure 55: Whetstones*

*Millstone*

An almost complete but quite worn upper millstone (Fig 56) had been reused as a hearthstone in the early medieval building on the lower terrace in the northern churchyard (Structure Y, *186*; *Ch 2*,

*pp 33-5*). The central perforation incorporates a crossbar or rynd socket, clearly indicating that the stone was power-driven. It is, however, difficult to date; obviously not Roman, it has been assumed, on the basis of its reuse in an early context, to be

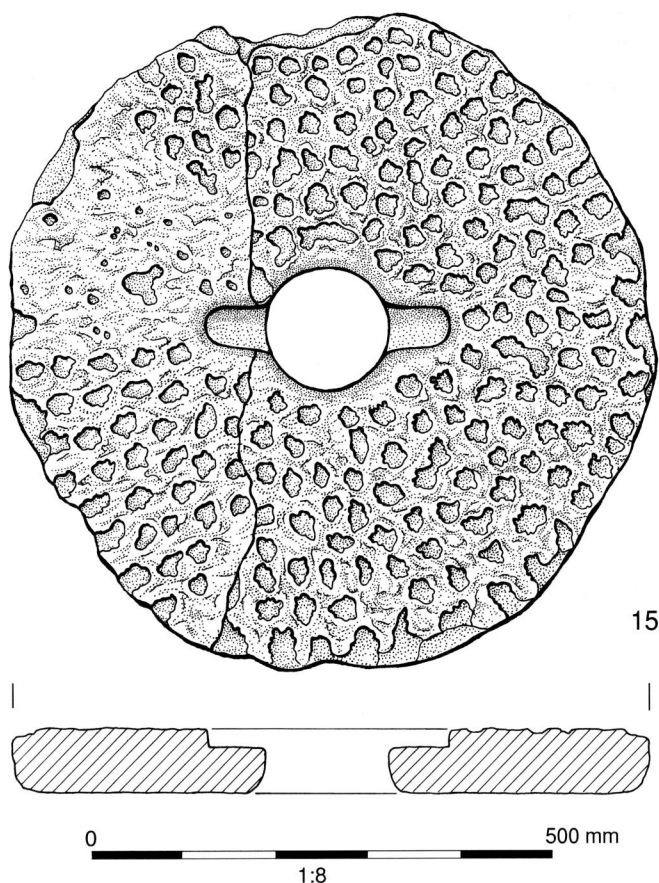

*Figure 56: Millstone*

pre-Conquest in origin. Although Anglo-Saxon watermills are well-attested archaeologically in both Britain and Ireland (Rahtz 1974; Rynne 1989; Rahtz and Meeson 1992), millstones are often not present, but there is evidence from a late tenth-century context at Goltho (Beresford 1987) for the reuse of a worn or redundant upper millstone as a hearth. The surface of that stone, now worn smooth (Smith 1987, 195-6, no 6), was probably originally pecked, like that from Dacre, and small fragments of pecked stones were found at St Peter's Church, Barton-upon-Humber (Gaunt and Cool 2011). It is clear that such complex pecking, whilst perhaps unusual, is not unique, since it was noted, when describing domestic horizontal watermills in Shetland, that `the grinding surface of both stones is renovated from time to time by sharpening with a pick. Diagonal grooves.... are not known' (Goudie 1889, 276).

Watermills are known from the Roman period onwards (Wilson 1976). Irish examples suggest that the horizontal waterwheel, which powers the millstone direct, is an early form, appearing there no later than the sixth century AD, and it is clear that mills employing such waterwheels persisted in

the Scottish Isles until the nineteenth century. They require much less power and resource than vertical watermills, like that excavated at Tamworth (Rahtz 1974), and in Shetland (Goudie 1886) appeared in a purely domestic context, one per homestead.

Grindstones driven by horizontal wheels tend to be smaller than those driven by vertical wheels, and the Dacre example, at 700 mm in diameter, is marginally smaller than the size range given for Shetland examples (approximately 750-900 mm), but larger than the lower stone of an eighth-century mill at Drumard, Co Derry, which measured only 550 mm in diameter (Baillie 1975). Whilst one millstone cannot be considered as anywhere approaching conclusive evidence for a mill in or very near the excavated area, it would seem reasonable to suggest that such a structure was not far away, presumably on the Dacre Beck. Pragmatism suggests that a worn-out millstone was not a valuable item and its weight would mean that it would not have travelled far.

15 Upper or male millstone made from of Old Red Sandstone. It is almost complete, though now in two pieces. One face is pecked, and has a crossbar socket.
Diam: 700 mm; Th: 50 mm
Site 2, *186*, hearth, Structure Y, Early medieval, OR 985

81

*Unworked white quartz*

There is persistent evidence to suggest that the accumulation and deposition of white quartz in or around graves was in some way significant at times within the pre-Conquest period (Craig-Atkins 2012). In northern Britain, especially, there is a strong apparent link with marking graves (see, for instance, Hill 1997; Maldonaldo Ramirez 2011). White quartz was present in a number of early contexts at Dacre, and excavations exploring an apparently early medieval cemetery on Lindisfarne (Dig-Ventures 2021) have emphasised this association.

## The glass
*H Quartermaine*
### Vessel glass

A few pieces of vessel seem to be pre-Conquest in date. In total, there are five vessel fragments (**1-5**) but only one of these is of recognisable form; three (from early medieval occupation layer *172*, and later hillwash *32*) are small, extremely thin body fragments; and the fourth (from late hillwash *71*) is part of a simple indented base. Fragment **1** (Fig 57) is part of the fire-rounded rim of a tall beaker or small bowl, decorated with opaque white, marvered trailing, from early medieval layer *533* in the south-western part of the northern churchyard, the area which also produced most of the pre-Conquest metalwork and window glass (*Ch 2*). Beaker fragments with similar white trailing have been found at Melbourne Street, Southampton (Hunter 1980, 63 (GL10) and 65 (GL38/39)), with single examples from Northampton (Hunter 1979, 298 (GL40)), Portchester (Harden 1976, 234:1), and, in a Celtic context, the Mote of Mark (Harden 1956, 150, 10 and 11).

This type of decoration is common in the Anglo-Saxon milieu, particularly in the period before 700 (J R Hunter *pers comm*). Fire-rounded rims seem to have developed in the fifth to sixth century on the Continent (Harden 1983) and seem to have been largely superseded by folded lips by the eighth century. Although it is impossible from such a small fragment to be specific as to form, and therefore date, this vessel is likely to have been made in the seventh century or earlier.

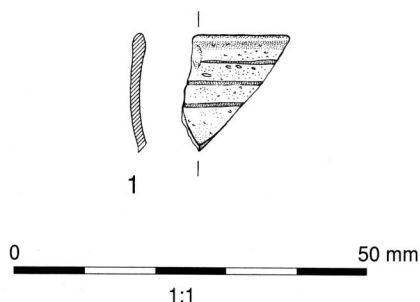

1

0                                    50 mm

1:1

*Figure 57: Glass vessel fragment*

1    Rim fragment in natural, pale blue bubbly glass, probably part of a tall cone beaker or small bowl. It is decorated externally with an applied opaque, white-trailed thread 0.6 mm wide, below the rim, which is fire-rounded. There is another trailed thread immediately inside the rim. Good condition, unweathered.
L: 16 mm; W: 13 mm; Th: 1.25 mm
Site 2, *533*, layer, Early medieval, OR 1300, probably seventh century

2    One very small vessel fragment in natural bluish glass. Good condition, unweathered.
L: 9.5 mm; W: 4 mm; Th: 0.5 mm
Site 2, *172*, occupation layer, Structure Y, Early medieval, OR 807

3    One very small fragment in dark blue glass, probably early. Good condition, unweathered but slightly abraded.
L: 13 mm; W: 8 mm; W: 2.5 mm
Site 2, *32*, hillwash, Medieval, OR 76

4    One fragment in very thin natural bluish bubbly glass. Good condition, unweathered.
L: 16 mm; W: 22 mm; Th: 0.5 mm
Site 2, *121*, hillwash, Medieval, OR 480

5    One fragment of dark bluish-green bubbly glass, possibly a fragment of an indented base. Good condition, unweathered but slightly abraded. Some irregular grozing.
L: 40 mm; W: 17 mm; Th: 3 mm
Site 2, *71*, hillwash, Post-medieval, OR 1305c

### Beads and other glass objects

The most distinctive bead from the site is large and cylindrical (**6**; Fig 58), with reticella decoration, found in a grave (*568*) in the early cemetery (*Ch 2, p 26*). It is a rare type, but widely distributed in Britain, though probably a Continental import, possibly via Kent, where they are relatively common (Matthews and Chadwick Hawkes 1985, 97). Similar beads have been found at South Shields and Usk in Roman contexts (Guido 1978, 101, fig 38 and 232, 237), but on the Continent they are known to have been current in the sixth- to eighth centuries (Brugmann 2004, 37, type A2b), mostly during the period 530-80, although they continued in use later in Northern France and south-west Germany (*ibid*).

They have been found in Merovingian graves at Lumes, Mazery, and Dieue-sur-Meuse, dating from 600-70 (Périn 1980, 227-31, figs 58, 75, 88, 110), and at Martray, Giberville, in a cemetery dating from the late fifth- to the seventh century (Pilet 1981, no 62). In southern Germany, at the cemetery site of Schretzheim near Stuttgart, the same type of bead was found in graves dating to 565-630 (Koch 1977, 211, figs 4-5, pl 4). Examples have also been found in a grave at Dover (Evison 1967, 82 and 105, fig 2b), dated to the sixth century, and at Morning Thorpe, Norfolk (Green *et al* 1987, fig 360), the pagan cemetery at Cheesecake Hill on the Yorkshire Wolds (Mortimer 1905, 286-93), Orphir in Orkney (Batey with Freeman 1986, 297-8), and at Chessell Down

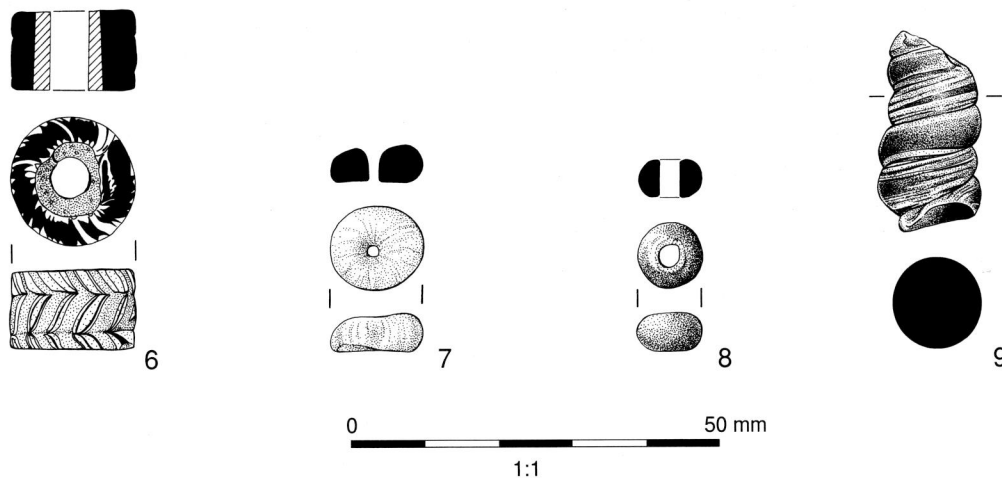

*Figure 58: Glass beads and twisted-glass rod fragment*

on the Isle of Wight (Arnold 1982, 71). Horace Beck describes the type (1928, 67, fig 71) but gives no provenance. A plaque of very similar design, but with blue and amber twists, was found at Whitby (Peers and Radford 1943, fig 22, 72 and 73). It is notable that, with the exception of the Whitby plaque and the Orphir bead, all parallels come from pagan contexts, particularly cemetery levels, the beads from Dover and Chessell Down being thought of as sword beads in the Frankish tradition (Evison 1967, 64-84).

The two annular beads (7-8) cannot be closely dated by form, but their association with the earlier medieval cemetery (fill *1261* of grave *1262*; although tenuous in the case of **8**, which is unstratified) would, however, suggest that they were contemporary. Indeed, annular beads in similar colours were components of a necklace within grave 2 in the Viking-age cemetery of Cumwhitton (Paterson *et al* 2014, 71), only 16 km to the north-east, dated to the early tenth century.

The *millefiori* rod fragment (**9**) from late hillwash *27* is of interest, in that it was found in isolation, rather than in association with evidence for the manufacture of beads or other glass artefacts. Such objects more usually occur in fairly large assemblages of cullet, wasters, and rod fragments destined for reuse. Groups of such material have been identified predominantly on upland sites in northern and western Britain, for example the Mote of Mark and Dinas Powys, and date to a period between the fifth and eighth centuries AD (Hunter 1981, 143; *pers comm*). A similar fragment, showing the impression of pincers, is amongst evidence of glass-working from Jarrow (Cramp 2006c, 264). Whilst it is not unknown for isolated pieces to be encountered, this fragment had clearly moved

downslope in hillwash from its original site of deposition, and thus its presence might suggest a manufacturing site in the vicinity.

6     Large cylindrical bead with reticella decoration. There is a central wound core of poor-quality dark green natural glass, over which has been laid spiral twisted canes of opaque yellow and red; their twists are opposed to give a herringbone pattern. There is some weathering and abrasion.
L: 10 mm; Diam: 16.5 mm; Diam (perf): 6 mm
Site 2, *567*, fill of grave *568*, Early medieval, OR 1376

7     Annular bead of natural green glass, undecorated. It has been hand-perforated (Guido 1978, 8) while warm, causing the base to flatten slightly. Such beads can date from the Roman period through to the sixth century AD (*op cit*, 66-7).
L: 4.5 mm; Diam: 13 mm; Diam (perf): 3 mm
Site 2, *1261*, fill of grave *1262*, Early medieval, OR 2201

8     Annular bead of bubbly blue glass, undecorated. Dating ranges between the Iron Age and the eighth century AD (Guido 1978, 66).
L: 6 mm; Diam: 10 m; Diam (perf): 3.5 mm
Site 2, *162*, Unstratified, OR 1829

9     Fragment of twisted glass rod, cut at one end, the other showing pincer marks where it may have been held. The cane comprises twisted natural dark blue and green rods, with white and light blue within the blue rods.
L: 44 mm; Diam: 24 mm
Site 2, *27*, hillwash, Post-medieval, OR 51

## Window glass

Unpainted window glass is not generally easy to date with accuracy and the criteria are, of necessity, general. That from Dacre has been divided into four broad date ranges on the basis of metal type, colour, and method of cutting. Of the 130 fragments, 22 (**10-31**) have been assigned to the pre-Conquest period, and all but two of these (**10, 31**) came from the south-western part of the northern churchyard, in the vicinity of Structure Y (*Ch 2, p 33*). All the early fragments are very small, and mostly in a natural bluish metal, probably reused soda-glass of Roman date, perhaps obtained locally.

The amount of early medieval glass from the site is not large in comparison to the assemblages from Wearmouth and Jarrow, at 298 and 1756 fragments respectively (Cramp 2006c). Indeed, there was only a single fragment from the Orchard (layer *52, Ch 4, p 112*; **10**; Fig 59), in a bubbly colourless metal streaked with red, which is almost identical to material from the monastic sites at Wearmouth and Jarrow (Cramp 1970, 328; 1975, 91; 2006c), and ranges in date from the seventh- to ninth century. It would seem reasonable to assign that from Dacre to the same period, although it was found in a disturbed context, but its physical proximity to an eighth-century strap-end (*p 52*) must strengthen the case for early medieval activity in this area.

The fragments from the northern churchyard are generally quite thin; many have grozed or partially grozed edges and probably come from quarries of small dimension. Although the range of colours is quite restricted when compared with the material from Wearmouth and Jarrow (Cramp 1970; 2006c), the natural blues, dirty dark blue, royal, and peacock blue all find parallels in that assemblage and also in material from Whithorn (Cramp 1997).

Only two fragments of the glass from the northern churchyard were found associated with graves (**11-12**; fill *535*, layer *665*), the rest coming from occupation layer *172*, associated with Structure Y (*Ch 2, p 33*), and later contexts. None of the material was abraded, perhaps indicating that little lateral movement had taken place, and it is of note that most of the early medieval metalwork (*pp 51-8*) was found in the same area, in similar contexts, as was part of a baked clay loomweight (*pp 85-6*), implying considerable activity in the area during the pre-Conquest period. Only one small fragment was found in the southern churchyard (*1010*, the occupation underlying the early medieval drain; *Ch 2, p 43*), and it is perhaps of significance that it was from within the same phase and same general area as bangle fragment **4** (*p 49*).

Despite the lack of variety in colour, the presence of early window glass at Dacre implies the existence of at least one decorative window. This is of considerable significance, bearing connotations of high status, wealth, and important connections with other monastic centres.

The pre-Conquest tradition of, and expertise in, glazing seems to have been introduced in its entirety, and quite deliberately, from Europe by high-ranking members of the ecclesiastical establishment (HA, bk 5;

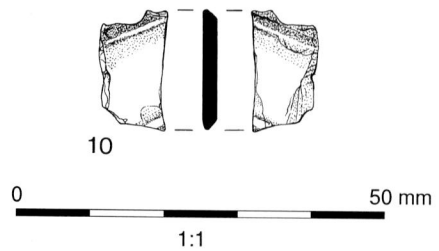

0                                                              50 mm
1:1

*Figure 59: Coloured window-glass fragment*

Giles 1845; King 1930). It appears that craftsmen were imported on an almost individual basis, to undertake specific commissions rather than to re-establish a lost craft (Hunter 1981, 144). It is, in consequence, unlikely that glazed windows would have appeared in any contemporary domestic context and therefore the presence of early glass at Dacre must indicate the existence of at least one important building on the site, possibly an earlier church. Despite the presence of glass, no lead kame was found in direct association, although numerous fragments of melted lead are known from the site (*p 75*). Interestingly, little or no kame has been found with the early glass at Whithorn (Cramp 1997, 329) and it may be that other means of fixing the glass were employed, or that lead was more sought-after, more easily retrieved, and therefore more recycled as a commodity than small glass fragments.

10      One small quarry fragment in bubbly colourless glass with dark red streaks (Fig 59). Good condition, unweathered. One, possibly two, edges are grozed, meeting at an obtuse angle.
        L: 15 mm; W: 16 mm; Th: 2 mm
        Site 1, *52*, layer, Medieval?, OR 172

11      One quarry fragment in natural bluish glass. Good condition, slight weathering, slightly abraded. Fits with **28**.
        L: 35 mm; W: 16 mm; Th: 1.5-2 mm
        Site 2, *535*, fill of grave *536*, Early medieval, OR 1545

12      One small fragment in bubbly natural bluish glass. Good condition, unweathered.
        L: 14 mm; W: 11 mm; Th: 1 mm
        Site 2, *665*, cemetery level, Early medieval, OR 1609

13      One small fragment in natural bluish glass. Good condition, unweathered.
        L: 15 mm; W: 5 mm; Th: 1.5 mm
        Site 2, *172*, occupation layer, Structure Y, Early medieval, OR 482

14      One small fragment in bubbly natural blue-green glass. One surface is uneven and pitted. Good condition, unweathered.
        L: 13 mm; W: 10 mm; Th: 1.75 mm
        Site 2, *172*, occupation layer, Structure Y, Early medieval, OR 790

15      One small quarry fragment in bubbly natural green-blue glass. Good condition, unweathered. One, possibly two, edges are grozed.

L; 16 mm; W: 8 mm; Th: 1.75 mm
Site 2, *172*, occupation layer, Structure Y, Early medieval, OR 821

16     One small fragment in natural bluish glass. Good condition, unweathered.
L: 27 mm; W: 1 mm; Th: 2 mm
Site 2, *172*, occupation layer, Structure Y, Early medieval, OR 825

17     One very small fragment in natural blue-green glass. Good condition, unweathered.
L: 7 mm; W: 4 mm; Th: 2 mm
Site 2, *172*, occupation layer, Structure Y, Early medieval, OR 857

18     One small fragment in bubbly blue glass. Good condition, unweathered. One edge is probably grozed.
L: 10.5 mm; W: 7 mm; Th: 1.25 mm
Site 2, *172*, occupation layer, Structure Y, Early medieval, OR 951

19     One small fragment in bubbly blue glass. Good condition, unweathered. One edge is possibly grozed.
L: 10.5 mm; W: 7 mm; Th: 1.75 mm
Site 2, *172*, occupation layer, Structure Y, Early medieval, OR 1016

20     One small fragment in peacock-blue glass. Good condition, unweathered. One edge is possibly grozed.
L: 16 mm; W: 8 mm; Th: 1.25 mm
Site 2, *534*, churchyard boundary bank, Eleventh/twelfth century, OR 1370

21     One small quarry fragment in natural bluish glass. Good condition, almost unweathered. One edge is grozed.
L: 16 mm; W: 12 mm; Th: 1.55 mm
Site 2, *44*, churchyard boundary bank, Eleventh/twelfth century, OR 91

22     One small quarry fragment in bubbly blue glass. Good condition, unweathered. One edge is grozed.
L: 13 mm; W: 5 mm; Th: 2 mm
Site 2, *169*, hillwash, Medieval, OR 487

23     One small quarry fragment in natural green glass. Good condition, unweathered but abraded. One edge is grozed.
L: 15 mm; W: 11 mm; Th: 1.75 mm
Site 2, *169*, hillwash, Medieval, OR 732

24     One small fragment in bubbly natural blue-green glass. Good condition, unweathered.
L: 19 mm; W: 8 mm; Th: 1.75 mm
Site 2, *169*, hillwash, Medieval, OR 749

25     One very small fragment in bubbly natural blue-green glass. Good condition, unweathered.
L: 9 mm; W: 7 mm; Th: 1.5 mm
Site 2, *181*, hillwash, Medieval, OR 478

26     One small quarry fragment in bubbly natural blue-green glass. Good condition, unweathered. One edge is grozed.
L: 18.5 mm; W: 7.5 mm; Th: 1.5 mm
Site 2, *291*, hillwash, Medieval, OR 884

27     One small quarry fragment in natural greenish glass. Good condition, unweathered, slight abrasion. One edge is grozed.
L: 21.5 mm; W: 8 mm; Th: 2 mm

Site 2, *152*, rubble to south of churchyard wall, Medieval, OR 366

28     One quarry fragment in natural bluish glass. Good condition, slight weathering, slightly abraded. Fits with **11**.
L: 25 mm; W: 29 mm; Th: 1.5-2 mm
Site 2, *382*, stone spread, Medieval, OR 1244

29     One quarry fragment in very bubbly natural greenish glass. Medium condition, unweathered. It has one grozed edge.
L: 31 mm; W: 23 mm; Th: 2 mm
Site 2, *36*, hillwash, Post-medieval, OR 2621

30     One quarry fragment in natural blue-green glass. Good condition, unweathered. Three edges are grozed, and it was probably originally triangular.
L: 14 mm; W: 24 mm; Th: 1.5 mm
Site 2, *26*, Topsoil, OR 1185b

31     One small fragment in natural green-blue glass. Good condition, unweathered.
L: 11 mm; W: 8.5 mm; Th: 1.75 mm
Site 3, *1010*, layer pre-dating drain, Early medieval, OR 1793

## Clay loomweights

*H Quartermaine*

Fragments of six clay loomweights were recovered, one from occupation layer *172* (in the south-west of the northern churchyard), which also contained material clearly deriving from early medieval activity (*Ch 2, p 33*), the remainder (**2-5**) coming from hillwash or unstratified. All can be assigned a pre-Conquest date, and fall into the 'bun-shaped' group, regarded typologically as the latest in the sequence of development first defined by John Hurst (1959). Such loomweights are not uncommon on pre-Conquest sites in Britain, and parallels can be drawn from a large number of sites, including, locally, Fremington (Howard-Davis 1996c), and, further afield, at Whitby (Peers and Radford 1943, 83), York (Walton Rogers 1997), Flixborough (Walton Rogers 2009), and to the north-east, at Yeavering (Hope-Taylor 1977, 182-4, fig 86). Those from Whitby were dated to the eighth-to tenth centuries, and such a date would accord with the pre-Conquest activity at Dacre.

The presence of such diagnostic early finds in a fairly localised area might indicate some domestic textile production on the site, especially when linked to the presence of lead and stone spindle whorls (*p 73; pp 77-8*), but whether this can aid an understanding of the function of the site is open to debate. To apply modern preconceptions on gender-differentiated domestic tasks is often misleading, especially in single-sex establishments where certain tasks have to be carried out, whether or not they are an activity normally associated with members of that sex.

1     Incomplete bun-shaped loomweight of fired clay (Fig 60; identification J G Hurst).

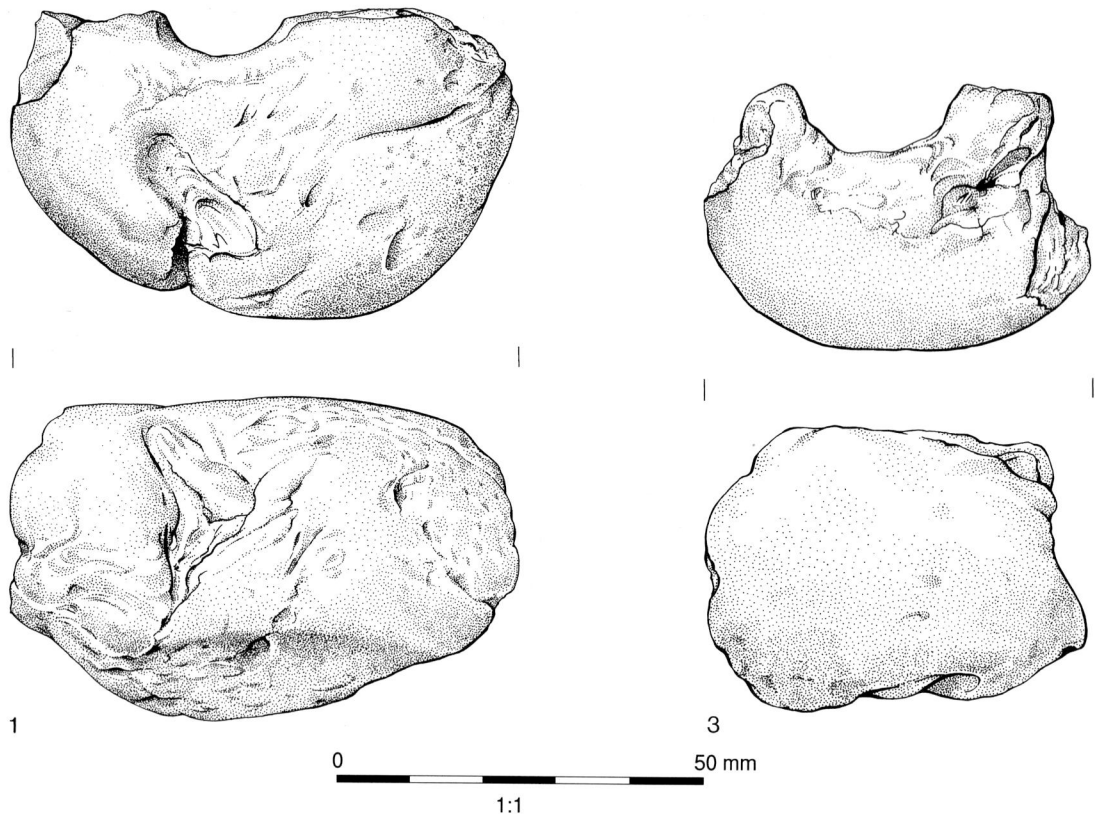

*Figure 60: Ceramic loomweights*

W: 33 mm; Th: 39 mm; Diam: 69-75 mm
Site 2, *172*, occupation layer, Structure Y, Early medieval, OR 470

2    Incomplete bun-shaped loomweight in a grey fabric, tempered with large grits, with an oxidised and burnished surface.
     L: 41 mm; W: 25 mm
     Site 2, *121*, hillwash, Medieval, OR 615

3    Incomplete (approximately 20%) bun-shaped loomweight of fired clay (Fig 60; identification J G Hurst). Grey oxidised fabric with some large grits; evidence of grass tempering and probably grass-burnishing.
     W: 23 mm; Th: 25 mm; Diam: 60-65 mm; Diam (perf): 22 mm
     Site 2, *36*, hillwash, Post-medieval, OR 770

4    Loomweight? or fragment of unworked sandstone. It appears to retain the edge of a central perforation; the height appears to be greater than the diameter, which suggests that it may have been bun-shaped. It is, however, very irregular in shape and may simply be a rounded piece of sandstone.
     W: 50 mm; Th: 44 mm; Diam (perf): 35-40 mm
     Site 2, *71*, hillwash, Post-medieval, OR 336

5    Incomplete loomweight in a pale grey fabric, tempered with black grit, and with an oxidised and burnished (with grass?) surface.
     L: 28 mm; W: 22 mm
     Site 2, *80*, hillwash, Post-medieval, OR 2493

6    Two fragments of fired clay, possibly loomweights, in a dark grey fabric with few inclusions. They have an oxidised and burnished surface.

i) L: 26 mm; W: 19 mm
ii) L: 32 mm; W: 22 mm
Site 2, *162*, Unstratified, OR 2500

## Building stone

*H Quartermaine*

A considerable amount of dressed building stone, principally red sandstone, was recovered from the site. All the fragments are effectively undatable, but some can be suggested as early, given their stratigraphical position.

1    Worked red sandstone fragments with dressed faces. The largest may have been used in a building.
     L (largest frag): 125 mm; W: 98 mm; Th: 71 mm
     Site 2, *687*, rubble spread west of early cemetery, Early medieval, OR 1921

2    Worked red sandstone, with a deep groove cut through the reverse. The edges of this are not straight, nor are they parallel, and they may well have been exaggerated by water action. One edge has incised cuts.
     L: 105 mm; W: 92 mm; Th: 38 mm
     Site 2, *1111*, fill of grave *1110*, Early medieval, OR 1873

## The human teeth

*by S Bullion*

Human bones and teeth were identified from 62 contexts within the northern churchyard (Site 2), 35 relating to graves associated with the early cemetery (*Ch 2*). The human remains were in a very poor state of preservation, with an absence of complete skeletons and very little articulating skeletal matter. All bone was fragmentary and usually so badly eroded that in many cases the teeth alone survived. This poor degree of preservation was likely to have arisen through the chemical nature of the soil rather than physical disturbance resulting from human activity, such as the disturbance of burials by later interments.

It was possible to divide the remains into two separate groups on the basis of the level of their preservation. The first group (termed preservation level 1) comprised the greater proportion of specimens, and included all but one of the remains from the early cemetery. Only a small amount of bone was present and this was very badly decayed so that identification was rarely possible; the teeth therefore played a dominant role in the analysis, although even they show evidence of advanced post-mortem decay. The maxillary and mandibular bone surrounding the teeth was absent in all but one case (grave *888, Ch 2*), which had a complete but heavily eroded maxilla. More significantly, of the dental hard tissue, the dentine was usually absent, leaving only the enamel crowns. By virtue of its exceptionally high degree of mineralisation (85%), enamel is often the tissue which is preserved best on archaeological sites. Because enamel comprises the tooth crown, however, it is still possible to extract the same information concerning the age at death, diet, general health, and also dental diseases, as it would if the tooth were complete and in the jaw.

The second group (termed preservation level II) displayed a markedly better degree of preservation. In all cases, there was a significant proportion of undecayed bone present, which was mostly possible to identify. The teeth too were complete, with all the dental tissues present. Apart from two cases (graves *528* and *536*), all specimens belonging to this group were associated with the medieval and post-medieval activity on the site.

## Analysis of the early cemetery material
### Biases and problems
The poor degree of preservation made it impossible to analyse the bone attributed to preservation level I; a detailed study was therefore carried out on the teeth, which mostly survived in the form of enamel shells. The brittle nature of the specimens, lacking in supportive dentine, made handling extremely difficult, and the specimens were cleaned simply by immersing in water and floating the dirt away from the surfaces. Information was recorded on dental attrition, dental diseases, age at death, and enamel hypoplasia, which is an indicator of growth disturbances.

Dental attrition seemed to have caused a major bias in this sample, since advanced attrition causes the tip of the enamel crown to be worn away and the dentine exposed underneath. This occurs as a single spot in incisor and canine teeth, but where teeth have two or more cusps, such as premolars and molars, the crown may become worn away and perforated at a number of separate places. As attrition advances in the living human, these perforations grow larger until the whole of the incisal and occlusal surface wears away, leaving an enamel rim around the periphery. It is unlikely that teeth with such extreme cases of attrition would survive under the poor preservation conditions existing at Dacre. Given that attrition advances with age, it is likely therefore that there may be a bias towards younger individuals in the sample.

The appearance of the crowns themselves was rather misleading, since, in the absence of dentine forming the roots, the tooth fragments could be mistaken for teeth in the process of formation (deciduous teeth form *in utero*, permanent teeth from birth up to about 12-16 years; Hillson 2005). In all but one case, however, the crowns were complete, and they did not appear to be in the process of formation at the time of death, although the crowns of the third molars of one individual (in grave *888*) appeared to be only partially formed. No dentine was present inside the crowns, which would have been expected in a developing tooth, although the lack of dentine was probably a result of chemical processes. Many groups of teeth occurred which could not possibly have been found together if they had been in the process of formation, since teeth such as the first incisor and the second molar develop at widely different times (*ibid*).

## Number of bodies per grave
There were few cases where there was evidence of more than one individual within a grave in the early cemetery. The exceptions to this were graves *672, 942, 964,* and *996* (Fig 61), where two individuals per grave may have been present. This may have been due to a failure to recognise the exact position of impinging graves, since grave *964* had another cut into it (*714*), within which no human remains were found, and grave *942* formed part of a complex mass of graves within which there were several graves where no human remains survived. Another group of two-plus individuals were found in a layer (*691*) contemporary with the cemetery and closely associated with the west ends of two graves.

The presence of more teeth of any one type than normal is the best guide to multiple individuals in a grave, but tooth size and attrition patterns can also

*Figure 61: Graves containing dental remains mentioned in the text*

be important. In the case of grave *996*, all teeth except an upper third molar were thought to have belonged to the same individual, since two other upper third molars in the group were similar both in size and in their patterns of attrition. Grave *672* contained two finds of human dental material, which are likely to have belonged to separate individuals based on these criteria, as well as the physical distance between the finds. Similarly, these criteria can be used to indicate the likelihood of the remains of a single individual scattered over an area, since two separated finds of human dental material from cemetery layer *665* probably represent the same individual, based on attrition patterns and tooth morphology.

**Age at death**
It is striking that the dental material comprised permanent teeth alone and in no cases were deciduous teeth found in contexts relating to the early cemetery. This might suggest that the burial group was mainly composed of adults, with the youngest age at death being greater than 11 years ±9 months (Schour and Massler 1941). Such assumptions, however, should be treated with extreme caution in the case of the Dacre material, since the enamel of deciduous teeth is more permeable and easily worn down, so that an advanced degree of attrition in these teeth could have limited the survival. Also, the depth of the enamel is thinner in deciduous teeth (0.5-1.0 mm) than in permanent teeth (2.0-5.0 mm). Therefore, it can only be stated that, whilst there appeared to be no young individuals associated with the early cemetery, in the presence of such extreme levels of decay it cannot be certain that they were completely absent from this burial group.

It was only possible to assign an age, based on the evidence of teeth, to eight individuals, all contained within graves, out of 55 studied from the early cemetery. The crowns of the upper third molars in grave *888* appeared to be only partially complete and therefore may have been in the process of forming at the time of death. This indicates an age at death of 7-16 years; as the crowns were almost completely calcified, the age was likely to have been towards the upper end of this range. The third molars in graves *672* and *920* were complete but did not show any signs of occlusal wear. These teeth erupt into the oral cavity at around 17-21 years and this may be suggested as a likely range for the age at death. Bodies in graves *361, 371, 374, 888,* and *898* were all aged 17-25 years, according to the classification of age given by Donald Brothwell (1981) for neolithic to medieval humans, based on variation in molar attrition.

## Attrition

Attrition of the teeth was recorded as patterns of dentine exposure, based on the sequence given by Murphy (1959). It appeared that there were no cases of completely unworn teeth in the sample, but this may be a result of post-mortem changes, which caused the teeth to appear worn. Moreover, the teeth did not exhibit extreme cases of occlusal wear; at most, the tips of the cusps were worn away in the canines, premolars, and molars, leaving a perforation in the crown where the dentine had been exposed, and only the incisal edge was worn in the incisors, more extreme cases of attrition being unlikely to have survived because the enamel crowns are too fragile without the support of the underlying dentine. It is normally assumed that there is a continual increase in attrition as the individual becomes older. The ages at death, using a method based on molar attrition (Brothwell 1981), are no greater than 25 years. Although the average life expectancy was likely to be considerably less in the past (30-5 years) compared to modern times (Roberts and Cox 2003), it cannot be discounted that the dental remains of older individuals have not survived on this site.

## Caries and calculus

The disease dental caries occurs in response to prolonged phases of low pH in the mouth, the prerequisite for this being the presence of plaque deposits and fermentable carbohydrates in the diet (Hillson 2005). When low pH levels do not predominate, perhaps because sugars are not eaten in quantity, these can mineralise, leading to the build-up of noticeable calculus deposits on tooth surfaces. These mineralised deposits are also associated with periodontal disease, which, when severe, can cause the loss of the alveolar bone.

The level of caries was observed to be low in the sample of 47 specimens capable of study, occurring in only four individuals and in a total of seven teeth. Caries was present in the cervical region of the mesial and distal surfaces of a lower second premolar in the individual in grave *361*, which was thought to be associated with a hypoplastic lesion, and also on the buccal surface of the lower right third molar. Caries was also found on the buccal surface of an upper first premolar from the individual in grave *942*, on the cusps of the occlusal surface of an upper left first molar from the individual in grave *888*, and also on the buccal surfaces of the lower right first and second molars, and associated with a fissure in the occlusal surface of a lower right third molar, in *964*. Because of the high degree of post-mortem decay associated with this site, however, all cases of caries were treated with caution.

Calculus deposits were observed to be common, occurring in 42 individuals. It was only possible to describe calculus deposits on the enamel crown itself, since no information was available for root-surface deposits. There was no surviving evidence of periodontal disease either, as the alveolar bone was consistently absent. Calculus deposits occurred on all tooth surfaces (mesial, distal, buccal, and lingual), except for the occlusal surface, where it rarely occurs in normal circumstances. These deposits were found on the main body of the tooth, termed 'smooth surface', the cervical margin (normally quite close to the gingival tissue in the living person), and also in the area of contact between the mesial and distal surfaces of two adjacent teeth. The high incidence of calculus suggests that sugars are unlikely to have been an important feature of the diet.

## Enamel hypoplasia

Enamel hypoplasia can be described as incomplete or defective enamel, resulting from damage to the enamel-forming cells during formation of the enamel matrix (Hillson 2005). Such a growth disturbance is normally systemic, affecting all teeth forming at the time of the disturbance, and is often associated with an episode of poor diet or disease. Enamel hypoplasia can appear as pitting or grooves in the normally smooth enamel surface and is generally associated with a reduction in thickness of the enamel. By applying information about the timing of crown formation, it is possible to estimate the age of occurrence of hypoplasia episodes.

Enamel hypoplasia was observed in 12 individuals (25.5%). In each case, the position of the lesion was in either the incisal/cuspal, central, or cervical thirds of the buccal surface. This information was then applied to the crown zonation diagram of Bullion (1987), which determines the chronological ages of hypoplasia episodes. At best, this method produces results to half-yearly intervals, although this is dependent on there being at least four teeth available, some of which should be from the anterior dentition.

The hypoplasias were seen to have occurred between 1¾ and 6½ years, but were most frequent at 4-4½ years. However, it is difficult to draw conclusions about the health of this population from such a small sample. The level of hypoplasias in this group appeared to be quite low (25.5%) when compared with the 82% found in the population of the medieval cemetery of St Helen-on-the-Walls, York (*ibid*), but it should not be forgotten that teeth exhibiting severe hypoplastic lesions may be weaker and hence not survive in the soil conditions existing at Dacre.

**Conclusions**
No juveniles were identified nor, where ageing was possible, individuals older than 25. The high incidence of calculus deposits adhering to the enamel suggests that sugars were unimportant in the diet, and the low levels of enamel hypoplasias implies that systemic disorders during the formative years were not common. However, the biases and problems arising from the nature of preservation on this site means that these conclusions must be treated with caution and that comparisons with other sites are likely to be difficult, given the unusual nature of the material.

# 4

# LATER MEDIEVAL AND POST-MEDIEVAL ACTIVITY

## The Northern Churchyard

### The establishment of the medieval churchyard

Either after, or at the time, that the early medieval cemetery seems to have fallen out of use, a major boundary, a bank (*151*) with a ditch (*215*) to the north (Fig 62), was constructed in the southern part of the site, extending for the whole 45 m width of the trench, and clearly related to features to the south of the excavated area. Despite the proximity of the church in that direction, the bank and ditch seemed to have marked the extent of the medieval churchyard, since no obviously medieval or later graves were found beyond them, and, indeed, the land to the north was not consecrated until later in the twentieth century

(K Smith *pers comm*). The bank sealed a dense mass of graves from the early cemetery (*Ch 2*) and ditch *215* clearly cut these graves.

The core of the bank, comprising a dark brown loam, varied in width, at 1.50-2.50 m, and was 0.20-0.55 m in height, having been created by upcast from ditch *215*, approximately 1 m to the north. Some disturbance of the underlying graves was noted, but whether this material derived from the cutting of ditch *215*, or from the spreading of subsequent churchyard debris on the top of the bank, remains uncertain. The crest of the bank had been covered by a spread of material containing many small stones (*378*), most obvious in the western part of the site, probably soon after bank *151* had been constructed. A further spread (*96*), above bank core *151* and *378*, particularly on its north side, increased the overall height of the feature

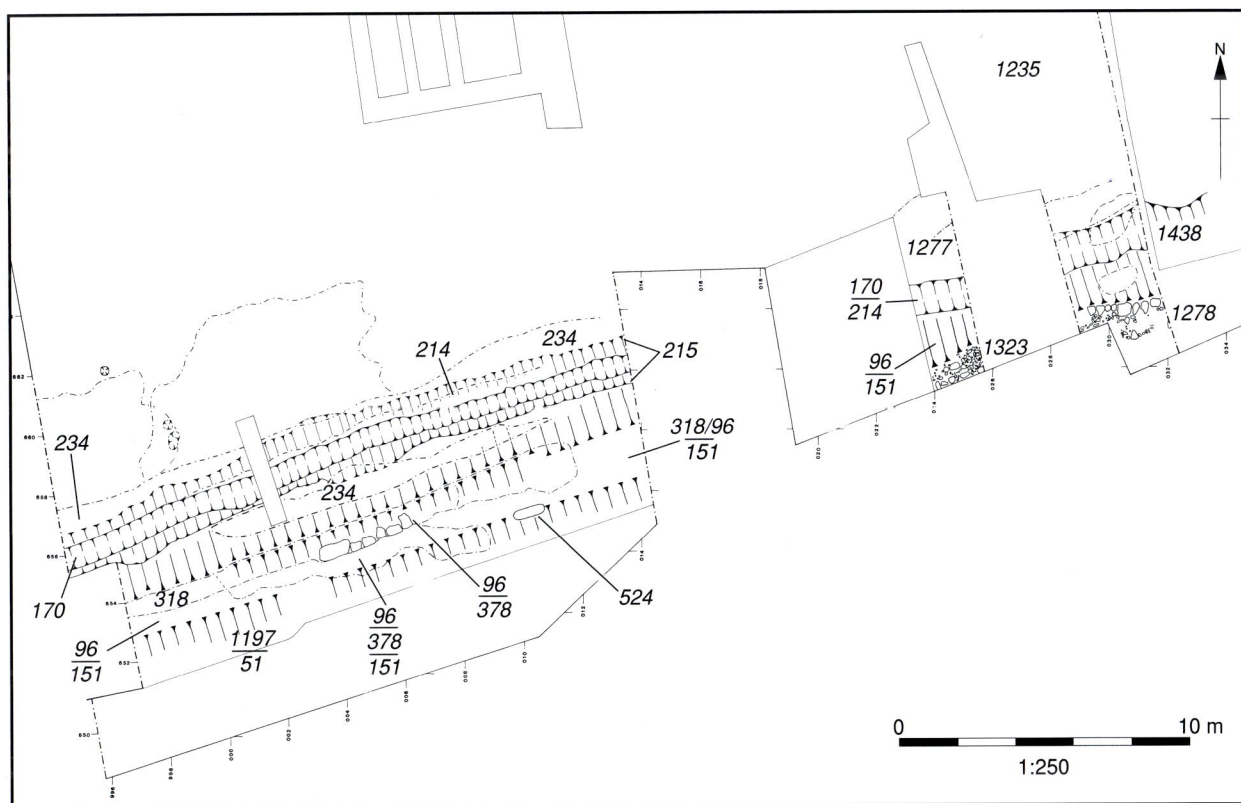

*Figure 62: The excavated bank and ditch in the northern churchyard*

*Plate 36: The bank under the medieval northern churchyard boundary wall*

to approximately 0.70 m. Deposit *96* may perhaps have been produced by some attempt at cleaning out ditch *215*, but it also seems to represent the decay of bank *151* and the slippage of some material down into the ditch (Pl 36).

A similar spread (*1197*) was found on the south side of bank *151*. It was, however, difficult to identify subtle changes due to the limited area excavated, and the same layer appeared to lie both beneath and against the south side of the later churchyard wall *28* (*pp 96-7*), which had been placed on the crest of the bank. This may account for some apparent contamination, as a minute fragment of post-medieval pottery was found, but this may also have resulted from animal activity. Some stone roofing tiles were also found amongst the stones.

Ditch *215* followed a roughly straight line from south-west to north-east (Pl 37), and varied in width (1.25-1.80 m), being widest in the western part of the site; it was probably about 0.50 m deep when first cut. A much stonier narrow layer (*297*), largely comprising glacial erratics, was identified above the primary fill of silty loam (*214*) in the western part of the site.

Grave *524* had been dug into the southern side of bank *151/96*, approximately 1 m to the south of the crest, and aligned at 55° from north. There was no evidence of any coffin, and the size of the cut (1.20 x 0.42 x 0.25 m) points to the burial of a child. It was

the only burial to cut the churchyard boundary, and its size, orientation, and position clearly indicate that it did not belong to the early cemetery.

Surface *234* comprised a narrow spread of gravel and small pebbles, lying parallel to the medieval churchyard boundary. It clearly pre-dated the final slumping into ditch *215* (*170, p 94*), yet overlay its primary fill. Its relationship with bank *151* proved harder to establish, as much of this area was removed by machine, but it seems likely that the surface post-dated it, yet pre-dated its upper element, *96*. Similarly, surface *1277* to the east comprised a compact layer of small, rounded pebbles, again parallel to the churchyard boundary. This surface also lay across the northern edge of ditch *215*, dipping down and disappearing amongst the slumping into the top of the ditch (*1316, 170*). There was no direct relationship between this possible surface and bank *151*. It is also not certain that *234* and *1277* represent the same surface, or that they were contemporary, although their presence may suggest that there was occupation in the east of the site from a slightly earlier date than that of the medieval croft found there (*p 98*) and that a path led to an entrance into the churchyard somewhere further to the west.

**Dating**
The dating evidence for the churchyard boundary ranges from the pre-Conquest period through to the twelfth- to fourteenth century, the earlier material

*Plate 37: Ditch 215*

reflecting the age and use of the deposits excavated to form the bank. The western part of bank *151*, close to the position of Structure Y (*Ch 2, p 33*), produced the shank of a pin (*Ch 3*, copper-alloy **10**), and part of a jet bangle (*Ch 3*, stone **4**), and a baluster-headed pin (*Ch 3*, copper-alloy **9**), were found in upper layer *96*. All are early medieval in date. A broken stylate pin (*Ch 3, p 54*), belonging to the same tradition of craftsmanship as the copper-alloy objects from the bank, was also associated with ditch fill *297*. The amount of early metalwork spread through the western part of the bank was probably connected with Structure Y, some 2 m to the north (*Ch 2, pp 33-5*), which had been disturbed in its creation, since neither stone spread *263*, nor wall *644* (*Ch 2, p 35*), directly beneath the bank, produced similarly dated objects.

The pottery from bank *151* was of twelfth- to fourteenth-century date (*Ch 5*) and the greatest amount was found in the western part of the site, close to the church; in contrast, there was a general lack of pottery in the eastern stretch of the bank. The dating evidence for upper layer *378* was similar to that from *151*, and the pottery from *96*, again concentrated heavily at the western end, was of

thirteenth- to fourteenth-century date, as was the single sherd from *1197*. Some fragments of ceramic roofing tiles were also recovered from that part of the bank. Contamination of upper layer *96* may have occurred when churchyard wall *28*, built on its crest (*pp 96-7*), was demolished in *c* 1950, or, on the northern side, by the removal of the overburden of hillwash (*80*) by machine during the excavation, since two fragments of possibly post-medieval glass were found. The only finds within the primary fill of ditch *215* were two sherds of twelfth- to fourteenth-century pottery, both from the central western part.

The fill of grave *524* contained a single fragment of human bone, together with two sherds of twelfth- to fourteenth-century pottery and a scrap of possible roofing lead. Eight sherds of pottery of a similar date were found in layer *234*, mostly to the south of the upper silting (*170*) of ditch *215*, and the eastern part of surface *1277* contained a single sherd of pottery, twelfth- to thirteenth-century in date.

These features thus contained the first substantial deposits of medieval pottery. All the sherds appear to belong to the period between the twelfth- and early fourteenth centuries, although stratigraphically this activity is unlikely to be later than the thirteenth century (*pp 97-8*).

## Hillwash

The lower terrace to the north of bank *151/96* had been covered by a slow build-up of soil, which had washed down the slope from the north, presumably as a result of agricultural activity, and had accumulated in the lower part of the site, its continued progress being blocked by the bank (Fig 63). The very nature of the continuous soil creep had mixed once stratified finds, an effect demonstrated by the three-dimensional plotting of material from within the hillwash. The soil could, however, be divided into two vertical zones, *32* and *27*, on the basis of the finds they contained, rather than on textural or colour differences; indeed, there seemed to be a relatively clear horizon, below which there was little contamination by post-medieval material. The upper band (*27*) was much thinner than the lower (*32*) and had been deposited relatively recently.

The lower hillwash (*32*) had sealed the early cemetery, although the northern part of the site on the upper terrace had suffered from erosion, which had removed any traces of occupation associated with the structures there (*pp 103-4; Ch 2, p 32*). Some finds within *32* were clearly early, including fragments of possibly early medieval glass from above layer *172* (*Ch 2, p 33; Ch 3, p 82*), a sherd of Roman coarseware (*Ch 3, p 48*), and a large number

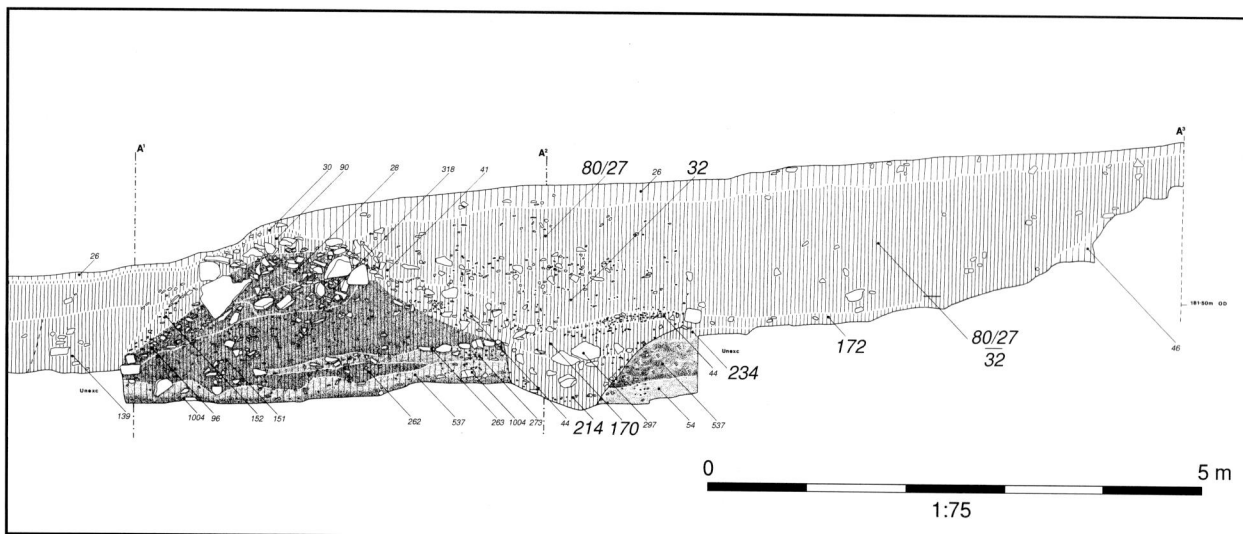

*Figure 63: Section through the first medieval churchyard boundary, showing the build-up of hillwash against it*

of coffin fittings, presumably from disturbed early medieval graves, or, perhaps, from the tops of unrecognised grave cuts. A large quantity of pottery was recovered from *32*, primarily sherds of twelfth- to fourteenth-century date, but also a few later sherds and a few post-medieval finds. Some of these objects may have resulted from contamination by the machine removal of the majority of the hillwash (*80*). Layer *32* also produced a relatively large amount of evidence for smithing, and also some evidence of possible smelting in the vicinity, unless this was residual from early medieval activity (*Ch 2, p 35*).

Layers *1235* and *1514*, to the north of ditch *215* in the eastern part of the site, where the terrace edge faded, could both be identified stratigraphically as belonging to this activity. Layer *1514*, which was indistinguishable from the upper material in the churchyard bank to the south, also clearly post-dated graves in the early medieval cemetery and partially overlay ditch *215*, indicating that it had been building up at the time ditch *215* was cut and subsequently silted, slumping over its primary fill. Layer *1235*, to the east, overlay the easternmost graves and the possible early medieval cemetery boundaries (ditches *1356*, *1414*, and *1306*; *Ch 2, p 23*). It was sealed by the layers and structures associated with the medieval croft (*p 98*) and had perhaps built up in part against the medieval churchyard wall to the south. The finds from layer *1235* were very mixed and included a *styca* of *c* 820 (*Ch 3, p 50*), a number of coffin fittings, and a large amount of twelfth- to fourteenth-century pottery (*Ch 5*). Some mixing of *1235* with layer *736* (*p 98*) above had obviously taken place, since sherds from the same medieval pottery vessel were found in both.

Layer *219* in the western part of the site, on the lower terrace below hillwash *32*, sealed the upper

cemetery level (*110*) and presumably resulted from the hillwash, although it could have represented the horizon below. It contained a single sherd of post-medieval pottery, found close to the terrace edge, which probably resulted from disturbance during the machine removal of the overburden.

## Modifications to the churchyard boundary

Ditch *215* may have been recut as *171* (Fig 64) after it had largely silted up, but this apparent recutting was only visible in the western part of the trench and may merely have been the break between the primary fills of the ditch and later slumping (*170*). A lens of charcoal-rich soil (*1316*), which probably represented the spread from a fire or hearth, lay on the interface between bank *151* and the slumping into the ditch (*170*) in the eastern part of the site, and there were also two skims of material on the north side of the ditch in the same area, which seemed to be slumping into it. Both of these (*1329* and *1439*) appeared to lie beneath slumping *170*, yet were above the primary ditch fill.

Spreads of rubble (*318, 1278, 1323*; Fig 62) sealed layer *96* on the top and north side of churchyard boundary bank *151*. In parts, these appeared simply as a jumble of stones, but at intervals the impression was gained of a deliberate, orderly deposition (*318, 1278*) along the crest of the bank. Rubble *318*, to the west, was composed of large cut blocks of red sandstone (3.40 x 0.60 m), laid in an east-west alignment, over a distance of 3.40 m. These tipped downwards to the south, following the slope of the underlying bank. The orderly alignment degenerated to the west and north into patchy, though discrete, areas of sandstone. Rubble *1323* to the east contained a great deal of red sandstone and limestone, which appeared to have been worked but had been deposited haphazardly.

94

*Figure 64: Northern churchyard boundary wall 28, and associated features*

Layer *1278*, further east still, which clearly underlay the north side of medieval churchyard boundary wall *28* (*pp 96-7*), though on the same alignment, also seemed to have been laid deliberately. It comprised large boulders and broken fragments of red sandstone masonry over a length of 2.40 m, with a possible parallel alignment of much smaller stones to the south. This was separated from the overlying medieval wall, *28*, by a series of lenses (*1217*, *1234*, *1250*, and *1298*). The lowest, reddish silty loam *1298*, was immediately above and against the south side of *1278*, whilst dark sandy-silt lens *1250* spread across the western stones of *1278* and seemed to represent a fairly natural build-up of soil, butting against reddish silty-loam lens *1234*. Both these lenses were overlain by dark silty-loam *1217*, immediately below wall *28* and to the south of it, above layer *1197* (*p 92*). These lenses may represent a gap in time between the creation of layer *1278* and the construction of wall *28*, or they could simply have resulted from dumping. The precise purpose of the stone alignments remains obscure, although they may represent an attempt at a boundary wall on the bank before wall *28* was built.

Rubble spread *44* (Fig 64) was concentrated along the northern slope of bank *151* and above slumping *170*, yet underlay wall *28*. This would suggest that it was contemporary with rubble alignment *318* (*p 94*), although the precise relationship remains uncertain. The amount of broken and discarded masonry within it points strongly to it being the debris from a demolished structure, and it may well have been associated with a rebuilding programme in the church. The church dates largely from the twelfth-thirteenth centuries (Hyde and Pevsner 2010, 320) and there were clearly relatively frequent campaigns of rebuilding and extension throughout this period. Rubble spread *46* to the north was at the same stratigraphic level as rubble *44*, but it was much less densely packed and seemed to have been separated from it by an area without stones. The two spreads may, however, have been the result of the same action, and they were probably contemporary. Rubble spread *1274* to the east again appeared to be immediately below part of wall *28* and to have covered the north side of bank *151*.

The majority of the finds from these layers were sherds of pottery, mostly of twelfth- to fourteenth-century date. That from slumping *170* was concentrated in the western part of the trench and had the same date range as the material in the core of the churchyard boundary bank (*151, 96, 378*) and the primary ditch fill (*214, 297*). This may reflect the lack of refinement of the pottery typology, however. Several sherds of similar pottery were also found in slumping *1316*, and stone spread *44* produced a large

amount (54 sherds), as did similar spread *1274* to the east. Possible alignment *318* produced three sherds of thirteenth- to fourteenth-century pottery, with a date range relatively equivalent to the rest of the pottery in the bank, although the fabrics and forms seem to be slightly later than those in bank *151/96*. Rubble spread *1234* also contained a single fragment of similar pottery. In contrast to *44* to the south, only four sherds of thirteenth/fourteenth-century pottery were found within rubble spread *46*. The only other ceramic find was a single fragment of roofing tile from rubble *1274*. Other fragments of roofing tile were found within the core of wall *28* (*pp 96-7*), and in association with the decay of the medieval croft (*p 110; 1016, 1097, 1186*). These may have come from a demolished or refurbished structure beyond the limits of the excavation, or it may be that the earliest phase of the croft dated from before the construction of wall *28*.

Large pit *336* (2.20 x 1.60 x 0.80 m), at the lip of the terrace in the west of the site, seemed to cut the deliberately enhanced terrace edge (*341, Ch 2*) and also the early cemetery levels (*110* and grave *389*; Fig 13). Although it contained two distinct fills, the lack of any datable finds makes its phasing and purpose uncertain.

## The churchyard boundary

Following the partial decay of the churchyard boundary bank (*151/96*), a new churchyard wall (*28*) was constructed along the crest of bank (Pl 38) during the period when ditch *215* was silting up. Wall *28* comprised two roughly coursed faces, largely of rounded river-worn boulders, with a rubble core containing a large quantity of red sandstone, some clearly worked. The wall was on average 1.70 m wide and generally survived to a height of about 0.70 m, particularly on the south side, where it appeared to be more deeply set. The northern face had been constructed on the apex of the bank and the southern face therefore required more courses to level it up. Towards the east, it seemed to bend slightly towards the south, and thus the part to the east may have been a slightly later addition, perhaps associated with an eastern extension of the churchyard, or perhaps simply a rebuilding. This wall remained the northern boundary of the churchyard until *c* 1950, when this was extended into the field to the north (K Smith *pers comm*). It seems that the majority of the stones from it were used to build the present northern churchyard boundary wall.

Wall *28* appeared to continue beyond the western edge of the excavation, along the line of the bank visible in the churchyard, and it may be the same as wall *18* in the Orchard (*p 112*). The recovery of large blocks of red sandstone (*64*) from graves dug along

Plate 38: Northern churchyard wall 28, on the crest of bank 151

the projected line of the wall (K Smith *pers comm*) supports this hypothesis.

A spread of rubble (*310*) lay in a slight depression at the upper terrace edge, covering pit *336* (*p 96*). It was overlain by hillwash *32* and probably represents the dumping of building material, possibly associated with one of the refurbishments of the church.

Cobbled surface *1390*, in the south-east corner of the site, was sealed by the collapse of a wall which seemed to have marked the southern extent of the medieval croft (*47*; *p 98*) and to have lain along the northern lip of a ditch (*1438*), which suggests that this surface and the ditch were probably roughly contemporary. Ditch *1438*, of which only a small element (0.68 m) was present in the excavated area, was aligned roughly east-west and appeared to have terminated in a rounded butt end to the west. It clearly cut into the upper fill of ditch *215* (*170, p 94*) and it may have been contemporary with, or slightly later than, medieval churchyard wall *28*. It appears to have performed the same boundary function as that wall, which followed the same alignment and had partially collapsed into the top of the fill, perhaps suggesting that ditch *1438* may have been an early boundary feature of the medieval croft immediately to the north (*p 98*). The ditch appeared to continue in an easterly direction beyond the excavation and

may in fact be the same as that visible in the field beyond the churchyard, which appeared to form the southern boundary of the platform containing the excavated farm buildings.

Stone spread *1422* overlay the primary fill of ditch *1438*. No finds were associated with it and the limited area excavated only indicated that it may have been a surface. Its stratigraphical position suggests that it belonged to the earliest activity in the medieval croft to the north of the churchyard.

The majority of the pottery associated with wall *28* was similar in date (twelfth- to fourteenth century) to that from the layers forming the underlying bank, although there was less than half the quantity. There was also a significantly later group of sixteenth-century sherds from the eastern part of *28*, immediately to the south of the croft (*p 108*), which supports the possibility that this section may have been a later rebuild. A well-preserved short-cross penny (*Ch 5, p 123*) from the reign of John was found in the western part of the wall. The dating evidence, particularly that of the pottery, would suggest that wall *28* was built before 1400, in all probability in the earlier thirteenth century. The amount of reused stones within the wall may suggest that its construction coincided with a period of rebuilding of the church, only some 5 m to the south, although it is possible that it was quarried entirely from stone spread *318* immediately below it.

Stone spread *310* contained a copper-alloy pin (*Ch 3, p 54*) and a corroded *sceatta* of *c 738-57* (*Ch 5, p 50*), both clearly pre-Conquest in date, but also a buckle plate (*Ch 3, p 53*), a single piece of medieval vessel glass, and three sherds of twelfth- to fourteenth-century pottery, which suggests that the pre-Conquest material was residual. The six sherds of pottery associated with rubble spread *1390* and the majority of the large amount from ditch *1438* were similarly dated. Although the range of pottery from these features is generally twelfth- to fourteenth-century in date, they were stratigraphically slightly later than those associated with the boundary bank and it therefore seems likely that they date from either the thirteenth or fourteenth century.

## The medieval croft

A set of farm buildings forming a croft was constructed immediately to the north of the medieval churchyard, largely in the east of the site (Fig 65). This farmstead seems to have been contemporary with slight modifications to the churchyard boundary, and was visible in the field to the east as a platform, seemingly fronting onto a hollow-way. A similar platform was visible to the north, close to the north-eastern corner of the present churchyard, and this also extended into the churchyard, being visible as a flat area surrounded by a slight ditch (*p 103*).

The foundations of a wall (*47*; 0.80-0.90 m wide) lay above the north side of ditch *1438* in the south-east corner of the site (Fig 66), and although these also extended to the west of the ditch, the wall appears to have followed its alignment fairly closely. The eastern part of wall *47* had collapsed, presumably due to the instability of its foundations, having been built into the unconsolidated ditch fill. The surviving part was constructed with two faces of apparently reused worked red sandstone, mixed with occasional substantial boulders; between these faces was a core of smaller stones, the whole seemingly dry-bonded. The relationship of this wall to churchyard wall *28* remains uncertain, in that both only survived at foundation level, although wall *47* seemed slightly later stratigraphically and may have butted wall *28* above the ground level. Although wall *47* was well-made, there was no evidence that it formed any part of a building, rather seeming to have formed the southern boundary of the croft, in succession to ditch *1438*, although why it was deemed necessary to construct a wall so close to the existing churchyard boundary cannot readily be understood.

A spread of stones (*1196*), dominated by yellow sandstone and lying immediately to the west of the

surviving remains of wall *47*, may represent part of its decay. Two abutting layers of friable reddish sandy silt (*1379, 1380*) seemed to have formed the uppermost silting of ditch *1438*. Layer *1379* may have formed part of the slumping from churchyard bank *151* to the south, whereas *1380* seems to have filled a central hollow in the primary fill.

Surface *1204* overlay the upper silting of churchyard boundary ditch *215* to the west, and was also found above rubble spread *1274* (*p 96*), which seems to indicate that it was contemporary with the construction of churchyard wall *28*, or slightly later. It comprised a closely packed spread of small stones, 1.23 m wide, and its proximity to wall *28* and the croft might suggest that it formed an access route into the churchyard.

Although the dating evidence appears to be very similar to that associated with the modifications to the medieval churchyard boundary, these features were clearly later on stratigraphical grounds. Each element contained some pottery, all from the thirteenth/fourteenth century; it was found in abundance in association with wall *47* and layer *1380*, but only a few sherds came from surface *1204* and layer *1379*. The date attributed to the pottery, particularly from wall *47* and layers *1379* and *1380* (*Ch 5*), suggests that the silting of ditch *1438* was a relatively rapid process.

The main features of the medieval croft were found in the eastern part of the site, where the terrace was not so pronounced. They cut into an accumulation of soil (*736*) similar to the deeper hillwash to the north and west (*32*), although it appears to have had a fairly limited period of deposition, apparently dating from a time after the development of the medieval churchyard boundary. Layer *736* extended over the area in which the structures forming the croft stood and contained a large amount of pottery, particularly towards its base. The vast majority of this dated from the twelfth- to fourteenth century, except for two sherds of fifteenth/sixteenth-century date from the upper levels, which have parallels in the demolition phase of the croft (*p 110*). Similarly, a fragment of clay pipe indicates some disturbance. The presence of daub may imply the layer continued to accumulate during the construction and occupation of the structures it surrounded.

A group of postholes and other enigmatic cuts, largely below a building associated with the croft, may have been part of an earlier structure on the site, although they formed no coherent pattern, and extended beyond the later structure (Structure C, *p 106*; Fig 66). These varied in size and shape, from 0.17 m (*786*) to 0.72 m (*826*) and from round to oval, and the westernmost of

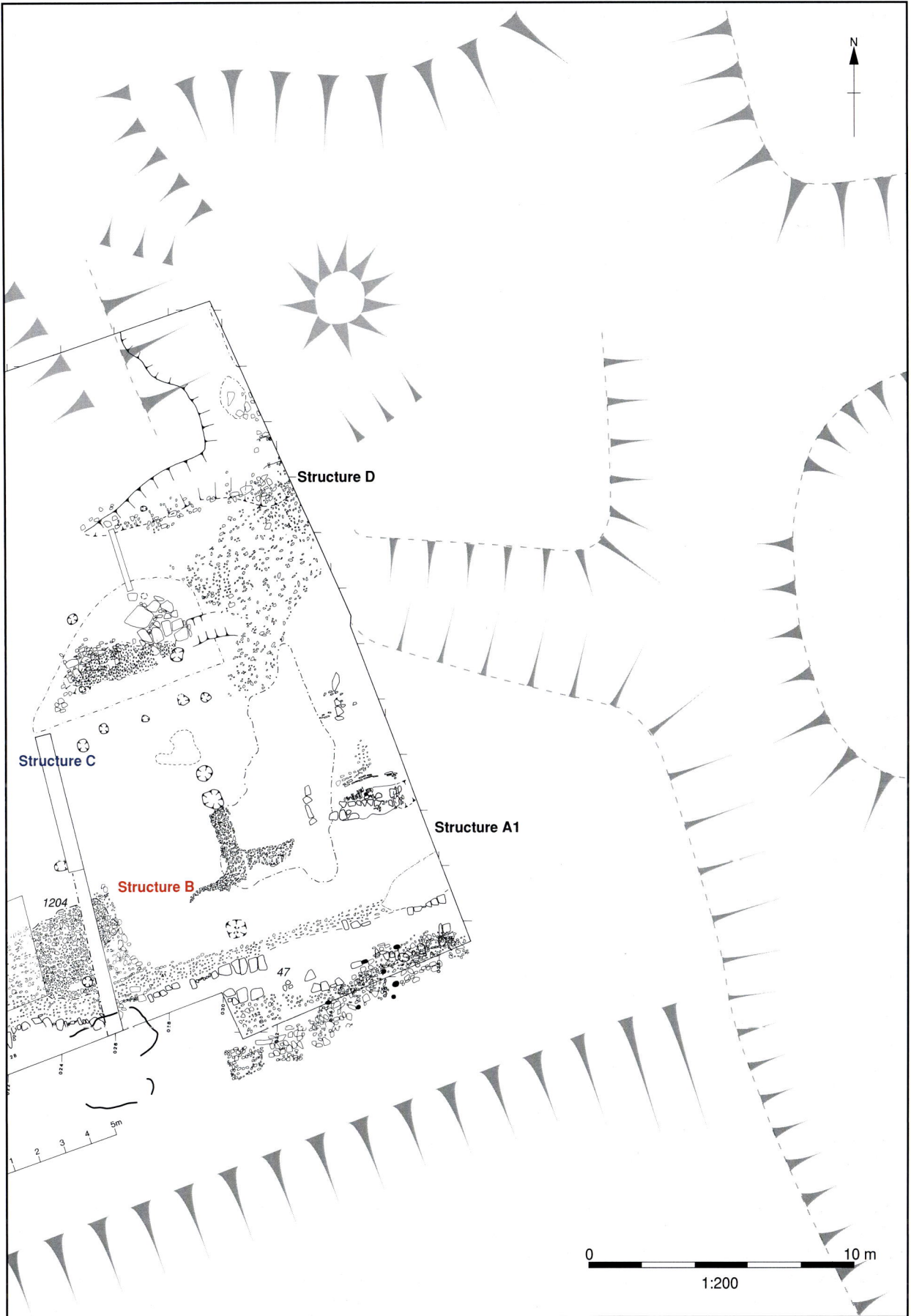

Structure D

Structure C

Structure A1

Structure B

1204

47

5m

1 2 3 4

0             10 m

1:200

*Figure 65: Structures A, B, and C in relation to the earthworks to the east*

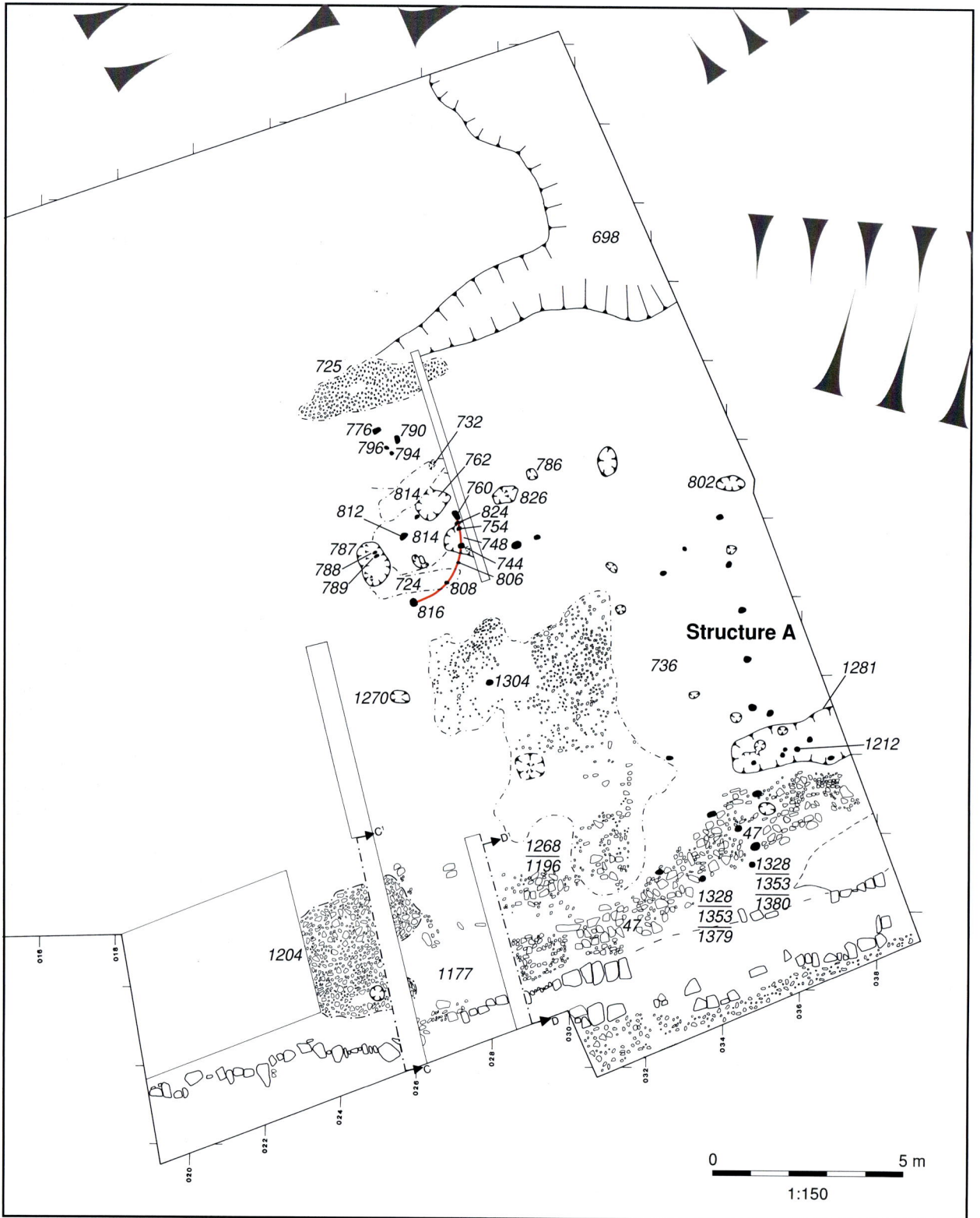

*Figure 66: Features in the east of the site around the croft*

these (*787*; 1.1 x 0.71 m) contained two deeper centres (*788, 789*), as if stakes had been driven into it. Posthole *802*, however, in the far east of the site, could have been a modern intrusion. These postholes seemed to be associated with a group of stakeholes, many of which formed a roughly semi-circular curve with a diameter of approximately 2 m (*eg 744, 754, 760,*

*806, 808, 816*). Stony layer *724*, within this arc, which could perhaps be regarded as a metalled surface, and sandy layer *814* to the north, were both cut by these stakeholes. Other postholes, some 2.5 m to the south, including *1270* and *1304*, which cut early cemetery ditch *1276* (*Ch 2, p 24*), were overlain by *736*, but were otherwise undatable.

Several groups of postholes, and also some isolated examples, in the north-east of the site, contained no dating evidence, but their position stratigraphically suggests they were associated with the croft, although they did not form any obvious structural patterns. A group of small postholes (776, 790, 794, and 796), immediately to the south of the western continuation of ditch 698 and surface 725 (p 107), were not identified above the level of the subsoil, apart from 796, which cut early medieval grave 798. Isolated posthole 732, 1 m to the south-east, cut layer 814 (p 100) and may have been associated with Structure C (p 106), whilst two postholes (760, 812) in the same area were separated by an irregular shallow depression (762) and may have been contemporary with the group of postholes associated with layer 814 underlying Structure C (p 100). Nearby, post-pit 748, containing two small postholes within it, which may or may not have been contemporary, seemed to cut stakehole 824. The lack of dating evidence for any of them means that their association with medieval activity is tenuous, particularly when no clear structure could be recognised in any of the groups.

Ditch 698, in the north-east corner of the site, was wide and shallow (at 5.70 m long by 4.80 m wide, though only 0.13 m deep), and could be seen as an earthwork in the field to the east of the churchyard. The excavated section bifurcated, one branch continuing the east-west alignment of the earthwork until it faded out, the other turning to the north. Both cut the subsoil, with no trace of them in the overlying hillwash (27). The ditch formed the northern boundary of the excavated croft and the northern branch seemed to have formed the western side of a smaller house platform, which appears to have been relatively contemporary, although little of this was within the area excavated.

Layers 1268 and 1353, both to the south, seemed to have slumped down from the north into the hollow created by the silted-up churchyard boundary ditch (215) in the eastern part of the site. The former appeared to have been stratigraphically akin to the early accumulation of hillwash layer 736 (p 98), which overlay it on its northern side, and 1353 was identified above the collapse of wall 47 and the upper silting of ditch 1438 (p 98). Small patches of clay (1324) at the top of 1353 could have come from either a roof or a wall, but it was not certain that they related to wall 47. Layer 1328 overlay 1353 and may have slumped down from churchyard boundary bank 151/96, since it contained stones that appeared to have been tumble from wall 28. Rubble 1177 may also relate to the decay of wall 28 and its repair in the medieval period, or possibly to the construction of the buildings forming the croft to the north-east.

The pottery from these layers again indicates a date of the thirteenth-fourteenth century for their formation, although five sherds of sixteenth-century wares from rubble 1177 may indicate that this layer continued to accumulate throughout the occupation of the croft. A *styca* of c 837-41 (*Ch 3, p 51*), from layer 1328, must surely be residual.

Red sandstone blocks (43; 1.60 m long by 0.80 m wide) in the west of the site could conceivably have formed a step on the north side of churchyard wall 28 (Pl 39), since they were situated close to the north door of the church (now blocked) and the upper surface of each was heavily worn. All were obviously reused and two retained faint traces of decoration.

Two postholes and two pits in the vicinity of Structure X (*Ch 2, pp 31-2*) may belong with the croft. The two pits (113 and 164; Fig 67) were found within the area of the structure in the north-west of the site, but were probably not contemporary with it, since pit 113 cut across the alignment of postholes forming the eastern side of the building. Both were large, that part of pit 113 within the excavation being 0.97 m long by 0.95 m wide, whereas pit 164 was 2.5 x 1.32 m, both being aligned approximately north-south. Pit 164 was, however, very irregular in shape and more than 0.50 m deep, whereas pit 113 had a much more regular outline and was very shallow, at only 0.09 m deep. Two postholes (127 and 138) in the same area also did not seem to belong with Structure X, both in terms of their positions and the finds from them, although posthole 127 could potentially have been part of the structure's north wall or an internal sub-division. Each of these features contained a small amount of pottery, again of thirteenth/fourteenth-century date.

*Plate 39: Red sandstone step 43*

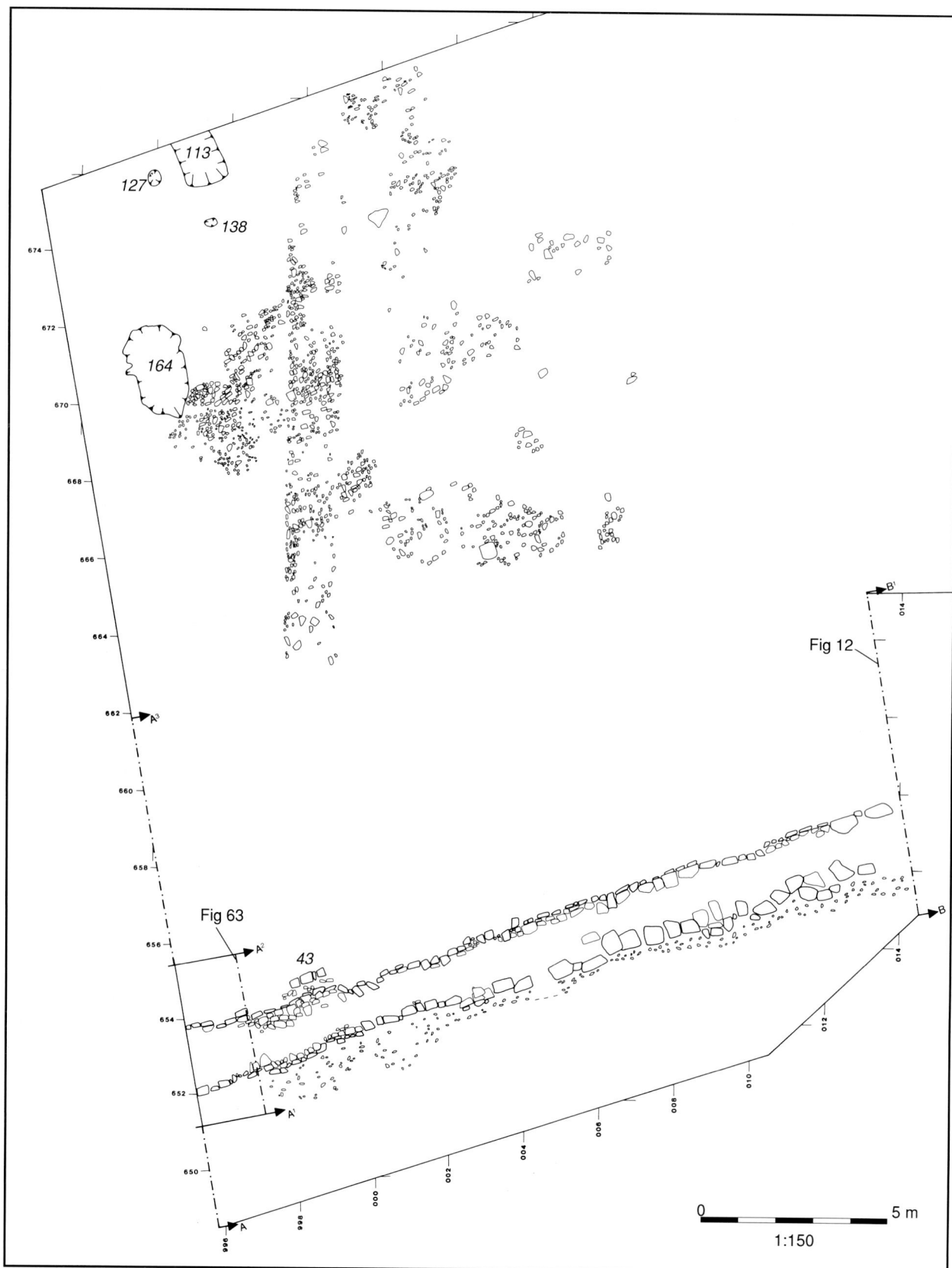

*Figure 67: Features in the west of the site*

## Structure A

An apparently rectangular timber structure (A) was constructed to the north of the collapse of wall 47 in the east of the site (Fig 66). An alignment of six postholes (*1174, 1178, 1180, 1182, 1184, 1232;* Fig 68) fitted stratigraphically between the earliest activity connected with the croft and the use of stone in the farm buildings (*pp 103-4*), one of which (*1232*) lay

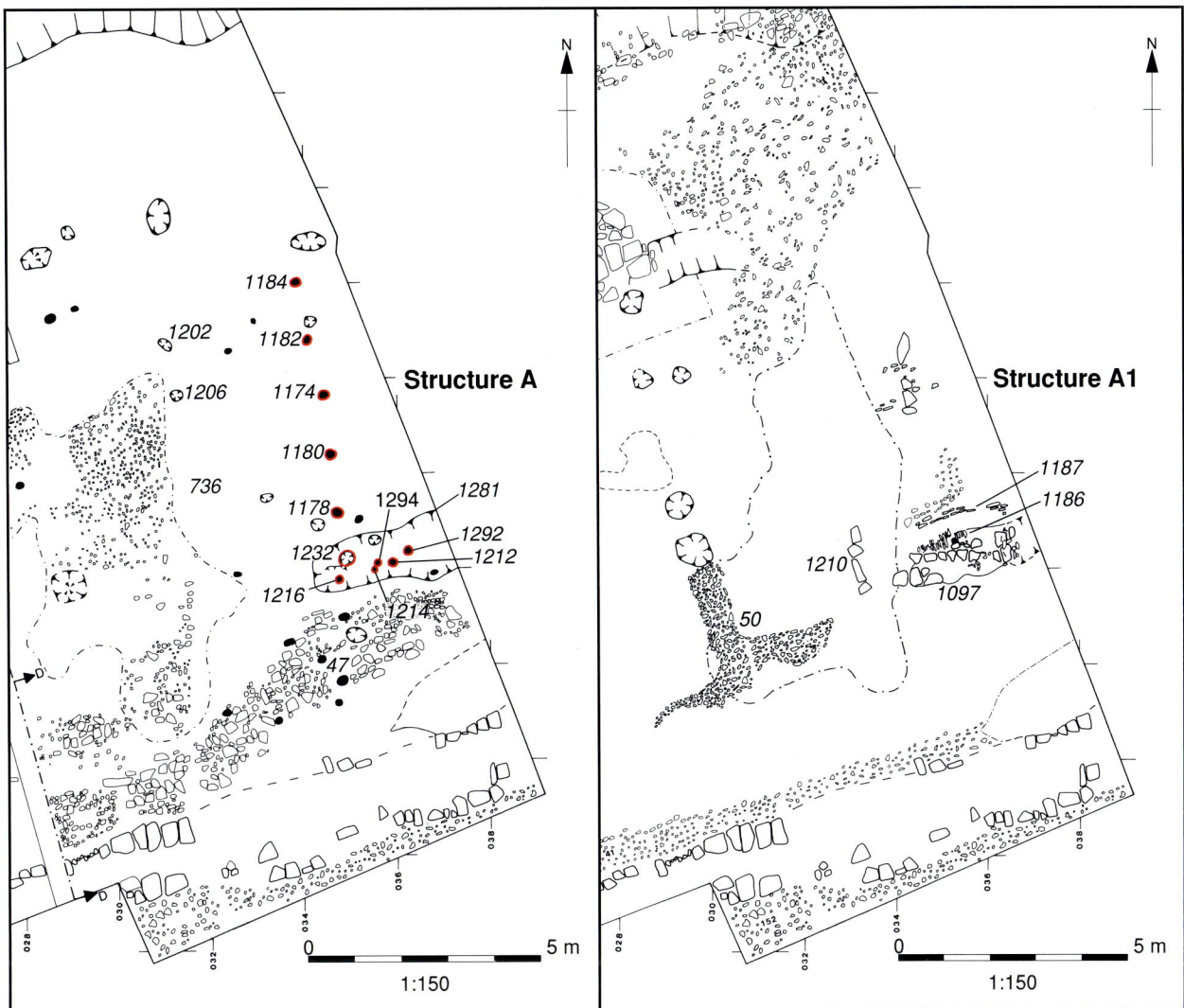

*Figure 68: Structures A and A1*

within the area defined by cut *1281* (*below*). This linear cut, at the southern extreme of the croft, may have acted as a trench into which the timber uprights for the gable end of the structure were placed. The posthole alignment seemed to have formed the western wall of a timber structure, some 7 m long, a large part of which lay beyond the excavated area, and thus there was no clear evidence either of internal features or an occupation horizon. Some other postholes and a dump of roofing stone appeared to be stratigraphically contemporary. Five postholes to the south (*1212*, *1214*, *1216*, *1292*, *1294*), all within cut *1281*, were sealed by a later stone wall (*1097*, *p 104*) and may have formed part of the gable of the structure, since they were approximately at right-angles to the alignment. Several other postholes (for instance, *1202* and *1206*) to the west may have been connected, but they did not seem to have been part of the main structure. All clearly cut layer *736*, and all were small, ranging from 0.11 m to 0.20 m in diameter, with only postholes *1202* and *1206* to the west, and *1232*, within cut *1181*, being larger, at 0.28 m

and 0.44 m respectively. No obvious occupational material was associated.

*Structure A1*

A probable half-timbered structure, aligned north-south, was identified above Structure A. Its main feature was a stone wall (*1097*; Pl 40), 2.44 m long, which had been constructed above the group of postholes defining the potential southern wall of the earlier structure. Wall *1097* comprised large dry-bonded angular blocks of red sandstone, only an average of 0.25 m wide, forming a straight northern face, although traces of a fragmentary southern face were also visible at its western end, suggesting its actual width was more like 0.60 m. A shallow linear cut, with a very irregular outline, surrounded these stones, apparently forming a foundation trench for them. This wall would appear to represent the complete rebuilding of the southern gable of the existing timber structure in a slightly different place, probably when the decision had been made to construct a fireplace against it (*p 104*).

*Plate 40: Structure A1, looking south*

The fireplace that may have led to the construction of wall *1097* was identified as hearth *1186*, with a probable edging (*1187*), 0.7 m to the north. This hearth, at least 1.2 m long, and possibly 1.80 m, was composed of small slabs of limestone, set upright, which clearly butted against wall *1097* (Pl 41), although it seems probable that its construction followed immediately on the completion of the wall. Edging *1187* comprised flat slabs of red sandstone set upright, with a few cobbles acting as chocking stones on the northern side. There was no evidence to indicate the superstructure of the fireplace, although a hood rather than a stone surround might be thought more likely.

A possible return (*1210*) for wall *1097*, 0.60 m to the west, comprised three large blocks of worked red sandstone in a fragmentary alignment, 1.5 m long, although no further stones were identified to the north. It could perhaps be thought of as a screen to protect hearth *1186*, built against wall *1097*, although this suggests a doorway at the south-western corner of the structure. Further to the west, a localised group of stones may have formed the last remnants of the south-west corner of the building (Pl 42), although it is possible that these were simply tumble, as they seemed partially to overlie what apppeared to have been an external metalled surface to the west of the

building. There was no other evidence, by way of either postholes or stone foundations, for a west wall to this structure, since the posthole alignment interpreted as the west wall of the earlier structure (Structure A) could not have formed an external wall for Structure A1, as it was partially sealed by hearth *1186*. There was, however, no evidence of any other external walls; removal of stone after the croft had been abandoned (*p 110*; *1099*) may have been responsible for this, although it is quite possible that the majority of the building was half-timbered, perhaps built on ground-laid sill beams, and the east wall would appear to have lain beyond the excavated area. The structure was presumably approximately the same size as its predecessor, and more than 4 m wide, given its position on the lower terrace. The only other clue to its width was perhaps in the shape of the nearby demolition deposits, such as *50* (*p 110*), which could suggest that it was up to 6.5 m wide. Again, no obvious occupational material was associated, and no floor level survived.

Ten sherds of pottery were associated with wall *1097*, ranging in date from the thirteenth/fourteenth century to the fifteenth/sixteenth century, the spread of dating perhaps representing the length of time the structure was in use, or perhaps the earlier group could have been associated with the wall of timber

*Plate 41: Fireplace and hearth* 1186

*Plate 42: The slight remains of the possible west wall of Structure A1*

Structure A (*1211*). Alternatively, the later pottery may have been connected with the demolition or collapse of the structure. Pottery dating from the thirteenth/fourteenth century was also found in rubble demolition layer *1099* above the building, and it has been suggested (*Ch 5, p122*) that this may have stemmed from the collapse of wattle walls, containing broken pottery as a binding agent, giving the date of construction rather than its demolition. It cannot be certain, though, whether these putative wattle walls were connected with Structure A or Structure A1. Four fragments of ceramic roofing tile and a stone roofing tile were also found, as well as a single fragment of ceramic roof tile between the stones of hearth *1186*.

## Structure B

A possible timber structure (B) was identified, at least 5.5 m long, and perhaps as much as 6.5 m, by some 4 m wide, built approximately at right-angles to, and some 3 m to the west of, Structure A1 (Fig 69). An east-west alignment of five postholes (*1142*, *1144*, *1072*, *1070*, *1068*) formed the north wall, covered by later hillwash (*27*). Postholes *1068*, *1142*, and *1144* cut layer *736*, and *1070* and *1072* cut layer *702*. This was above layer *736* (*p 98*) and was in turn covered by deposits associated with the decay of the medieval croft (*56*, *531*, *p 110*). It is therefore likely that *702* was accumulating during the main period of occupation of the buildings.

Two further postholes (*1114*, *1162*) may have formed part of an eastern return, although they did not align exactly with *1068* and both were larger, at 0.60-0.74 m in diameter, as opposed to 0.26-0.46 m, than the postholes in the east-west alignment. Both cut metalling *45* (*p 107*) and also contained clear post-pipes, unlike most of the other postholes on the site. Indeed, while unlikely, it is just possible that these were connected with Structure A1 and that the two buildings were physically linked. There was little trace of any part of the south side of Structure B, although a large posthole (*1310*), adjacent to posthole *1114* and again containing a post-pipe, could signify the south-east corner of the structure, and *1222*, a rather enigmatic hollow to the west that may have been the base of a posthole (0.13 m deep), could conceivably have marked its western extent. Again, there was no obvious occupational debris associated. No datable finds came from these postholes, but some possible daub was found in the lower fill of *1114*. This could perhaps be linked to clay spread *1074* (*p 110*), which may represent the collapse of this structure.

105

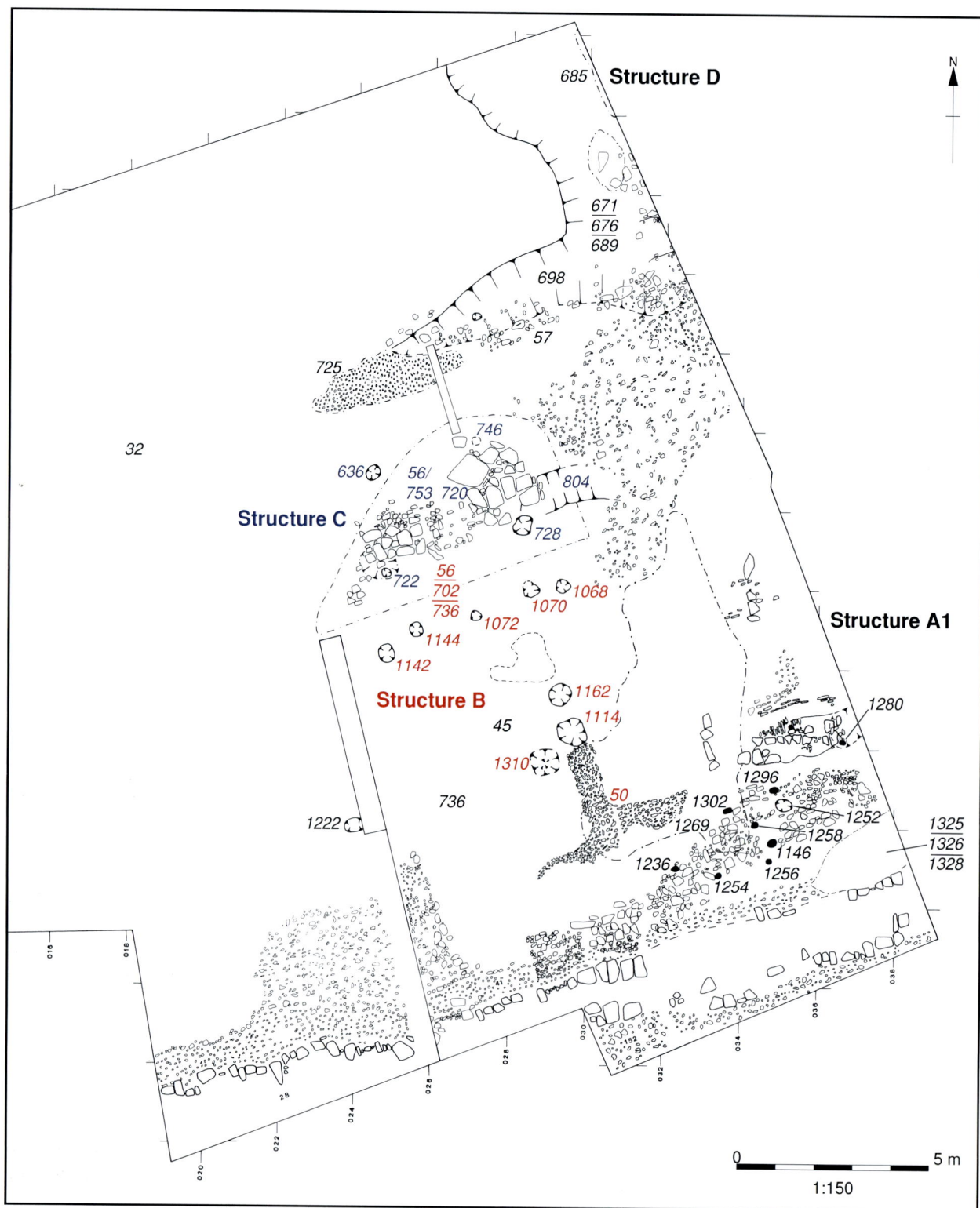

*Figure 69: Structures B, C, and D, and features to the south of Structure A1*

## Structure C

A stone floor (720), situated 2 m to the north of Structure B, marked the site of a further building, measuring some 5 x 2.5 m. It was composed of irregularly shaped flat slabs, mostly sandstone, laid fairly randomly (Pl 43). The eastern edge of the floor was slightly bowed and it also appeared to have sunk into cut 787 (p 100) at its western end.

It was divided into two, although it was uncertain whether this gap had been created during the use of the structure or during its decay. There was little evidence for the walls surrounding this surface, and thus they were probably formed of timber or turf, since four small postholes were identified (636, 746, 728, and 722; 0.18 m to c 0.40 m in diameter), two seemingly forming each wall line. These seemed to

*Plate 43: Structure C*

form a trapezoidal pattern, with a larger posthole opposed to a smaller one, perhaps to hold a basic frame such as a pair of crucks. Floor *720* partly overlay the post-pits of postholes *722* and *728*, but the floor was nevertheless probably contemporary. It had been covered by a spread of rubble (*56*; *p 110*), representing the collapse of the structure. An irregular linear depression (*804*) extended from under the south-eastern side of *720* and appeared to have formed a drain for the building, 1.9 m long by 0.90 m wide, suggesting that it may have housed animals. No finds or occupational debris were associated.

Clay layer *753*, to the south of ditch *698*, was stratigraphically below the level of floor *720*, although it did not underlie it. It sealed posthole *732* (*p 101*) and was in turn sealed by the decay of the later structure (*56*; *p 110*). Its compactness would suggest that it represented the remains of a surface, possibly an earlier floor, although the fact that no trace of it was found below floor *720* makes this interpretation less likely.

**Structure D**

Traces of a closely packed stone surface (*685*) projecting from the section in the north-eastern corner of the site, on the upper platform that was only just clipped by the excavation, probably related to the building platform visible as an earthwork in the field to the east. No finds were associated and too small an area was available for excavation to establish much of its character, but it was probably either an external metalled surface or an internal floor. Ditch *698* apparently continued to silt up (*676*, *671*) during this phase, possibly as a result of some decay of the platform, but there were no finds to aid dating.

**Other features**

Metalled surface *45*, to the west of Structure A, was not directly associated with any building and it perhaps represents the remains of a yard. Another metalled area (*725*) to the north, which partially sealed the primary fill of the western extension of ditch *698* (*p 101*), was probably also a yard. The phasing of this feature remains uncertain, given the lack of dating evidence associated with both it and the underlying ditch.

To the south of the structures, three postholes (*1236*, *1296*, *1302*) cut the northern side of the collapse of wall *47*, approximately following the alignment of this wall. They varied greatly in size (from 0.14 m to 0.33 m in diameter) and their purpose is not immediately obvious. In the same area, sandstone

107

spread *1326* lay in the bowl-shaped hollow to the south of Structure A, and of collapsed wall *47*, and above layer *1328* (*p 101*). The stones appeared to be broken roofing tiles, similar in size and shape to those associated with the collapse of Structure A1 in this area, though stratigraphically earlier. Those in layer *1326* did not seem to have resulted from the collapse of a roof, but had probably been dumped and were possibly connected with the construction of a building, a supposition supported by the presence of two distinct layers of stone within the spread. Layer *1325* had accumulated in the top of the depression largely filled by *1326* and both layers appeared to butt against the base of churchyard wall *28*.

Several features appeared to have been at the same stratigraphical level, but contained no dating evidence. Clay *1269* seems to have accumulated to the south of timber Structure A, filling the hollow created by the raised churchyard boundary and the natural slope of the ground. Six apparently randomly distributed small postholes (*1146*, *1252*, *1254*, *1256*, *1258*, *1280*) in the area of collapsed wall *47* cut layer *1269* and lay beneath deposits associated with the decay of the croft (*eg 1016*; *p 110*). These might also have been associated with postholes *1236*, *1296*, and *1302* (*p 107*).

Stones *57* comprised an east-west alignment of large limestone blocks, 1.5 m long, along the southern side and partly over the fill of ditch *698* (*p 101*) in the north-eastern corner of the site. It appears to have formed the northern boundary of the croft, although the type of superstructure the stones could have supported remains unclear.

Only layer *1269* and surface *45* contained pottery. This appears to suggest a thirteenth/fourteenth-century date, although two sherds of fifteenth/sixteenth-century pottery in *45* may reflect the length of time the surface was in use, or perhaps some later disturbance.

Soil creep seems to have been a constant action down the slope throughout the medieval period. It is therefore generally impossible to define it in terms of individual phases, although in certain parts of the site, accumulations can be identified as continuing over limited periods. Similarly, the decay of the churchyard boundary was not rapid, but continued over many years.

Stone spread *35* (Fig 70), in the north-west of the site on the upper terrace, included notable concentrations of red sandstone. The density varied greatly, probably at least partly due to the machine removal of hillwash in 1983, which also distorted

its shape, but nevertheless it seems too irregular to have formed any sort of surface; it may in fact relate to activity beyond the excavated area. Its phasing is difficult, since *35* lay above earlier hillwash *32*, which in turn partially covered debris from the decay of churchyard wall *28* (*41, below*), and the relatively few finds from the spread as a whole, which were mostly from the southern part, included six sherds of twelfth- to fourteenth-century pottery, whereas *41* contained a large quantity of sixteenth-century pottery, although much of this was from the eastern part of the site, near the croft.

Stone spread *1190* clearly lay above metalled surface *1204* (*p 98*) in the south-eastern part of the site, and in turn was partially covered by the decay of the churchyard wall (*41, below*). The pottery assemblage, which was found only in the eastern part of the layer, was dominated by sherds of fifteenth/sixteenth-century date, although ten sherds of thirteenth/fourteenth-century pottery and also two sherds of post-medieval pottery were found. It seems possible, given this assemblage, that the spread was contemporary with the decay of the medieval croft.

## Decay

Some decay of churchyard boundary wall *28* appears to have begun during the occupation of the croft and to have continued intermittently into the post-medieval period. In its earliest form, it comprised rubble layer *152*, to the south of the wall. The pottery contained was mostly of thirteenth/fourteenth-century date, although two sherds of fifteenth/sixteenth-century date were found. Other finds included a silver short-cross penny (*Ch 5, p 123*) and a similar halfpenny, which are likely to have been deposited originally in the thirteenth century. The coins came from the lowest element of the rubble and are roughly contemporary with the coin from the wall core (*p 97*). This may suggest that the lowest rubble represents debris from the construction of wall *28*, rather than its early decay. Two sherds of post-medieval pottery and some human bone were also found amongst the stones, which probably came from the dumping of material from grave digging around the edge of the medieval and modern churchyard. The presence of post-medieval pottery, unless it was intrusive, indicates the length of time during which the layer accumulated.

A spread of rubble (*41*) of varying width was also found along the northern side of the churchyard wall. Many sherds of pottery were found within this, dating from the thirteenth century through to the nineteenth century. The area to the south of the croft produced most of the pottery, as well as five fragments of ceramic roofing tile. The range of finds indicates that, although it is possible that

*Figure 70: Later deposits in the northern churchyard*

some of the finds were residual, since much of the rest of the site shows evidence of the mixing of finds through soil creep, the accumulation of *41* was not rapid and probably represents several periods of decay and repair, particularly immediately to the north of the church. There may also have been an element of contamination from the machine removal of hillwash to the north (*80*).

Spreads of rubble (*42, 56, 1016, 1099, 1157*) from the decay and robbing of the ruined croft covered its buildings. The largest spread (*1099*) was associated with Structure A1 (*p 103*), as was a scatter of red sandstone (*1157*), which may have been related to the decay of the putative firehood over hearth *1086*. Rubble *1099* was partially covered by the remains of what appeared to have been a collapsed roof (*50*), comprising a spread of yellow sandstone with some glacially derived stone in a sticky reddish silty-loam, and obvious stone roofing tiles were also found amongst it. The box-like *1169* in the area of Structure A/A1, some 0.78 x 0.32 m, comprised several flat slabs of red sandstone which, despite the lack of peg holes, were probably roofing material which had collapsed downwards into the centre of the structure. These spreads were covered by layer *1016*, which had been affected by the decay of the croft beneath, but probably represented the beginning of hillwash from the north, bringing earlier material into the upper levels of the site.

Clay spread *1074*, to the south of the putative north wall of Structure B, contained a lens of burnt material and probably represented the wall of a collapsed structure, presumably Structure B, rather than the remains of a floor. Rubble spread *56* covered floor *720* and the area to the east, and this concentration suggests that the stones came from Structure C, although there was no surviving evidence of stone being used in its construction, except for its floor. It was sealed by layer *531*, containing patches of red clay, again possibly from the structure, although this layer probably at least partly accumulated as a result of hillwash.

A large amount of pottery (89 sherds) was found within layer *1016*, in contrast to collapse *1099* below it (16 sherds), although most of the material from both layers was earlier than the seeming decay of the croft, being largely thirteenth- or fourteenth-century in date, with only a single sherd from the fifteenth-sixteenth century present in *1016*. The date range of the pottery from these layers in the area may reflect the use of broken vessels as a binding agent in wattle walls (*p 105*, Structure A1), the decay of which is reflected in the rubble spreads (*Ch 5, p 122*). Layer *1016* in particular may also have included material washing down the slope

from the north. Single sherds of fifteenth/sixteenth-century pottery were associated with clay *1074* and rubble spread *56*, and a few sherds of similar date, as well as later material, were found in layer *531*, above Structure C, which would seem to indicate the continuing accumulation of this into the post-medieval period. A similar conclusion could be drawn from the finds from rubble spread *42*, although it is likely, given the assemblage, that this largely formed during the sixteenth- or seventeenth century. The presence of a sherd of fifteenth/sixteenth-century pottery amongst stone alignment *57* (*p 108*) suggests that it was constructed only shortly before the site was abandoned, since the lack of post-fourteenth-century material within the structural elements and occupational levels of the croft would perhaps indicate that it decayed from the fifteenth century onward, presumably as the settlement either shrank or moved westwards towards the present site of the village.

## Burial within the post-medieval churchyard

Layer *139* formed the earlier of two churchyard levels associated with modern graves within the small part of the medieval churchyard within the excavation (Fig 71). The upper part clearly sealed rubble layer *152* (*p 108*) so it was probably forming in the later medieval period. Sherds of twelfth- to fourteenth-century pottery were found, although later medieval and post-medieval fabrics were also represented, which would suggest that grave-digging could have disturbed earlier layers beneath, or perhaps that the layer began to accumulate shortly after the churchyard was formally laid out, with bank *151* as its northern boundary (*p 91*). Hillwash *27* represented soil creep from the north (Pl 44). The finds from it were therefore extremely mixed and included prehistoric, Roman, pre-Norman, medieval, and post-medieval material.

The latest activity on the site seems to have occurred in the seventeenth century or later. A group of burials within the medieval churchyard, to the north of the church, cut layer *139*. Most contained evidence for coffins and all the skeletons were relatively well preserved, in contrast to the lack of preservation within the early cemetery (Ch 3, *pp 86-7*). A sequence could be discerned within the group, the earliest, *289*, being accurately oriented, whereas the others were parallel to the church. Neither grave *289*, nor *284*, which was also early in the sequence, had visible remains of coffins and this, together with the decayed state of the skeletons, suggests that these burials could be of medieval date rather than modern. Grave *148* also had no evidence of a coffin, but it was clearly late in the sequence. The other burials were all within coffins, which had collapsed, and had well-preserved skeletons associated.

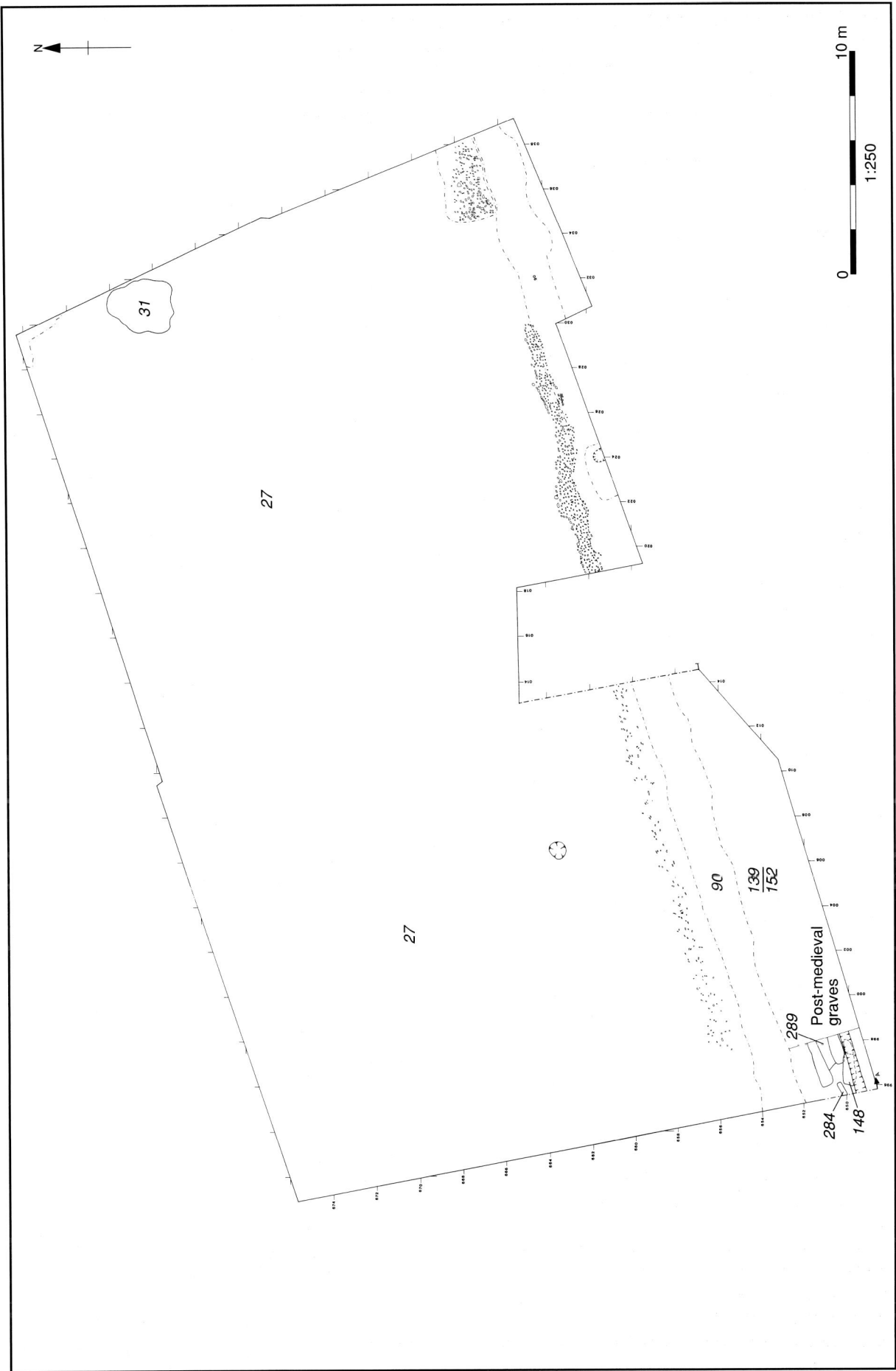

*Figure 71: Burials within the post-medieval churchyard*

111

*Plate 44: The deep hillwash, butting against the medieval northern churchyard boundary*

Churchyard boundary wall *28* is known to have stood until *c* 1950, when the churchyard was extended to its present dimensions (K Smith *pers comm*). The wall was then demolished (*90*) and many of the stones used to construct the new northern boundary. Stone spread *31*, in the north-east corner of the modern churchyard, and containing large quantities of human bone, lay immediately below the topsoil and clearly resulted from the dumping of debris from grave digging in the older part of the churchyard.

## The Orchard

### The medieval churchyard boundary?

Wall *18* ( Fig 72), in the north-east corner of the Orchard, butted against wall *17* to the south (*Ch 2, p 38*; Pl 45), and seemed to have been built while the latter was still standing. It survived at foundation level as a double line of boulders with a rubble core, aligned north-south. The character of *18* was very similar to, though slightly narrower than (1.2 m as opposed to 1.7 m), the thirteenth-century churchyard boundary wall to the north of the church (*28, p 96*), and it seems likely that it once performed the same function. Two sherds of fourteenth- to sixteenth-century pottery were found within its core.

Layer *52* appeared to have accumulated around the base of wall *18* to its east, and the north face of kerb *51* (*Ch 2, p 40*). It formed a thin skim immediately above the subsoil to the north but deepened and seemed to extend over other early features (for instance, hollow *114*; *Ch 2, p 38*) to the south, where the subsoil dipped downwards. A range of medieval pottery and also two sherds of post-medieval pottery were found within it. The latter suggests that there was an intrusion to the east of wall *18* that was not identified, or that subsequent gardening activity was in some places deeper than was recognised.

Layer *68*, again to the east of wall *18*, contained a large amount of worked stones, many of which seemed to lie against the wall. These were probably tumble from it, but it is also possible that they might represent the demolition of an earlier building, not identified in the excavated area. The stones seemed to have sunk into the upper fill of hollow *124* below (*Ch 2, p 38*).

A deep deposit of hillwash (*5*) throughout much of the Orchard seems to have been building up whilst putative early medieval wall *17* and its possible rebuild, wall *116* (*Ch 2, p 40*), were still standing, although it was at its thinnest in the northern part of the site. Two sherds of late medieval pottery and an abraded sherd of samian ware were recovered from

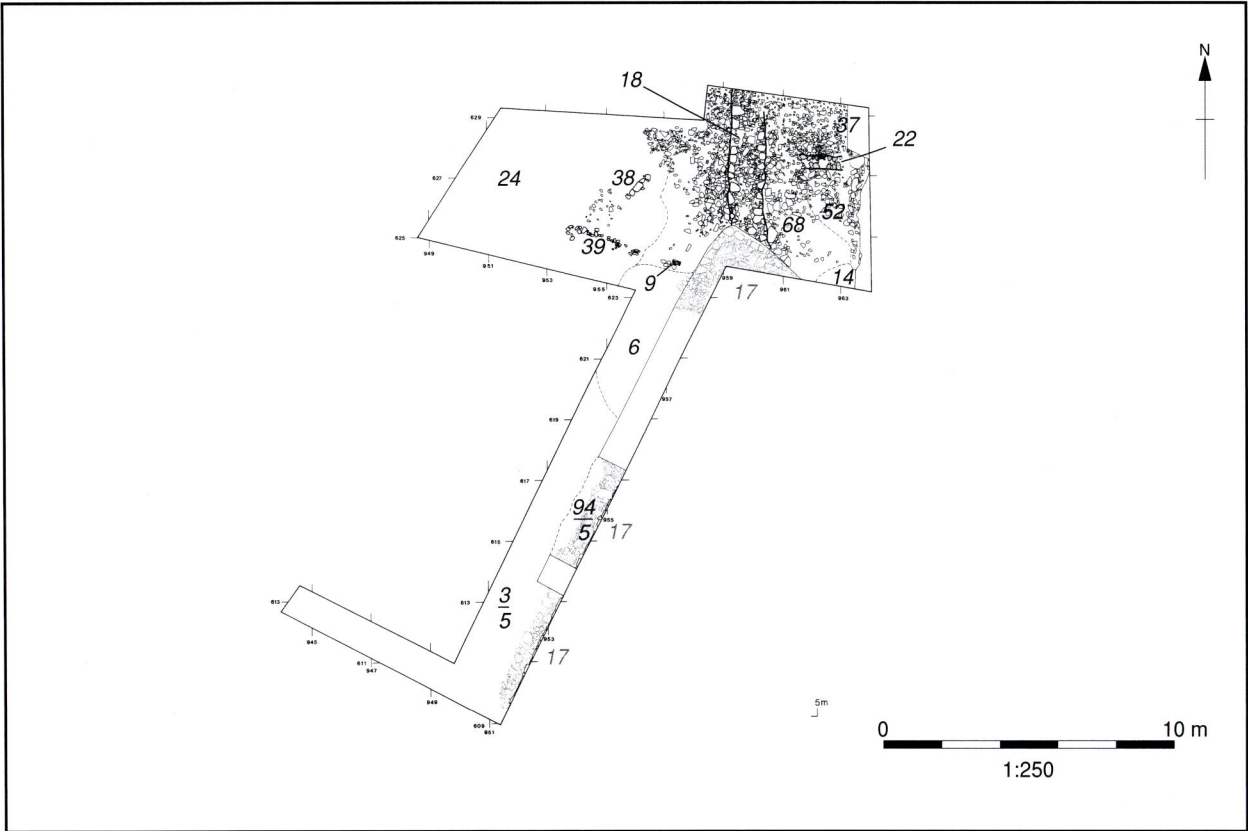

*Figure 72: The medieval activity in the Orchard*

*Plate 45: Wall 18 in the Orchard, butting against earlier wall 17*

this. These finds contrast with the lower elements of the hillwash (59), which contained no datable objects, and the upper hillwash (3), which contained both medieval and post-medieval pottery.

## A structure within the medieval churchyard

Two distinct areas of activity, which fit into a general 'medieval' phase, could be identified in the northern part of the site, although the two cannot be linked stratigraphically. Wall 22, to the east of, and at right-angles to, wall 18, comprised a double row of mixed rounded stones, with neatened outer faces (Fig 73). No relationship between the two walls could be established, since 22 degenerated into a mass of rubble at the junction with wall 18, perhaps indicating the position of a doorway. There was no sign of a continuation of wall 22 to the west beyond wall 18, or of any other return to it. This implies that wall 18 acted as the west wall of the structure of which 22 was an element, suggesting that it would have been greater than 4 m in each direction, although the difference in its width and construction makes it unlikely that this was its primary use.

The width of wall 22 (0.50 m) perhaps implies that it was no more than a single storey high, or that it formed the stone footings for a timber superstructure. Alternatively, the wall perhaps constituted an internal division within a structure, the external walls of which, apart from wall 18, lay outside the excavated area. If wall 18 did originally form the western boundary of the churchyard, then this structure was built on once-consecrated ground. It could therefore have been a dwelling for someone connected with the church, perhaps the parish priest; whatever its function, its construction seems to have led to the removal of a small part of the churchyard from its primary use, which would help to explain the strange shape of the northern part of the Orchard. The absence of graves there would point to a very early date for the removal of this parcel of land from the churchyard.

Posthole 9, to the south-west of wall 18, contained upright red sandstone packing on three sides, and a line of stones, set vertically (39; Fig 72; Pl 46), stretched to the west from it for a distance of 4 m; another alignment (38) extended from the western end of 39 north-eastward at an acute angle for a further 3 m. Although both proved insubstantial, alignment 39 appeared to have marked the line of a fence or some other obstruction, and despite the lack of any other postholes, it is probable that alignment 39 and posthole 9 were related. These might have formed parts of a timber structure, or possibly an enclosure, although the acute angle between alignments 38 and 39 seemed to

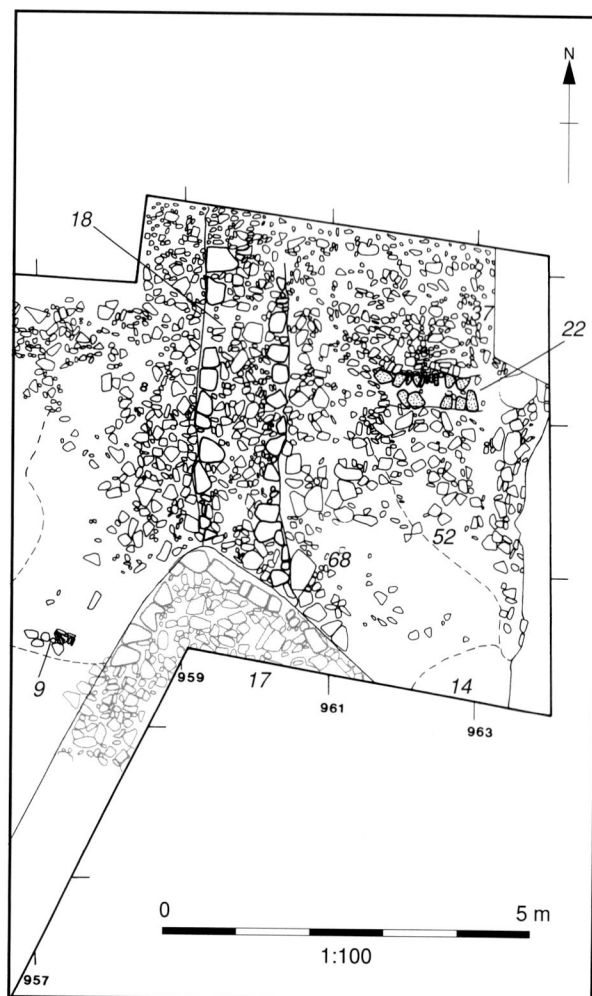

*Figure 73: Wall 22 in the Orchard*

preclude them from being two sides of the same structure. The purpose of these features, and their relationship with other elements of the site, remains uncertain.

To the south, layer 6, similar in composition to other hillwash but clearly affected by the activity to the north and east, perhaps formed the associated ground surface. It was found to contain only medieval pottery, but the other features lacked any dating evidence, although all were sealed by layers containing both medieval and modern pottery, the latter clearly connected with the overlying gardening activity.

Layer 24 was similar to layer 6, and had built up around stone alignments 38 and 39 in the north of the site. The finds suggest that this had accumulated from the fifteenth century onwards and yet it lay directly upon undisturbed subsoil. This may imply a large amount of erosion in this northern, uphill area prior to its development.

An area of closely packed rubble (37) butted the north side of wall 22 and could possibly have

*Plate 46: Alignment 39*

formed the base for a floor within the putative building. The spread became less dense to the north and there it resembled demolition debris. The only find was a single sherd of thirteenth/fourteenth-century pottery.

The uppermost hillwash (*3*) probably continued to form until the relatively recent past, since it contained substantial quantities of both medieval and post-medieval pottery. A relatively large quantity of yellow sandstone fragments (*94*) at its eastern extremity had clearly tumbled from wall *17* during its decay.

## Decay

The uppermost activity related to both the decay of the structure (layers *21*, *23*, *8*) in the north-eastern corner of the site, and the build-up of soil over them (layers *7*, *2*), caused by gardening activity, although layers *7* and *23* may have acted briefly as surfaces. Both the decay and gardening activity seem to have been relatively recent events, since the associated finds were largely post-medieval. Stone dumps, in the south of the site and to the north (*14*), were probably associated with the construction or renovation of the present churchyard wall, which was clearly relatively modern, since it bounded the nineteenth-century southern churchyard extension as well as the older part of the churchyard.

# The Southern Churchyard

## Robbing of the drain

Three features seemed to have been created in the southern churchyard after the primary use of drain *913* (*Ch 2, p 44*). An irregular cut (*932*; Fig 74) lay close to the surviving capping stones and appeared to have disturbed layer *946* (*Ch 2, p 46*), and a similar cut (*930*) was identified to the west, although this seemed to lie at a slightly higher level, cutting layer *867* (*p 116*). It seems probable that these were connected to the presumed medieval robbing of the capping stones of *913*. No dating evidence was recovered from *930*, but *932* contained seven small sherds of twelfth- to fourteenth-century pottery, from at least four different vessels.

Traces remained of the possible deliberate backfilling, rather than natural silting, of drain *913* in the small area that had not been excavated in *c* 1929 (Hudleston 1932). A dump of loosely packed large boulders (*917*) close to the present churchyard wall appeared to have been tipped into the drain in a haphazard fashion, and lay immediately above thin silt layer *865* (*Ch 2, p 46*). The photograph of the *c* 1929 excavation (*op cit*, 76) shows a heap of large stones by the side of the trench, and a large

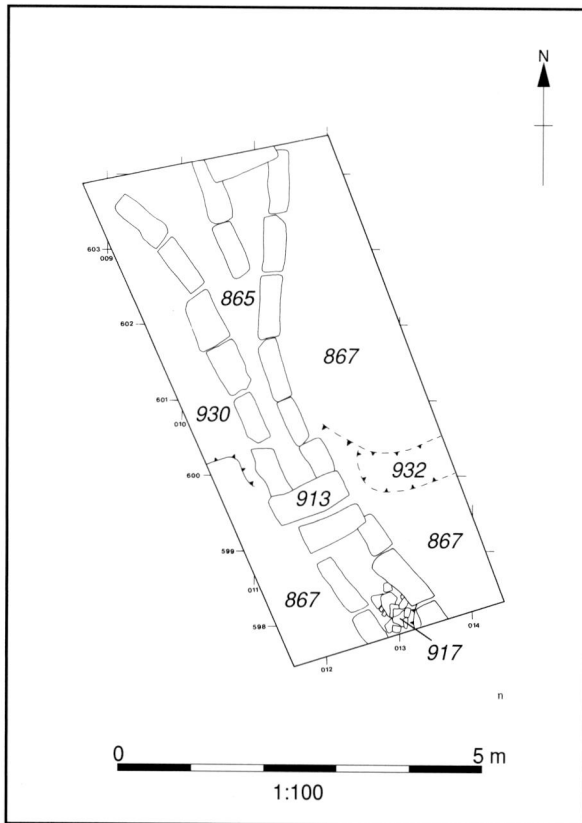

Figure 74: Deposits around drain 913

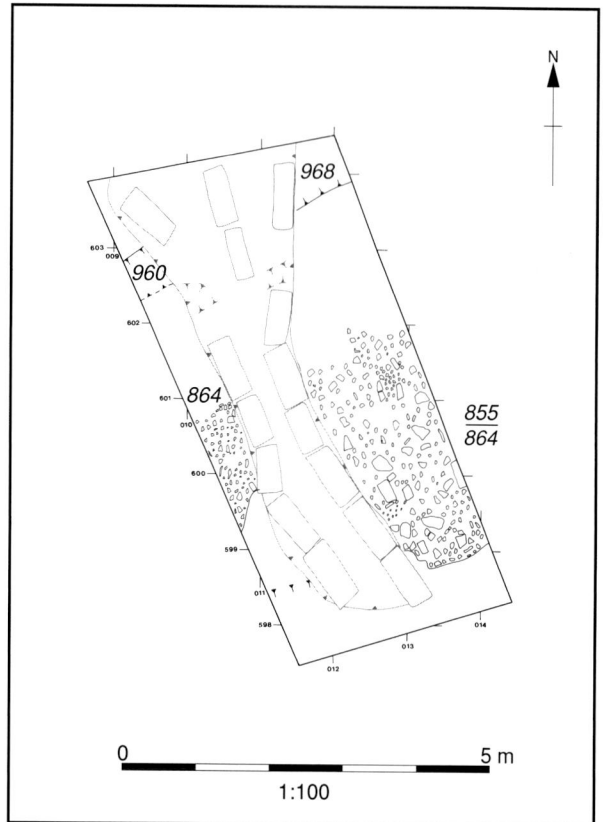

Figure 75: Later deposits in the southern churchyard

quantity of stones of the same size and shape were found within the backfilling of these excavations (835; p 117). Given that the c 1929 excavations do not appear to have examined anything outside the drain itself, it would seem that at least part of the drain had contained a large amount of stone.

It can be argued that this perhaps implies a conscious backfilling, rather than that the drain was stone-filled whilst it was in use, although it could equally indicate that it was later reused as a field drain at some period. Layer 867, a reddish gravelly sandy silt, seems to have covered drain 913 and the surrounding area. There is evidence in the southern part of the site for a cut at the base of this into underlying layers 946 and 998 (Ch 2, p 46), which was probably again associated with the robbing of the capping stones of the drain, as it seems logical that the layers dumped around it at the time of its construction would once have covered it completely. Twelve sherds of thirteenth/fourteenth-century pottery, mostly from a single vessel, were found close to the surface of 867 and it can be presumed that the layer was an accumulation contemporary with, and subsequent to, the robbing of the drain.

## Later activity
A metalled surface (864; Fig 75) had been constructed across the line of drain 913, to the

south of the medieval churchyard boundary and, on the east side of the c 1929 excavation, a gravel and sandstone spread (855) seemingly represented a resurfacing. There was no evidence to suggest that this was not post-medieval and a precursor of the existing field track from Stainton to Dacre, which is situated immediately to the south of the present churchyard wall.

Two linear cuts of uncertain phase were excavated to the north of metalled surface 864. Cuts 960 and 968 seemed to have been stratigraphically later than layers 998 and 946 (Ch 2, p 46) respectively, although 968 seemed to be at a slightly higher level than 960, but they may nevertheless have been parts of the same feature. There was no dating evidence associated with either cut, but stratigraphically they belonged to a period after drain 913 ceased to be used. It seems probable that these cuts served some drainage function, or were connected with the robbing of stone from drain 913.

## Post-medieval activity
The more recent events within the excavated area are likely to have belonged to a relatively long period. Hollow 990 (Fig 76) contained several large flat pieces of red sandstone, which presumably came from the drain and were possibly parts of the capping stones. The hollow may therefore have been connected with stone robbing from the

116

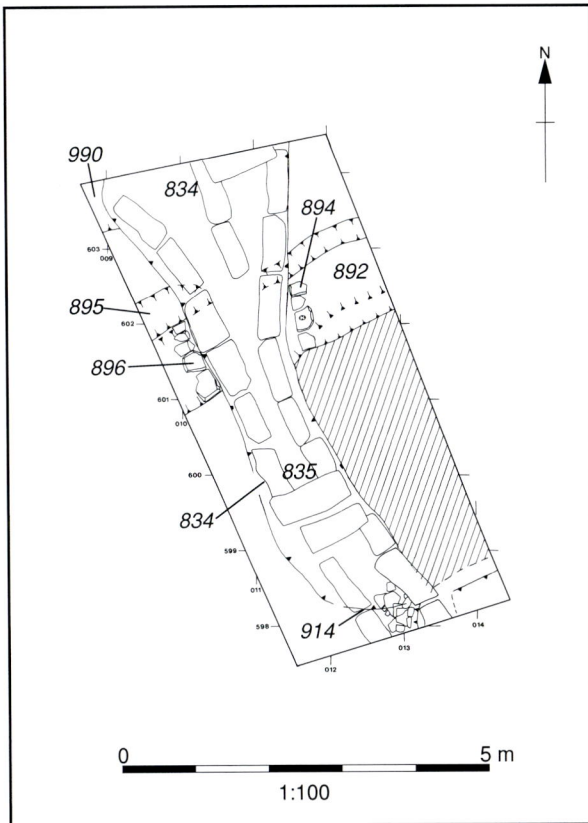

Figure 76: Latest deposits in the southern churchyard

Plate 47: Modern red sandstone blocks 834, marking the position of the drain in the southern churchyard, laid following excavation in the 1920s

drain, or, more probably, related to grave-digging activities which disturbed it by accident. No dating evidence was associated, but the stratigraphy indicated that it was a modern feature.

A deep drainage trench (892) cut through all the archaeological levels, aligned east-west. The terracotta pipe at the base appeared to have been rammed beneath drain 913, implying that the position of the early drain was known, or had been discovered during the laying of the pipe. A line of stones (894, 896) was found in the upper fill on either side of 913. These had been placed where the digging of drain 892 ceased on either side of drain 913 and presumably acted as revetments to stop the drain stones from toppling into the modern cut. A parallel, narrower, stone-filled gully (895), to the north of 892, was probably also connected with drainage.

An irregular cut (914), roughly following the outer edge of drain 913, clearly marked the limit of the c 1929 excavation, confirmed by the published photograph of the excavation (Ch 1, Pl 1). The backfill (835) within it contained a substantial amount of large, rounded stones, which probably formed the original backfill of drain 913 (917, p 115). The position of the stones forming the drain had been marked at the conclusion of the excavation with blocks of red sandstone (834; Pl 47), cut to the approximate size of each original, which had subsequently sunk into the turf and been lost.

The pre-Norman copper-alloy objects found in the excavation backfill included a decorative escutcheon (Ch 3, pp 56-7), possibly from a book, and a stylus similar to those found at Jarrow and Whitby (Cramp et al 2006; Peers and Radford 1943). Since the edges of the c 1929 excavation have been proved to lie exactly above the outer edges of drain 913, it follows that these objects almost certainly came from either within or above this feature. The stylus therefore takes on importance when considering the date of the drain. A gold ring (Ch 3, p 56), similarly pre-Conquest in date, also came from this area, although it was unstratified.

# 5

# LATER MEDIEVAL AND POST-MEDIEVAL OBJECTS

## The Later Medieval Artefacts

### The medieval pottery and tile
*M R McCarthy and C M Brooks*

In all, some 2200 sherds of medieval pottery were examined. Many were very small (substantial numbers being less than 80 mm² in area) and severely abraded, and this, considered alongside the very limited amounts from many of the individual contexts, and the nature of the contexts themselves (with much of the pottery coming from hillwash), substantially restricted the range of analysis possible. In addition, it made quantification by weight potentially rather uninformative, and in consequence the assemblage was quantified by sherd-count alone (this work was undertaken in the 1980s, long before the modern guidelines were introduced; PCRG *et al* 2016). Thus, the more sophisticated methods of analysis were not thought appropriate, and the reason for counting the sherds was simply to provide an indication of the size of the ceramic assemblage in each phase. The sherds from each context and phase have been quantified, identified to fabric, and, where possible, to form. The pottery is discussed by site, so inevitably the principal assemblage is that from the northern churchyard.

Whilst the pottery undoubtedly lies within a wider regional ceramic tradition, firmly identified comparators are few. Indeed, it is probable that most of the medieval pottery at Dacre is of relatively local manufacture, though exactly where remains unclear, as few production sites are known, and for the most part they are unexplored (Newman and Newman 2007), with the exception of a possible kiln at Cumwhinton, near Carlisle, where numerous wasters were recognised in a rural assemblage (Bradley and Miller 2014). A few later regional imports have been recognised, notably the sixteenth-century Cistercian- and Hambleton-type wares (Fabrics 9 and 10; *Appendix 1*), and possibly an earlier, slightly sandy whiteware (Fabric 8), dated to the thirteenth-fourteenth century. Dacre is very close to an ancient trans-Pennine routeway, marked now by the A66, where, at sites such as Brougham Castle, Yorkshire-made wares were represented amongst the fifteenth- to seventeenth-century pottery (McCarthy and Brooks 1992). Indeed, the fourteenth-century connections of the Dacre family, then at least partly resident in Dacre Castle, but also holding estates in Yorkshire (Ferguson 1880), might lead one to expect the presence of Scarborough and/or other North-Eastern wares within the pottery assemblages from the locality.

### Site 1: the Orchard
Only 139 sherds came from the Orchard. A roughly made, perhaps rather workaday, late-medieval greenware (Fabric 1) was present in contexts including some of the earliest activity (regarded on other grounds as pre-Conquest), as well as most of the subsequent phases. It is thus likely that all were contaminated in antiquity. All the common local wares were found, including decorated jugs, one bearing a graffito (Fig 77.7).

### Site 2: the northern churchyard
Sixteen sherds from cooking pots and a jug were recovered from contexts pre-dating the creation of the churchyard during the medieval period. A sherd of red gritty ware (Fabric 7) from the upper fill (*103*) of grave *104 (Ch 2, p 30)*, and an everted rim from layer *633*, are both typologically early, although not necessarily earlier than the twelfth century. Many sherds are very small, several to the point of being unidentifiable, which may suggest a long period of exposure before they were incorporated within deposits, thus probably post-dating the use of the early cemetery (*Ch 2*), and reflecting deposition during a subsequent period of disuse.

Of the 138 sherds from contexts associated with the first medieval churchyard boundary, approximately a third (31%) are attributable with some confidence to the thirteenth-fourteenth century (Fabrics 4-5, 8). They include examples of glazed jugs decorated with brown strips and thumbing on the underside of the base (Fabric 4). Fabric 6, an off-white to pinkish fabric in the Northern Gritty tradition, provided over half the pottery (57%). Many of these sherds

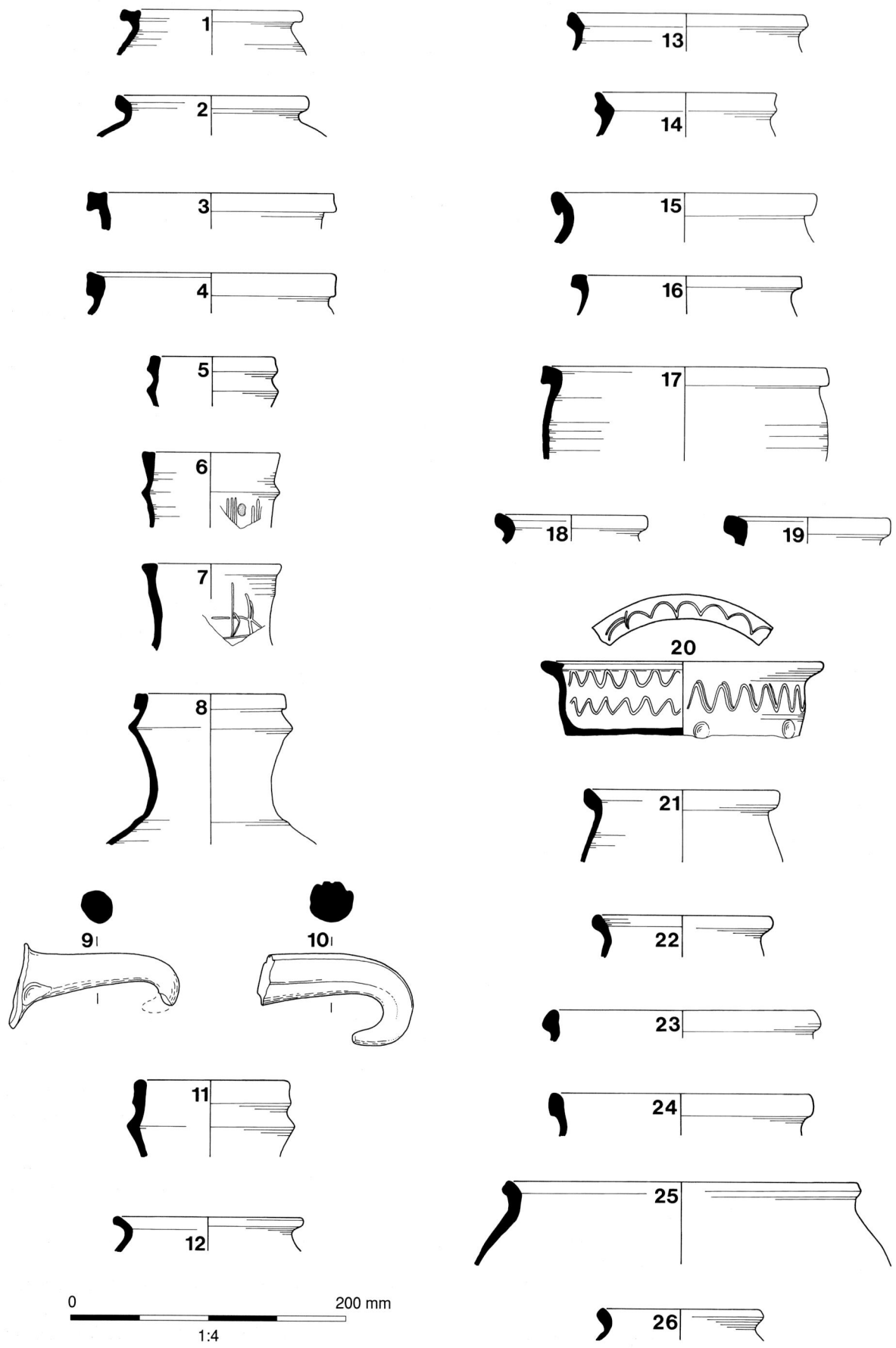

*Figure 77: Selected medieval pottery*

are from square-rimmed cooking pots attributable to the twelfth century, although it is possible that jugs in this same fabric may be a little later.

There are several examples of joining sherds which link the lower, middle, and upper levels of the churchyard boundary bank. Although none of these, when joined, make up as much as 25% of any individual pot, their size may, nonetheless, imply only a short period of exposure before they were incorporated in the bank. Furthermore, assuming the bank to have been constructed of material in its immediate vicinity, the discovery of so much pottery within it probably indicates the presence of domestic rubbish accumulating close by.

Hillwash deposits produced an appreciably wider range of pottery, comprising approximately 24% of the thirteenth-fourteenth-century red gritty wares (Fabric 7), and up to 12% of the fifteenth-sixteenth-century reduced greenwares (Fabric 1), although no fabric was particularly dominant. This seems to suggest its accumulation over a prolonged period of soil and rubbish movement down the hillslope.

Layer *1235*, an accumulation beneath the medieval croft (*Ch 4*, *p 94*), contained 96 sherds, of which over half (53%) belong to cooking pots and jugs in thirteenth-fourteenth-century Fabric 4. The presence of only six sherds (6.25%) of Fabric 7 (twelfth-century gritty redware) is of interest, and they should probably be considered alongside the small percentage (13.6%) derived from the overlying levels. Whilst it is impossible to be sure what, if anything, this means, it is clear that the type was not accumulating on this part of the site before or during the occupation of the croft.

Pottery found in the vicinity of the churchyard boundary came from contexts associated with the bank, but beneath the medieval churchyard wall built on top of it. They produced a largely thirteenth-fourteenth-century collection, made up of Fabric 4 jugs and cooking pots (32%), and Fabric 5, almost entirely from rubble spread *1274* (*Ch 4*; 22%), as well as Fabric 6, attributed to the twelfth-fourteenth century. Fabric 7, an especially gritty twelfth-century redware, accounts for only 20%.

The occurrence of several examples (6.8%) of late reduced greenware (Fabric 1), and a single sherd of slightly sandy oxidised Fabric 3, dated to the fourteenth century or after, confirms the fact that the churchyard boundary wall (*28*) survived into the later medieval period. The presence of sherds which join with those from the underlying bank seems to imply that its construction must have entailed some disturbance to the extant bank. The pottery is

otherwise a standard twelfth- to fourteenth-century assemblage, in which Fabric 4 comprises 35% and the earlier fabric, Fabric 7, 24%. The fill (*1421*) of a ditch (*1438*) to the north contained a range of similarly dated pottery, amongst which are sherds from a highly decorated jug.

This area produced the only example of a bowl from the site (Fig 77.20). This is most unusual in being thickly glazed and decorated, both inside and out. Unlike cooking pots and jugs, which are ubiquitous in assemblages of the twelfth-fourteenth century, bowls occur much less frequently and, in some areas, do not seem to exist in earthenware. In Cumbria, it can be inferred, in view of their rarity as a ceramic form, that bowls were usually made from wood.

Pottery incorporated in the collapsed wall just to the north of the churchyard in the east of the site (*Ch 4; 47, 1267*) was almost identical to that in the nearby fill of the boundary ditch (*1421*) to the north. Metalled surfaces and accumulations against the north side of the wall, as well as features related to the medieval croft and its buildings, yielded 296 sherds, in which medieval Fabrics 4-8 are dominant. About 2% can be attributed with confidence to the later fifteenth or sixteenth century, but one of these fabrics (Fabric 1) also came from contexts through which the 'croft' was cut; these may, however, have come from an intrusive feature not seen in excavation. It is noticeable that less than 2% of the total assemblage from these features was associated with postholes and features related to the buildings. In other words, the bulk of the pottery was found in external deposits, which implies that rubbish was not allowed to accumulate inside the buildings. This reflects the practice seen in medieval villages elsewhere in the country (for instance, at Goltho, Lincolnshire; Coppack 1987, 164).

The pottery associated with buildings in the croft comprised the same range of fabrics as in the external assemblage. The earthenware vessels used in the buildings apparently included glazed jugs as the most important single type, with cooking pots as a minor item. This is consistent with the impression gained from Carlisle, as well as in Scotland, that after the initial period of pottery introduction in the twelfth century, when cooking pots were, if not the most important form, then certainly of equal status with jugs, they were gradually supplanted in importance by jugs (McCarthy and Brooks 1992). Indeed, this trend is observable nationally, although in some parts of the country it is less apparent, as pipkins and skillets took the place of the simple cooking pot (McCarthy and Brooks 1988). At Dacre, pipkins have been recognised by two handles (Fig 77.9-10).

The proportion of late medieval reduced greenware (Fabric 1) stands at over 50% of the pottery associated with the final stages and abandonment of the croft. Significantly, it is associated with Fabrics 2 and 9, both thought to date to the sixteenth century. Over 620 sherds of pottery were recovered from deposits associated with demolition debris, or incorporated in soil accumulations, including hillwash overlying the former buildings. Ceramic evidence places the final occupation of the buildings to the fifteenth or sixteenth century, perhaps ending in the sixteenth. The pottery present includes a range of types, the latest being early post-medieval, and includes Staffordshire and possible Low Countries slipwares. Late medieval reduced greenware (Fabric 1), however, at 30%, still provided the largest single element within the group. Whilst it is clear that much of the pottery originated in hillwash, another origin must be sought for some of the remaining material. One possibility is that, if the buildings had cob walls (a common building technique in Cumbria; Jennings 2003), pottery could have become incorporated in the wall when the mud was mixed and applied, being redeposited once the wall collapsed. Several medieval sherds were recovered from the uppermost layers on the site, reflecting the date of the structures beneath, and supporting the idea of abandonment of the settlement at the end of the Middle Ages.

## Site 3: the southern churchyard

Only 29 sherds were recovered from the small excavation in the southern churchyard. The material surrounding the early medieval drain (998) contained a large sherd of fifteenth-sixteenth-century reduced greenware (Fabric 1), whilst another (946) had a fragment from a thirteenth-fourteenth-century Fabric 4 jug. Although it is impossible to date contexts conclusively on the basis of single sherds, it would be reasonable to assume that these features cannot be placed much earlier than the thirteenth century, unless the pottery is intrusive. Much of the pottery from 946, however, including the Fabric 4 jug, came from near the surface, where medieval robbing was evident, and it may therefore relate to this event, rather than the construction of the feature.

## Illustrated catalogue

1    Cooking pot, Fabric 4; partially sooted externally (seven sherds), rim and body (Fig 77).
     Site 2, 1203, layer, Medieval, OR 1994; 1235, layer, Medieval, OR 2082; 1235, layer, Medieval, OR 2472

2    Cooking pot, Fabric 4, rim; patchy pale olive glaze externally (Fig 77).
     Site 2, 1203, layer, Medieval, OR 2057

3    Cooking pot, Fabric 4 (two sherds), square rim (Fig 77).
     Site 2, 1268, layer, Medieval, OR 2177

4    Cooking pot, Fabric 4, rim (Fig 77).
     Site 2, 101, rubble, churchyard boundary bank, Medieval, OR 281

5    Jug, Fabric 4, square rim; partially glazed olive externally (two sherds; Fig 77).
     Site 2, 1267, wall, Medieval, OR 2298

6    Jug, Fabric 4, rim; olive glaze externally, decorated with applied brown pellets and vertical combing (four sherds; Fig 77).
     Site 2, 1177, layer, Medieval, OR 2073

7    Jug, Fabric 4, rim and body; graffito incised before application of brown external glaze (Fig 77).
     Site 1, 40, demolition layer, Medieval/Post-medieval, OR 97

8    Jug, Fabric 4, square rim; abraded olive glaze externally below carination on neck (14 sherds; Fig 77).
     Site 2, 1235, layer, Medieval, OR 2327

9    Pipkin handle, Fabric 4 (Fig 77).
     Site 2, 1177, layer, Medieval, OR 1981

10   Pipkin handle, Fabric 4 (Fig 77).
     Site 2, 152, tumble, churchyard wall, Medieval/Post-medieval, OR 1168

11   Jug, Fabric 5, rim (Fig 77).
     Site 2, 45, surface, Medieval, OR 130

12   Cooking pot, Fabric 6; rim, partially sooted externally (Fig 77).
     Site 2, 1235, layer, Medieval, OR 2185

13   Cooking pot, Fabric 6 (two sherds), rim (Fig 77).
     Site 2, 1380, ditch fill, Medieval, OR 2346

14   Cooking pot, Fabric 6, rim; sooted externally, occasional glaze spot externally (Fig 77).
     Site 2, 1380, ditch fill, Medieval, OR 2361

15   Cooking pot, Fabric 6, rim (Fig 77).
     Site 3, 933, fill, Medieval?, OR 1734

16   Cooking pot, Fabric 6; square rim, splash of olive glaze over the rim (Fig 77).
     Site 2, 1235, layer, Medieval, OR 2186

17   Cooking pot, Fabric 6, square rim (Fig 77); traces of pale yellowish-green glaze on interior towards the base (not drawn; the basal angle does not survive), and occasional glaze spots externally (46 sherds).
     Site 2, 358, churchyard boundary bank, Medieval, OR 1235; 530, churchyard boundary bank, Medieval, OR 1279; 530, churchyard boundary bank, Medieval, OR 1282

18   ?Small cooking pot or jug, Fabric 6, rim (Fig 77); partial brown glaze and sooting externally.
     Site 2, 162, Unstratified, OR 2462

19   ?Small cooking pot or jug, Fabric 6, rim (Fig 77); olive glaze over interior and exterior of rim, and covering the broken surface, making this a probable waster.
     Site 3, 933, fill, Medieval?, OR 1734

20   Bowl, Fabric 6, rim, body, and base; olive glaze and wavy combed decoration internally and externally (26 sherds; Fig 77).

Site 2, *1267*, wall, Medieval, OR 2272; *1380*, ditch fill, Medieval, OR 2370; *1421*, ditch fill, Medieval, OR 2482

21    Cooking pot, Fabric 7 (seven sherds), rim (Fig 77).
      Site 2, *316*, upper fill, churchyard boundary ditch, Medieval, OR 1048

22    Cooking pot, Fabric 7, rim (Fig 77).
      Site 2, *633*, layer, Early Medieval, OR 1464

23    Cooking pot, Fabric 7, rim (Fig 77).
      Site 2, *69*, hillwash, Post-medieval, OR 2497

24    Cooking pot, Fabric 7, rim (Fig 77).
      Site 2, *93*, tumble, churchyard wall, Medieval/Post-medieval, OR 2490

25    Cooking pot, Fabric 7 (two sherds), rim (Fig 77)
      Site 2, *139*, layer, churchyard, Medieval/Post-medieval, OR 624

26    Cooking pot, Fabric 8, rim (Fig 77); sooted externally.
      Site 2, *1269*, layer, Medieval, OR 2313

## The medieval tile

In addition to the pottery, there were 66 fragments of tile. All were from ridge tiles in a fabric resembling Fabric 5 but coarser, with a higher sand content, oxidised surfaces, and reduced cores. No complete tile profile was found, however. Most of the fragments were very small, but many showed traces of a clear lead glaze, especially on the uppermost part of the ridge, although there was no sign of crests or other decorative finials. No fragments of flat roof tiles, or indeed floor tiles, were recognised. It seems, therefore, that the medieval buildings at Dacre were probably roofed with organic materials, protected at the ridge by ceramic tiles. Tiles of this kind are almost impossible to date, although their association with the medieval croft might suggest a general thirteenth-fourteenth-century date.

## The medieval coins

*M M Archibald*

Five silver coins have been identified as medieval, all dating from the late twelfth- to the mid-thirteenth century. Three, all short-cross pennies or cut halfpennies of King John, seem to have been lost during the construction of the north wall of the medieval churchyard (*Ch 4, p 96*); the remaining two are unstratified.

1    HENRY II (1154-89)
     Cut-halfpenny, 'Tealby' type, 1158-80 (Seaby and Seaby 1988, 84), class uncertain but early.
     Mint: London; Moneyer: Ricard or Rodbert.
     Rev: +R (   )N D(?)
     Wt: 0.59 g
     Although an early class (the precise details required for a finer classification are not visible), this coin is considerably worn and so was probably lost during the later period of the currency of the 'Tealby' issue, perhaps *c* 1170-80, although abnormal wear at an early period remains a

possibility.
Site 2, *162*, Unstratified, OR 2003

2    RICHARD I (1189-99)
     Cut-halfpenny, Short Cross type, class 4a (*op cit*, 86).
     Mint: Winchester; Moneyer: uncertain; Osbern or Willelm.
     Rev: +(   ):ON:WIN
     Wt: 0.67 g
     Class 4 is dated 1194-1204, so the earliest group probably falls within the reign of Richard I (*ibid*), although when exactly the sub-types ended has not been established. This is a good, unclipped, halfpenny and not worn, so it was probably lost before 1204, although later survival must be allowed for. In any case, the coin must have been deposited before the Short Cross type was superseded in 1247 (*op cit*, 88).
     Site 2, *162*, Unstratified, OR 636

3    JOHN (1199-1216)
     Penny, Short Cross type, class 5c (*op cit*, 87).
     Mint: London; Moneyer: Abel.
     Rev: +ABEL.ON.LVNDE
     Wt: 1.34 g
     This coin is unclipped but shows some wear. Class 5 was issued between 1205 and 1210, so this coin was probably lost at some time between *c* 1210 and *c* 1230, but a later survival cannot be ruled out until the end of the type in 1247 (*op cit*, 88).
     Site 2, *324*, core of medieval churchyard boundary wall *28*, Medieval, OR 1039

4    JOHN (1199-1216)
     Cut-halfpenny, Short Cross type, class 5b (or, less likely, 5c; *op cit*, 87).
     Mint: Canterbury; Moneyer: Goldwine.
     Rev: +GOLDWINE (   ) very double struck
     Wt: 0.80 g
     The class means that the coin must be by Goldwine of Canterbury (*ibid*) rather than the moneyer of that name at London. Its poor appearance is the result of double striking. This coin is just a little worn and so is likely to have been deposited *c* 1210-30, but a later survival cannot be ruled out.
     Site 2, *315*, tumble from medieval churchyard boundary wall *28*, Medieval, OR 1141

5    JOHN (1199-1216)
     Penny, Short Cross type, class 7b (*op cit*, 88-9).
     Mint: Canterbury; Moneyer: Roger.
     Rev: very double struck, ( ) ROGER ON C ( )
     Wt: 1.18 g (chipped)
     The poor appearance of this coin is a result of poor striking; it is not clipped and is little worn. The dating of the sub-groups of the long-lived class 7 has not been established, so it is not possible to suggest narrow limits for the currency of this penny. It was probably lost within the period *c* 1230-48, and earlier rather than later within that bracket is the more likely.
     Site 2, *315*, tumble from medieval churchyard boundary wall *28*, Medieval, OR 998

## Copper alloy

*D Tweddle and C Howard-Davis*

There is only a small group of medieval copper-alloy objects, comprising three buckle frames and a belt loop (**1-4**), a finger-ring (**5**), two pins (**6-7**), four lace tags (**8-11**), a padlock (**12**), a rumbler bell (**13**), and undiagnostic fragments of sheet metal.

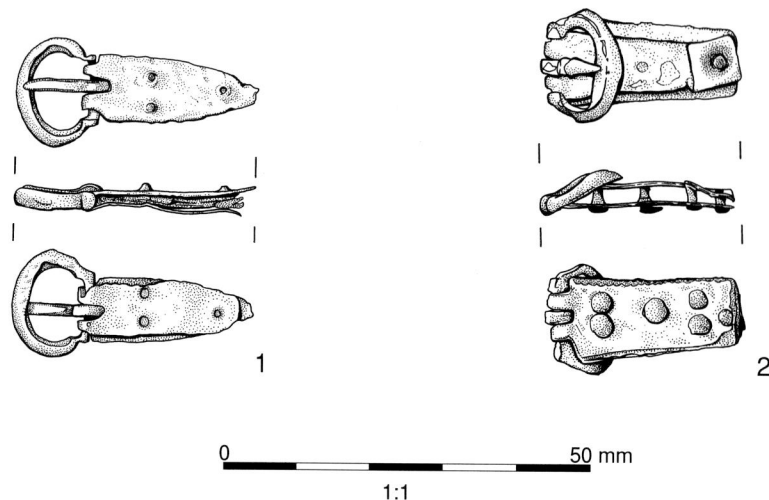

*Figure 78: Copper-alloy buckles*

## Personal adornment

Two buckles were found in rubble spread *1274* on the north side of the earliest churchyard boundary in the east of the site (*Ch 4*). Both (**1** and **2**; Fig 78) probably belong to a common type of single-looped D-shaped buckle with an offset bar, which seems to have come into use in the late twelfth- or early thirteenth century and continued until the late fourteenth century (PAS 2016a). Buckle **1** has three rivets in the buckle plate, and the loop is very close in form to Meols type 2, examples (such as SOM-BB843B; PAS 2017a) being well known. In contrast, buckle **2** has been gilded, and there is a smoother junction with the offset pin bar. It also has a moulding at the junction between the loop and shaft of the pin, and five rivets in the plate, all of which make it remarkably similar in form to a buckle from the Somerset area (WILT-DDE14C (PAS 2017b). The Dacre example seems to have undergone a rudimentary repair to the strap attachment, with an additional rivet and plate section added on the back of the buckle plate.

1      Buckle. The loop, of D-shaped section, is roughly oval, with the inner ends projecting a short distance at right-angles and joined by the straight pin bar. The buckle plate is folded over the offset pin bar and its corners are cut away to accommodate the ends of the loop. There is a rectangular slot for the tongue; towards the opposite end the plate tapers. The leather strap, probably *c* 14 mm wide, was held in place by three copper-alloy rivets, one at the narrow end, and a pair half-way along the length of the plate. The wire tongue is simply folded around the pin bar. It is likely to date to the twelfth- to fourteenth century.
L: 32.9 mm; W: 14 mm; Th: 4 mm
Site 2, *1274*, churchyard boundary bank, Medieval, OR 2239

2      Buckle, gilded. The loop is oval and of plano-convex section, tapering towards the junction with the straight pin bar. The loop and the pin bar are separated by projecting cuboids. The tongue is folded over the pin bar and is parallel-sided before being shouldered, and then tapers to a point. The buckle plate is formed from a single sheet folded over the pin bar with a slot cut for the tongue, and shoulders cut to accommodate the cuboid projections. The strap was held in place by five copper-alloy rivets. The front of the buckle plate tapers towards a square end and is decorated with an undulating incised line paralleling the edge. The rear plate is narrower and tapers more sharply. At the far end, a separate rectangular copper-alloy sheet has been riveted on from the back. The single copper-alloy rivet penetrates the front face.
L: 26.8 mm; W: 14.9 mm; Th: 4.4 mm
Site 2, *377*, churchyard boundary bank, Medieval, OR 1172

An unstratified detached buckle loop (**3**, Fig 79) is most probably of medieval date. It is essentially oval, with one slightly straightened side forming the pin bar, from each end of which develops a short oblique projection or ear. It appears to be a well-known if not particularly common form, probably of the fourteenth century (Whitehead 2003), with examples from London, where the form is assigned a mid-fourteenth- to mid-fifteenth-century date (Egan and Pritchard 1991, fig 11, fig 43, no 285), and from The Bedern, York (Ottaway and Rogers 2002, fig 1466, no 14304).

3      Copper-alloy buckle loop. It is oval, with a pointed ovoid section. The pin bar is straight and at each end is a stubby oblique projection.
L: 26.7 mm; W: 20.2 mm; Th: 2.1 m
Site 3, *835*, backfill of excavation trench, Modern, OR 1641

Object **4**, from late medieval accumulation *1016* in the northern churchyard (*Ch 4, p 110*), is a D-shaped strap loop. A broadly similar example from Winchester came from a sixteenth- to eighteenth-century context (Hinton 1990, fig 143, no 1362), but the form, effectively a buckle without a pin bar, appeared in Winchester and elsewhere during the fourteenth century (*ibid*). The discontinuous projections may have allowed the accommodation of a strap with the relatively bulky decorative metal mounts fashionable at that time (Egan and Pritchard 1991, 231).

124

3   4

5

0 _____ 50 mm
1:1

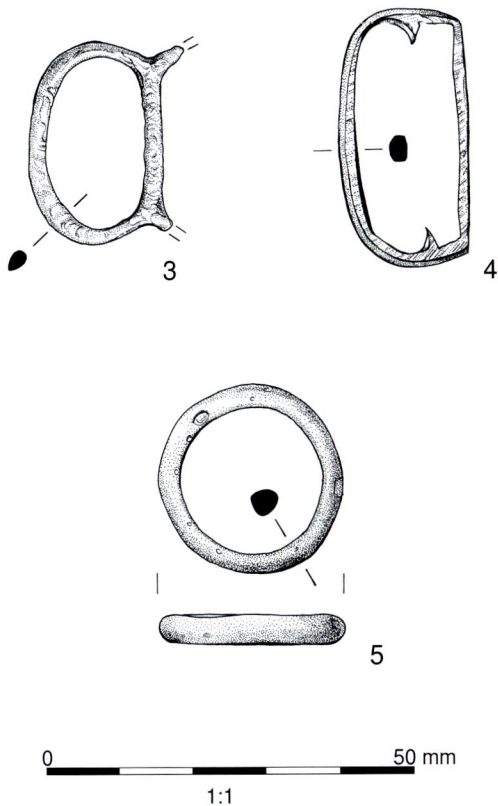

*Figure 79: Copper-alloy buckle, strap loop, and ring*

4   D-shaped strap loop. The straight bar is of rectangular
    section, the loop of D-shaped section. Small, pointed
    projections jut from the inside at each end of the loop,
    close to the junction with the pin bar.
    L: 33.9 mm; W: 17.7 mm; Th: 3.8 mm
    Site 2, *1016*, decay of the croft, Late medieval, OR 1855

The ring (**5**), from medieval hillwash, has a D-shaped
cross-section, but is otherwise undecorated. The
section allows it to be identified as a finger-ring, as
medieval brooches, which are often of approximately
the same size, have a flat or circular profile, not
the D-shape seen here (Egan and Pritchard 1991).
The context of this find suggests a medieval date,
but the simplicity of the object makes closer dating
impossible.

5   Copper-alloy finger-ring of D-shaped section.
    Undecorated.
    Diam: 25.4 mm; Th: 4.3 mm
    Site 2, *121*, hillwash, Medieval, OR 1358

There are two dress pins (**6-7**), both with double-
wound heads, although they vary somewhat in size.
Such pins were produced in England from the late
thirteenth century onwards, but they were mostly
imported from Europe, in huge numbers, with the
trade continuing well into the post-medieval period
(Egan and Forsyth 1997, 224). They were used in
large quantities in day-to-day life (*ibid*), as well being
used as shroud pins, and large numbers have been
recovered, for example, from the cemetery of the

0      10 mm

*Plate 48: Copper-alloy wound-headed pin* **6**

church of St Helen-on-the-Walls, York, which went
out of use in 1549-50 (Dawes and Magilton 1980). In
general, the longer the pin, the more likely it is to
be medieval, and it is of significance that the longer
of the two is from an early context in the north-east
corner of the Orchard (*58*; *Ch 2, p 40*). Heads that have
been rendered spherical by crimping, like the other
pin, are most likely to be sixteenth- to seventeenth
century in date (Oakley and Webster 1979, 260).

6   Copper-alloy pin with a double-wound head (Pl 48).
    L: 40.1 mm; Diam (head): 3 mm
    Site 1, *58*, layer, Early medieval?, OR 157

7   Copper-alloy pin with a double-wound head.
    L: 27.8 mm; Diam (head): 1.9 mm
    Site 2, *90*, demolition, churchyard boundary, Post-
    medieval, OR 978

There are also four lace tags or aglets (**8-11**), all from
medieval and later contexts in the Orchard. They
are all made from sheet metal, rolled into a tapering
tube around the lace and probably held in place by
a rivet at the open end, although, with the exception
of **8** from layer *52*, this does not survive. They are a
common form, corresponding to Type 1 of Oakley's
typology (Oakley and Wester 1979), and can be dated,
in the main, to the fifteenth or sixteenth century, when
they appear to have been used in abundance (Egan
and Forsyth 1997, 224), although use continued at a
low level into the following century, and some are
known from seventeenth-century contexts. A wider
date-range has been suggested, however; at King
John's Hunting Lodge, Writtle, Essex, for example,
lace tags were found in all the major phases spanning
the period 1211-1521 (Rahtz 1969, 87, fig 49, 86-92).
In this case, however, a fifteenth-century date would
not seem inappropriate.

*Plate 49: Copper-alloy lace tags 8 and 9*

8    Copper-alloy lace tag (Pl 49). It takes the form of a piece
     of sheet rolled into a slightly tapering tube, with a rivet
     through the widest end.
     L: 24.2 mm; Diam: 2 mm
     Site 1, *52*, layer, Early Medieval/Medieval, OR 163

9    Copper-alloy lace tag. It consists of a sheet-metal tube,
     tapering towards the lower end, and roughly broken away
     at the upper end.
     L: 21.3 mm; Diam: 3.4 mm
     Site 1, *21*, demolition material, Medieval/Post-medieval, OR 6

10   Copper-alloy lace tag similar to **8**, though bent (Pl 49).
     L: 24.2 mm; Diam: 3.4 mm
     Site 1, *21*, demolition material, Medieval/Post-medieval,
     OR 89

11   Copper-alloy lace tag similar to **8**.
     L: 16.2 mm; Diam: 2.9 mm
     Site 1, *18*, churchyard boundary wall, Medieval, OR 84

**Domestic objects**
There are few domestic objects, of which a padlock
case (**12**; Fig 80) came from the upper silting of the
medieval churchyard boundary ditch (*1439*) in the
northern churchyard. A small harness bell or rumbler
(**13**) was recovered from the medieval churchyard
wall (*28*) in the same area.

The padlock case is of octagonal section, with
the barrel decorated with rocker ornament. Such
padlocks, in a number of different forms and with
slightly differing mechanisms, were widely used
from the pre-Conquest period and on into the later
Middle Ages (PAS 2019), examples being known
both in copper alloy and iron, the latter often
tinned or brazed. An octagonal example similar
to this padlock, though lacking the decoration,
came from a thirteenth-century context in London
(Egan 1998, 93, fig 66, no 244). Perhaps the closest
parallel is, however, that from North Elmham,
Norfolk, though unstratified (Wade-Martins 1980,
502, fig 263.3), and there is a similar example from
Goltho, Northamptonshire, dated only to the late
medieval period (Beresford 1975, 93, fig 94.91), while
an example from Rayleigh, Essex, is dated more
closely to *c* 1070-1350 (Francis 1913, 163-4, pl B.I).
This evidence confirms a later medieval date for the
Dacre example, but does little to refine it further.

Object **13** (Pl 50) is the upper half of a spherical
rumbler bell made from sheet metal. Two-piece bells
like this example, soldered at the central joint, and
characteristically with no holes in the upper body,
seem to have been introduced in the late thirteenth
century, falling out of use in the fifteenth century
(Egan and Pritchard 1991, 336-7; Goodall 1981). It
is probable that this example derives from a horse
harness, but similar bells were also used on dog
collars and on belts, at least in the fifteenth century
(Goodall 1980, 70), as well as on other clothing (Egan
and Pritchard 1991, 336-7).

12   Cylindrical padlock. The case is of octagonal section and
     tapers slightly. Each of the lower three faces of the exterior
     is decorated with an incised line in parallel with the ends.
     Inside these is an undecorated zone, separated, by more
     incised transverse lines, from a field decorated with a single
     line of rocker ornament. A T-shaped slot in the wider end
     admitted the key and at this end, from the upper face,
     emerges a parallel-sided fin. At the upper end, this joins
     on to a bar of circular section, originally paralleling the
     case, but now largely broken away. A circular plate fits
     into the narrow end of the case, within the top of which

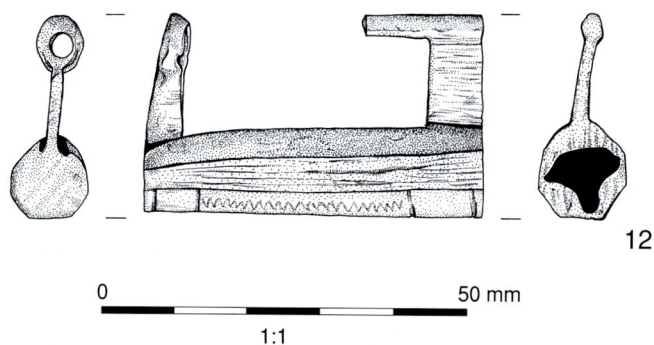

0                                                    50 mm

1:1

*Figure 80: Copper-alloy padlock*

*Plate 50: Rumbler bell*

is a narrow projecting fin accommodated by a slot in the upper face of the case. This fin terminates in a circular loop, which originally fitted over the end of the lost circular bar in parallel with the case.
L: 46 mm; W: 27 mm; Th: 12 mm
Site 2, *1439*, fill of churchyard boundary ditch, Medieval, OR 2388

13    Rumbler bell. It has a projecting moulding around the lower edge, and a D-shaped suspension loop is soldered on to the top. The whole is crushed and the lower hemisphere is now missing.
Ht: 13 mm; W: 22 mm; Th: 13 mm
Site 2, *28*, churchyard boundary wall, Medieval, OR 974

The group of copper-alloy finds of medieval date is small, and largely of a personal nature. They probably represent casual losses on a site of considerably reduced prosperity when compared to that of the early medieval activity (*Ch 3*). This implies that the nature of the site had changed radically from the pre-Conquest period, with the medieval metalwork appreciably poorer both in quality and quantity.

## Ironwork
*P Ottaway*

The majority of the recognisably medieval material was of a domestic nature (Fig 81), being mostly identified from X-ray only (see *Appendix 2* for a complete catalogue). Object **305** is a strap terminal, probably part of the fittings of a small box, of later medieval date. There is a small pruning hook (**6**), and several knives (**7-12**) are represented. One (**8**) is a scale-tang knife of late- or post-medieval date. Object **3** is a wool-comb tooth, similar to those from the earlier phases of the site. Objects **20**, a strike-a-light, and **21**,

a socketed candleholder, may be of medieval or post-medieval date. Object **346** is a key of late medieval type.

Whilst not precisely datable, several tools were recovered from medieval contexts, and three, **1** (a punch), **4** (a small drawknife), and **5** (a small auger or spoon bit), are metal- or woodworking tools. Two large and crudely made door hinges, **337** and **338**, are probably of medieval or early post-medieval date.

Two of the horseshoes, **369** and **376**, have the characteristic wavy edge, which suggests a twelfth- to thirteenth-century date (Clark 1995, 95-6, figs 80-1). Two of the four arrowheads (**378** and **380**) are of the thirteenth- to fifteenth centuries, used for hunting, while arrowhead **381** is medieval. Object **379** is the tip of an arrow of a type used in a longbow of late medieval date (Ottaway and Rogers 2002, 2969).

1       A tanged punch consisting of a tapering tang and working arm (Fig 81). The latter has a rounded tip.
L: 128 mm; W: 11 mm
Site 2, *46*, stone spread, Medieval, OR 159

3       A wool-comb tooth, with a rounded cross-section and a missing head.
L: 70 mm; W: 2 mm
Site 2, *359*, churchyard boundary bank, Medieval, OR 1278

4       A drawknife blade, with a tang projecting upwards on each end (Fig 81). It is now incomplete.
L: 59 mm; W: 16 mm; Th: 8 mm
Site 2, *355*, churchyard boundary bank, Medieval, OR 1150

5       A spoon bit or auger with a missing tip and a short triangular tang (Fig 81).
L: 96 mm; W: 15 mm; Th: 6 mm
Site 2, *36*, hillwash, Medieval/Post-medieval, OR 1818

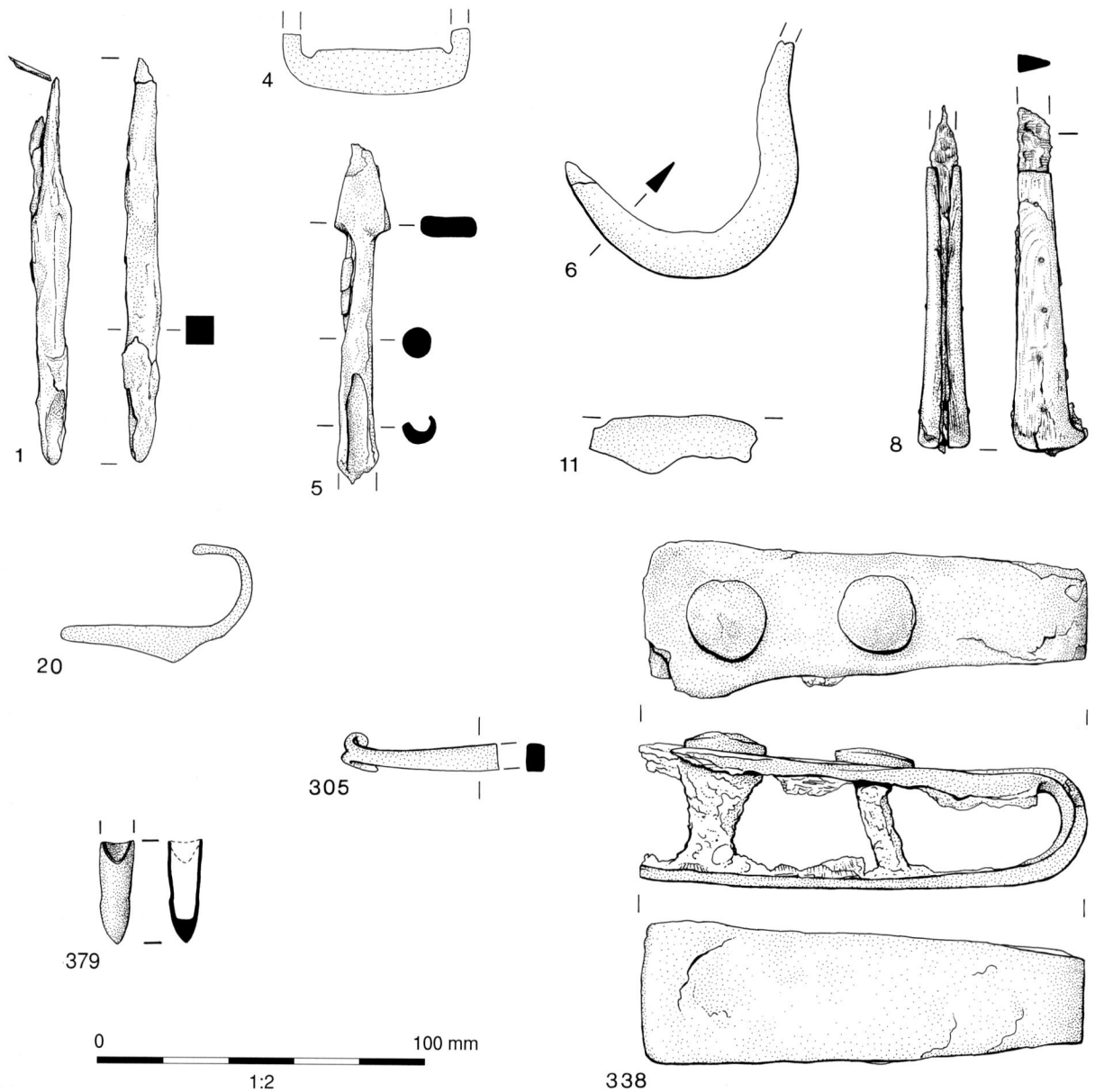

*Figure 81: Iron objects*

6    A pruning hook with a C-shaped blade (Fig 81). The cutting edge is on the concave side, and the tang is incomplete.
L: 46 mm; W: 10 mm
Site 2, *310*, stone spread, Medieval, OR 99

7    Two fragmented knives were found in association. The first consists of a short piece of a blade and bolster. The second is a blade with a convex back, straight cutting edge, and a missing tip. Only a fragment of the tang survives.
i) L: 47 mm; W: 14 mm
ii) L: 52 mm; W: 20 mm; Th: 5 mm
Site 1, *52*, layer, Early Medieval/Medieval, OR 181

8    A knife fragment with a scale tang (Fig 81), the handle held in place with five non-ferrous rivets. The blade is largely missing.
L: 115 mm; W: 12 mm
Site 1, *21*, demolition material, Medieval/Post-medieval, OR 100

9    A knife fragment consisting of a blade and incomplete tang. The object is very corroded.
L: 40 mm; W: 14 mm; Th: 5 mm
Site 2, *151*, churchyard boundary bank, Eleventh/twelfth century, OR 376

10   A fragment of knife blade.
L: 39 mm; W: 10 mm; Th: 3 mm
Site 2, *534*, churchyard boundary bank, Medieval, OR 1389

11   A knife fragment consisting of a blade, broken at the junction with the tang (Fig 81). The back is straight, before it curves down towards a missing tip. The cutting edge is S-shaped.
L: 54 mm; W: 16 mm; Th: 6 mm
Site 2, *178*, stone spread, Medieval, OR 618

12   A knife fragment consisting of a blade with a straight back, which curves down towards a missing tip. The cutting edge is corroded and the tang is incomplete.
L: 42 mm; L (blade): 32 mm; W: 14 mm; Th: 6 mm
Site 2, *1235*, layer, Medieval, OR 2213

20   A strike-a-light consisting of a slim striking plate, with a curved arm on one end (Fig 81).
L: 60 mm; W (across arm): 34 mm; Th: 4 mm
Site 2, *310*, stone spread, Medieval, OR 1002

21   A candleholder consisting of an incomplete shank with a socket on one end.
L: 70 mm; L (socket): 20 mm; Diam: 25 mm
Site 2, *1016*, Decay of croft, Medieval/Post-medieval, OR 1909

305   A strap, broken at one end, narrows towards the other, where there is a bifurcated terminal, the arms of which are recurved (Fig 81).
L: 58 mm; W: 8 mm; Th: 3 mm
Site 2, *26*, Topsoil, Post-medieval, OR 1206

337   A U-eyed hinge, the straps widening away from the eye. Each strap is pierced twice, the nails still *in situ*.
L:137 mm; W: 45 mm; W (straps): 52 mm; L (nails): 52 mm, 43 mm; W (heads): 22 mm, 30 mm; Th (shanks): 6 mm
Site 2, *1204*, surface, Medieval, OR 2439

338   A U-eyed hinge (Fig 81). The straps widen away from the eye. Each strap is pierced twice, the nails still *in situ*. There are wood remains.
L: 133 mm; W: 39 mm; W (straps): 45 mm; L (nails): 44 mm; W (heads): 24 mm; Th (shanks): 8 mm
Site 2, *1204*, surface, Medieval, OR 2440

346   Key, the bow largely missing. The stem is solid up to the tip, where it is hollow. The bit is incomplete.
L: 50 mm; W (at bit): 15 mm; Th (stem): 6 mm
Site 2, *1197*, stone spread, Medieval, OR 2091

369   The branch end of a horseshoe. This has a wavy outer edge and two countersunk holes.
L: 55 mm; W: 16 mm
Site 2, *147*, fill of grave, Post-medieval, OR 362

376   The branch end of a horseshoe. It probably has a wavy edge, part of one countersunk hole, and a calkin.
L: 53 mm; W: 23 mm; Th: 8 mm
Site 2, *162*, Unstratified, OR 2432

378   Barbed and socketed arrowhead.
L: 50 mm; W (blade): 19 mm; Diam (socket): 8 mm
Site 2, *121*, hillwash, Medieval, OR 471

379   Arrowhead, socketed and bullet-shaped (Fig 81). It has been copper plated.
L: 30 mm; Diam: 10 mm
Site 2, *36*, hillwash, Medieval/Post-medieval, OR 1203

380   Barbed and socketed arrowhead.
L: 62 mm; W (blade): 20 mm; Diam (socket): 10 mm
Site 2, *36*, hillwash, Medieval/Post-medieval, OR 1811

381   Socketed, tapering blade, with a rectangular cross-section.
L: 105 mm; Diam (socket): 15 mm
Site 2, *139*, churchyard layer, Medieval/Post-medieval, OR 873

## Lead
### Window kame
*H Quartermaine*

Window kame, recognised by its diagnostic H-shaped section, was found in both medieval and later contexts, although the majority was unstratified. It has been broadly dated on the basis of the depth of its section, following the typology proposed by Knight (1985). In general terms, medieval kame is cast and has a shallow H-shaped section, whilst post-medieval/modern examples are generally milled, and have a much deeper and narrower cross-section. Using these criteria, fragment 1 (Fig 82) and other unstratified fragments are probably medieval in date, whilst 2 (from a late layer (*24*) in the Orchard; *Ch 4, p 114*), though post-medieval, might be earlier rather than later in the period, as it is unlike the narrow H-shaped nineteenth-century pieces, such as 3 (from the post-medieval churchyard (*139*)), and other unstratified pieces, which are post-medieval or modern. All of that identified as medieval is covered by a thick layer of white corrosion products, whilst much of that regarded as more modern is almost unaffected.

The flanges on the medieval examples are only 1-2 mm deep and have been cast, whilst on the later fragments they are considerably deeper (*c* 3 mm), and, having been milled, the flanges are much less robust. Only one unstratified example (4) gives

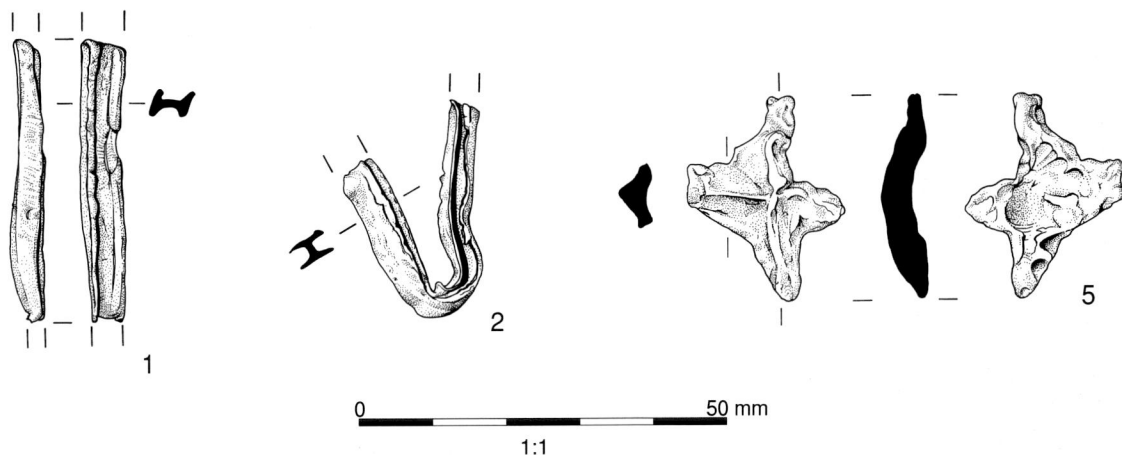

*Figure 82: Lead window kames and ventilator grill*

any indication of the shape of the glass quarry which it supported; it appears to be an extempore repair to the corner of a broken quarry, probably triangular in shape, which has been patched with thin lead sheet.

1    Kame fragment with distorted H-profile (Fig 82).
     L: 32 mm; Th: 1 mm
     Site 1, *52*, layer, Medieval?, OR 184

2    Kame fragment (Fig 82), bent. Probably post-medieval.
     L: 52 mm; Th: 3 mm
     Site 1, *24*, layer, Post-medieval, OR 10

3    Fragment of window kame, post-medieval or modern.
     L: 71 mm; Th: 3.5 mm
     Site 2, *139*, churchyard layer, Medieval/Post-medieval, OR 359

4    A corner fragment of window kame framing remnants of thin lead sheeting and glass (Pl 51).
     L: 45 mm; Th: 21 mm
     Site 2, *162*, Unstratified, OR 1633

*Plate 51: Fragment of lead kame with an apparent patch*

## Ventilator grille

Object **5**, from medieval layer *1235* in the northern churchyard (*Ch 4, p 94*), appears to be a small fragment from a cast-lead window ventilator. Complete examples of these decorative grilles are known widely, for instance, from Battle Abbey (Hare 1985), and, in the North West, Norton Priory in Cheshire (Brown and Howard-Davis 2008, 401, fig 279), amongst many others.

5    A cross-shaped cast fragment without an H-shaped profile (Fig 82).
     L: 23 mm; W: 21 mm; Th: 7 mm
     Site 2, *1235*, layer, Medieval, OR 2404

## Sheeting and other items used in construction

It appears possible to divide the lead sheet tentatively on the basis of thickness, two groups being identified:

sheet 1-2 mm thick, which includes narrow strips, off-cuts from the production of such strips, and perforated sheet; and heavier-gauge sheet, 2.5-3.5 mm thick. It is not impossible that the sheet was cast on site, as required, although there is no archaeological evidence to support this.

Five of these fragments may have been used as flashing, or are scraps of roof covering, as they have been pierced by substantial nails. Three further pieces are of a similar nature but have no nail holes. Almost all of them have been carefully folded, perhaps indicating that they had been removed and replaced in the course of repairs and, as scrap, were intended for recycling. The stratified material all came from medieval contexts in the vicinity of the medieval northern churchyard boundary.

Fourteen off-cuts with at least one tool-cut edge, 11 fragments of strip, and five torn fragments were recognised. Several of the narrow strips had probably been used as ties, and two further pieces seem to have been discards from the production of such strips. Two other strip fragments had been folded.

Three objects were formed from tightly rolled sheet which was then cut with a sharp tool, two being covered with mortar. This clearly suggests their use as galleting in a mortared wall. The majority of this material was unstratified, but several ties and off-cuts were from medieval contexts in the northern churchyard.

6    Off-cut with remnants of three cut strips (Fig 83).
     Th: 2 mm
     Site 2, *32*, hillwash, Medieval, OR 52

7    Off-cut of rolled or tightly folded sheeting (Fig 83).
     Th: 2.5 mm
     Site 2, *162*, Unstratified, OR 1714

Apart from roofing nails, which bear a strong resemblance to those from Monkwearmouth and Jarrow (Type IV, Trueman 1985, 12 and fig 1), little of the lead can be identified. Several objects are probably wedges used in masonry and **8** may be a leaden cap for a nail, or alternatively packing for a button or decorative nail head.

8    Hemispherical object with a hollow centre (Fig 83). Possibly a protective or decorative cap.
     Diam (base): 13.5 mm; Th: 8.5 mm
     Site 2, *162*, Unstratified, OR 1012

## Thin lead discs

Object **9**, from the upper material in the boundary bank (*96; Ch 4, p 91*) of the medieval churchyard, is the most complete item from a group of thin lead discs. It is a thin disc of sheet metal, 52 mm in diameter, with a small perforation (*c* 2 mm

130

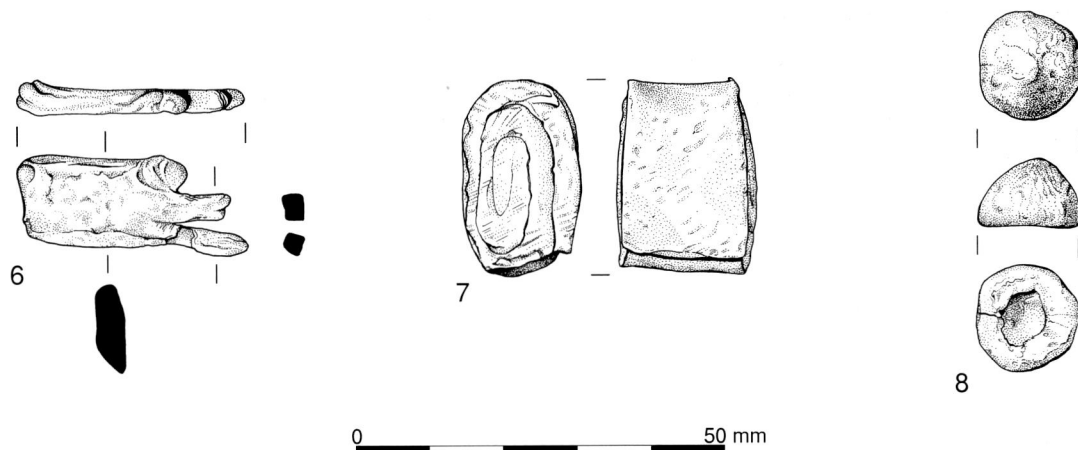

*Figure 83: Other lead objects*

in diameter) close to the edge; despite the considerable distortion, it possibly bears a crude repoussé cross. It is clear that **12** also had a single nail hole. Neither **10** nor **11** are complete enough to establish whether they were perforated, but their overall similarity suggests that it was likely. The function of these pieces is not obvious, although the possible decoration on **9** implies a religious significance, perhaps a pilgrim token. They appear to have been intended to pivot on a single nail or rivet, perhaps acting as loose covers. It is not impossible that they were crude seals, but none bear inscriptions and it is perhaps more likely that they were intended to protect more fragile wax seals, or that they performed some more practical function, such as closing a door spy-hole; it is interesting to note that **12** is distorted as if

torn upwards from its pivot. Such interpretations, however, must remain tentative.

9    Circular sheet of lead with a single perforation (Fig 84). This may be a seal or cover pivoting on a single rivet or nail.
     Diam: 52 mm; Th: 1 mm; Diam (perf): 2 mm
     Site 2, *96*, churchyard boundary bank, Eleventh/twelfth century, OR 274

10   Circular sheet fragment (Fig 84). No perforation.
     Diam (estimate): 40 mm; Th: 1.5 mm
     Site 2, *122*, hillwash, Medieval, OR 968

11   Circular sheet with some probably accidental score marks and associated stress marks (Fig 84). This piece has no perforation but bears a strong resemblance to **9**.
     Diam: 45 mm; Th: 1-1.5 mm
     Site 2, *139*, churchyard layer, Medieval/Post-medieval, OR 359b

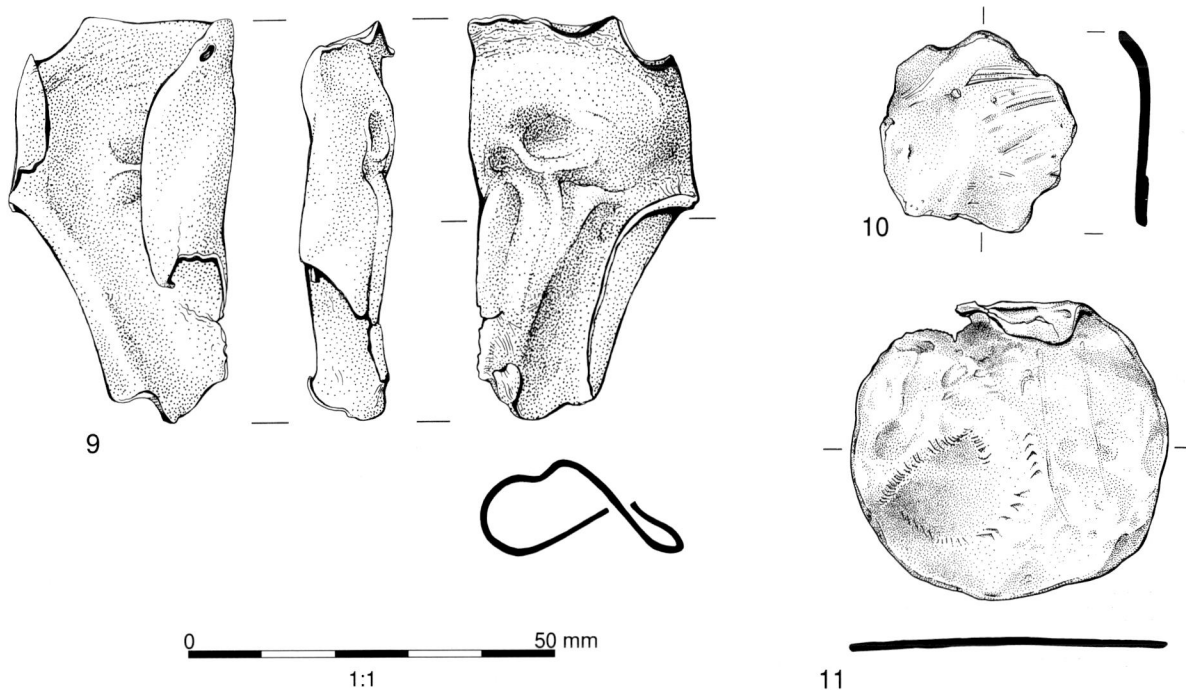

*Figure 84: Circular lead discs*

131

12      Curved sheeting, torn. Undecorated.
Diam (estimate): *c* 40 mm; Th: 1 mm; Diam (perf): 2 mm
Site 2, *90*, demolition of churchyard boundary wall, Post-medieval, OR 1118

## Pricket candleholder

Object **13** (Fig 85), from a lower level of the medieval churchyard boundary bank (*359; Ch 4, p 91*), can be identified as the weighted base of a simple pricket candleholder, as the remnant of an iron spike is set in the lead base. A second, similar, though less complete, object came from the medieval churchyard wall (*28; Ch 4, p 96*) on top of the bank. These seem to have been in relatively widespread use during the medieval period, and a somewhat more elegant stone example, still retaining its central iron spike, is known from Nonsuch Palace (Goodall 2005, fig 190.97).

13      Pricket candleholder or stand. A truncated pyramid in form, it has a central circular depression, *c* 5 mm deep, in the upper surface. An iron shaft is fixed within this depression.
L (base): 54 mm; W: 51 mm; Th: 20 mm; L (top): 26 mm; W (top): 25 mm; Wt: 380 g
Site 2, *359*, churchyard boundary bank, Medieval, OR 1308

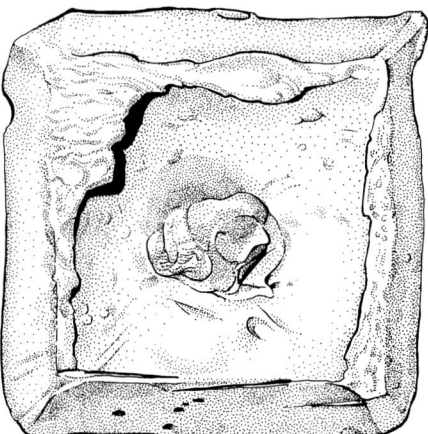

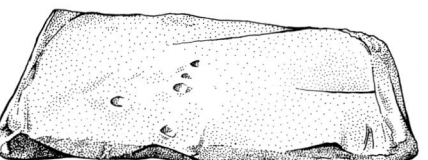

56

```
0 _____ 50 mm
        1:1
```

*Figure 85: Pricket candleholder or stand*

14      Square object with one complete edge. The centre of the upper surface has a circular recess. On the complete side, a thin square sheet, 7 x 7 mm, had been fixed when soft. On the base is an area of copper-alloy corrosion. The object seems to be a stand or holder.
L: 34 mm; Th: 11 mm
Site 2, *28*, churchyard wall, Medieval, OR 1060

The remainder of the lead is largely unidentifiable. It probably represents utilised off-cuts, discard, and accidental loss of scrap in the course of day-to-day maintenance or building work.

## Glass

*H Quartermaine*

### Vessel glass

There are three small fragments (**1-3**) of vessel glass in a greenish-natural metal, two of them heavily weathered. All three are probably fragments of small 'ribbed and wrythen' beakers, although their extremely small size precludes confident identification. Such beakers were most common in the late sixteenth- and seventeenth centuries (Willmott 2002, type 4) and were a well-attested product of the northern glasshouses (Crossley and Aberg 1972; Hurst Vose 1994; 1995). Two of the fragments (**1-2**) came from the Orchard, both from late contexts (*23* and *21*), from the same as the majority of the post-medieval window glass, thus reinforcing the date of deposition for that material. The third fragment was from a medieval layer (*310*) on the terrace edge in the northern churchyard (*Ch 4, p 97*).

1      Rim fragment in thin natural pale green vessel glass with spiral ribbing (Pl 52). Late sixteenth or seventeenth century.
Site 1, *21*, demolition material, Post-medieval, OR 9

2      Body fragment of very thin moulded vessel glass. Weathered but possibly originally tinged blue-green. Late sixteenth or seventeenth century.
Site 1, *23*, layer, Post-medieval, OR 2619

3      Fragment of very thin natural olive-green vessel glass with internal bubbling, and moulded ribbing. Late sixteenth or seventeenth century.
Site 2, *310*, rubble spread, Eleventh/twelfth century, OR 1003

### Window glass

Only ten fragments of later medieval window glass were found, nine from the Orchard (from garden soil (*7, 11*) or later layers (*21, 40*)). All were plain quarry fragments and all but the single fragment from a late demolition layer (*1190*) in the northern churchyard (**12**) were very badly weathered, in the manner typical of the products of the northern glass houses (Willmott 2002, 7). It was not possible to ascertain the method of manufacture but the thinness of the glass can be taken to imply a date in the latest part of the medieval period, perhaps the fifteenth or sixteenth century. The fragments from the Orchard came from a very localised area (6 x 4 m) in the north-eastern part of

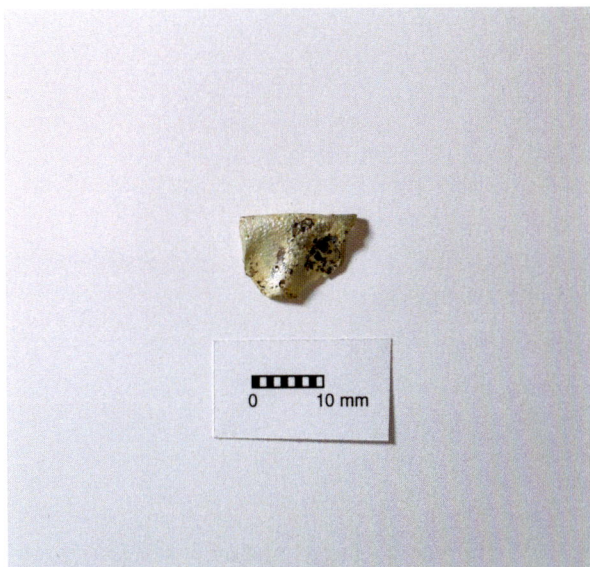

*Plate 52: Rim fragment (1) of a glass vessel*

the site, and were associated with the demolition of the small structure there (*Ch 4, p 115*).

4    One fragment in thin natural greenish glass. Poor condition, brown sugary weathering.
L: 32 mm; W: 19 mm; Th: 1 mm
Site 1, *7*, layer, Post-medieval, OR 90

5    One quarry fragment in thin natural greenish glass. Poor condition, brown sugary weathering. One edge grozed.
L: 29 mm; W: 16 mm; Th: 1.5 mm
Site 1, *21*, demolition material, Post-medieval, OR 7

6    One fragment in thin natural greenish glass. Poor condition, brown sugary weathering.
L: 30 mm; W: 18 mm; Th: 1.5 mm
Site 1, *21*, demolition material, Post-medieval, OR 8

7    One quarry fragment in thin natural greenish glass. Poor condition, brown sugary weathering. One edge grozed.
L: 24 mm; W: 22 mm; Th: 2 mm
Site 1, *21*, demolition material, Post-medieval, OR 88

8    One quarry fragment in thin natural greenish glass. Poor condition, brown sugary weathering. One edge grozed.
L: 30 mm; W: 21 mm; Th: 1.5 mm
Site 1, *21*, demolition material, Post-medieval, OR 102a

9    Two fragments in thin natural greenish glass. Poor condition, brown sugary weathering. One edge of one fragment grozed.
i) L: 23 mm; W: 13 mm; Th: 1 mm
ii) L: 11 mm; W: 13 mm; Th: 1 mm
Site 1, *40*, demolition material, Post-medieval, OR 98

10    One quarry fragment in natural greenish glass. Poor condition, brown sugary weathering.
L: 26 mm; W: 20 mm; Th: 4 mm
Site 1, *40*, demolition material, Post-medieval, OR 1104a

11    One quarry fragment in natural greenish glass. Poor condition, brown sugary weathering. Thickness uneven. Grozed along thickest edge.
L: 31 mm; W: 21 mm; Th: 1-1.5 mm
Site 1, *11*, garden soil, Post-medieval, OR 2620

12    One small fragment in natural greenish glass. Good condition, slight weathering, slightly abraded. One edge part-grozed.
L: 15.5 mm; W: 11.5 mm; Th: 1.5 mm
Site 2, *1190*, stone spread, Medieval, OR 1997

## The Post-medieval Artefacts

### The pottery
*A J White*

The late pottery (1646 sherds) represents a useful sample of the post-medieval ceramics made, or available, in this part of Cumbria over a period of some five centuries. There is nothing momentous in the assemblage, and the circumstances of the site do not suggest any important structural events in the period, although the presence of some small sherds of terracotta is interesting, perhaps coming from a structure such as a tomb, rather than a vessel. There are, however, several sherds of imported sixteenth- and seventeenth-century German stoneware, and a single sherd from a Martincamp flask, probably imported from Northern France (Jennings 1981). Elsewhere in England, these are relatively common finds on sites of all levels of status, but in the North West their relative scarcity makes them worthy of note. Another significant feature is the quantity of slip-trailed black- and brown-glazed earthenware which cannot as yet be ascribed to particular kilns, and which may well have had a local, as yet undiscovered, source. Penrith or Kirkoswald are likely sources, being, respectively, five (8 km) and 14 miles (22 km), to the north-east.

The great majority of sherds are from utilitarian vessels in a coarse earthenware, glazed brown or black, depending on the iron content. Such vessels exhibit little development over a period of centuries and seem to have been made very widely. They are virtually impossible to attribute to particular kilns, and some of them may, indeed, have been produced in local brickyards.

In general, the presence of much of the material is explicable as the results of accumulated hillwash, the encroachment of the churchyard on earlier secular rubbish tips, the dumping of broken vessels from church-ales or the like, and the attrition of pots of all types used as flower holders on graves, or in the church itself. There are many sherd-joins between different contexts.

### The clay tobacco pipes
*A J White*

Only four of the 212 fragments of clay tobacco pipe were marked, two having the very common incuse 'TW' mark, which belongs to the late nineteenth century and probably represents a Glasgow maker adopting a stamp first used in Edinburgh (Gallagher 2016). One stem mark, 'THE MEERSCHAUM', is a type name of the same period, while the single marked seventeenth-century example is fragmentary. It was almost certainly by the 'IB' maker or makers who cannot now be identified, but it is a bulbous type probably from the Rainford area of South Lancashire (Higgins 2015). There are several other bulbous seventeenth- to early eighteenth-century bowls, but none with marks.

Apart from Lancaster, Whitehaven, and north Cumbria, there seem to have been no local manufacturers to serve the Lake District and its environs until the nineteenth century. It is likely that Liverpool and south Lancashire provided most of the needs before *c* 1700. One 'navvy' pipe may be of Irish origin, but the style was much copied in England.

## The post-medieval coins and token
*A J White*
The earliest post-medieval coin is of 1560-1, in the reign of Elizabeth I, and there is one seventeenth-century coin, of James I or Charles I, both from hillwash in the northern churchyard. The relatively high proportion of coins of George II is perhaps of note, though these are in any case disproportionately common (University of Notre Dame 1997, 3). Equally, the absence of any coins of George III or any contemporary tokens is a little curious. Most of the copper-alloy coins are in poor condition. Loss of surface appears in general to be due to soil conditions rather than wear.

## Post-medieval fine metalwork
*D Tweddle*
There are 12 items of fine metalwork which can be assigned a post-medieval date, and a further 14 fragments which cannot be dated. The post-medieval objects include an unstratified rectangular buckle of sixteenth- or seventeenth-century date (Whitehead 2003, no 145), whilst a rectangular shoe buckle from the topsoil in the northern churchyard is later, probably dating to the eighteenth century. There is also a ring of uncertain purpose. Only two of the five buttons were from stratified contexts, from garden soil (*11*) in the Orchard, and from late hillwash (*36*) in the northern churchyard. The two thimbles are from

late hillwash (*71*) and the topsoil. The post-medieval and undatable material emphasises the diminished and still declining status of the site at this time, as well as reflecting reduced activity over most of the area. Again, it appears to represent the casual loss of a small number of personal items of little worth. The metalworking debris, although undated, is of some interest, providing a tantalising hint of copper-alloy working somewhere in the vicinity.

## Glass
### Vessel glass
*H Quartermaine*
All the remaining vessel glass from the site lies within a date range from the early eighteenth century to the present day. There are several fragments of the dark olive-green wine/beer bottles so characteristic of eighteenth-century domestic assemblages (Hurst Vose 2008), their distribution being focused on the northern part of the Orchard, particularly in the north-eastern corner of the site, and on the churchyard boundary wall and the hillwash in the western part of the northern churchyard, where bottles and other vessel glass may have been deposited after church ales. Modern vessel glass in this vicinity is likely to have come from the periodic removal of rubbish, including flower containers, from the churchyard.

### Window glass
The remaining 98 fragments of window glass can be broadly divided into two groups: one, a thin, natural greenish metal, largely unweathered; and a group of high-quality, almost or completely colourless metals, which are unweathered. The first group is typical of seventeenth- to early nineteenth-century triangular and lozenge-shaped window quarries in the locality (Howard-Davis 1992). It is of interest that many of the pieces show evidence of diamond-cutting and differential weathering, which marks the line of the lead kame and allows the depth of the H-shaped section to be estimated. Both of these elements allow the group to be dated more closely to, at the earliest, the later eighteenth century, when diamond glass-cutters came into more general use. There is perhaps sufficient material to suggest some refurbishment of the church windows around the beginning of the nineteenth century. The second group is clearly modern.

# 6

# DISCUSSION

## Early Medieval Sites in Cumbria

The site around the church at Dacre has provided one of the very few archaeologically excavated sequences in north-west England that can be clearly associated with the early medieval period. Over the last half century, excavations have added to the known sites, but the evidence from Blackfriars Street (McCarthy 1990), and west of the Cathedral (Keevil 1989; McCarthy 2014), in Carlisle, provide the only evidence for proto-urban activity, on the ruins of the Roman *civitas*, and there are isolated rural structures at Kentmere (Dickinson 1985) in southern Cumbria, Ribblehead (King 1978; 2004), and west Craven more generally (Johnson 2012; Ingleborough Archaeology Group 2015a; 2015b), just over the border into North Yorkshire, and in the Shap (Heawood and Howard-Davis 2002) and Brougham areas (Oliver *et al* 1996; Heawood and Howard-Davis 2002; Fig 86). Improvements in radiocarbon dating since the Dacre excavations have resulted in more sites being identified, no longer having to rely on typology alone, of which a small settlement to the north of Carlisle, at Stainton, is perhaps significant, as it was dated to the eighth- to tenth century and hints at some nucleation (Brown *et al* in prep).

The eighth-century documentary reference to a monastery at a place called Dacre (Bede, HE, bk 4, ch 32; Colgrave and Mynors 1969) lifts the site to an enhanced status, although Cumbria is unusual in having three other references, the other three being at Carlisle (VSC, xxvii; Colgrave 1940), Heversham (HSC, 147; *ibid*), and an unlocated site, although presumably relatively close to Carlisle (VSC, xxvii; *ibid*). The study of the development of Christianity in Cumbria has, however, a long tradition (*eg* Collingwood 1927) and the stone sculpture at more than 30 church sites (Bailey and Cramp 1988), including Dacre, is the most visible evidence for the early medieval habitation of the modern county. In addition to the work at Dacre, however, the burials excavated to the west of the Cathedral in Carlisle

(McCarthy 2014), and at St Michael's Church, Workington (Zant and Parsons 2019), have provided important evidence, both having benefited from the survival of human bone, which has meant that radiocarbon dating has been possible. At Carlisle, several burials were dated to the eighth- to tenth centuries (Batt 2014), while at St Michael's, two clearly separated phases of burial were established, one in the seventh- to ninth centuries, and the other tightly dated to the first half of the eleventh century (Marshall *et al* 2019).

The other remarkable category of sites from Cumbria, which gives some colour to the picture of life in the early medieval period, is that of furnished 'Viking' burials, of which Cumbria has more definite and possible examples of this rare site type than anywhere else in England (Richards 1991). These were only known from casual, and antiquarian, reports (Edwards 1998), however, until the discovery of a grave in 2004 by a metal detectorist, which led to the excavation of a small cemetery of six graves, only some 16 km (ten miles) to the north-east of Dacre, at Cumwhitton (Paterson *et al* 2014; Pl 53). This is important for Dacre in that it confirms how different the metalwork and beads were at these sites, which in turn aids the dating of the early medieval activity at Dacre.

## Early Medieval Northumbrian Monasteries

When the site at Dacre was excavated in the early 1980s, there had been relatively little work published on sites with which it could be compared (Cramp 1974; 1976). In the intervening years, however, the seminal report on the sites of Monkwearmouth and Jarrow (Cramp 2005; 2006d), the home of the Venerable Bede, Whithorn, in Galloway (Hill 1997), and Hoddom, in Dumfriesshire (Lowe 2006) have been published, to add to reports on work at Tynemouth (Jobey 1967), Hartlepool (Cramp and Daniels 1987; Daniels 1988; Daniels and Loveluck

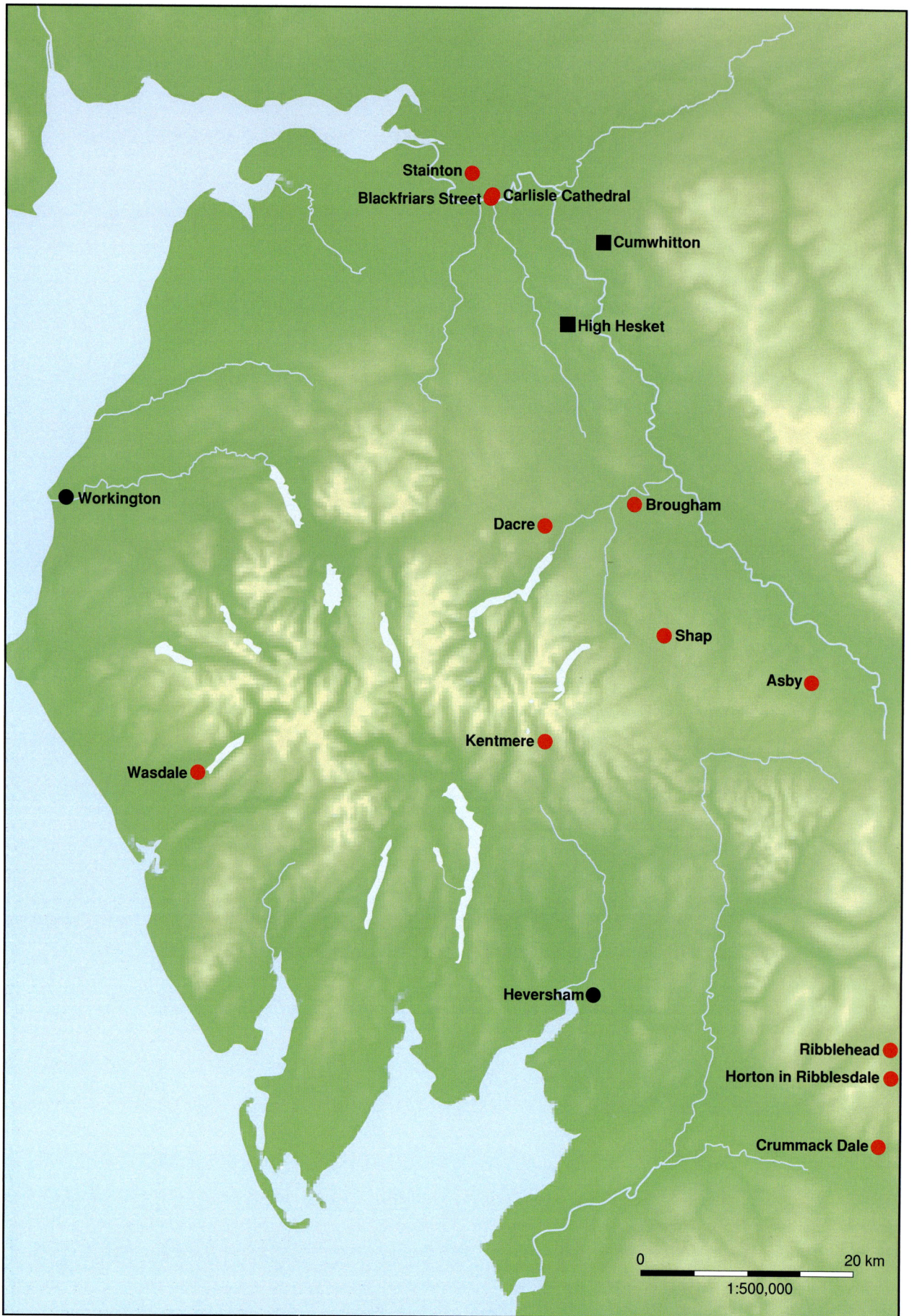

*Figure 86: Early medieval sites in Cumbria and the surrounding areas*

*Plate 53: The main group of burials at the Cumwhitton Viking-age cemetery*

2007), Beverley (Armstrong *et al* 1991), and Whitby (Peers and Radford 1943; Fig 87). All of these sites have, in some fashion, literary references to the existence not just of a church, but of an early ecclesiastical community, and many were refounded as monasteries after the Norman Conquest. During the same period, however, other sites without literary signposts to their monastic origins have been examined, for instance, in Scotland at Portmahomack (Carver 2004; 2008), and in Lincolnshire, at Flixborough (Loveluck 2007). These have challenged the criteria for interpreting a site as monastic in the early medieval period, other than from literary references, although Portmahomack supports one important criterion: the presence of early stone sculpture; while Flixborough, although being interpreted as a 'high-status' settlement for much of its life, is nevertheless tentatively associated with ecclesiastical ownership, perhaps an estate centre of a monastery, in the ninth century, when evidence for literacy, in the form of styli, was recovered and craft production was at its peak. This raises the possibility of dynamic changes in the function of a site through time (*op cit*, 162-3).

A site called *Dacore* certainly fulfils the first and most important criterion of being mentioned by the Venerable Bede in the *Historia Ecclesiastica*

as a monastery known to him through its abbot, Thrydred (HE, bk 4, ch 32; Colgrave and Mynors 1969). Bede, of course, does not give a more detailed location for this site. It has generally been assumed, though, that it was within the bounds of the kingdom of Northumbria, and, indeed, the only two places with this name (although that does not exclude the possibility that other places of that name once existed) are found within the former kingdom, near Pateley Bridge in North Yorkshire, and in Cumbria, just to the west of Penrith. That in North Yorkshire, however, has no other criteria to suggest that an early medieval site may have existed there, in contrast to Dacre in Cumbria, where early medieval stone sculpture of considerable sophistication had been found (*Ch 1, pp 12-13*) prior to the excavations.

These excavations have produced a wealth of evidence that can be examined in the light of the debate on the function of sites, including the layout, structural remains, and other key features, and also the artefactual assemblage. In terms of patterning, it is suggested (Hill 1997, 40-8) that the early medieval remains at Whithorn followed a defined layout that was somehow recognisable as monastic, in other words amongst such sites within Northumbria. There is, however, clearly no easily defined pattern at this time, to match the relatively

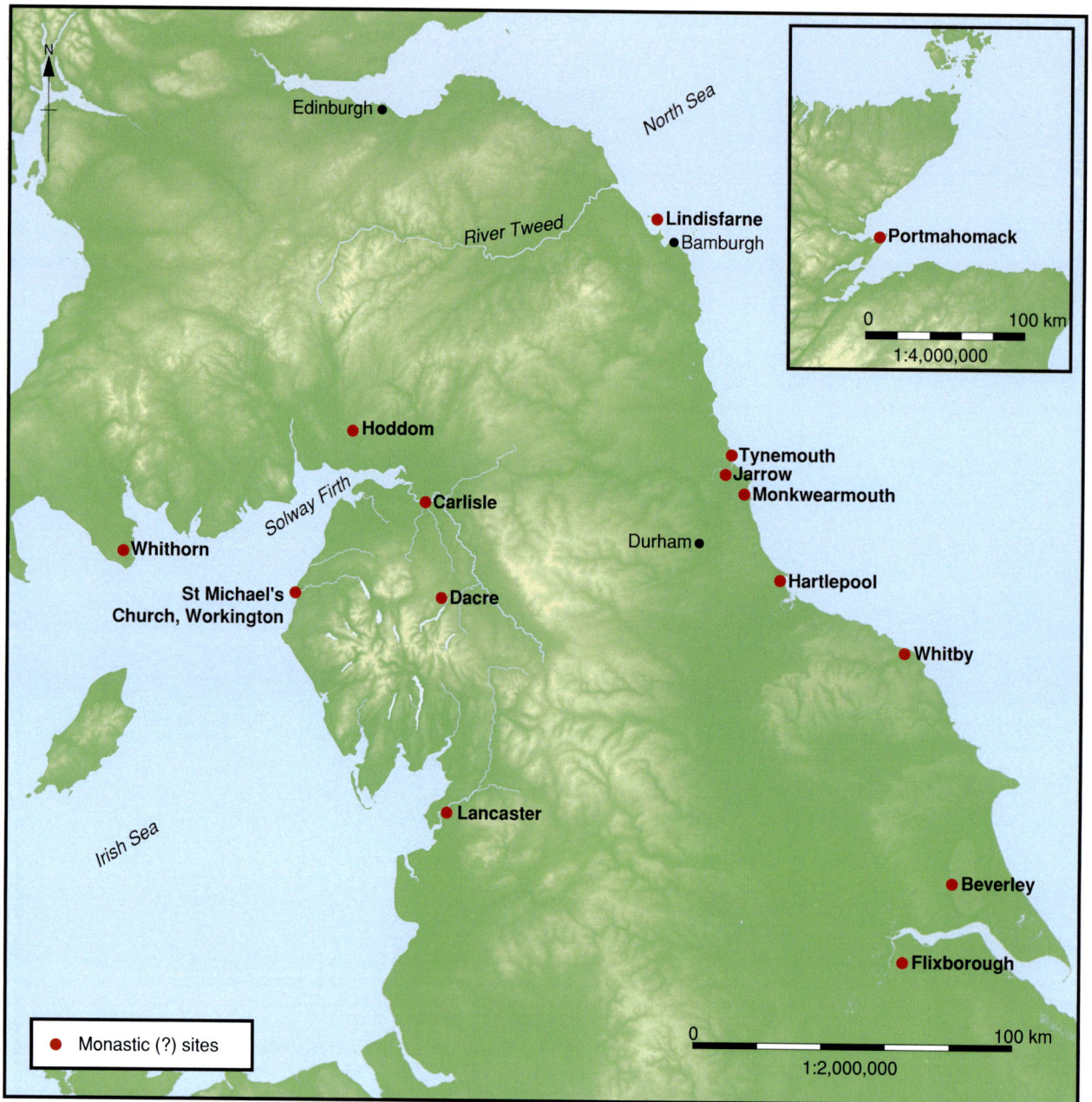

*Figure 87: Northumbrian documented and possible monastic sites*

standardised layout of medieval monasteries, where a visitor to a site would instantly recognise the relationship between the church and cloister, and know reasonably well the function of each element of the claustral and ancillary buildings (Blair 2005). This first becomes visible in the plan of St Gallen from the ninth century (UCLA 2012).

The subtle differences in layout between Jarrow and Monkwearmouth indicate that even in monasteries founded by the same individual there are few points of comparison, perhaps as much to do with the areas available for excavation as in reality. The buildings that have been excavated did, however, have order to them and stood to the south of what may have been several churches, built end on, as can been proven at Jarrow (Cramp 2005, 138), a layout also

interpreted at Whithorn (Hill 1997). Even extensive excavations, as at Whithorn, have examined only a small part of the site, and thus the samples known are necessarily biased.

Perhaps the most comparable sites are Wearmouth and Jarrow, where the areas immediately to the south of standing early medieval churches were examined, but whereas at Jarrow two large buildings were excavated, aligned east-west and forming a row on the terrace to the south of the church, with no evidence of a physical link with the church, at Wearmouth there was evidence of buildings akin to a proto-claustral arrangement, to the south of the church, and aligned on it, a link between them having been formed by a covered walkway (Cramp 2005, 111-13; Fig 88), similar in plan to a late antique villa.

138

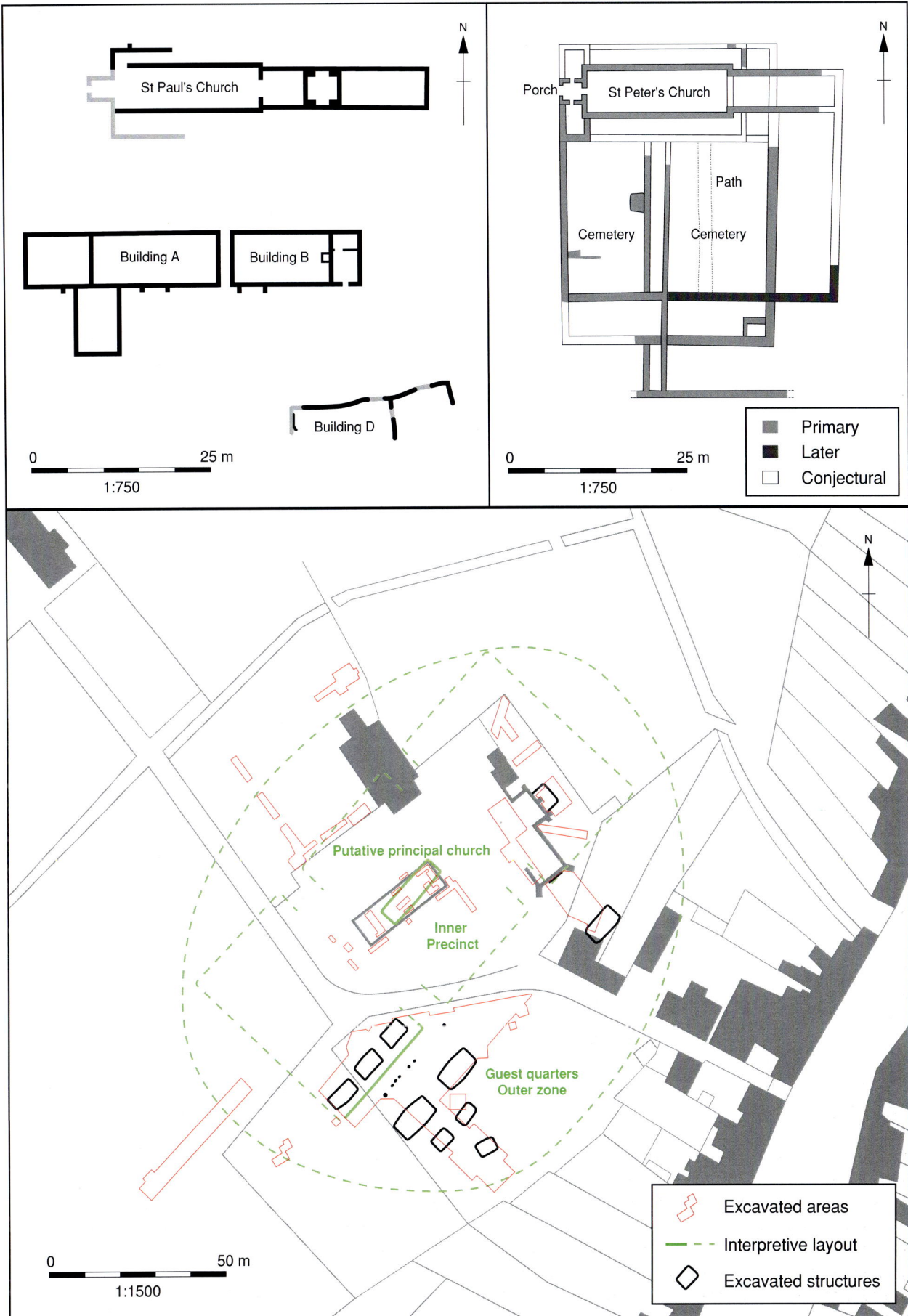

St Paul's Church

Building A    Building B

Building D

0                    25 m

1:750

Porch    St Peter's Church

Cemetery    Path    Cemetery

Primary
Later
Conjectural

0                    25 m

1:750

Putative principal church

Inner
Precinct

Guest quarters
Outer zone

Excavated areas
Interpretive layout
Excavated structures

0                    50 m

1:1500

*Figure 88: The layout of the monastic sites at Jarrow, Monkwearmouth, and Whithorn*

The establishment of a layout at many sites is constrained, as at Dacre, by the presence of a medieval parish church, and in several by a medieval monastery having been founded on the earlier site following the Norman Conquest (as, for example, at Wearmouth and Jarrow, Tynemouth, Whitby, and Whithorn). If it can be assumed that these medieval churches were normally rebuilds of an earlier structure, as at Jarrow, where the early medieval 'basilican' church was rebuilt, seemingly first in the eighteenth century, and then again in the nineteenth century on the same basic footprint as its predecessor (Cramp 2005, 139-44), and that these later churches were surrounded by a burial ground, then what might be considered the heart of the early site will be largely unavailable for large-scale study. This was certainly the case as Dacre, where the areas that could be excavated might be interpreted as peripheral to the presumed early complex now buried beneath the medieval churchyard.

## The Case for the Early Medieval Monastery at Dacre

### The cemetery

The most prominent element of the early ecclesiastical site at Dacre was undoubtedly the cemetery, containing well over 200 graves, found to the north of the medieval parish church. The lack of survival of human bones, however, severely limited the information that could be gained from this, although there are still some important points that can be made. All the graves were relatively accurately oriented, although there were subtle shifts in alignment that hinted at perhaps three phases of burial (*Ch 2, p 28*). Orientations slightly off true east-west are not unusual in the early medieval and medieval periods (see, for instance, Maldonado Ramirez 2011, 157-8; Boddington 1996, 31-2), as variation would occur depending on the time of year the primary burial, or the structure on which it was aligned, was established. This, and also slight variations in alignment over time, was seen too in the seventh- to ninth-century phase of burial at St Michael's Church, Workington (Parsons *et al* 2019, 122). Indeed, it has been suggested that an alignment more north-east to south-west is not an uncommon feature of the earliest burials known from the early medieval period in northern England and southern Scotland, and radiocarbon dating of sites in the latter has demonstrated that these graves cluster round the middle of the first millennium AD, eventually being overtaken in numbers by graves with a more truly east-west orientation (Maldonado Ramirez 2011, 157).

*Plate 54: The side face of bead **6**, unusually apparently ground and polished through the twisted canes at the side of the bead*

Where it could be established, where teeth were found *in situ*, the bodies had been placed in a supine position with their heads at the west end of the grave. While such an orientation cannot automatically be taken as indicating that these burials were Christian, as there is considerable evidence that burial to face the rising sun was a common practice in Europe from prehistory onwards (Gräslund 1980, 46-7), the fact that there were almost no artefacts associated with the graves is perhaps telling.

Indeed, the only material apart from iron fittings from the graves was a very distinctive bead (*Ch 3, p 82*), rare in Britain except in Kent, but similar to those found in Merovingian graves of the seventh century (Périn 1980, 227-31) and somewhat earlier in southern Germany (Koch 1977, 211). In the North, similar beads have been found in a pagan context at Cheesecake Hill on the Yorkshire Wolds (Mortimer 1905, 286-93). It is, however, unique, in that it appears to have been modified, the sides having been polished (Pl 54), perhaps to repair damage (A Parsons *pers comm*). Even the surrounding cemetery levels contained very few finds, with only an early coin, an annular bead, a frit melon bead, a copper-alloy pin head, a possible iron ringed pin, and a few whetstones coming from the layers cut by, or sealing, the graves (*Ch 3*). All of these artefacts could have been associated with clothing that the deceased was buried in, a custom known from clearly Christian cemeteries elsewhere in the North (for instance, from the cemetery west of Carlisle Cathedral; McCarthy 2014; and Thwing; Ottaway nd b).

The graves all seem to have contained adults, as there were no juvenile teeth in the assemblage, though of course it must be admitted that deciduous teeth, and, indeed, juvenile bones, would not survive as well as adult examples (Hillson 2005). The size of the cuts, however, which were almost all in the range of 1.50-2.20 m in length, with only a few larger, and predominantly 0.40-0.70 m in width (*Ch 2, p 26*), supports the lack of juveniles in the excavated area. This suggests either that this was a cemetery reserved for adults, though these cannot be sexed on the surviving evidence, or that there was zoning within the cemetery so that the part excavated had been reserved for a particular element of the population.

Indications of the general health of the population from the teeth were limited. Enamel hypoplasia, a condition indicative of periods of illness during childhood (*ibid*), was present in 12 instances, but in comparison with other medieval cemeteries, its incidence was quite low, possibly indicating relatively good living conditions (*Ch 3, pp 89-90*). Representation of caries was also low, and calculus relatively high, suggesting a diet that was not particularly rich in sugar or other sweet luxury items.

The relative paucity of child burials in many early medieval cemeteries, both associated with ecclesiastical sites and so-called field cemeteries, is, however, not unusual (Welch 1992, 76; Maldonado Ramirez 2011). This lack of juveniles has a parallel in the seventh- to ninth-century burials at St Michael's Church, Workington, where 7.89% of the assemblage were juvenile, though only a single example was less than 12 years of age (Parsons *et al* 2019, 125), in contrast

to a similarly dated assemblage from west of Carlisle Cathedral, where 16.67% were young (McCarthy 2014), as were 35.47% and 42.9% at Wearmouth and Jarrow from the same period (Anderson *et al* 2006, 482), where there was no evidence of zoning. Whilst taphonomic processes might be argued for the lack of children in many assemblages, the universally large size of the grave cuts argues against this being the reason for this lack at Dacre.

It has been suggested that, at least during the later medieval period, deliberate spatial segregation may have taken place in some churchyards, with a trend towards a preference for adult women and children being buried in the southern element (Gilchrist and Sloane 2005, 70; Dawes and Magilton 1980, 33-6), this, of course, being an area not available for excavation at Dacre. At other sites, such as Raunds (Boddington 1996, 40) and the Hirsel, in the Scottish Borders (Cramp 2014, 319-20), small children have been found buried close to the church, within the eaves-drip, the reasons for which could include religious beliefs, financial constraints, lack of social status, or even the time of year in which burial took place (Anderson *et al* 2006, 484; Halcrow and Tayles 2011, 345). All this leads to the conclusion that there was considerable variation in organisation and cultural expression in early medieval cemeteries, although there also seems to have been a temporal aspect to these differences.

There was clear evidence of organisation within the cemetery at Dacre (Pl 55), both in terms of the neat

*Plate 55: The northern part of the cemetery*

rows visible in some parts (*Ch 2, p 26*), although others demonstrated a rather more haphazard arrangement (Pl 56), particularly towards the peripheries, although nowhere did the organisation break down completely. Whilst there was some inter-cutting of graves, this was mostly in the form of one grave clipping another, rather than the destruction of one grave by a later burial, perhaps suggesting that the position of the earlier grave had been forgotten (Drinkall and Foreman 1998), or that there was a need to squeeze as many burials as possible into the available space, without disturbing earlier burials too much (Boddington 1996, 50). Indeed, there was little evidence amongst the teeth for the remains of more than one individual to be in a grave (*Ch 3, pp 87-8*). This differs from the earlier phase of burial at St Michael's Church, Workington, where there was at least one sequence of five individuals buried at least partially one on top of the other (Parsons *et al* 2019, fig 60). Despite this clear evidence of organisation, though, there was no indication that the graves had been marked individually, except, presumably, for a mound of earth for some time after the interment had taken place, although it must be admitted that the degree of truncation would have meant that any marker, unless deeply dug into the ground, would have left no evidence in the cemetery levels excavated.

The graves were at their densest in the western part of the site, becoming more spread out to the north-east, where there were hints that the natural edge of the cemetery had been reached, in contrast to the north-west, where the graves clearly continued to the north, beyond the modern churchyard, at least in a narrow band. In the south, they seemed to be focused on something to the south of the excavation, perhaps slightly to the south-east, as they were at their very densest below the later medieval churchyard boundary bank. It is presumably no coincidence that the medieval parish church now occupies this space.

A large amount of ironwork was found in association with the cemetery, which proved to be fittings from wooden chests (*Ch 3, p 68*), in other words, a box with a hinged lid, sometimes with metal straps, and locks (Craig 2009, 138). Although there were very few nails at Dacre, suggesting that these boxes were jointed with wooden dowels and pegs, there were large numbers of hinges of a distinctive type, some still retaining their integrity, which would have been nailed onto the container, as would corner brackets (Fig 89). This accords with contemporary practice for the construction of chests, often found associated with burials, such as in the Oseberg ship (Grieg 1927, 121-3), but not used to contain the dead, and in other circumstances, such as the Mästermyr tool chest (Arwidsson and Berg 1983).

Burial in such containers is proving to be a widespread, though still rare, burial rite in northern cemeteries within the Kingdom of Northumbria, with at least 18 other sites being known, both associated

*Plate 56: Intercutting graves in the central part of the cemetery*

142

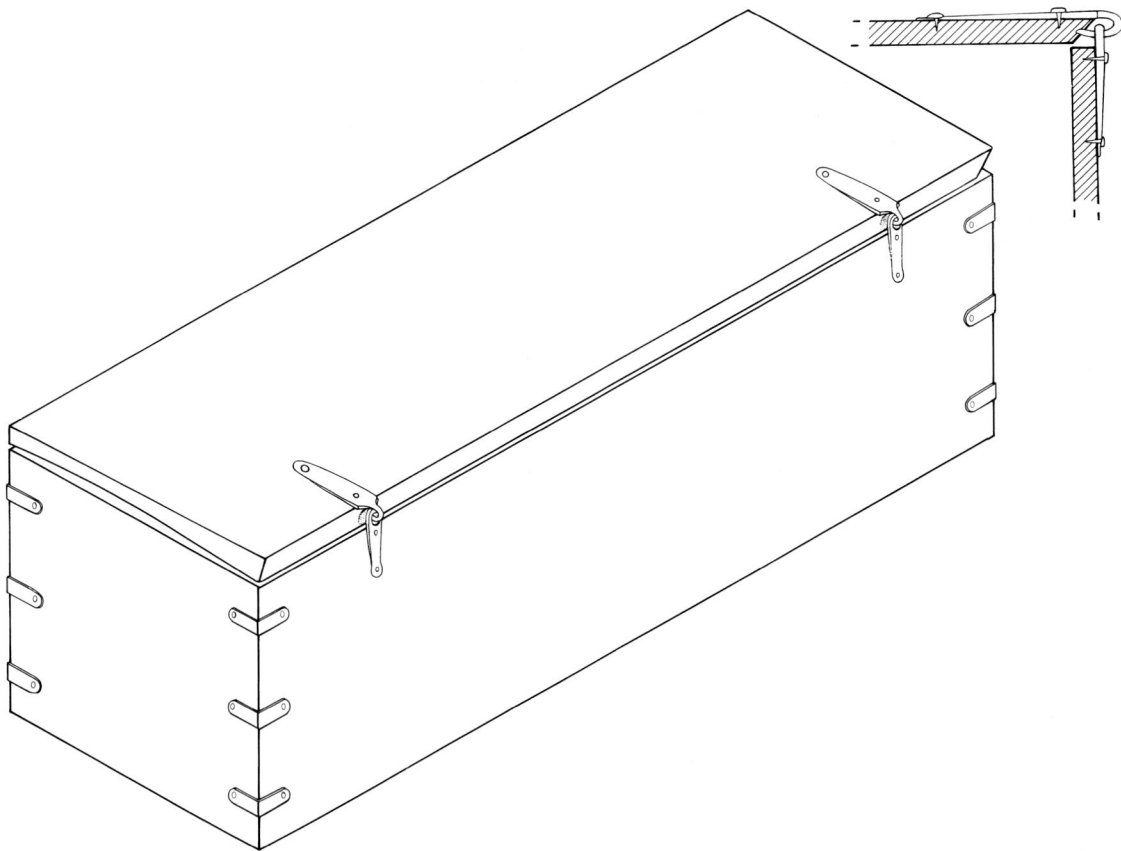

*Figure 89: Reconstruction of a hinged box, using the fittings found at Dacre*

with important documented church sites such as York Minster (Phillips and Heywood 1995, 83), Monkwearmouth (Clogg 2006), and Ripon (at Ailcy Hill; Hall and Whyman 1996), and sites without documentary evidence, such as Thwing (Ottaway nd b). These are mostly to the east of the Pennines, although this perhaps reflects the sites excavated rather than an accurate distribution, and all that have been subject to radiocarbon dating indicate a date range in the eighth- to ninth century. There are, however, differences in the detail of the hinges, with some sites containing cruder versions than others (Craig 2009, 365). Many of these chests have been found to have contained locks with, less frequently, keys, such as those from Ailcy Hill, Whithorn, and Thwing, but also Spofforth and Norton (*op cit*, 371). In most cases, the chests were locked, where the position was recoverable (*ibid*). The symbolism of locks and keys within early Christian beliefs has linked their presence to St Peter, as the keeper of the gates to Heaven, and doors appear frequently in Christian imagery, leading to the suggestion that the grave was being seen as a doorway (Thompson 2004, 129-31).

The precise form of the hinge straps is a significant indicator of date, since parallels can be found readily in pre-Conquest material, but rarely from later sites. Component A straps, which narrow to a point at

the base (*Ch 3, p 59*), occur in most of the cemeteries in which chests have been found, and elsewhere in Europe on, for example, the Førlev chest (Brøndsted 1936, 191-2, fig 102), an eighth-ninth-century coffin from Dunum, Friesland (Schmid 1970, abb 8.3b), and the coffin from Fyrkat (Roesdahl 1977, fig 191). A second form, with a rounded pierced terminal, is also common in the Northumbrian cemeteries, except for Monkwearmouth (Clogg 2006), where, for some reason, it does not appear.

Component B straps (*Ch 3, p 59*), the heads of which have been drawn out and then curved over to make a loop, are very characteristic of the pre-Conquest period, and are virtually unknown later. This form is also common in the cemeteries producing chests, and may be seen on a pair of late seventh- or eighth-century hinges from Yeavering, Northumberland (Hope-Taylor 1977, fig 90 4-5), the hinge strap from Tamworth (Ottaway 1992b), and straps from 16-22 Coppergate, York (Ottaway 1992a). Straps which narrow towards a pointed curved-over base or to a rounded terminal again occur widely in other cemeteries, and Scandinavian examples of the former include those from Førlev and Fyrkat. The parallel-sided Yeavering straps can be paralleled at Dacre (*Ch 3, pp 59, 65, 71*), and examples are also known from other cemeteries, again with the exception of Monkwearmouth (Clogg 2006). Other straps from

Dacre are, however, not so easy to find parallels for; those with distinctly convex sides over much of their length, and a pair of holes arranged transversely at their widest point, appear at present to be peculiar to this site, although similarly paired holes can be seen on a strap from Ripon (Ottaway 1996). The non-ferrous plated nails are extremely unusual, the only parallel being at Spofforth (NAA 2002, 60). Holes made in hinges by punching through the head of the strap are less common in the pre-Conquest period, although there are several examples from Monkwearmouth (Clogg 2006), and another strap with a flat top, narrowing towards the base, can only be paralleled at Monkwearmouth (*op cit*).

Intact corner brackets (*Ch 3, p 65*) were scarce at Dacre, as elsewhere, although several forms were noted. Those where the arms narrow from the corner towards distinct rounded terminals are paralleled on the Garton Slack coffin (Mortimer 1905, pl 91) and another example from a tenth- or eleventh-century context at Castle Green, Hereford (Shoesmith 1980, 37-8, fig 32, 9). Brackets with parallel-sided arms and rounded pierced terminals occur in numbers in the Repton and Ripon cemeteries (Ottaway 1996), and examples with simple rounded ends at Hereford (Shoesmith 1980, 37-8, fig 32, 3, 11-2).

The locks from Dacre, with sprung sliding bolts (*Ch 3, p 68*; Fig 90), seem to have been a long-lived form, apparently originating in the Roman period (Manning 1985, O66; Ottaway 1992a). Amongst the earliest post-Roman examples known is a group of eight (six with a central axial slot) from the sixth- to seventh-century cemetery at Buckland, Dover (Evison 1987, 100-1, figs 17, 21, 30, 33, 34, 39, 51, 124), where several of the locks employing this form of bolt came from contexts dated to the eighth- to tenth centuries. There was an example on the Garton Slack coffin (Mortimer 1905, pl 91), several have been found in the Ripon and Thwing cemeteries (Ottaway 1996; nd b), and they also occur on coffins from York Minster (Kjølbye-Biddle 1995). Three such locks were found in a domestic context, at 16-22 Coppergate, York (Ottaway 1992a), two in tenth-century contexts, and one, with a central slot, from the eleventh- to twelfth century, where it was probably residual. No bolts of this type are known from medieval sites without evidence for prior, pre-Conquest occupation. Continental examples appear to be scarce but they include one on the Førlev chest, and several, with central slots, from the Dunum cemetery (Schmid 1970, abb 8.3d). The hasp from Dacre cannot be paralleled exactly, although hasps are known on coffins from Repton, Ripon, Thwing, and York Minster (*above*), and a late ninth-century grave in the Cathedral Green cemetery at Winchester (Goodall 1990).

**A**

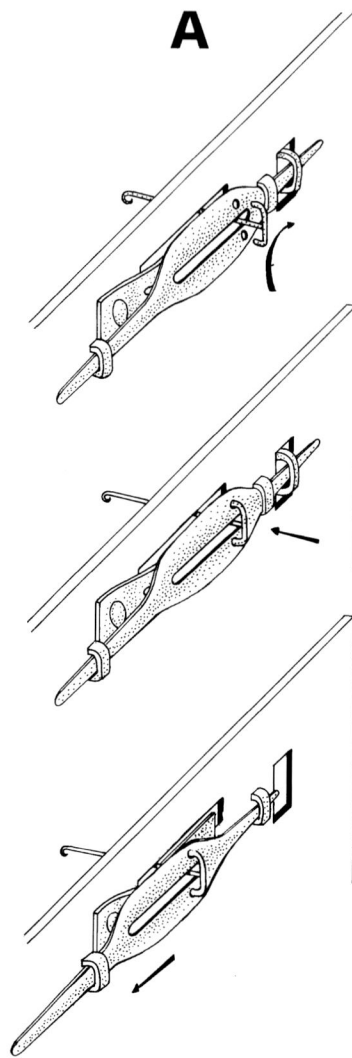

Approximate length of lock 150 mm

*Figure 90: The functioning of one of the locks found at Dacre*

Whilst evidence of such fittings was widespread amongst the graves and within the cemetery levels at Dacre, it could not be said that every burial had been contained within such a container, and it has been suggested that their use might reflect the personal attributes of the individuals (Hadley 2000, 163), though this does not necessarily reflect a higher social status, although it does, perhaps, suggest conspicuous consumption, which was probably limited to wealthier groups. In all of the cemeteries in which they have been found, these chest burials are in the minority (Craig 2009, 363), and seem largely to have been reserved for adults, and, where sex was established, of both men and women (*op cit*, 376). Whether these were purpose-built containers or reuse of domestic storage chests, perhaps even once they had broken (Kjølbye-Biddle 1995, 517; Nicholson 1997, 413), remains a vexed question, although there is some evidence to suggest that at least some were not initially constructed for use in funerary practices. At Ailcy Hill and

Thwing, for instance, unusual collections of nails may indicate a repair (Hall and Whyman 1996, 93; Ottaway nd b), and at the latter site, one chest also contained a large lead patch in the base. The use of a chest for the transport of a body is of course documented, when St Cuthbert was moved from his grave at Lindisfarne and transported across northern England for several years (Colgrave 1940, 290-5).

In general, such chest burials have been linked to higher-status contexts, many associated with documented early ecclesiastical centres, as at Dacre, Whithorn (Nicholson 1997, 415), Ailcy Hill (Ottaway 1996, 113), Wearmouth (Clogg 2006), and York Minster (Lucy and Reynolds 2002, 16), although Thwing was rather associated with what seems to

have been a high-status settlement (Manby 1986) that contained structures analogous to the royal site at Yeavering (Hope-Taylor 1977). It is clear that important lay burials took place at monastic sites from the beginning, and at both Insular and Anglo-Saxon foundations, the burial of members of royal or noble families conferring a validity to the monastic landholding, which often proved necessary to be maintained (Cramp 2005, 355). The vast majority of chest burials have been found within the bounds of the Kingdom of Northumbria (Fig 91), although occasional occurrences have been noted elsewhere, particularly in Mercia, at Hereford (Shoesmith 1980, 36-7) and Repton (Ottaway 1996, 99), as well as Winchester (Goodall 1990). These, however, seem to be later than those within Northumbria, dating

*Figure 91: High-status chest burials within the Kingdom of Northumbria*

145

to the tenth-and eleventh centuries (*ibid*), and there are also differences in the construction, as slotted hasps are more commonly used, rather than the locks found in northern cemeteries (Ottaway 1996, 113).

Few of these cemeteries had excavated boundaries, although this may have more to do with the areas excavated (Hirst 1985, 20-4) than a real absence. A clear boundary was, however, defined on the northern and eastern edges at Church Walk, Hartlepool (Daniels and Loveluck 2007, 84), and a post-in-trench fence and a timber palisade have been identified at Pontefract and Thwing respectively (Youngs *et al* 1987, 172; Roberts and Whittick 2013; Manby 1986). At Dacre, most of the boundaries identified were ditches, and such a feature was also identified to the west of burials at the Bowl Hole, Bamburgh (Groves 2011), although the graves seemed to peter out towards the ditch. Another possible boundary ditch was identified at Thornton Steward by geophysical survey, where all but one of the excavated early medieval burials were found to the south of it (Adamson and Abramson 1997). The extent of burial seemed to have been

reached at Adwick-le-Street on all four sides, with no indication of any formal boundary surviving (Craig 2009, 118), although this does not entirely rule out the use of simple barriers that would not survive in the archaeological record.

This makes the boundaries at Dacre unusual at the least, and wall *644* (*Ch 2, p 23*), in particular, currently unique. The cemetery seems to have been defined along much of its circumference by insubstantial ditches (*Ch 2, pp 21-3*), although it appears that not all were contemporary with the earliest burials, since other ditches were found in the south-east of the cemetery that perhaps imply expansion in that direction, unless they marked distinct zones of burial (Fig 92). It was notable, however, that ditch *160* cut grave *320*, indicating at least some expansion to the west. Evidence for possible zonation was in the form of ditch *1276* (*Ch 2, p 24*), the only such feature to be aligned east-west. This was identified near the apparent eastern extremity of the cemetery, some 3 m to the north-east of one of the densest concentrations of graves. Its proximity to ditch *1356*, which would have met it at right-angles, if this relationship had

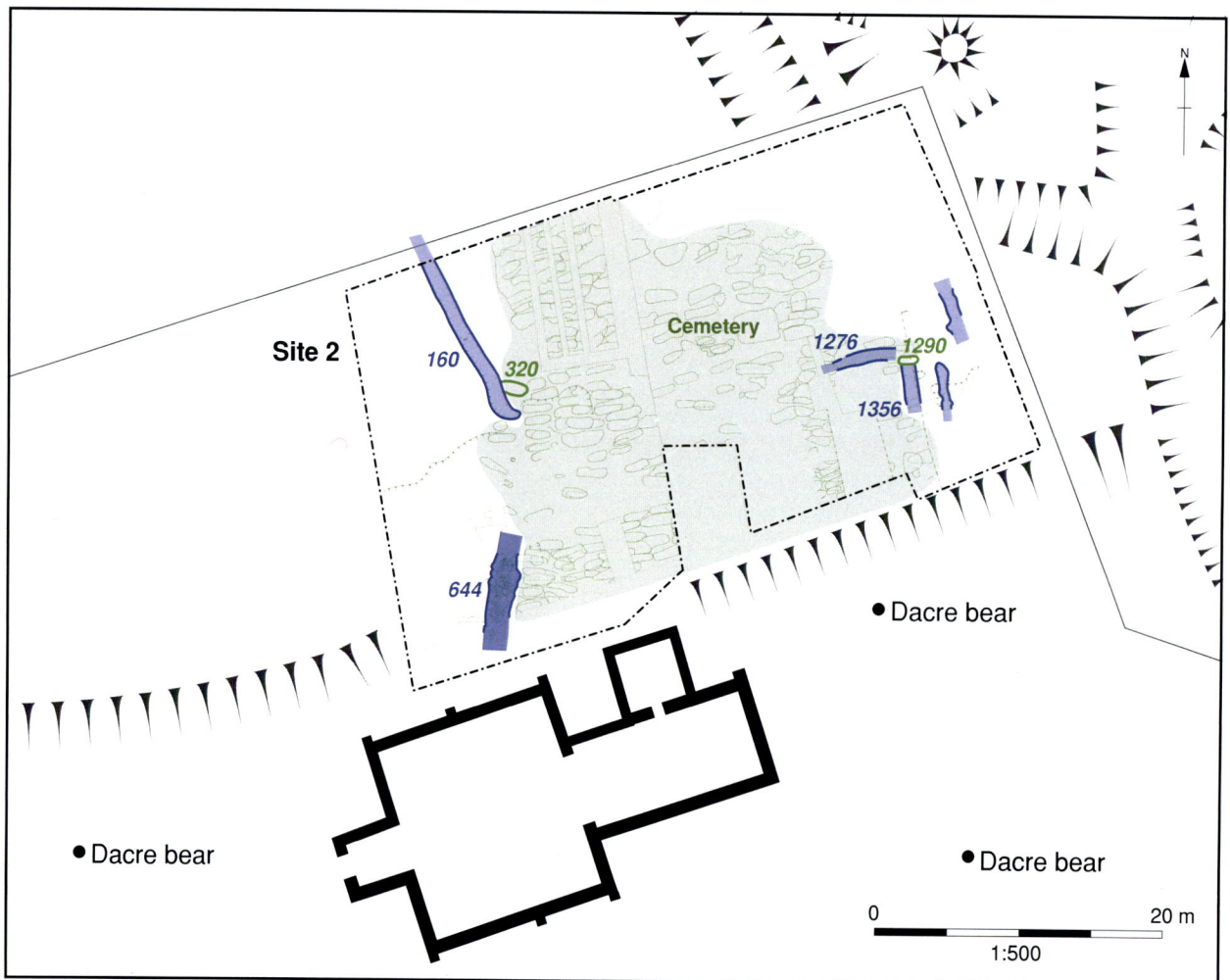

*Figure 92: Boundaries within the cemetery at Dacre*

not been removed by grave *1290*, suggests that this either once formed the north-eastern corner of the cemetery, which was subsequently expanded, or that this was an indication that in places, at least, there were internal divisions, as have been found at a few other cemeteries, such as the late Roman site at Poundbury, Dorset (Farwell and Molleson 1993).

Whilst only a short stretch of wall *644*, and in this only the foundations, could be excavated, this seemed to have been well made, with faced stones and a rubble core. Tantalisingly, there was a hint that it was turning eastwards, in towards the cemetery, at the point that it was cut by the earliest medieval churchyard boundary, in the form of ditch *215* (*Ch 4, p 91*), perhaps suggesting an entrance at this point. That it was sealed by the upcast from this ditch, in the form of bank *151*, demonstrates that the two could not have been contemporary, however. The presence of a stone wall, to the west of which there was no evidence of graves, the area instead providing indications of more 'domestic' activity, does suggest that this was a more 'important' boundary than the ditches elsewhere. It would be logical, since the density of

burials was at its greatest immediately to the east of this, apparently focusing on something to the south, that this might have been a visible feature in a more public space, rather than simply a utilitarian division. If, indeed, the focus of the cemetery was on a church to the south, and that, as, for instance, at Wearmouth, the cemetery contained a mixed population of both men and women, then it might be expected that an access point into it would be close to the western, presumably more public, end of the church, placed close to the scarp between the upper and lower terraces, adjacent to Structure Y (*Ch 2, p 23*).

## The structures

It is thus perhaps no coincidence that the buildings (Structures X and Y, and putative Structure Z; *Ch 2, pp 31-5*) associated with early medieval activity in the northern churchyard were immediately to the west of the apparent cemetery boundary (Fig 93), although these differed in both shape and alignment, and also in the amount of material culture associated with them. Structure Y is unusual in both shape, although its dimensions and exact footprint cannot be confirmed, as only an element lay within the

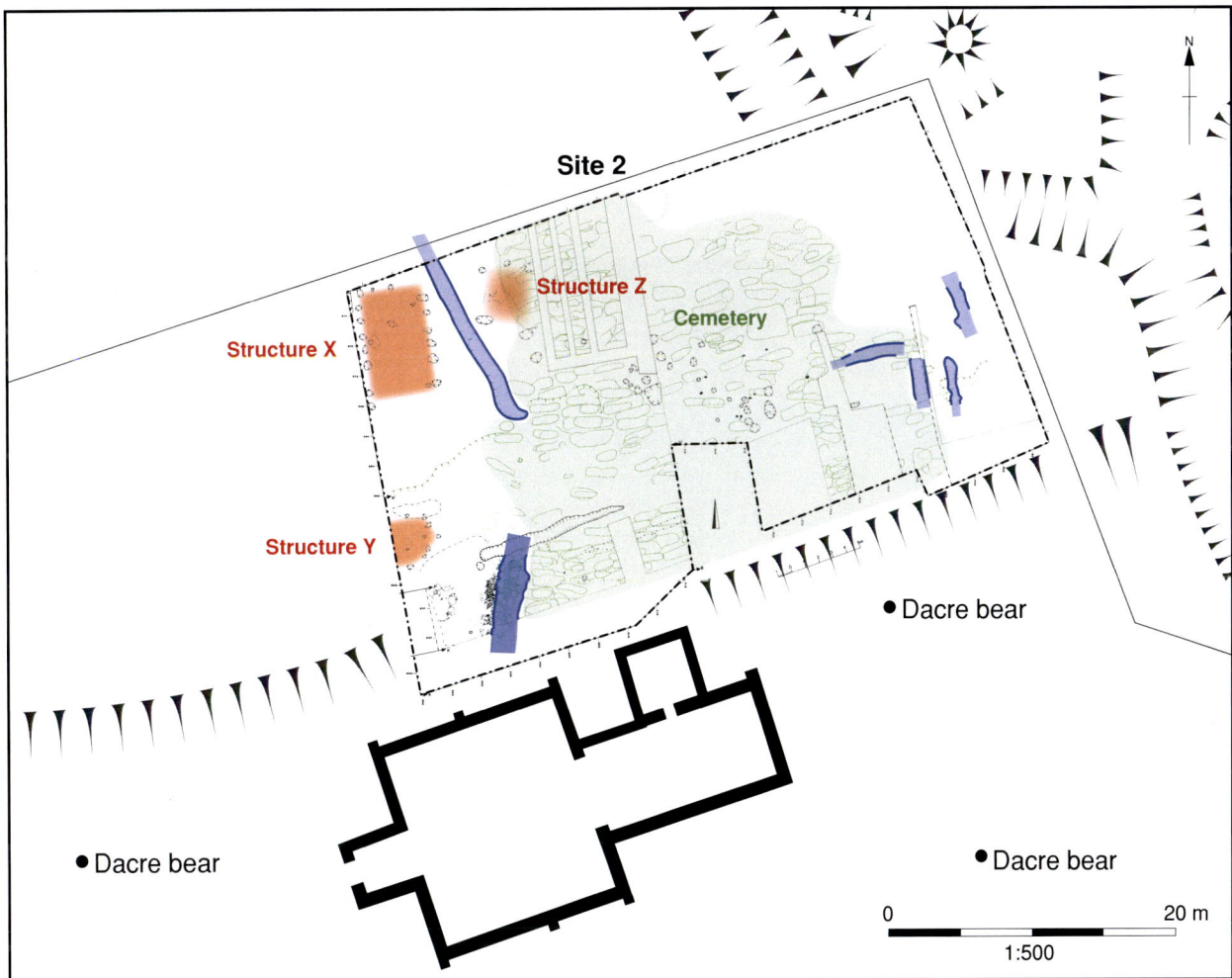

*Figure 93: The early structures in relation to the cemetery*

excavation, and the amount of early medieval material associated with it. It was built of timber and appeared to have a semi-circular eastern end, apparently aligned east-west. It had seemingly been rebuilt after some time, to contain two sequential stone hearths close to its eastern end. These suggest 'domestic', perhaps public, accommodation of some sort, an interpretation strengthened by its position close to what may have been the formal entrance to the cemetery.

The shape of the building, as far as it can be established, is unusual in a pre-Norman context; certainly, sub-circular buildings are not generally found in association with specifically Anglo-Saxon sites. Oval or round-ended structures have, however, been found at probable monastic sites at Burgh Castle, Norfolk (Johnson 1983), Tynemouth (Jobey 1967), and also at Wykeham, in North Yorkshire (Moore 1966), although the existence of those at Burgh Castle has been questioned (Johnson 1983, 37-9). In addition, the circular structures recorded at Tynemouth were stratigraphically lower than the rectangular structure that was thought to be monastic (Jobey 1967, 35-41). This suggests that they continued the long-lived tradition of circular buildings known from the Bronze Age through to the Roman period, and possibly beyond, in rural contexts in the North (Higham and Jones 1975; Gates 1983).

The first hearth in the sequence in the apparently rebuilt or refurbished structure was a conventional flat piece of red sandstone, which had clearly been much used, as it was decayed and had lost much of its original shape (Pl 57). This had been replaced by a millstone, a relatively unusual feature in its own right in an early medieval context (Ch 3, pp 80-1), although one has been found with a similar secondary use as a hearthstone in an eleventh-century context at Goltho, in Lincolnshire (Beresford 1987, 75, 195-6).

The area over and around this structure also contained the largest concentration of early medieval material in any of the excavations at Dacre, both in the layer associated with its rebuild and in the area to the south. This included fine metalwork, in the form of pins (Pl 58), strap-ends, and buckles, and also a spindle whorl and loomweight, and both vessel and window glass (Pl 59). The overlying hillwash also produced more evidence of loomweights and glass (Ch 3). This is clearly a significant assemblage, and much larger than might have been expected in such a context; it is certainly larger than any other assemblage from a single site in Cumbria.

Many of the copper-alloy objects are small, and sometimes valuable, personal items, presumably lost by visitors, as their intrinsic value makes it unlikely that they would have belonged to the inhabitants

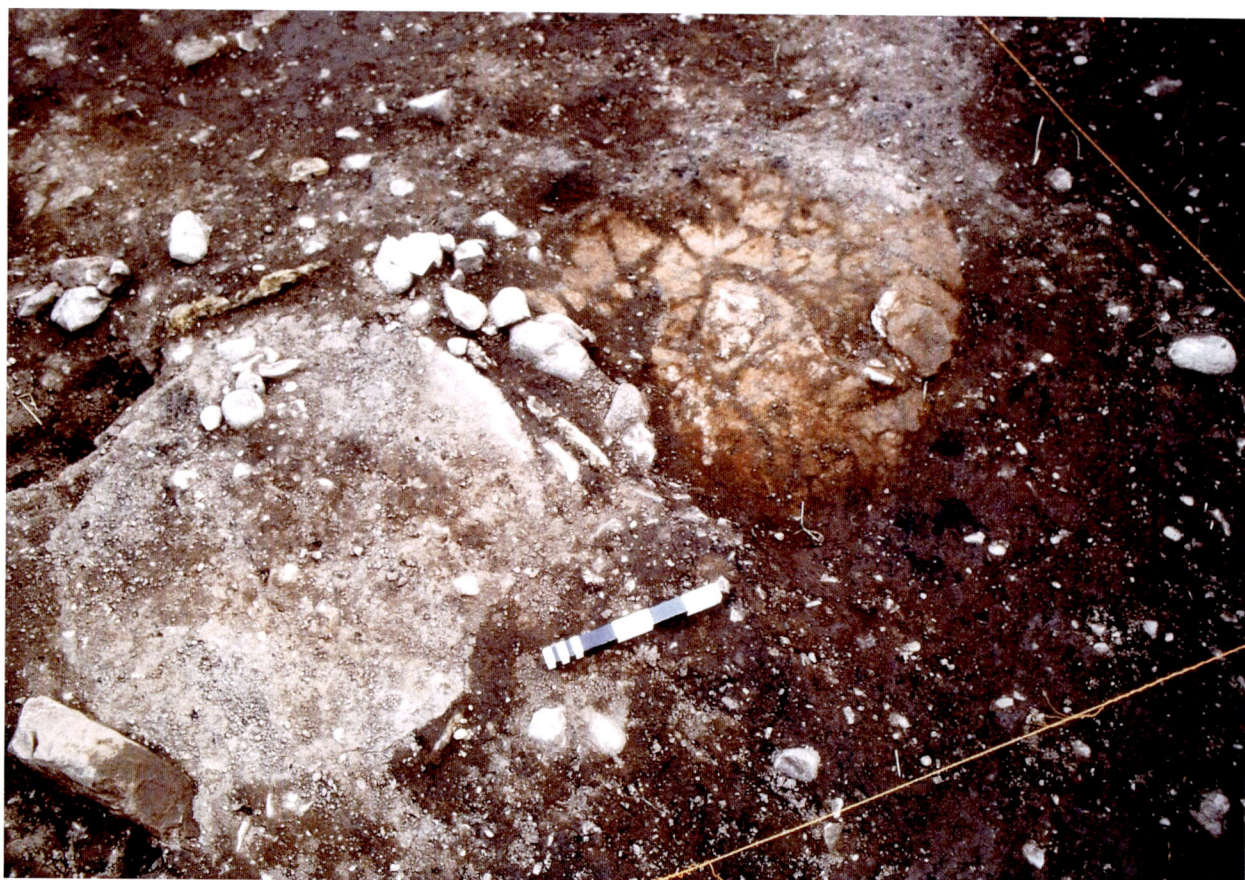

*Plate 57: The millstone reused as a hearth in Structure Y, adjacent to the earlier hearthstone*

*Plate 58: Early pins associated with the area over and around Structure Y*

*Plate 59: Early window glass, mostly associated with Structure Y*

of a monastery, who had, presumably, renounced worldly goods. The dating evidence seems to be focused on the eighth- to mid-ninth centuries, also reflecting the dates of the early medieval coins from the site (one *sceatta* and five *stycas*; *Ch 3, pp 50-1*), the sceatta dating to the mid-eighth century and the stycas to the second quarter of the ninth century.

The mixture of personal possessions, more utilitarian items, such as spindle whorls and loomweights, and window and vessel glass suggests a high-status building, perhaps such as a guest hall. Window glass, in particular, is thought to have been rarely used, Bede recording that Benedict Biscop sent to Gaul in 674, when the church at Wearmouth was almost complete, for glaziers, because the art of making glass was at that time unknown in Britain (HA; King 1930, ch 5). He asked them to glaze the windows of the church, *porticus*, and refectories, and also make glass vessels (Cramp 1975).

Jarrow and, to a lesser extent, Wearmouth have indeed produced the greatest amount of window glass, associated not only with the churches, but with the buildings to the south, including the long, apparent gallery at Wearmouth, and in addition to Buildings A and B at Jarrow, on the terrace to the south of the churches, also Building D, which has caused its original interpretation as a workshop to be revised (Cramp 2006c). However, growing numbers of sites across the country have now produced such glass, most associated with an ecclesiastical function, including in Northumbria, of course, Wearmouth and Jarrow (Cramp 2006d), but also Escomb (Cramp 1971), Whitby (Evison 1991, 143-4), Whithorn (Cramp 1997), and Flixborough (Cramp 2009), and slightly further afield, Repton (Cramp and Heyworth forthcoming). It is noticeable that the glass from most of the ecclesiastical sites is pale to light blue, and green-amber, while secular sites have so far produced only colourless glass (Cramp 2006a, 79). A few sites, mostly in Northumbria, including Dacre, have also produced red-streaked glass, such as Beverley (Henderson 1991), Flixborough (Cramp 2009), Whithorn (Cramp 1997), and York (Cramp 2006a), with similar material known from Repton, Glastonbury, and Winchester (*ibid*).

Structure X and putative Structure Z were in many ways more conventional, being timber buildings, aligned north-south on the upper terrace, Structure X overlooking Structure Y on the lower terrace. They were both built of relatively evenly spaced posts, presumably with wattle panelling between, and neither contained any material culture that would confirm their dating. This lack of material, however, and, indeed, of any associated surface, would seem to be the result of taphonomic processes, in that the upper terrace had been subject to greater erosion than the lower. Indeed, it might be argued that at least some of the early medieval material found on the lower terrace apparently associated with Structure Y, and to its south, might as easily have been eroded from Structure X on the upper terrace.

149

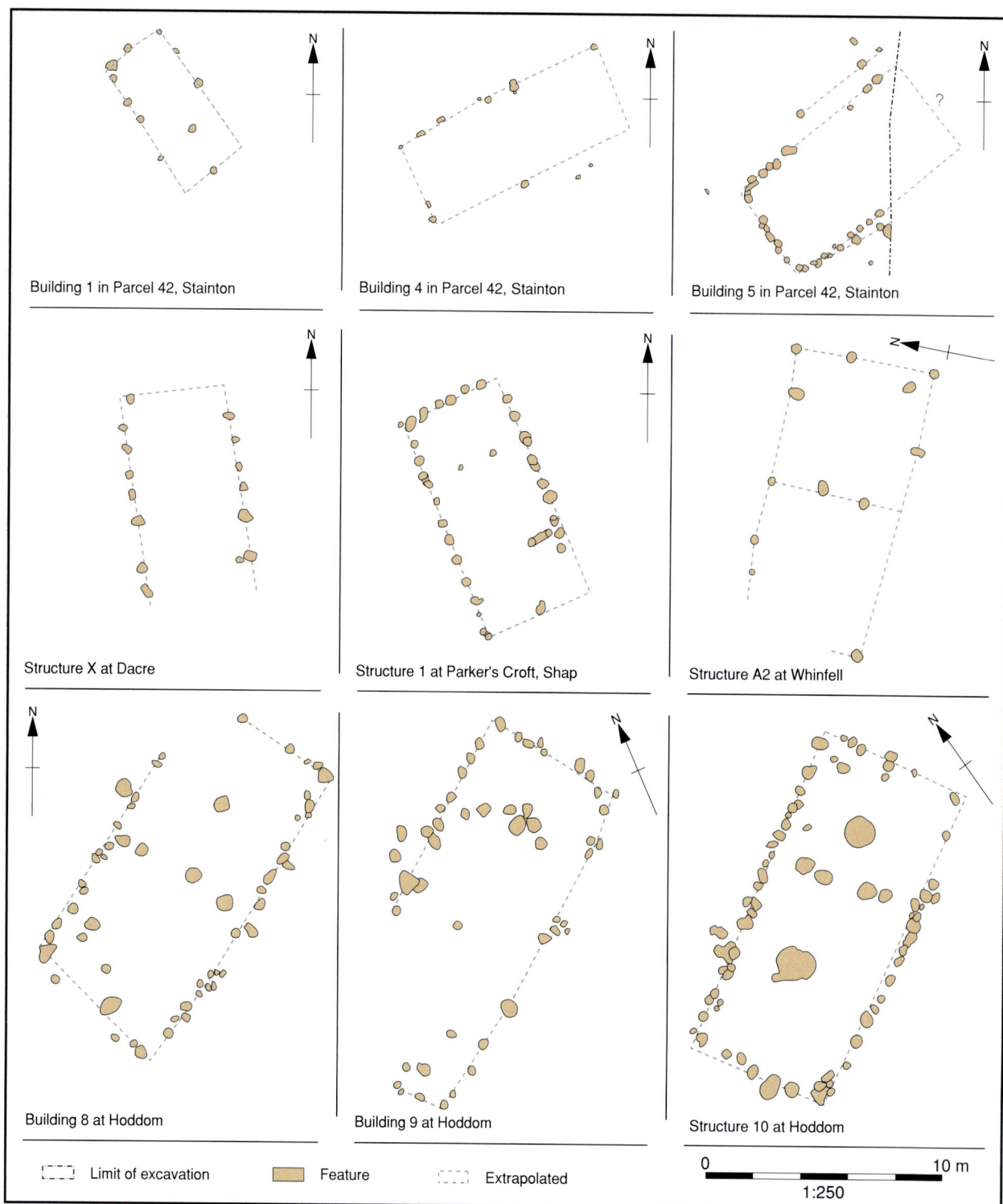

*Figure 94: Comparative early medieval rectilinear structures from Cumbria and Dumfriesshire*

Parallels for these structures in the North West were few at the time of excavation, but have steadily grown into a significant corpus since (Fig 94). Sites in a rural context, at Shap, Whinfell, and Fremington, all in the Penrith area (Heawood and Howard-Davis 2002; Oliver *et al* 1996), and Stainton, the latter to the north of Carlisle, have produced relatively similar timber structures, the latter radiocarbon-dated to the eighth- to mid-tenth centuries (Gregory in prep). The structure at Shap was dated to the seventh- or

eighth century from the presence of distinctive loomweights, of a type also found at Dacre (*Ch 3, pp 85-6*), and Whinfell was postulated as being early medieval by analogy (Heawood and Howard Davis 2002), while that at Fremington was dated to the early medieval period by the presence of four *grubenhauser*, spindle whorls, and loomweights, the latter again of a similar type to those from Dacre (*Ch 3, pp 85-6*), whetstones, and a copper-alloy 'garment hook' of probable eighth-century or

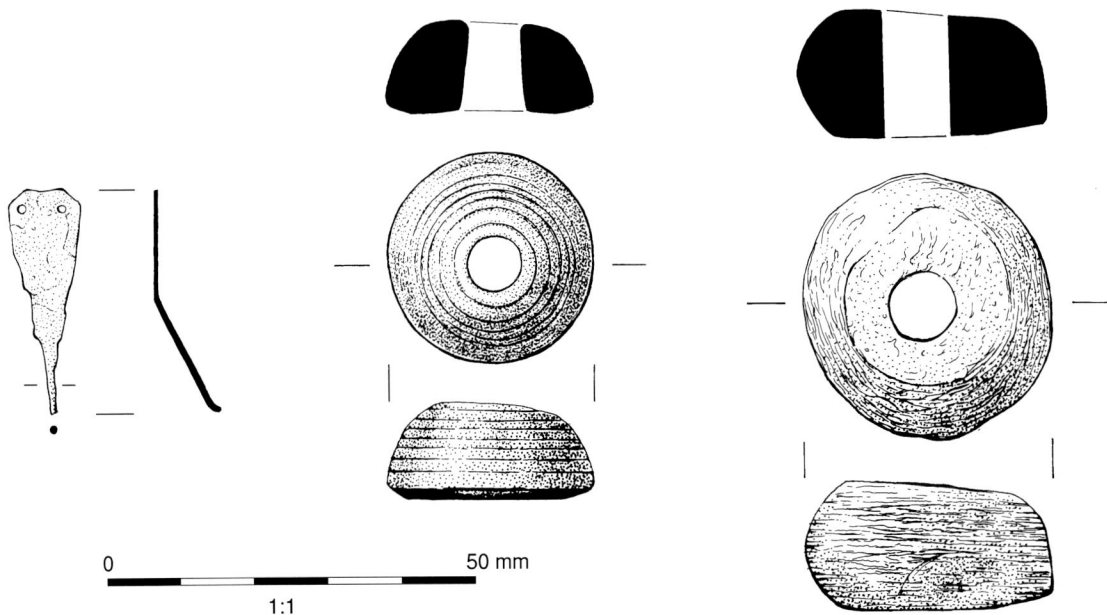

*Figure 95: Early medieval finds from the nearby site at Fremington*

slightly later date (Fig 95; Oliver *et al* 1996). These buildings varied quite considerably in size, from *c* 6 m long to 14 m, and 3-4.8 m wide, depending on the reconstruction, so the Dacre structures, at *c* 8.50 m long and *c* 5 m wide, were well within the range. A timber structure of apparent early medieval date, dated from finds of the seventh- to ninth centuries, has been found at Blackfriars Street, Carlisle (McCarthy 1990, 70-1), within the bounds of the Roman settlement. This was at least 11 x 5 m, but was of stone-filled slot construction, with presumably a timber superstructure.

Timber 'hall-type' structures are common further afield, those at Dacre being comparable to the secular early medieval building tradition (James *et al* 1984; Blair 2018), and are not dissimilar in size to timber buildings excavated at Tynemouth (Jobey 1967, 42-9) and Hartlepool (Cramp and Daniels 1987, 424-8). The ancillary buildings at Hoddom tended to be somewhat larger, at *c* 11-15 m long, and up to 6.6 m wide (Lowe 2006), although also post-built, while those at Whithorn, as far as they could be ascertained, were about 12 m long (Hill 1997), though mostly built in a post-in-slot technique.

The standard module of such buildings is thought to have been a square, and therefore doorways are often found opposed, at the junction between two modules at the centre of the building (James *et al* 1984, 186, fig 4), although as more buildings of the period are excavated, the position of doorways seems to have become more varied. The use of wall trenches also seems to have been slightly more common in the early medieval period, although all the North

Western examples have proved to be post-built, and at Hartlepool, where both types of construction were found, those built of individual postholes seemed to be earlier (Cramp and Daniels 1987, 424-6).

Although so little could be recorded of wall *17* in the Orchard, as it in effect formed the edge of the trench, beneath the modern churchyard wall in the north-eastern corner of the site (*Ch 2, pp 38-40*), the impression gained from its external face was that it had been constructed with considerable care, in effect in ashlar, in a type of yellow sandstone not local to the area, or used elsewhere on the site. It seemed to have formed the north-west corner of a building, now wholly lost under the medieval churchyard. A wall very similar to the northern medieval churchyard boundary had been built against it (*18; Ch 4, p 112*), demonstrating its early date. It is perhaps notable that the modern churchyard wall had been built over the corner of wall *17*, and it may well have dictated the shape of the churchyard at this point.

## The position of the church?

The focusing of the early graves in the south of the northern churchyard on something to the south, and perhaps slightly to the east of the medieval church, suggests that an earlier building or buildings stood on this approximate position. Some evidence, in the form of a cluster of red sandstone building material in the south-west corner of the site, may add weight to this hypothesis, since this clearly pre-dated the construction of the medieval churchyard boundary and seemed to have come from a stone building. Given that no evidence for such a building existed in the northern churchyard, and the stone was of different type from that constituting wall *17* in the Orchard, and the drain in the southern churchyard, it seems likely that this came from a building within the present churchyard, the most likely candidate being a church. Indeed, the evidence from Jarrow, Wearmouth, and Whithorn demonstrates that these were all placed on rising ground, as was Dacre, with the ecclesiastical buildings surrounded by a cemetery, with other buildings to the south (Cramp 2005, 348).

## The drain and other features in the southern churchyard

Perhaps the most surprising structure at Dacre had been known for some considerable time: the drain in the southern churchyard. This was first excavated in the later 1920s (Hudleston 1932), when the rumour was that there was a tunnel to the medieval Dacre Castle, to the south. This excavation had done no more than expose the top of the stones and empty the interior, to allow the form of the stones to be recorded, and to identify the structure as a large, stone-built drain (Fig 96). Re-excavation in 1985, of a slightly larger area than the original, and analysis, has identified the stones as originally coming from a Roman structure, perhaps a bridge or mill (*Ch 2, p 46*; P Hill *pers comm*). They had subsequently been crudely reworked, by pecking one side, the other being left smooth (Pl 60). The crudely pecked sides each contained a lewis hole, to aid with the

*Plate 60: The worked stone blocks forming the drain*

manoeuvring of the pieces into place, which seems likely to have originally been laid flat, so that their present position is (as they still remain *in situ* within the churchyard, though reburied) at 90° to the original.

No Roman bridges are known for certain in the North, apart from that at Corbridge (Breeze 2006, 427), and those at Willowford in Cumbria and Chesters in central Northumberland, that carry Hadrian's Wall across the Rivers Irthing and Tyne (*ibid*), although there obviously must have been many more (for instance, the Roman name for Newcastle, *Pons Aelius* (Bridge of Hadrian)), of varying sizes. Mills are also rare, being known only on Hadrian's Wall at Haltwhistle Burn (*op cit*, 268), until one was excavated at Papcastle, following the major flooding of the River Derwent in 2009 (Apperley 2016). In either case, it is perfectly possible that a structure could have existed close to Dacre, on the Dacre Beck or the River Eamont to the east (*Ch 2, p 46*), that could have been quarried for good stone, and, indeed, the Eamont could conceivably have been used to transport material from further away, such as from the fort at Brougham, some six miles (9.6 km) to the north-east, which stood on the south bank of the river (Fig 97).

Roman sites made good quarries for building stone in the early medieval period, particularly for churches, and stone from Hadrian's Wall was clearly used to build the early medieval crypt at Hexham, with material from the Roman fort at Binchester being used in the construction of Escomb church in County Durham in the late seventh- or eighth century (Taylor and Taylor 1965), that perhaps from the eastern terminus of Hadrian's Wall being used at Jarrow (Bidwell 2006b). All these sites demonstrate the capacity of early medieval groups to move stone over quite significant distances; that used at Hexham

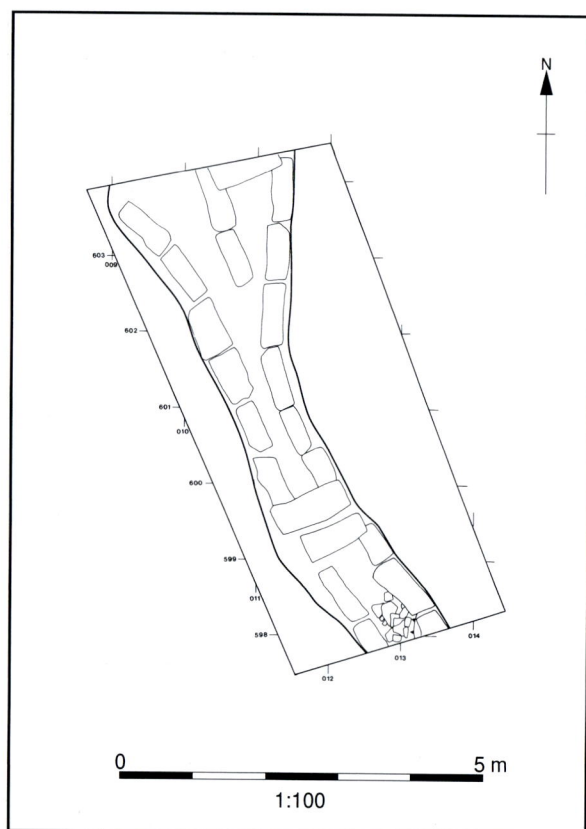

*Figure 96: The extent of the excavation of the drain in the 1920s*

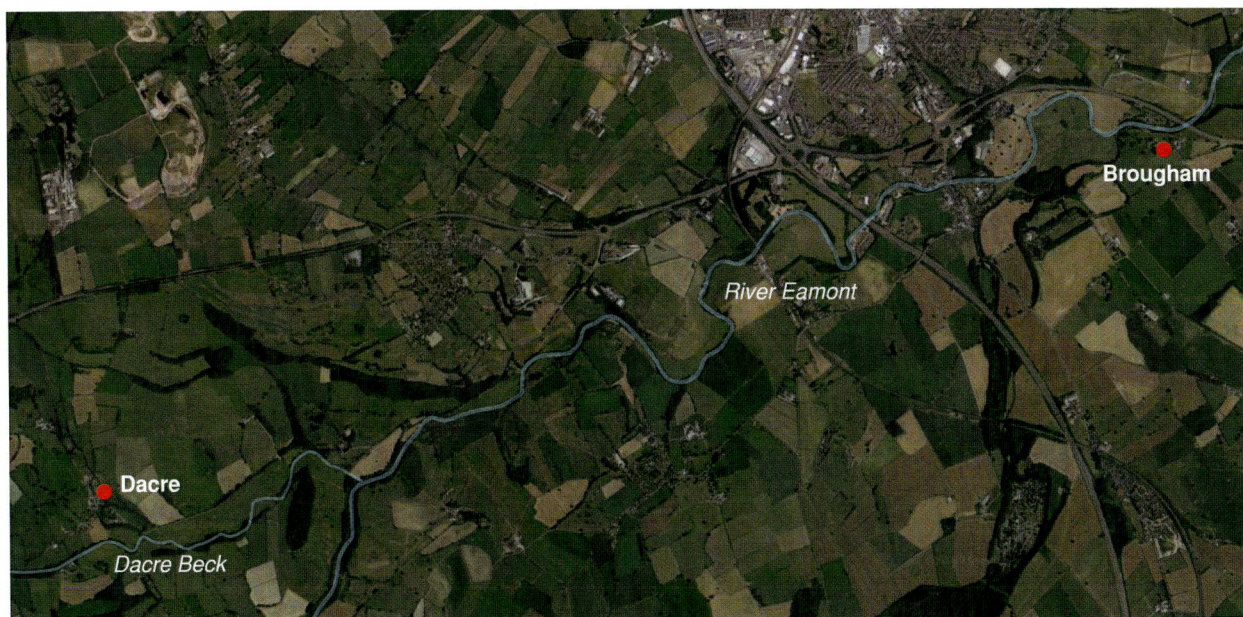

*Figure 97: The sites at Dacre and Brougham, in relation to the River Eamont and the Dacre Beck*

would have to have been moved over land, unless the stone came from the site at Corbridge, some five miles (7 km) to the east.

The drain proved to be exposed at the place where two channels came together from points further to the north. These quite monumental stones would seem to have been over-engineering of anything other than a significant conduit, though the fact that it issued from the churchyard, and beyond that, the area of the early medieval cemetery, might suggest that the channels carried foul water rather than clean. Whilst stratigraphically it is conceivable that the drain could have been medieval in origin, it seems highly improbable that anyone would go to this amount of trouble to drain a parish churchyard. It seems more likely that it drained buildings that stood on the terrace, presumably to the south of the medieval church, which is likely to have been built on the site of an earlier church.

This is, perhaps, reminiscent of the layout excavated at Jarrow (Cramp 2005), where two major buildings (*op cit*, buildings A and B) were found, built in line east-west (Fig 98), on a terrace similar to that at Dacre, also to the south of the early medieval churches. It is notable that if the alignments of the channels at Dacre were extended to the north, then one would head for the approximate junction of the present nave and chancel of the church, whilst the other would point some way to the west of that structure, providing some support to the contention that they drained buildings no longer in existence (Fig 99). Indeed, the buildings at Jarrow were placed centrally to the western, basilican, church, the Eastern church, now the chancel of the parish church, projecting further to the east (Cramp 2005,

356; Pl 61). No parallels have been found for such extensive drains in an early medieval context, the most similar perhaps being those that flushed medieval monasteries, although these tended to be even bigger (see, for instance, those at Furness Abbey or Fountains, which could be walked through; Pl 62).

Whilst no early finds came from secure contexts associated with the drain, the material from the backfill of the earlier excavation, which only excavated between the stones and directly above them (*p 152*), was entirely early medieval, and of significant quality. This included an escutcheon, that could have come from a book or wooden object, a gold ring, and the only stylus from the site (*Ch 3*; Pl 63). This goes some way to confirm the early medieval date of the feature and also the status of the buildings the channels were draining.

The unexpected feature of the re-excavation of the drain was that it proved not to have been the earliest presence in the southern churchyard. It clearly sealed activity that seemed to focus to the south, beyond the bounds of the churchyard, where earthworks are visible in the field. Indeed, the drain seems to cut through these, taking an arcing course away from what might have been expected as the shortest route to a watercourse, as though it perhaps serviced other buildings there. The ground at the southern extreme of the trench was waterlogged, unlike anywhere else excavated, and this tantalisingly preserved a wattle fence or wall panel forming the southern trench section, and quite significant quantities of wood, which appeared to have been dumped (*Ch 2, p 43*). Where identifiable, this was of oak, and was perhaps building debris, again relating to activity to the south.

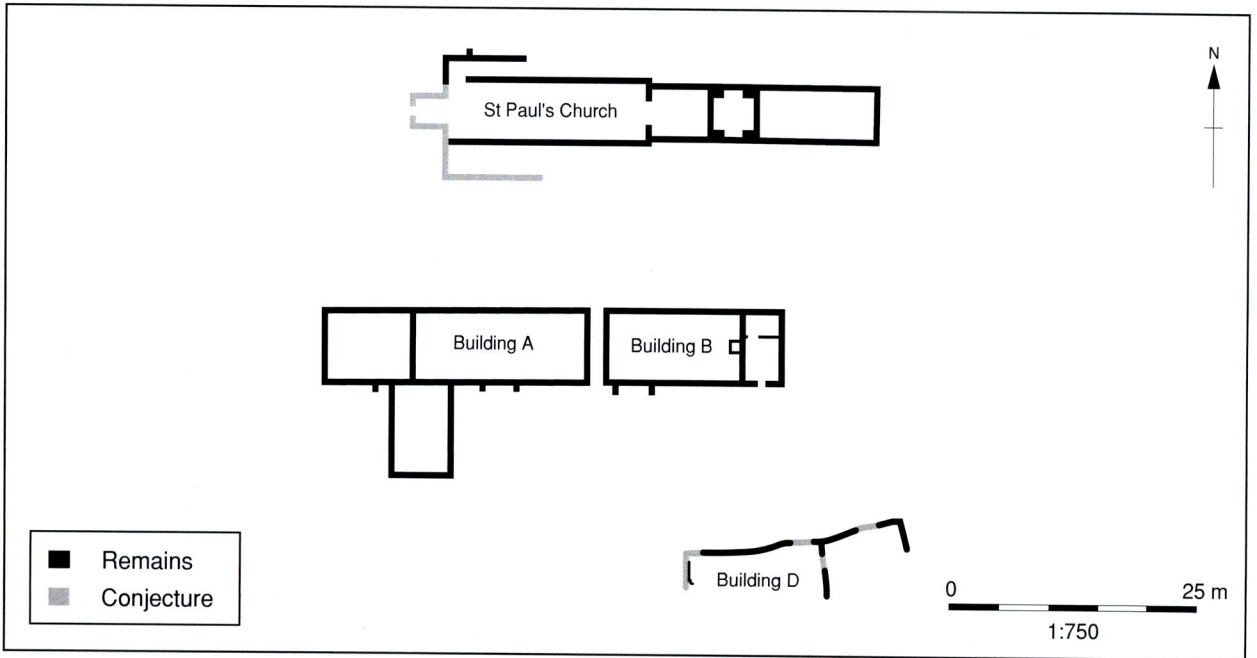

*Figure 98: The layout of the buildings excavated at Jarrow in relation to the church*

St Paul's Church

Building A

Building B

Building D

■ Remains
■ Conjecture

0    25 m
1:750

N

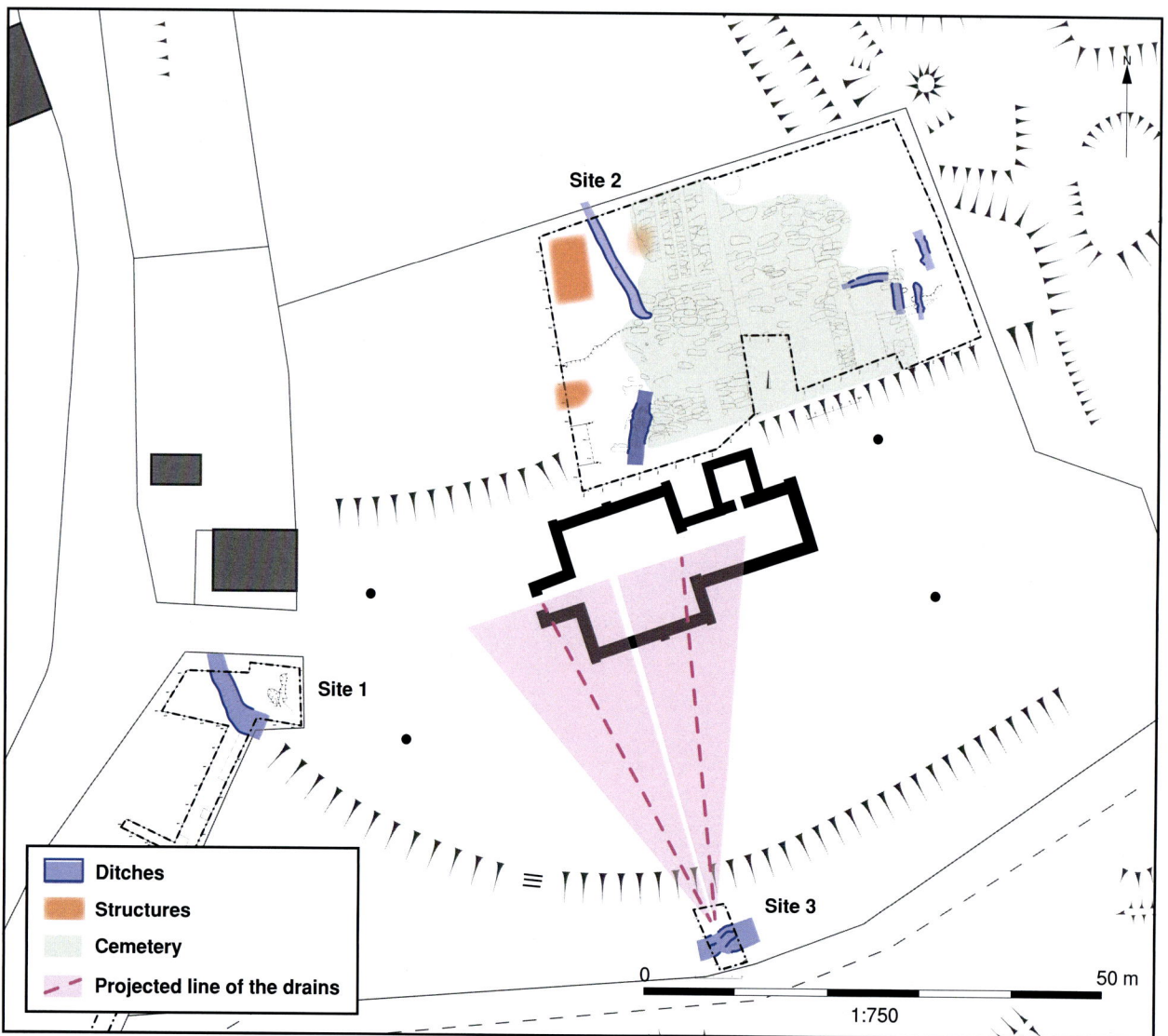

*Figure 99: The early medieval features at Dacre in relation to the church*

Site 2

Site 1

Site 3

Ditches
Structures
Cemetery
Projected line of the drains

0    50 m
1:750

N

154

*Plate 61: Model of the excavated early medieval buildings at Jarrow*

*Plate 62: One of the major drains at Furness Abbey*

*Plate 63: The stylus*

This in turn had partially infilled a ditch, which proved to be the primary activity on the site. Whilst different from that excavated in the Orchard in a similar, primary, position, in terms of the shape of the cut, these had a similar relationship to the bank forming the southern medieval churchyard boundary, and seemed to form a relatively similar arc, though admittedly not an absolute fit. No evidence of a similar ditch in a primary position was noted in the northern churchyard, and, indeed, if the logical curve of these ditches were to be followed, this would be no surprise, as the curve would take such a feature to the west and north of the present churchyard (Fig 100).

The question of the origin and meaning of circular enclosures around churches is a vexed one, once having been claimed as evidence of Celtic, rather than Northumbrian (following the Roman tradition), Christian sites (Thomas 1971a, 50; 1971b, 109). This cannot be proven but the link to early medieval sites remains (O'Sullivan 1980; 1985, 32), many clearly ancient sites having evidence that they were once enclosed in such a manner, as at Ninekirks, some seven miles (10 km) to the north-east (St Joseph 1978). Whilst the ideal of enclosing such sites with a formal barrier might well have been by use of topographical features, if not entirely notional, there is growing evidence for enclosures of *c* 150-300 m in association

(Blair 2005, 198). Documentary evidence suggests that monastic sites would have contained a multiplicity of buildings, probably zoned, as in later monasteries, perhaps visible at Hoddom (Lowe 2006), Whitby (Peers and Radford 1943), and Hartlepool (Daniels 1988). Indeed, at Hoddom, aerial photography has indicated an enclosed area of around 8 ha (20 acres; Lowe 1991), accentuating how little of such sites has actually been examined archaeologically.

## Conclusions

The wealth of evidence of early medieval activity, when added to the documentary reference for a monastery at Dacre, demonstrates that the site can be included in the growing corpus of such sites in Northumbria. The material accords well with the site having been established, probably, in the late seventh century: it was certainly in existence before 731, when Bede completed the *Historia Ecclesiastica* (HE, bk 4; Colgrave and Mynors 1969). However, it also demonstrates that without the documentary evidence, whilst the early medieval date of the cemetery and associated buildings would not be in doubt, the nature of the site still would be; in other words, can a monastic, as opposed to any other form of ecclesiastical site, be recognised from archaeological features and the material culture alone, without documentary support? This has been debated for sites such as Flixborough

156

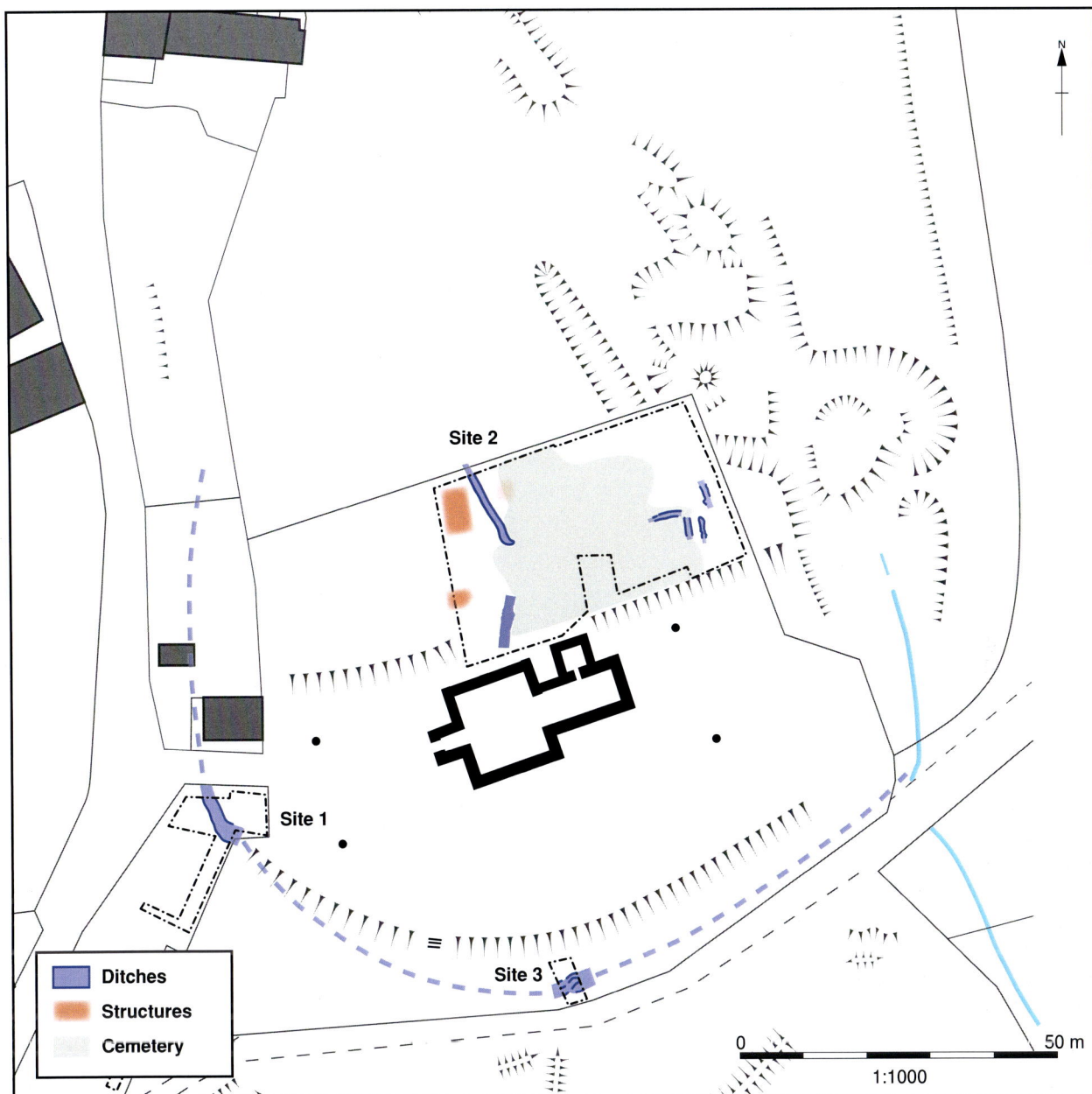

*Figure 100: The southern churchyard and Orchard boundaries in relation to the excavated features*

in particular, in terms of what criteria denote a primarily ecclesiastical as opposed to primarily secular site (Loveluck 2007), and in an ecclesiastical context, in terms of what constitutes a monastery, at St Michael's Church, Workington (Zant and Parsons 2019). This is exacerbated by the necessarily small, and presumably biased, samples of such sites that have been excavated.

It is clear from cemeteries at other documented monasteries that these also served a wider populace than the traditional view of an adult male community, as both women and children have been found buried at, for instance, Whithorn and Monkwearmouth (Hill 1997; Cramp 2005). This of course begs the question as to whether the 'traditional' view of a monastic cemetery can be applied at this time. Indeed, medieval

burials in monasteries provide a remarkable variety of people, of both sexes, and adults and children, apart from in the area reserved for the brethren (*eg* Furness Abbey (Rowland *et al* in prep) or Norton Priory (Brown and Howard Davis 2008)). The exclusively adult occupants of the graves at Dacre, as far as can be ascertained, may suggest that the excavated cemetery was in some way 'special', or simply that there was zonation, and the area reserved for children was not within the excavated site.

The amount of early medieval finds marks Dacre out from other sites in Cumbria, including church sites, excavated to date, yet, despite the quality of the material, it is quite sparse in comparison with sites such as Flixborough, which, it has been suggested, was a lordly settlement except for a

*Plate 64: The four intricately carved faces of the ninth-century cross-shaft (Bailey and Cramp 1988, Dacre 1)*

period in the ninth century (Loveluck 2007, ch 9). Indeed, the 'cleanness' of monastic sites has been remarked upon (Cramp 2005, 360). The presence of a stylus, indicating literacy, had been thought to indicate a monastic settlement, but again, the site at Flixborough has challenged this, although admittedly the greatest amount of evidence for literacy came from the period where a monastic interlude has been posited (Loveluck 2007).

The quality of the sculpture at Dacre is certainly very high, the early ninth-century cross fragment having highly unusual iconography, in the form of the figures inhabiting the vinescroll on one face, with the remarkable 'lion' associated (Bailey and Cramp 1988, Dacre 1; Pl 64). Whilst there are parallels for individual elements seen on the fragment, the cross itself in its entirety cannot be paralleled. It has been suggested that there was a good Classical model for its inspiration, and that the alternation of interlace and fret patterns on other faces drew its inspiration from contemporary manuscripts (*ibid*).

## Dacre in the Tenth- and Eleventh Centuries

After the documentary reference in the *Historia Ecclesiastica* (Bede HE, bk 4, ch 32; Colgrave and Mynors 1969), no further mention was made of Dacre until William of Malmesbury (*c* 1135) stated that it was the site of the meeting, in 927, between King Æthelstan and the kings and lords of the provinces to the north of his expanding kingdom (Giles 1876, ii, 6), which in the Worcester (D) recension of the *Anglo-Saxon Chronicle* is said to have taken place 'at Eamont' (*aet aemotum*; Earle and Plummer 1892, 107). William's account of the meeting describes the baptism of the son of Constantine, king of the Scots, 'at the sacred font' (Giles 1876, 133), although whether this refers to an existing church or a place consecrated specifically for the occasion may be debated.

It seems clear that William had some knowledge that Dacre was a place with a Christian tradition attached to it and, since Bede did not give precise details as to where the monastic site of Dacre was, it seems impossible that the knowledge that a place called Dacre lay close to the River Eamont was gleaned solely from a reading of the *Historia Ecclesiastica*. Given that William explicitly stated his reliance on earlier sources for his account of the event (Mynors *et al* 1998), it can be assumed that he had access to information about the exact site of the meeting between Æthelstan and the kings which has subsequently been lost.

There is no archaeological or documentary evidence for the date at which the monastery at Dacre ceased to function as such, although monasticism in Northumbria was clearly declining even in the eighth century (Sayles 1964, 64; Blair 2005) and had become almost invisible in the North by the end of the ninth century (Bailey 1980, 82) during the political implosion resulting from the incursions of Viking raiders and settlers, and the collapse of the Anglian royal house. Certainly, monasteries were not static entities, and changed through time to reflect the attitudes of the lay world to those communities (Cramp 2005, 360): there seems to have been less commitment to the austere life advanced during the period of conversion, but it is clear that many continued to function in some form, though seemingly impoverished (Blair 2005, 320). By the tenth century, patronage of the tradition of Christian stone sculpture had been taken over by others, and became a largely lay art (Bailey 1980, 82), associated with lordly church sites, and with Anglo-Scandinavian tastes, epitomised in Cumbria, at any rate, by the great cross at Gosforth (Pl 65).

Plate 65: The Gosforth cross (courtesy Adam Parsons)

Cumbria of that time, which shows 'a novel and thoughtful approach to Christian doctrine' and which seems to have been used to proclaim the faith (Bailey 1977, 69-70), although in comparison to the earlier fragment, its style of carving was cruder. It is generally agreed that 'Viking-age' sculpture, as distinct from the preceding Northumbrian examples, was under the control of secular patrons and was used more in funerary contexts than previously (Bailey 1980, 82-3). The presence of such a cross at Dacre may therefore indicate either the continuing use of the early cemetery, or a part of it, for Christian burial, by this time with at least some of the graves marked by stone and also possibly wooden crosses, or else the establishment of a new churchyard on approximately the same site, probably because of a continuing tradition, even in the form of an existing community, that it was a religious place.

The erosion that had obviously taken place above the early cemetery in the northern churchyard seems to have removed all trace of old ground surfaces from a period before the thirteenth- or fourteenth century, so that the impression is given of a period of abandonment before the formal laying out of the medieval churchyard. The first churchyard boundary to the north of the church (bank 151/96; Ch 4, p 91) not only overlay the graves, but also clearly post-dated some of this erosion, since the graves, as excavated, were plainly not as deep as when they had first been dug.

The kingdom may have disintegrated, but there is no archaeological evidence for a dramatic end to the pre-Conquest activity at Dacre. Indeed, there is little datable evidence from the site to indicate any activity in the period of the two centuries before the Norman occupation of the area in 1092, apart from the sculptural fragment from the church. Without firm dating, however, much of the archaeological evidence remains equivocal. Pollen analysis from southern Cumbria indicates that some woodland regeneration took place in the eleventh century (Hodgkinson *et al* 2000, 47-9), and the possibility of some desertion and movement of settlements in the same period is implied by place-names, particularly 'old-by' (Winchester 1987, 38), which may represent a disruption in the development of the landscape (*op cit*, 133). It may be noted that the large farm of Aldby, first documented in 1203 (Armstrong *et al* 1950, 186), which seems to have had quite extensive lands to the east, forms the next settlement to the north of Dacre.

The Dacre Stone (Pl 66), the fragment of cross-shaft of tenth-century date found during the rebuilding of the eastern wall of the chancel in 1875 (Mathews 1891, 226), is the only clear evidence for the continuance or re-establishment on the site of Christian teaching in the Viking Age in the period before the Norman occupation of Cumbria in 1092. The shaft is a piece, unusual amongst the surviving sculpture from

Plate 66: The Dacre Stone (Bailey and Cramp 1988, Dacre 2)

The constant soil creep down the slope to the north of the church had resulted in a deposit 1.3 m deep, which had built up against the formal churchyard boundaries (firstly against bank *151*, subsequently against wall *28*). The creation of this deep deposit had presumably been accelerated by medieval ploughing, although the field to the north of the church seems to have been turned over to permanent pasture in the sixteenth century (E H A Stretton *pers comm*), giving a period of no more than 400 years for the accumulation of the deposit. This demonstrates the potential scale of the erosion in the 200 or 300 years before the medieval churchyard was formally defined.

No particular evidence of soil creep, however, was identified in the southern churchyard, either in the form of eroded surfaces or deposits of hillwash, which suggests that the problem was not so severe there, presumably because there was no agricultural activity immediately up the slope. This has relevance for the evidence of erosion below the churchyard boundary, since it would indicate agricultural activity on the steep slope to the north of the church before the thirteenth century.

## The Development of the Parish of Dacre

The development of parishes in Cumbria seems largely to have taken place by the thirteenth century, although it appears to have resulted from a process which had begun by the tenth century at the latest (Winchester 1987, 23). It is generally accepted that most churches in rural areas had originated between the eighth and eleventh centuries, the oldest as minster churches, often originally monastic foundations, although the majority as proprietary chapels attached to manor houses (Rodwell 1981, 140-2). The forces which produced a widespread parochial system of small units from these beginnings, normally coterminous with single villages or manors (Addleshaw 1970, 11), can be traced in parts of southern England, where contemporary documentary sources survive, if not in abundance, at least in sufficient numbers to demonstrate the manner of its creation (Blair 2005, 158-60, 298-306). In the North, where documents are scarce, these developments are less easy to identify and the point at which many churches ceased to be entirely in the private possession of the lord of the manor is unknown. The payment of tithes, however, to a certain church gave a territorial dimension to the parish and the jealousy with which priests guarded their right to tithes led to the hardening of parish boundaries by the early Norman period (Winchester 1987, 23).

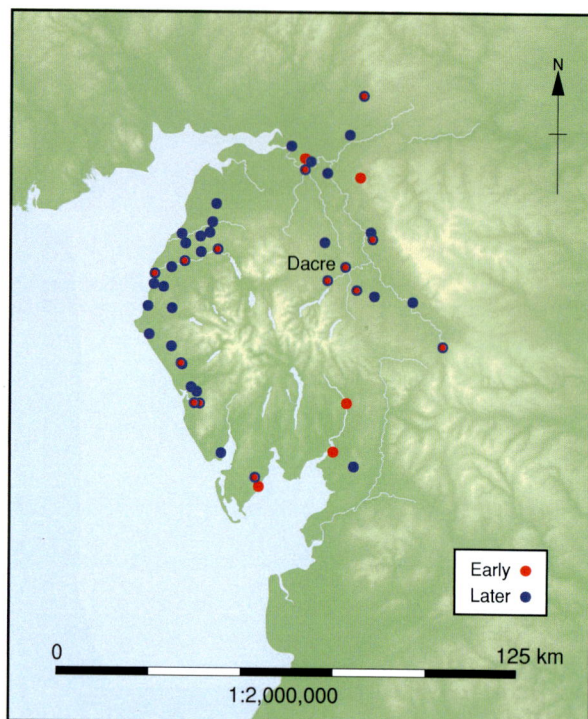

*Figure 101: The sites with early medieval stone sculpture in Cumbria*

Some 36 churchyards in Cumbria contain fragments of stone sculpture of the eighth- to eleventh centuries (Bailey and Cramp 1988), mostly sited along the west coast and around the Eden Valley, which may be used to indicate the location of at least the majority of the pre-Norman churches of the county (Fig 101). It seems clear, however, that there was a revitalisation of the church in Cumbria after the establishment of Anglo-Norman lords in the early twelfth century (Rose 1982, 119), culminating with the foundation of the diocese of Carlisle in 1133.

There is also evidence for the re-emergence in the area of the cults of various Celtic saints, such as Kentigern and Ninian, which may have been an attempt to give the new Norman lords a sense of continuity with the past (*op cit*, 130); several lives of saints were written at this time, for example the *Vita Niniani* by Ailred of Rievaulx (Forbes 1874) and the *Vita Kentigerni* by Jocelin of Furness (*ibid*). It is less certain that this revitalisation should be seen as the refoundation of churches in a society which had come close to anarchy, lying as it did in a political no-man's-land between England and Scotland (Rose 1982, 122), or simply as a vigorous building campaign in functioning parishes as a reflection of the assertion of control, albeit by an act of piety, by new tenurial masters. It is, however, clear that a great many of the churches and chapels were built or rebuilt at this time (Bouch 1948, 9).

The parish of Dacre would appear geographically to have been carved out of the parish of Greystoke,

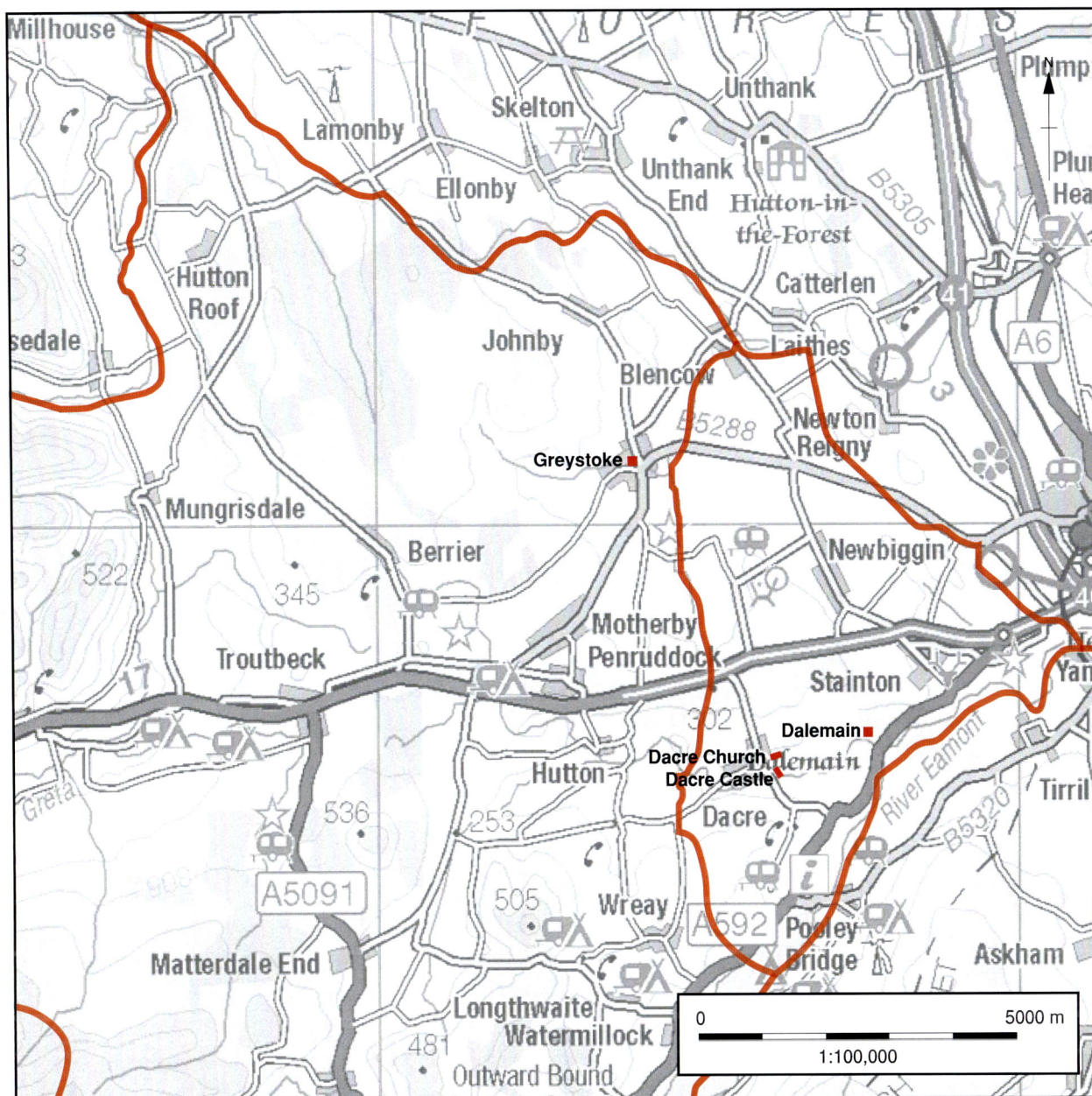

*Figure 102: The relationship between the parishes of Dacre and Greystoke, with Dalemain, and Dacre church and castle*

although given the evidence for a pre-Norman church at Dacre and the lack of evidence for a similar structure at Greystoke, the reverse may be true (Fig 102). Of the two, Dacre certainly seemed to be possessed of the better agricultural land, whilst Greystoke was formed of the higher, more marginal ground. The ecclesiastical entity seems to have more or less equated with the secular manor of Dacre, perhaps reflecting a reorganisation of religious boundaries to create a unit coterminous with the estate of a new lord. It is notable in Cumbria that there was frequently a relationship between a barony and a single parish church, presumed to be the successor to the pre-Norman mother church of the area (as at Kendal (the church of Kentdale) and Millom; Winchester 1987)), and the relationship of the barony of Egremont with the church of St Bees

could possibly be similar to that originally pertaining in Greystoke, where the mother church at Dacre was at some distance from the secular centre of power. The area around Penrith shows clear traces of the fragmentation of both ecclesiastical and secular power, connected with the creation of the royal forest of Inglewood, which may have distorted the original patterns of lordship there (*ibid*).

The deficiency of documentary sources is as great in connection with Dacre as elsewhere in Cumbria, the first reference to a priest (Nicholas de Appleby) not occurring until the late thirteenth century (Thompson 1906, I, 85); at that time the church was rectorial and the lord of the manor (the head of the Dacre family) held the advowson. In the late thirteenth century at least, Dacre and Greystoke were extremely rich in terms of the surrounding parishes in the Deanery of Cumberland, presumably reflecting the stable conditions of the preceding century: in 1291, they produced a third of the revenue from the Deanery for the Papal Taxation, although Dacre seems to have suffered more heavily from the uncertainties of the succeeding years, since its revenue had fallen from £13 6/8d in 1291, to 100/- (£5) in 1341 (*ibid*). In contrast, Greystoke had declined from £20 to £13, and Penrith only from £8 13/4d to £8 during the same period.

The creation of a churchyard at Dacre, with a formal boundary of, at first, a bank and ditch, then later a stone wall added to the crest of the bank, seems to have occurred at approximately the time of the religious revitalisation of the region. Presumably the wall was added as the ditch was no longer maintained, and a robust barrier was seen to be required to separate the churchyard from the fields and apparently agricultural activity to the north. The pottery evidence associated with both the bank and ditch (*151/215*), and the wall (*28; Ch 5*) dated from the twelfth- to fourteenth centuries, but the sequence suggests that the earlier boundary was in existence by the twelfth century, and coins associated with the wall indicated that it had been constructed before *c* 1300. The tower arch in the church is clearly twelfth century in origin (although reconstructed in 1810) and the chancel is constructed in a late Romanesque style (Pevsner 1967, 116), implying a general rebuilding programme within the site during the twelfth- and early thirteenth centuries, physical evidence for the earlier church being present in several voussoirs with zig-zag ornamentation visible in the church today (*pers obs*).

The position of the churchyard boundary is worthy of comment, since there is some possibility that its southern side was constructed on the approximate line of an earlier enclosure (*p 156*) and the northern side is unusual in having been so close to the church (only some 6 m to the north). Not only is this boundary exceptional in its proximity to the church, but its creation also effectively deconsecrated a part of the earlier cemetery. This could be explained, at least partly, by the supposition that either the whole cemetery, or more probably this northern part of it, had been abandoned at some time before the formal reconstitution of the sacred enclosure, the extent of the cemetery in use shrinking inwards towards its focus, presumably an earlier church on approximately the same site as the present structure. The rebuilding of an extant church, where there would be a reason to keep the exact position of the structure, coupled with the earlier abandonment of the northern part of an existing cemetery, could therefore produce such a phenomenon. The power of the lord to adjust the boundaries of all elements of a settlement was considerable (Roberts 1987), however, and should not perhaps be ignored in such a circumstance, particularly if there was some over-riding tenurial reason for the deconsecration.

If the supposition is correct that wall *18* in the Orchard (*Ch 4, p 112*) once formed part of the western boundary to the churchyard, why it ceased to perform this function is puzzling. The excavation demonstrated that a structure, probably half-timbered, had been constructed utilising wall *18* as its western end, possibly in the fourteenth- or fifteenth century. The erection of buildings within churchyards, particularly by inserting them into the perimeter wall, is perhaps unusual but by no means unique, as structures can form the churchyard boundary (as at Kirkby Lonsdale, or Lastingham; *pers obs*). The fifteenth-century rectory at Halsall, and the seventeenth-century grammar school in Leyland, both in Lancashire (Pevsner 1988, 135, 166), indicate that buildings actually in churchyards tended to be related to church activities, such as the provision of accommodation for the incumbent and, in the post-medieval period, a place for the education of the parish. Indeed, irregularities in many churchyards could have been caused by the severing of pieces from them (Roberts 1987).

It is possible that the structure at Dacre may have been a house for the priest, although there is no evidence for the location of the rectory before the mid-nineteenth century, so this must remain speculation. There was a very small amount of grozed window glass, its bubbly green metal suggesting it to be 'forest glass' (Hurst Vose 1980), thus possibly making it as late as the sixteenth- or seventeenth century, a small part from a lead ventilator grille, and the lead kame into which it was set. Most came from a layer (*21; Ch 4, p 115*) marking the decay the structure, and perhaps reflects a growing supply of window glass for lower-status domestic buildings (*ibid*).

## Dacre in the Later Medieval Period

In the medieval period, Dacre formed a mesne manor, held of the Barony of Greystoke by military suit and service (Whellan 1850, 523) and also in part by cornage (Nicolson and Burn 1777, II, 383), believed to be a render surviving from the pre-Norman period (Kapelle 1979, 51) and frequently used by historians to indicate a pre-Conquest estate. The village was one of five constablewicks (Dacre, Soulby, Stainton, Newbiggin, and Great Blencowe) within the larger parish (Hutchinson 1794, 467). Little, however, is known about the settlement itself in this period, and even the castle to the south of the church does not have convincing documentation associated with its construction, although it probably belongs to the early fourteenth century (Stretton 1994).

In 1286, the inquisition after the death of Ralph de Dacre (TNA C133/44/7) noted that the manor of Dacre contained a capital messuage, presumably the site on which the castle was constructed, 160 acres of demesne land, and 15 acres of demesne meadow, a park, a water mill, and a fulling mill. Twenty-four bovates, worth 3/3¼d each, and a number of cottagers (*cotarii*), who rendered 46/3d *per annum* for their cottages, are also listed. The manor was later destroyed by the Scots (Sharp and Stamp 1910, 19-35), but there is no documentary evidence of how long it took to recover, although the whole of Cumbria suffered a decline throughout much of the fourteenth century, from a combination of Scottish raids, pestilence of both man and animals, and, in the earlier part of the century, crop failures, creating famine conditions (Winchester 1987, 44-7).

By 1486, when Humphrey Dacre, lord of Dacre and Gilsland, died (TNA C142/1/12), the amount of demesne land had fallen to 30 acres of arable and six acres of meadow, and the water corn-mill was in ruins, although the fulling mill still appears to have been functioning, and the park is clearly recorded as having been walled. At this time, there were 12 messuages, with land and meadows adjacent, in the occupation of tenants at will, worth 3s each, and eight cottages with gardens, lands, and meadows adjacent, again in the occupation of tenants at will, worth 20d each. These brought in a rent that was not much greater than that from the *cotarii* 200 years earlier. Although the inquisition records that a certain tower had been newly built on the capital messuage (surely referring to a refurbishment rather than the reconstruction of the castle, which displays architecture from a century earlier; Stretton 1994), it is likely that by this stage the Dacre family rarely came to the manor, living mainly at Kirkoswald to the north (Brockington and Rose 2019).

The village was situated (and indeed still is) off the main routeways, but close to them, since it is less than five miles (8 km) from the main north-south route through Penrith (now the A6) and one of the major trans-Pennine highways (via Stainmore) also passed through Penrith, perhaps with a continuation towards Keswick via Greystoke. Since Dacre contained the parish church, it naturally formed the focus for a number of routes leading from the outlying hamlets of Soulby to the south-east, Stainton to the east, and Newbiggin and Great Blencowe to the north. Some of the routes have been remetalled in the twentieth century, but others survive merely as footpaths and bridleways. The present road system isolates the parish church in a cul-de-sac to the east of the main street, but it is clear that this once continued up the hill to Aldby, and probably also to Newbiggin, and that a further track skirted the southern side of the churchyard before leading to Stainton (Fig 103).

Most of the houses in the village now stand on the roads leading out of the valley towards the north and west, but the excavation of medieval structures, dating from the fourteenth- to the sixteenth century, immediately to the north-east of the church (*Ch 4, p 98*), has demonstrated that the settlement spread further to the east in the medieval period. The excavation also indicated that most of the numerous earthworks in the field to the east and north of the churchyard were likely to be of similar date, perhaps even forming a row of structures on platforms along a hollow-way which joined with the track to Stainton. The westwards shift of the village in the post-medieval period may simply have resulted from the shrinking of the settlement (Roberts 1987, 94), or possibly from the growing dominance of the roads that have survived as through routes, encouraging the construction of new dwellings along them.

The excavated structures, particularly in their latest form, had the appearance of being the major part of a small farmstead, the perimeter of which was bounded to the north and south by ditches, and apparently by the hollow-way to the east, beyond the excavated area (Fig 104). The axis of the holding seems to have been east-west, almost parallel with the churchyard wall, as the ditch (*Ch 4, p 96, 1421*) and later wall (*47*), which formed the southern limit, butted the churchyard at an acute angle and increasingly diverged from it to the east. On the northern side the ditch (*698; Ch 4, p 101*) and later possible wall (*57*) became indistinct towards the west and the great depth of hillwash in the south-western part of the northern churchyard, which was in marked contrast to that in the area of the medieval buildings, would suggest that ploughing took place in the vicinity. This leaves the position of the western boundary of the croft uncertain.

Three structures were identified within the area, two aligned east-west (Structures B and C), with the eastern building approximately at right-angles (Structure A/A1). All were constructed of timber, although there was evidence that Structure A had at least partly been rebuilt in stone, probably when a fireplace had been added to the southern gable (*Ch 4, p 103*). This provided the only indication of a domestic structure in the complex. Ceramic ridge tiles were found in association with its demolition spreads (*Ch 5, p 123*), implying that it had been roofed with thatch or reeds, and capped with tiles. A spread of decayed small micaceous roofing stones (*Ch 4, p 103, 50*) may have come from the post-in-posthole building (B) to the west, which was separated from the proposed

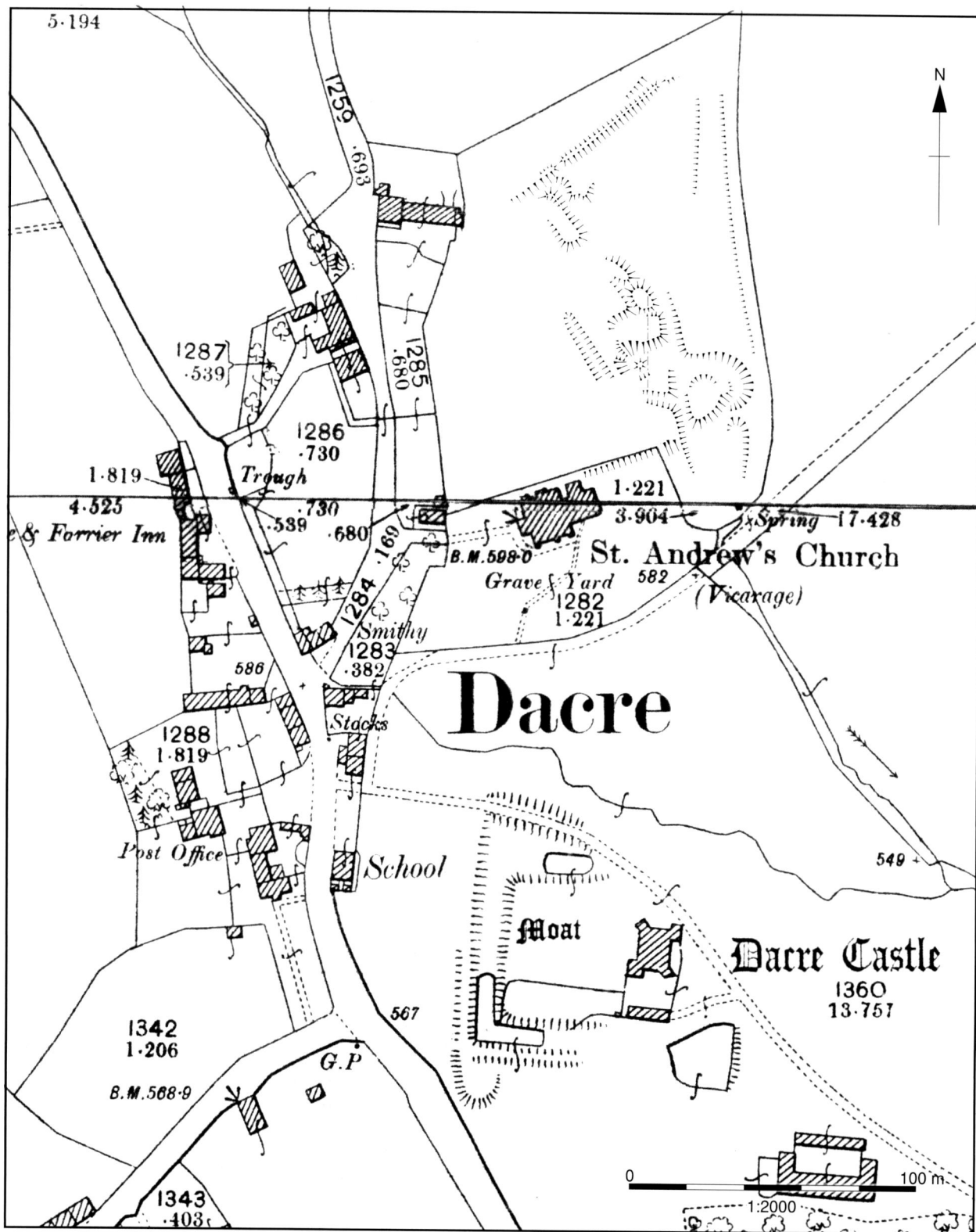

*Figure 103: Second Edition Ordnance Survey map (1900), showing Dacre as the hub of several routes*

domestic accommodation by a metalled yard (45), although its sharp angle towards Structure A1 might indicate the extent of this building and also that it had been at least partially roofed in stone. A few lead roofing nails were also recovered, but these cannot be unarguably linked to the medieval buildings on the site.

Both these structures were possibly constructed with clay walls, since a deposit of this material (1074) was associated with the decay of Structure B, and it has been suggested that the early date of some of the pottery in the demolition layers may have resulted from sherds being used as a binding agent in daub walls (*Ch 5, p 122*). Less is known about the northern

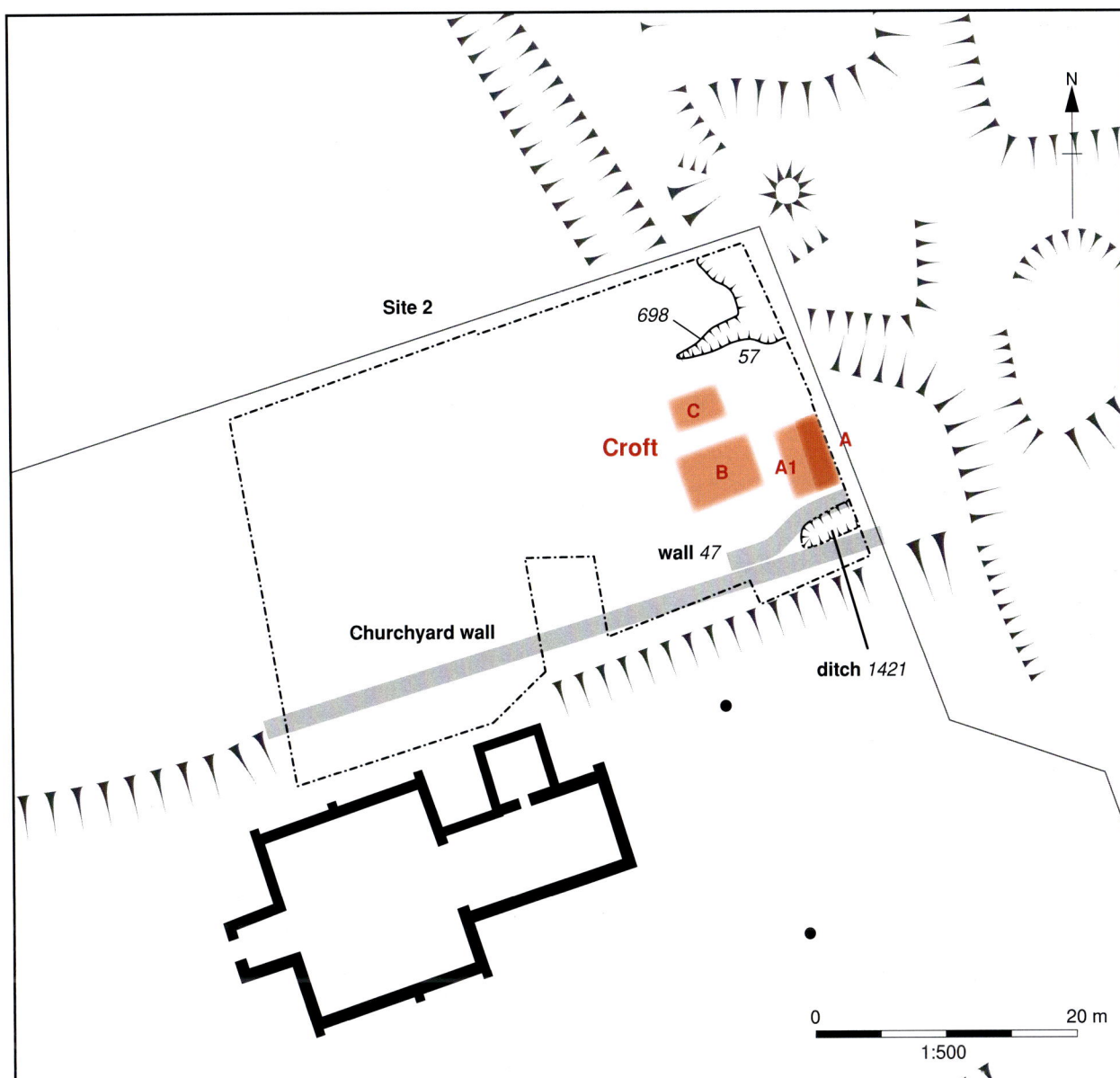

*Figure 104: Buildings A, B, and C, forming the croft in the eastern part of the site*

and apparently smallest structure of the group (C), although this had a stone floor with a drain leading from it, which perhaps indicates that it was a byre. It may have been turf-walled, with a timber frame, since it had a posthole at each of its four corners, but no other visible means of support. A further building platform to the north was seen to have a ditch (*698*) to the west and south, although none of the internal elements of this property lay within the excavated area.

The farmland of Dacre appears to have begun immediately to the north of the earthworks surrounding the church, since a large bank there separated them from a small area of ridge and furrow, which had survived modern ploughing and drainage. There is also some evidence of another field, bounded to the east and south by the modern village roads (CA Q/RE/1/46) and the settlement

may have been constricted to the east by the park, the perimeter of which is still visible in the modern field boundaries, particularly the massive wall to the east of the churchyard (Pl 67). If this were indeed the western boundary of the park attached to Dacre Castle (Cal Inq pm, Ralph de Dacre, 1286; TNA C133/44/7), mentioned by Daniel Sandford in *c* 1675; Ferguson 1890b, 34), the excavated structures would have lain in the confined space between the church and this park. The available evidence does not indicate why medieval structures should have been constructed there, so close to the perimeter of the churchyard, particularly when there was no obvious pressure of population, as in some urban centres, nor a lack of adequate land for building.

There is also no precise reason why this part of the settlement should have declined, probably during the sixteenth century, although this seems to have

*Plate 67: Looking north-east across the site to the earthworks, and the probable park wall beyond*

been a period of unsettled tenurial conditions in the county, culminating, in 1610, in the setting aside of tenant right and the substitution of 40-year leases in a number of Cumberland manors, including Dacre (Appleby 1978, 76). The Dacre lands were split after the death of Thomas, Lord Dacre, in 1458, many of his estates devolving to a female heir (Stretton 1994, 22). The manor of Dacre continued in the hands of the Dacres of Gilsland until the late sixteenth century (*op cit*, 28), although the family probably rarely visited it, and after the rebellion of Leonard Dacre in 1569 it became crown property; the castle was certainly tenanted by 1580 (*op cit, 55;* Brierley 1912, 89). Francis Lennard, Lord Dacre of the South, recovered some of the estates of the northern Dacres in 1657 but the manor was finally sold to the Hasell family of Dalemain in 1715 (Whellan 1850, 523). During the previous 150 years, only the Earl of Sussex, in the later seventeenth century, seems to have taken any direct interest in the estate, refurbishing the castle in *c* 1675 (Stretton 1994, 62).

The later sixteenth century would appear to have been a time of disease and even famine in the county, the parish registers indicating that the parish shared in the population crisis in the winter of 1587-8, possibly resulting from a typhus epidemic (Appleby 1978, 103). In the parish of Dacre, the death rate leapt from 22 in 1586 to 63 in 1587, declining to 37 in 1588; the majority of the deaths would seem to have been of adults (*op cit*, 105). The crisis may have been triggered by a bad harvest in 1586, coinciding with a dramatic fall in the price of wool, and it may be notable that the number of baptisms decreased during this period, even in parishes without heightened death rates, perhaps an indication of malnutrition (*op cit*, 107-8). Four successive bad harvests devastated much of England in 1594-7 and, again, this seems to have been reflected in the high mortality rate in the Penrith area, particularly from November 1596 to February 1598 (*op cit*, 112).

A final period of near-famine conditions may have existed in the area, following the unsettled situation created by the Civil Wars of the 1640s, although the area itself did not suffer from any major conflict. The harvests failed in 1647-9 and, in 1649, the death rate in the parish rose to 27, compared with an average of less than 14 in the years 1644-52 (*op cit*, 155). A combination of natural disaster and tenurial change may therefore have led to the desertion of the eastern element of the village.

## The growth of pottery use

Medieval pottery forms a significant part of the material assemblage from the later twelfth century onwards, and must reflect its growing use in local households; in urban centres such as Carlisle, pottery use clearly developed rapidly (McCarthy and Brooks 1992). In the more rural parts of the county, widespread pottery use does not seem to have taken hold as readily as in these growing urban centres, and its adoption as a part of normal household equipment by people living away from the major centres, especially in the scattered settlements which are a feature of Cumbria, may not have occurred until a considerably later date. Further south, in urban centres such as Chester, pottery dating from before the Norman Conquest is relatively well-known (Carrington 1975; Newman 2006, 109), but its use does not seem to have extended into Lancashire and further north. Indeed, its use in Cumbria appears, rather, to echo the situation further to the north in southern Scotland, and, indeed, there are strong similarities in some fabrics and forms (Miller 2011), which indicate that strong ties existed between northern Cumbria and Scotland. There, despite excavations in several of the Border burghs, no pottery earlier than the twelfth century has been recognised (McCarthy and Brooks 1988).

The chronology and development of the pottery industry within the region after its conquest by the Normans in 1092 (Earle and Plummer 1892) remains uncertain until more kiln sites are recognised and investigated. No doubt vessels in organic materials, principally wood and leather, and more expensively in copper alloy and iron, provided perfectly adequate vessels for cooking, handling, and storage, and the many other uses that have been posited for pottery (McCarthy and Brooks 1988). It is quite likely that the adoption of ceramic containers for storage, cooking, food preparation, and possibly decanting wine or ale, represented a significant departure from centuries-old domestic habits. Indeed, the introduction of pottery vessels may well have been seen as something of an innovation, perhaps accompanying other changes in diet and methods of cooking, amongst the incoming Norman regime as it took a firm hold in the early twelfth century.

There must have been an influx of potters amongst the numerous craftsmen who first built, and then serviced, the growth of urban centres, often linked to the new castles, and their hinterlands, which followed the establishment of Norman baronies (Winchester 1987, 124-7). Indeed, the increasing use of pottery would have led to the growth of potting as an added or alternative means of earning a livelihood in rural areas. As there is, however, a lack of clarity about the scale of production, and whether it was undertaken at an individual or more industrial scale, or the extent to which pots were brought in from elsewhere, the economic impact of this change should not be overstated.

Thus, it seems that pottery must have come into regular use, at least in the more urbanised parts of the county, during the twelfth and thirteenth centuries (Ch 5). The sources of this pottery still remain unclear, with much of the assemblage from Carlisle regarded as probably of local production (McCarthy and Brooks 1992). It is still the case that no kiln sites are known from Carlisle itself, although they are suspected on the evidence of wasters associated with burnt material from behind the Castle Street frontage (Jope and Hodges 1955). To the immediate east of the city, at Cumwhinton, substantial numbers of wasters implied a kiln or kilns nearby (Railton et al 2014). Only at Muckleground, near Waberthwaite on the west coast, at the edge of the south-western fells, have kilns been archaeologically attested (Cherry and Cherry 1984), while a documentary reference hints at others at St Bees in 1307 (TNA E101/370/16 f15v), although it is uncertain whether this refers to earthenware as distinct from metal potting, the term potter applying, at that time, to both (Fay 1920). Pottery production at or close to Penrith is possible, and may also have been the case for other Cumbrian towns. By the fifteenth- to sixteenth century, production of the ubiquitous reduced green-glazed pottery is known from the Silverdale and Docker Moor kilns in north Lancashire (Edwards 1977; White 1977; 2000).

This provides the background against which the pottery from Dacre must be seen. The earliest medieval material is probably represented by Fabrics 6 and 7 (Ch 5, p 119; Appendix 1), both characterised by a coarse gritty red and white/pink oxidised body, which in some instances may have been hand-made. These fabrics are closely related to the widespread Northern Gritty-ware tradition (McCarthy and Brooks 1988), and was almost certainly made in many places, on both sides of the Pennines. The most reliable dating has so far come from Yorkshire and the North East, between the mid-late eleventh- and thirteenth centuries (C Cumberpatch pers comm; Mace 2015, 36). Forms at Carlisle include both cooking pots and large globular jugs, not dissimilar to the twelfth-thirteenth-century tripod pitcher traditions further south (McCarthy and Brooks 1992). At Dacre, unglazed cooking pots have been found in the typical twelfth-century forms, and tended to appear earlier than jugs (occasionally decorated), indicated by the presence of a small number of glazed sherds and, much more rarely, bowls. These vessels essentially provided the kitchen and tablewares of the day.

From the twelfth century on, the pottery charted the slow changes in technology which characterised medieval pottery elsewhere (McCarthy and Brooks 1988), with the appearance of first partially reduced, and then, by the fourteenth century and later, completely reduced fabrics which again fall within the wider reduced green-glazed tradition of the North. Cookwares during this period of change became less important, and new forms were introduced, including pipkins and one or two dishes, perhaps reflecting the introduction of metal cooking vessels, and an increasing concentration on glazed vessels for the storage and serving of liquids. One such change was the gradual movement towards the production of a finer body with less deliberately introduced filler and, by the fifteenth and sixteenth centuries, the development of a fine reduced, green-glazed ware of a type ubiquitous throughout northern England and Scotland (at Dacre, Fabric 1; *Ch 5, p 119*; *Appendix 1*; *eg* Ellison 1981; Haggarty 1980).

Another trend was towards the use of highly decorated wares, sometimes incorporating anthropomorphic motifs, in the thirteenth-fourteenth century, followed by a preference for plainer forms. Yet another was the late medieval dominance of drink-related containers, of which jugs and bung-hole cisterns used for brewing are the most important local types (*Ch 5, p 122*); the rarity of Cistercian-ware cups (Fabric 9) at Dacre may reflect the distance to the nearest production centre rather than a cultural preference for drinking vessels in materials other than ceramic, although it should be noted that Cistercian ware was well represented among pottery from Brougham Castle, only some seven miles (11 km) to the east (McCarthy and Brooks 1992). A small amount of vessel glass

was also found at Dacre. Like the window glass, it was probably a product of the northern glasshouses, active in the sixteenth and seventeenth centuries (Willmott 2002, 45-50), and seems to have come from a small number of drinking vessels (ribbed and wrythen beakers) used at table.

## Other material

It is quite clear that the number and quality of items associated with dress are both much reduced for the medieval period, and it is of interest that the few which can be dated are confined to the fourteenth century or later. There are simple buckles, a strap loop, lace tags (aglets), and small dress pins (*Ch 5, p 125*), all commonplace additions to dress, but all very practical, and in no way susceptible to swift changes in fashion. There is, in addition, a single copper-alloy finger ring, from hillwash *121* in the northern churchyard, but no other items of jewellery. Other household items are equally few, from which only a fine barrel padlock (*Ch 5, p 126*) stands out (Pl 68); whilst by no means a close parallel, the decorative treatment is similar to that on a padlock from St Michael's Church, Workington (Zant and Parsons 2019, 63, fig 31.37), dated to the fourteenth to fifteenth century. One, possibly two, lead pricket candleholders were also found (*Ch 5, p 132*); these, although not closely datable, seem to have become more common in the medieval period, with an increased use of candles from the thirteenth century onward (PAS 2021), and are an obvious indicator of the use of artificial light.

0          10 mm

*Plate 68: The small medieval padlock from Dacre*

## Post-medieval Dacre

It seems likely that, by the end of the sixteenth- or early seventeenth century, deposition within the excavations had become very limited. Coins and small dress accessories continued to be deposited, but as these comprised common artefacts, for example copper-alloy buttons, they were probably lost by those attending church, working in the field immediately to the north, or maintaining the enceinte, including, for example, grave diggers.

Once the manor had been sold to the Hasell family, Dalemain, a mile (1.5 km) to the east of Dacre, became the centre of the estate (Fig 105), and Dacre Castle was converted into a farmhouse, subsequently becoming a ruin until restored some 50 years ago (E H A Stretton *pers comm*). The fields were enclosed in the late eighteenth century and the commons in 1808 (CA Q/RE/1/46). The parish as a whole is recorded as containing 151 families in 1747 (Nicolson and Burn 1777, II, 384), 712 inhabitants in 1801, rising to a population of 904 in 1821 (Parson and White 1829, 468), and 975 in 1841 (Mannix and Whellan 1847, 250), but Dacre, although still the centre of the parish, did not expand; of the latter population, only 204 lived in the township of Dacre itself and this declined to 163 people in 1851, out of a total of 954 (*ibid*).

The village is recorded in the nineteenth century as a small settlement, of which only the castle and a school were worthy of note (Parson and White 1829, 468). In contrast, the neighbouring village of Stainton, to the north-east, seems to have expanded to become the dominant member of the parish during the eighteenth century, an event reflected in the surviving structures of each settlement, since in Dacre almost no new building has been undertaken since the early nineteenth century, whereas in Stainton, all periods of architecture from the eighteenth to the twentieth centuries are visible.

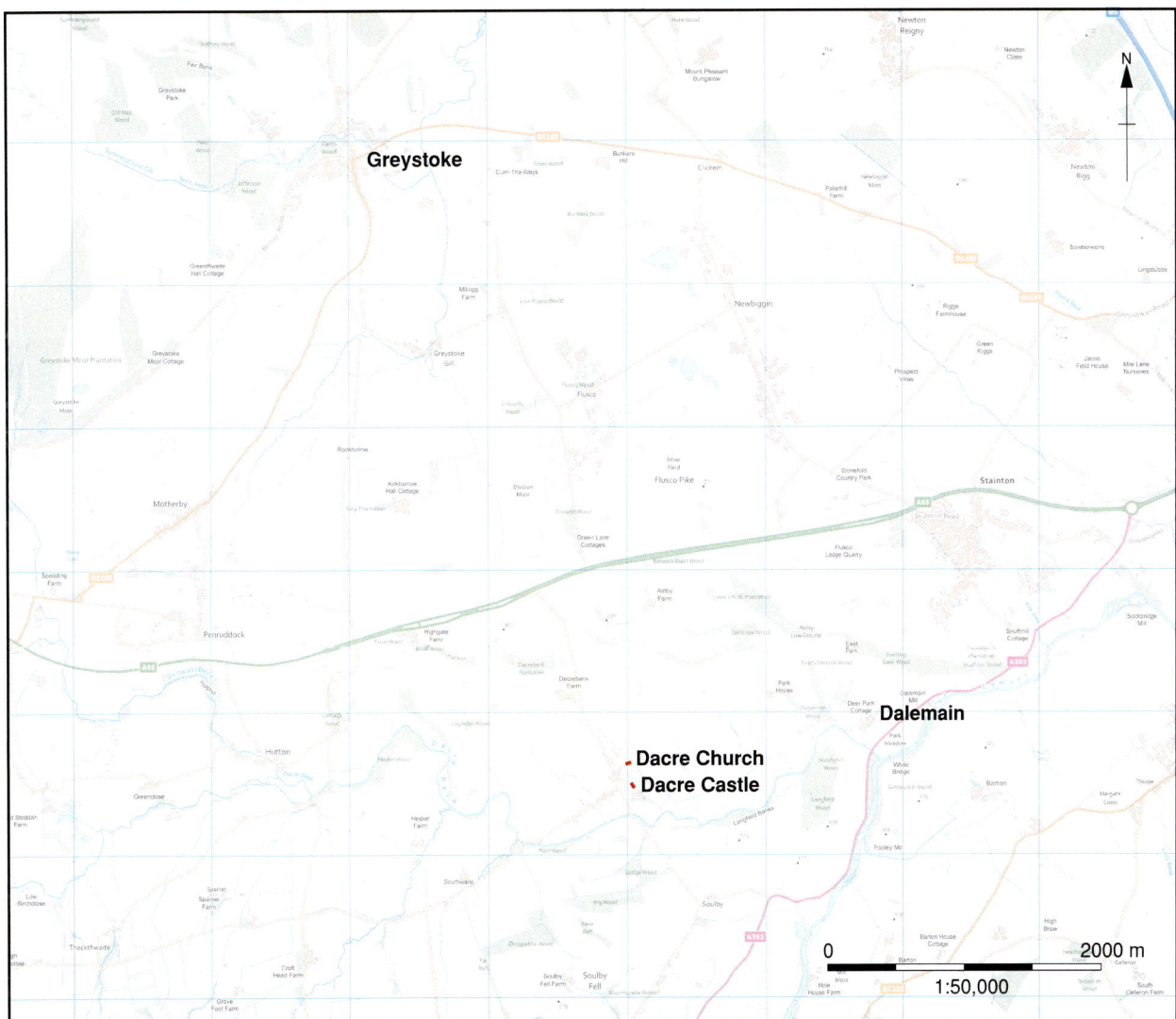

*Figure 105: The relationship between Greystoke, Dalemain, and Dacre church and castle*

# Conclusions

The excavations at Dacre have provided a wealth of evidence of both early medieval and medieval activity, periods relatively little studied until recently in the North West, particularly in a rural context (Newman 2006; Newman and Newman 2007, 97). They have also produced evidence of importance for debates beyond the county and the North West, such as exactly what criteria should be used to define an early medieval monastery (Blair 2005). Dacre can now be put alongside the sites at Jarrow and Monkwearmouth, Whithorn, Hoddom, Hartlepool, and Whitby, all of which have of necessity examined different elements of such sites, allowing some synthesis of the material.

The metal chest fittings are also of importance for an understanding of burial rites, seemingly for specific groups, that are particular to Northumbria at this period (Craig-Atkins 2012), apparently spreading later in small numbers into Mercia and perhaps Wessex. The corpus of early medieval finds is also important, as these are rare in the North, although the Portable Antiquities Scheme is revolutionising thinking on both the amount of metalwork in circulation and also the quality (Newman 2006). It is noticeable that when Dacre was first excavated, there were almost no northern parallels for the material, but it has now been possible to cite numerous comparators. Indeed, the weight of evidence that meets the criteria posited by John Blair for such sites (2005, 198-204) is remarkable, encompassing layout, enclosure, zonation, the quality of the finds, and the sculpture, to add to the documentary evidence that tends to link Dacre to the communities of the eastern heartland of Northumbria known to Bede.

Studies of medieval artefacts, and especially pottery, in north-west England continue to be sparse (Newman and Newman 2007), the most comprehensive views still being based on assemblages from Carlisle, where a series of significant interventions, producing large amounts of stratified pottery and other artefacts, has helped to create a relatively sound framework and a local pottery fabric series (see, for instance, McCarthy and Brooks 1992; Bradley and Miller 2009). The last decade or so in particular has seen significant progress. Within the city, publication of medieval material from the City Ditch in the Millennium Project (Bradley and Miller 2009), that at Rickergate (Miller 2011), and from the Lanes (Bradley and Howard-Davis in press) has, for the most part, supported and consolidated earlier work at Blackfriars Street (McCarthy and Taylor 1990) and St Nicholas Yard (Brooks 1999), and allowed analysis and understanding to be extended beyond the confines of Carlisle (McCarthy and Brooks 1992).

This has provided comparators for important pottery assemblages from urban centres such as Cockermouth (Miller 2012) and Penrith (Bradley 2015), and rural sites such as Cumwhinton (Bradley and Miller 2014), as well as groups from the south of the county, at Kendal (McCarthy and Brooks 1992; Whitehead *et al* 2013). Nonetheless, the medieval pottery and other artefacts from Dacre still remain an important addition to the meagre medieval corpus from Cumbria (McCarthy and Brooks 1992).

*Plate 69: Looking north to the church at Dacre, from Dacre Castle*

The parish church at Dacre (Pl 69) can demonstrate over 1300 years of relatively unbroken Christian worship, continuing on into the future. Such sites as this and, elsewhere in Cumbria, St Michael's Church, Workington (Zant and Parsons 2019), and Carlisle Cathedral (McCarthy 2014), are now demonstrating how this worship has changed over time, from the early beginnings in the seventh- to ninth centuries, through the political upheavals following the collapse of the Northumbrian kingdom, often most visible in the Scandinavian iconography of tenth- and eleventh-century stone sculpture, to the development of the parish system by the twelfth century, which continues to the present day. In this, the apparent continuity of alignment of boundaries, from the primary ditches in the southern churchyard and Orchard, through to the medieval churchyard boundaries that existed until the nineteenth- and twentieth centuries, is telling. A tranquil village such as Dacre seems superficially timeless, but when such sites are examined in detail, they provide important evidence of the great political and philosophical changes that have led to the country of today.

# BIBLIOGRAPHY

## Primary Sources

CA Q/RE/1/46 Cumbria Archives, *Enclosure award for Dacre and Soulby*, 1ˢᵗ October 1808

Ordnance Survey, 1900 25-inch: 1 mile map, Cumberland, LVIII.14, 2nd edn

TNA C133/44/7 The National Archives, *Inquisition Post Mortem, Ralph de Dacre, 1286*

TNA C142/1/12 The National Archives, *Inquisition Post Mortem, Humphrey Dacre, 1486*

TNA E101/370/16 f15v The National Archives, *Kiln at St Bees*

## Secondary Sources

Adamson, C, and Abramson, P, 1997 *Thornton Steward to Sowden Beck water pipeline: archaeological excavation and watching brief*, NAA, Unpubl rep

Addleshaw, G W O, 1970 *The development of the parochial system from Charlemagne (768-814) to Urban II (1088-1099)*, Borthwick Inst Hist Res, York

Addyman, P V, and Hill, D H, 1969 Saxon Southampton: a review of the evidence. Part II: Industry, trade and everyday life, *Proc Hampshire Fld Club Archaeol Soc*, **26**, 61-96

Allason-Jones, L, 1996 *Roman jet in the Yorkshire Museum*, York

Allen, J R, and Anderson, J, 1903 *The Early Christian monuments of Scotland*, **3**, Edinburgh

Anderson, S, Wells, C, and Birkett, D, 2006 The human skeletal remains, in Cramp 2006d, 481-545

Apperley, E, 2016 *Roman Papcastle (Derventio)*, Cockermouth

Appleby, A B, 1978 *Famine in Tudor and Stuart England*, Liverpool

Armstrong, A M, Mawer, A, Stenton, F M, and Dickens, B, 1950 *The place-names of Cumberland, part 1*, Engl Place-Name Soc, **20**, Cambridge

Armstrong, P, Tomlinson, D, and Evans, D H, 1991 *Excavations at Lurk Lane Beverley, 1979-82*, Sheffield Excav Rep, **1**, Sheffield

Arnold, C J, 1982 *The Anglo-Saxon cemeteries of the Isle of Wight*, London

Arwidsson, G, and Berg, G G, 1983 *The Mästermyr find: a Viking Age tool chest from Gotland*, Stockholm

Bailey, R N, 1977 The meaning of the Viking-age shaft at Dacre, *Trans Cumberland Westmorland Antiq Archaeol Soc*, n ser, **77**, 61-74

Bailey R N, 1980 *Viking Age sculpture in Northern England*, London

Bailey, R N, 2010 *The British Academy corpus of Anglo-Saxon stone sculpture, 9: Cheshire and Lancashire*, Oxford

Bailey, R N, and Cramp, R J, 1988 *The British Academy corpus of Anglo-Saxon stone sculpture, 2, Cumberland, Westmorland and Lancashire North-of-the-Sands*, London

Baillie, M G L, 1975 A horizontal mill of the 8th century AD at Drummond, Co Derry, *Ulster J Archaeol*, **38**, 25-32

Baker, F, 1988 *The occurrence of white quartz in ritual contexts in Scotland*, Unpubl BA diss, Univ Durham

Barker, D, 1993 *Slipware*, Princes Risborough

Barker, D, and Halfpenny, P, 1990 *Unearthing Staffordshire: towards a new understanding of 18ᵗʰ century ceramics*, Stoke-on-Trent

Batey, C E, with Freeman, C, 1986 Lavacroon, Orphir, Orkney, *Proc Soc Antiq Scot*, **116**, 285-300

Batt, C M, 2014 Radiocarbon dates, in McCarthy 2014, 236-9

Bayley, J, and Butcher, S, 2004 *Roman brooches in Britain: a technological and typological study based on the Richborough Collection*, Rep Res Cttee Soc Antiq London, **68**, London

Beck, H C, 1928 Classification and nomenclature of beads and pendants, *Archaeologia*, **77**, 1-76

Beresford, G, 1975 *The clay land village: excavations at Goltho and Barton Blount*, Soc Medieval Archaeol Monog Ser, **6**, London

Beresford, G, 1987 *Goltho: the development of an early medieval manor c 850-1150*, Engl Heritage Archaeol Rep, **4**, London

Biddle, M, and Kjølbye-Biddle, B, 1992 Repton and the Vikings, *Antiquity*, **66**, 36-51

Bidwell, P, 2006a Roman pottery from Jarrow, in Cramp 2006d, 325-6

Bidwell, P, 2006b Possible origin of the reused Roman building stone at Jarrow, in Cramp 2006d, 1-2

Bieler, L, 1952 *Libri Epistolarum Sancti Patricii Episcopi: introduction, text and commentary*, 2 vols, Dublin

Black, J, 2001 *British tin-glazed earthenware*, Princes Risborough

Blackwell, A, 2018 *A reassessment of the Anglo-Saxon artefacts from Scotland: material interactions and identities in early medieval northern Britain*, Unpubl PhD thesis, Univ Glasgow

Blair, J, 2005 *The church in Anglo-Saxon society*, Oxford

Blair, J, 2018 *Building Anglo-Saxon England*, Princeton

Boddington, A, 1996 *Raunds Furnells: the Anglo-Saxon church and churchyard*, Raunds Area Project, Engl Heritage Archaeol Rep, **7**, London

Booth, J, 1984 Sceattas in Northumbria, in D Hill and D M Metcalf (eds), *Sceattas in England and on the Continent*, BAR, Brit Ser, **128**, Oxford, 71-112

Bouch, C M L, 1948 *Prelates and people of the Lake Counties: a history of the Diocese of Carlisle 1133-1933*, Kendal

Bradley, J, 2015 Medieval and post-medieval pottery, in J Zant, *Penrith: the historic core*, Cumbria Archaeol Res Rep, **6**, Bowness-on-Windermere, 81-7

Bradley, J, and Howard-Davis, C, in press The medieval and post-medieval pottery, in J Zant and C Howard-Davis, *Roman and medieval Carlisle: the northern Lanes, excavations 1978-82. 2: the post-Roman period*, Lancaster Imprints, **31**

Bradley, J, and Miller, I, 2009 The medieval and post-medieval pottery, in C Howard-Davis (ed), *The Carlisle Millennium Project: excavations in Carlisle 1998-2001. Volume 2: finds*, Lancaster Imprints, **15**, Lancaster, 660-78

Bradley, J, and Miller, I, 2014 Medieval pottery, in Railton *et al* 2014, 74-88

Breeze, D J, 2006 J *Collingwood Bruce's Handbook to the Roman Wall*, 14th edn, Newcastle upon Tyne

Brierley, H (trans), 1912 *Dacre 1559-1716*, Cumberland Westmorland Antiq Archaeol Soc, Parish Register Ser, **1**, Kendal

British Geological Society (BGS), 2019 *1:250,000 UTM series of the United Kingdom and continental shelf, Lake District Sheet 54 N-04 W solid geology* [Online] Available at: http://www.largeimages.bgs.ac.uk/iip/mapsportal.html?id=1003815 (accessed 13 November 2019)

Brockington, R, and Rose, S, 2019 *Kirkoswald and Renwick*, Victoria County History Shorts, London

Brøndsted, J, 1936 Danish inhumation graves of the Viking Age, *Acta Archaeologia*, **7**, 81-228

Brooks, C M, 1987 *Medieval and later pottery from Aldwark and other sites*, Archaeology of York, **16/3**, London

Brooks, C M, 1999 The medieval and post-medieval pottery, in C Howard-Davis and M Leah, Excavations at St Nicholas Yard, Carlisle, 1996-7, *Trans Cumberland Westmorland Antiq Archaeol Soc*, n ser, **99**, 102-6

Brothwell, D R, 1981 *Digging up bones*, 3rd edn, British Museum (Natural History), Oxford

Brown, F, Clark, P, Dickson, A, Gregory, R A, and Zant, J, in prep *From an ancient Eden to a new frontier: an archaeological journey along the Carlisle Northern Development Route*, Lancaster Imprints

Brown, F, and Howard-Davis, C, 2008 *Norton Priory: monastery to museum. Excavations 1970-87*, Lancaster Imprints, **16**, Lancaster

Brugmann, B, 2004 *Glass beads from early Anglo-Saxon graves: a study of the provenance and chronology of glass beads from early Anglo-Saxon graves, based on visual examination*, Oxford

Bullion, S K, 1987 *Incremental structures of enamel and their applications to archaeology*, Unpubl PhD thesis, Univ Lancaster

Bu'lock, J D, 1960 The Celtic, Saxon and Scandinavian settlement at Meols in Wirral, *Trans Hist Soc Lancashire Cheshire*, **112**, 1-28

Burl, A, 1976 *The stone circles of the British Isles*, Newhaven and London

Carrington, P, 1975 Some types of Late Saxon pottery from Chester, *Chester Archaeol Bull*, **3**, 3-9

Carrington, P, 1994 *The English Heritage book of Chester*, London

Carver, M, 2004 An Iona of the East: the early-medieval monastery at Portmahomack, Tarbet Ness, *Medieval Archaeol*, **48**, 1-30

Carver, M, 2008 *Portmahomack: monastery of the Picts*, Edinburgh

Charles-Edwards, T, 2003 Nations and kingdoms: a view from above, in T Charles-Edwards (ed), *After Rome*, Oxford, 23-60

Charles-Edwards, T, 2013 *Wales and the Britons, 350-1064*, Oxford

Cherry, J, and Cherry, P J, 1984 Medieval pottery kiln at Muckleground, Waberthwaite, *Trans Cumberland Westmorland Antiq Archaeol Soc*, n ser, **84**, 267

Clark, J, 1995 *The medieval horse and its equipment c. 1150-c.1450*, Medieval Finds from Excavations in London, **5**, London

Clarke, G, 1979 *Pre-Roman and Roman Winchester part 2; Roman cemetery at Lankhills*, Winchester Stud, **3.2**, Oxford

Clifton Ward, J, 1878 Notes on archaeological remains in the Lake District, *Trans Cumberland Westmorland Antiq Archaeol Soc*, 1 ser, **3**, 241-65

Clogg, P, 2006 *Iron coffin fittings from Wearmouth*, in Cramp 2006d, 291-303

Colgrave, B (ed), 1940 *Two lives of St Cuthbert*, Cambridge

Colgrave, B, and Mynors, R A B (eds), 1969 *Bede's Ecclesiastical History of the English People*, Oxford

Collingwood, W G, 1912 Anglian cross-shafts at Dacre and Kirkby Stephen, *Trans Cumberland Westmorland Antiq Archaeol Soc*, n ser, **12**, 157-63

Collingwood, W G, 1923 An inventory of the ancient monuments of Cumberland, *Trans Cumberland Westmorland Antiq Archaeol Soc*, n ser, **23**, 206-76

Collingwood, W G, 1926 An inventory of the ancient monuments of Westmorland and Lancashire-North-of-the-Sands, *Trans Cumberland Westmorland Antiq Archaeol Soc*, n ser, **26**, 1-62

Collingwood, W G, 1927 *Northumbrian crosses of the pre-Norman age*, London

Cook, A M, and Dacre, M W, 1985 *Excavations at Portway, Andover 1973-1975*, Oxford Univ Cttee Archaeol Monog, **4**, Oxford

Coppack, G, 1987 Saxon and early medieval pottery, in Beresford 1987, 134-69

Craig, E, 2009 *Burial practices in Northern England c AD 650-850: a bio-cultural approach*, Unpubl PhD thesis, Sheffield Univ

Craig-Atkins, E, 2012 Chest burial: a middle Anglo-Saxon funerary rite from Northern England, *Oxford J Archaeol*, **31.3**, 317-37

Cramp, R J, 1969 Excavations at the Saxon monastic sites of Wearmouth and Jarrow, Co Durham: an interim report, *Medieval Archaeol*, **13**, 21-66

Cramp, R J, 1970 Decorated window glass and millefiori from Monkwearmouth, *Antiq J*, **50**, 327-33

Cramp, R J, 1971 The window glass, in M Pocock and H Wheeler, Excavations at Escomb Church, County Durham, *J Brit Archaeol Assoc*, **34**, 26-8

Cramp, R J, 1974 Anglo-Saxon monasteries of the North, *Scot Archaeol Forum*, **5**, 104-24

Cramp, R J, 1975 Window glass from the monastic site at Jarrow, *J Glass Stud*, **17**, 88-96

Cramp, R J, 1976 Monastic sites, in D M Wilson (ed), *The archaeology of Anglo-Saxon England*, London, 201-52

Cramp, R J, 1984 *The British Academy corpus of Anglo-Saxon stone sculpture*, **1**, *County Durham and Northumberland*, London

Cramp, R, 1997 The early medieval window glass, in Hill 1997, 322-6

Cramp, R J, 2005 *Monkwearmouth and Jarrow monastic sites*, 1, London

Cramp, R J, 2006a Bangles, beads and glass objects, in Cramp 2006d, 258-67

Cramp, R J, 2006b Lead objects, in Cramp 2006d, 303-7

Cramp, R J, 2006c The Anglo-Saxon window glass, in Cramp 2006d, 56-78

Cramp, R J, 2006d *Monkwearmouth and Jarrow monastic sites*, 2, London

Cramp, R J, 2009 Window glass and lead cames, in Evans and Loveluck 2009, 159-64

Cramp, R J, 2014 *The Hirsel excavations*, Soc Medieval Archaeol Monog, 36, London

Cramp, R, Cherry, J, and Lowther, P, 2006 Copper alloy and silver, in Cramp 2006d, 230-56

Cramp, R J, and Daniels, R, 1987 New finds from the Anglo-Saxon monastery at Hartlepool, Cleveland, *Antiquity*, 61, 424-32

Cramp, R J, and Heyworth, M P, forthcoming The window glass, in M Biddle and B Kjølbye-Biddle (eds), *Investigations at Repton*

Crossley, D W, and Aberg, F A, 1972 Sixteenth-century glass-making in Yorkshire: excavations at furnaces at Hutton and Rosedale, North Riding, 1968-1971, *J Post-medieval Archaeol*, 6, 107-59

Crummy, N, 1983 *The Roman small finds from excavations in Colchester 1971-9*, Colchester Archaeol Rep, 2, Colchester

Cunliffe, B, 1976 *Excavations at Portchester Castle*, 2, *Saxon*, Rep Res Cttee Soc Antiqs London, 33, London

Daniels, R, 1988 The Anglo-Saxon monastery at Church Close, Hartlepool, Cleveland, *Archaeol J*, 145, 158-210

Daniels, R, and Loveluck, C, 2007 *Anglo-Saxon Hartlepool and the foundations of English Christianity*, Hartlepool

Dawes, J D, and Magilton, J R, 1980 *The cemetery of St Helen on the Walls, Aldwark*, Archaeology of York: the Medieval Cemeteries, 12/1, London

Devenish, D, 1979 Excavations in Winding Street, Hastings, 1974, *Sussex Archaeol Coll*, 117, 125-34

Dickinson, S, 1985 Bryant's Gill, Kentmere: another 'Viking-period' Ribblehead?, in J R Baldwin and I D Whyte (eds), *The Scandinavians in Cumbria*, Edinburgh, 83-8

Dig-Ventures, 2021 *Site diary: our best discoveries on Lindisfarne so far (2019)* [Online] Available at: https://digventures.com/lindisfarne/timeline/types/diary/ (accessed 4 September 2021)

Downham, C, 2007 *Viking kings of Britain and Ireland: the dynasty of Ivarr to AD 1014*, Edinburgh

Drinkall, G, and Foreman, M, 1998 *The Anglo-Saxon cemetery at Castledyke South, Barton-on-Humber*, Sheffield Excav Rep, 6, Sheffield

Dymond, C W, 1891 Mayburgh and King Arthur's Round Table, *Trans Cumberland Westmorland Antiq Archaeol Soc*, 1 ser, 11, 187-219

Earle, J, and Plummer, C (eds), 1892 *Two of the Saxon chronicles*, Oxford

Edmonds, F, 2009 History and names, in J Graham-Campbell and R Philpott (eds), *The Huxley Viking hoard: Scandinavian settlement in the North West*, Liverpool, 3-12

Edmonds, F, 2015 The expansion of the kingdom of Strathclyde, *Early Medieval Europe*, 23(1), 42-66

Edwards, B J N, 1977 Medieval pottery in Lancashire, in P J Davey (ed), *Medieval pottery from excavations in the North West*, Liverpool, 108

Edwards, B J N, 1998 *Vikings in north west England: the artifacts*, Lancaster

Edwards, B J N, 2002 A group of pre-Conquest metalwork from Asby Winderwath Common, *Trans Cumberland Westmorland Antiq Archaeol Soc*, 3 ser, 2, 111-43

Edwards, D, and Hampson, R, 2005 *White salt-glazed stoneware of the British Isles*, London

Egan, G, 1998 *The medieval household: daily living c.1150-c.1450*, Medieval Finds from Excavations in London, 6, London

Egan, G, and Forsyth, H, 1997 Wound wire and silver gilt: changing fashions in dress accessories c.1400 – c.1600, in D Gaimster and P Stamper, *The age of transition: the archaeology of English culture 1400-1600*, Oxford, 215-38

Egan, G, and Pritchard, F, 1991 *Dress accessories c.1150-c.1450,* Medieval Finds from Excavations in London, **3**, London

Egan, G, and Pritchard, F, 2002 *Dress accessories c.1150-c.1450,* Medieval Finds from Excavations in London, **3**, rev edn, London

Ellison, M, 1981 The pottery, in B Harbottle and M Ellison, An excavation in the castle ditch, Newcastle upon Tyne, 1974-76, *Archaeol Aeliana,* 5 ser, **9**, 95-164

Elsworth, D, 2018 The extent of Strathclyde in Cumbria: boundaries and bought land, *Trans Cumberland Westmorland Antiq Archaeol Soc,* 3 ser, **18**, 87-108

Evison, V I, 1967 The Dover ring-sword and other sword-rings and beads, *Archaeologia,* **101**, 63-118

Evison, V I, 1987 *Dover: the Buckland Anglo-Saxon cemetery,* Engl Heritage Archaeol Rep, **3**, London

Evison, V I, 1991 Catalogue entries nos 66 (v)–(y), 67 (m)–(v), 107 (f)–(p), 108 (a)–(e), in L E Webster and J Backhouse (eds), *The making of England: Anglo-Saxon art and culture, AD 600–900,* London, 87–8, 90–3, 143–5, 146–7

Fanning, T, 1994 *Viking Age ringed pins from Dublin,* Medieval Dublin Excav 1962-81, Ser B, Dublin

Farwell, D E, and Molleson, T I, 1993 *Excavations at Poundbury, 1966-1982, volume 2: the cemeteries,* Dorset Natur Hist Archaeol Soc Monog Ser, **11**, Dorchester

Fay, A H, 1920 *A glossary of the mining and mineral industry,* USA Bureau Mines Bull, **95**, Washington

Ferguson, R, 2010 *The hammer and the cross,* London

Ferguson, R S (ed), 1877 *Miscellany accounts of the Diocese of Carlile (sic), with the terriers in to me at my primary visitation, by Bishop Nicolson, late of Carlile (sic),* Cumberland Westmorland Antiq Archaeol Soc, Extra Ser, **1**, London

Ferguson, R S, 1880 The Barony of Gilsland and its owners to the end of the sixteenth century, *Trans Cumberland Westmorland Antiq Archaeol Soc,* 1 ser, **4**, 446-85

Ferguson, R S, 1890a The bears at Dacre, *Trans Cumberland Westmorland Antiq Archaeol Soc,* 1 ser, **11**, 323-8

Ferguson, R S (ed), 1890b *A cursory relation of all the antiquities and familyes in Cumberland by Edmund Sandford* circa *1675,* Cumberland Westmorland Antiq Archaeol Soc, Tract Ser, **4**, Kendal

Field, D, and Legge, A, 2017 *Lead fixing for historic ironwork* [Online] Available at: https://www. buildingconservation.com/articles/lead-fixing-ironwork/lead-fixing-ironwork.htm (Accessed 23 March 2021)

Forbes, A P (ed), 1874 *Lives of St Ninian and St Kentigern,* Edinburgh

Foreman, M, 1991 Stone objects, in Armstrong *et al* 1991, 106-13

Francis, E B, 1913 Rayleigh Castle: new facts in its history and recent exploration on the site, *Trans Essex Archaeol Soc,* **12**, 147-85

Gaimster, D R M, 1997 *German stoneware 1200-1900: archaeology and cultural history,* London

Gallagher, D, 2016 *Morlaggan: clay tobacco pipes* [Online] Available at: https://highmorlaggan.files.wordpress. com/2016/05/high-morlaggan-pipes-report_dennis-gallagher.pdf (accessed 28 September 2021)

Garmonsway, G N (trans), 1975 *The Anglo-Saxon Chronicle,* London

Gates, T, 1983 Unenclosed settlements in Northumberland, in J C Chapman and H C Mytum (eds), *Settlement in North Britain 1000 BC-AD 1000,* BAR, Brit Ser, **118**, Oxford, 103-48

Gaunt, G, and Cool, H E M, 2011 Worked stone artefacts, in W Rodwell with C Atkins, *St Peter's Barton-upon-Humber, Lincolnshire – A parish church and its community. **1**: history, archaeology and architecture,* Oxford, 1027-33

Geddes, J, 1984 Decorative ironwork, in G Zarnecki, J Holt, and T Holland (eds), *English Romanesque art, 1066-1200: catalogue of an exhibition at the Hayward Gallery,* Arts Council, London, 296-7

Gilchrist, R, and Sloane, B, 2005 *Requiem: the medieval monastic cemetery,* London

Giles, J A (ed), 1845 *The lives of the holy abbots of Weremouth (sic) and Jarrow,* in *The Historical Works of the Venerable Bede,* **2**, London

Giles, J A (trans), 1848 *Six Old English chronicles,* London

Giles, J A (trans), 1876 *William of Malmesbury's Chronicle of the Kings of England,* London

Goodall, I, 1980 The iron objects, in P Wade-Martins, *Excavations in North Elmham Park*, E Anglian Archaeol, **9**, Gressenhall, 509-16

Goodall, I H, 1990 Locks and keys, in M Biddle, *Object and economy in medieval Winchester*, Winchester Stud, **7ii**, Oxford, 1001-36

Goodall, I H, 2005 Iron objects, in M Biddle, *Nonsuch Palace: the material culture of a noble restoration household*, Oxford, 373-411

Goodall, R, 1981 The medieval bronzesmith and his products, in D W Crossley, *Medieval industry*, CBA Res Rep, **40**, London, 3-71

Goudie, G, 1886 On the horizontal water mills of Shetland, *Proc Soc Antiq Scot*, **8**, 257-97

Graham-Campbell, J, 1973 The ninth-century Anglo-Saxon horn-mount from Burghead, Morayshire, Scotland, *Medieval Archaeol*, **17**, 43-51

Graham-Campbell, J, 1990 The metal objects, in McCarthy 1990, 181-3

Gräslund, A S, 1980 *Birka IV, the burial customs: a study of the graves on Björkö*, Uppsala

Green, B, Rogerson, A, and White, S G, 1987 *The Anglo-Saxon cemetery at Morning Thorpe, Norfolk*, 2 vols, E Anglian Archaeol Rep, **36**, Gressenhall

Gregory, R A, in prep Settlement and enclosure: the early and later medieval and post-medieval landscape, in Brown *et al* in prep

Grieg, S, 1927 Kongsgaarden, in A W Brögger and H Shetelig, *Osebergfundet*, **3**, Oslo, 1-286

Griffiths, D, Philpott, R A, and Egan, G, 2007 *Meols: the archaeology of the north Wirral coast. Discoveries and observations in the 19th and 20th centuries with a catalogue of collections*, Oxford Univ School Archaeol Monog Ser, **68**, Oxford

Groves, S, 2011 Social and biological status in the Bowl Hole early medieval burial ground, Bamburgh, Northumberland, in D Petts and S Turner (eds), *Early medieval Northumbria: kingdoms and communities, AD 450-1100*, Turnhout, 241-66

Guido, M, 1978 *The glass beads of the Prehistoric and Roman periods in Britain and Ireland*, Rep Res Cttee Soc Antiq London, **35**, London

Hadley, D, 2000 Equality, humility, and non-materialism? Christianity and Anglo-Saxon burial practices, *Archaeol Rev Cambridge*, **17**(2), 149-78

Haggarty, G, 1980 The pottery, in G Ewart, Excavations at Stirling Castle, 1977-1978, *Post-medieval Archaeol*, **14**, 36-45

Halcrow, S E, and Tayles, N, 2011 The bioarchaeological investigation of children and childhood, in S C Agarwal and B A Glencross (eds), *Social bioarchaeology*, Chichester, 333-60

Hall, D W, 1996 Blind date - Scottish medieval pottery industries, *Tayside Fife Archaeol J*, **2**, 126-9

Hall, R A, and Whyman, M, 1996 Settlement and monasticism at Ripon, North Yorkshire, from the 7th to 11th centuries AD, *Medieval Archaeol*, **40**, 62-150

Hamerow, H, 1993 *Excavations at Mucking 2: the Anglo-Saxon settlement: excavations by M U Jones and W T Jones*, Engl Heritage Archaeol Rep, **21**, Swindon

Harden, D B, 1956 Glass vessels in Britain and Ireland, AD 400-1000, in D B Harden (ed), *Dark Age Britain: studies presented to E T Leeds*, London, 132-67

Harden, D B, 1976 The glass, in Cunliffe 1976, 232-34

Harden, D B, 1983 The glass hoard, in Johnson 1983, 81-8

Hardy, W (ed), 1876 *Willelmi Malmesiriensis Monarchi Regum Anglorum at que Historia Novella*, **1**, London

Hare, J N, 1985 *Battle Abbey: the Eastern Range and the excavations of 1978-80*, Engl Heritage Archaeol Rep, **2**, London

Hawkes, S, and Dunning, G C, 1961 Soldiers and settlers in Britain, fourth to fifth century: with a catalogue of animal-ornamented buckles and related belt-fittings, *Medieval Archaeol*, **5**, 1-70

Heawood, R, and Howard-Davis, C, 2002 Two early medieval settlement sites in eastern Cumbria? *Trans Cumberland Westmorland Antiq Archaeol Soc*, 3 ser, **2**, 145-69

Hencken, H, 1950 *Lagore Crannog: an Irish royal residence of the 7th to 10th centuries AD*, Proc Royal Irish Acad, **53**, Dublin

Henderson, J, 1991 The glass, in Armstrong *et al* 1991, 124–30

Henstead, A, Hildyard, R J C, and Wood, P, 2010 *Nottingham salt-glazed stoneware 1690-1800*, Nottingham

Higgins, D A, 2015 Clay tobacco pipes, in S Rowe, J Speakman, and D A Higgins, Early post-medieval ceramics from No 91 Church Road, Rainford, in Philpott 2015, 138-58

Higham, N J, 1986 *The northern counties to AD 1000*, Harlow

Higham, N J, 1992a *Rome, Britain and the Anglo-Saxons*, London

Higham, N J, 1992b Northumbria, Mercia and the Irish Sea Norse, 893-926, in J Graham-Campbell (ed), *Viking treasure from the North West: the Cuerdale Hoard in its context*, Liverpool, 21-30

Higham, N J, 1993 *The kingdom of Northumbria, AD 350-1100*, Stroud

Higham, N J, 2004 *A frontier landscape: the North West in the Middle Ages*, Macclesfield

Higham, N J, and Jones, G B D, 1975 Frontiers, forts and farmers: Cumbria aerial survey, 1974-5, *Archaeol J*, **132**, 16-53

Hill, P, 1997 *Whithorn and St Ninian: the excavation of a monastic town 1984-91*, Stroud

Hillson, S, 2005 *Teeth*, Cambridge

Hinton, D A, 1974 *Catalogue of the Anglo-Saxon ornamental metalwork 700-1100 in the Department of Antiquities, Ashmolean Museum*, Oxford

Hinton D A, 1990 Belt-hasps and other belt-fittings, in M Biddle, *Object and economy in medieval Winchester*, 2, Winchester Studies, **7.ii**, Artefacts from Medieval Winchester, Oxford, 539-42

Hirst, S M, 1985 *An Anglo-Saxon inhumation cemetery at Sewerby, East Yorkshire*, York

Hoaen, A W, and Loney, H L, 2004 Bronze and Iron Age connections: memory and persistence in Matterdale, Cumbria, *Trans Cumberland Westmorland Antiq Archaeol Soc*, 3 ser, **4**, 39-54

Hodges, R, 1981 *The Hamwih pottery: the local and imported wares from thirty years excavations and their European context*, CBA Res Rep, **37**, London

Hodgkinson, D, Huckerby, E, Middleton, R, and Wells, C, 2000 *The lowland wetlands of Cumbria*, North West Wetlands Surv, **6**, Lancaster Imprints, **8**, Lancaster

Hodgson, C, 1832 An account of some antiquities found in a cairn, near Hesket-in-the-Forest, in Cumberland, in a letter from Mr Christopher Hodgson to the Rev John Hodgson, Secretary, *Archaeol Aeliana*, 1 ser, **2**, 106-9

Hollister, C W, 2001 *Henry 1*, New Haven

Hope-Taylor, B, 1977 *Yeavering: an Anglo-British centre of early Northumbria*, DOE Archaeol Rep, **7**, London

Howard-Davis, C L E, 1992 The glass, in J H Williams, Excavations at Brougham Castle, 1987, *Trans Cumberland Westmorland Antiq Archaeol Soc*, n ser, **92**, 118-19

Howard-Davis, C L E, 1996a The early medieval ceramics, in Oliver *et al* 1996, 149-51

Howard-Davis, C L E, 1996b The copper alloy, in Oliver *et al* 1996, 156-7

Howard-Davis, C L E, 1996c Ceramic objects, in Oliver *et al* 1996, 151-2

Howard-Davis, C L E, 2009 Other copper-alloy objects, in C L E Howard-Davis, *The Carlisle Millennium Project: excavations in Carlisle 1998-2001*, 2, *Finds*, Lancaster Imprints, **15**, Lancaster, 725-45

Hudleston, F, 1932 The recent find in Dacre churchyard, *Trans Cumberland Westmorland Antiq Archaeol Soc*, n ser, **32**, 75-7

Hunter, F, 1997 The jet, shale, and cannel coal, in Hill 1997, 441-3

Hunter, F, 2008 Jet and related materials in Viking Scotland, *Medieval Archaeol*, **52**, 103-18

Hunter, J R, 1979 The glass, in J H Williams, *St Peter's Street, Northampton: excavations 1973-1976*, Northampton, 298

Hunter, J R, 1980 The glass, in P Holdsworth, *Excavations at Melbourne Street, Southampton, 1971-76*, CBA Res Rep, **33**, London, 59-72

Hunter, J R, 1981 The medieval glass industry, in D W Crossley, *Medieval industry*, CBA Res Rep, **40**, London, 143-50

Hurst, J G, 1959 Middle Saxon pottery, in G C Dunning, J G Hurst, J N L Myres, and F Tischler, Anglo-Saxon pottery: a symposium, *Medieval Archaeol*, **3**, 13-31

Hurst, J G, Neal, D S, and van Beuningen, H J E, 1986 *Pottery produced and traded in North-west Europe 1350-1650*, Rotterdam Pap, **6**, Rotterdam

Hurst Vose, R, 1980 *Glass*, London

Hurst Vose, R, 1994 Excavations at the 17th century glasshouse at Haughton Green, Denton, near Manchester, *J Post-medieval Archaeol*, **28**, 26-30

Hurst Vose, R, 1995 Excavations at the c.1600 Bickerstaffe Glasshouse, Lancashire, *J Merseyside Archaeol Soc*, **9**, 1-24

Hurst Vose, R, 2008 Glass vessels, in Brown and Howard-Davis 2008, 358-70

Hutchinson, W, 1794 *The history of the county of Cumberland and some places adjacent*, Carlisle

Hyde, M, and Pevsner, N, 2010 *The buildings of England: Cumbria: Cumberland, Westmorland and Furness*, rev edn, Harmondsworth

Ifor Evans, B, 1940 *A short history of English literature*, Harmondsworth

Ingleborough Archaeology Group, 2015a *The Crummack Dale Project: excavations of three early medieval steadings and a lime kiln*, Ingleton

Ingleborough Archaeology Group, 2015b *Excavation of a multi-period site at Top Cow Pasture, Selside, Upper Ribblesdale*, Ingleton

James, S, Marshall, A, and Millett, M, 1984 An early medieval building tradition, *Archaeol J*, **141**, 182-215

Jarvis, R A, Bendelow, V C, Bradley, R I, Carroll, D M, Furness, R R, Kilgour, I N L, and King, S J, 1984 *Soils and their use in Northern England*, Soil Surv England Wales Bull, **10**, Harpenden

Jennings, N, 2003 *Clay dabbins: vernacular buildings of the Solway Plain*, Cumberland Westmorland Antiq Archaeol Soc, Extra Ser, **30**, Kendal

Jennings, S, 1981 *Eighteen centuries of pottery from Norwich*, E Anglian Archaeol, **13**, Norwich

Jobey, G, 1967 Excavation at Tynemouth Priory and Castle, *Archaeol Aeliana*, 4 ser, **45**, 33-104

Johns, C, 1996 *The jewellery of Roman Britain: Celtic and Classical tradition*, London

Johnson, D, 2012 *Excavation of an early medieval structure in Upper Pasture, Horton-in-Ribblesdale, North Yorkshire*, Ingleton

Johnson, S, 1983 *Burgh Castle: excavations by Charles Green 1958-61*, E Anglian Archaeol Rep, **20**, Gressenhall

Jope, E M, and Hodges, H W M, 1955 Medieval pottery from Castle Street, in R Hogg, Excavations in Carlisle 1953, *Trans Cumberland Westmorland Antiq Archaeol Soc*, n ser, **55**, 79-107

Kapelle, W E, 1979 *The Norman Conquest of the North: the region and its transformation 1000-1135*, London

Keevil, G D, 1989 Early medieval finds from Carlisle Cathedral, *Bull CBA Churches Cttee*, **26**, 16-18

Kilbride-Jones, H E, 1938 Glass armlets in Britain, *Proc Soc Antiq Scot*, **72**, 366-95

King, A, 1978 Gauber High Pasture, Ribblehead: an interim report, in R A Hall (ed), *Viking Age York and the North*, CBA Res Rep, **27**, London, 21-5

King, A, 2004 Post-Roman upland architecture in the Craven dales and the dating evidence, in J Hines, A Lane, and M Redknap (eds), *Land, sea and home: settlement in the Viking period*, Soc Medieval Archaeol Monog, **20**, Leeds, 335-44

King, J E (trans), 1930 *Baedae Opera Historica*, 2 vols, London

Kirby, D P, 1962 Strathclyde and Cumbria: a survey of historical development to 1092, *Trans Cumberland Westmorland Antiq Archaeol Soc*, n ser, **62**, 77-94

Kjølbye-Biddle, B, 1995 The finds: iron-bound coffins and coffin fittings from the pre-Norman cemetery, in Phillips and Heywood 1995, 489-521

Knight, B, 1985 Cames, in Hare 1985, 154-6

Koch, U, 1977 *Das Reinhengraberfelds bei Schretzheim*, Berlin

Kruse, S E, 1986 The Viking Age silver hoard from Scotby, the non-numismatic element, *Trans Cumberland Westmorland Antiq Archaeol Soc*, n ser, **86**, 79-83

Lang, J T, 2002 *The British Academy corpus of Anglo-Saxon stone sculpture, 6: North Yorkshire*, Oxford

Lawson, A, 1976 Shale and jet objects from Silchester, *Archaeologia*, **105**, 241-57

Leahy, K, and Coutts, C M, 1987 *The lost kingdom: the search for Anglo-Saxon Lindsey*, Scunthorpe

Leech, R H, and Gregory, R A, 2012 *Cockermouth, Cumbria: archaeological investigation of three burgage plots in Main Street*, Cumbria Archaeol Res Rep, **3**, Carlisle

Lewis, C P, and Thacker, A T (eds), 2003 *A history of the county of Chester, 5/1, the city of Chester: general history and topography*, Victoria County History, London

Lockett, T A, 1986 *Creamware and Pearlware: the fifth exhibition from the Northern Ceramic Society*, Stoke-on-Trent

Loveluck, C, 2007 *Rural settlement, lifestyles and social change in the later first millennium AD: Anglo-Saxon Flixborough in its wider context*, Excavations at Flixborough, **4**, Oxford

Lowe, C E, 1991 New light on the Anglian 'minster' at Hoddom, *Trans Dumfriesshire Galloway Natur Hist Archaeol Soc*, 3 ser, **66**, 11-35

Lowe, C, 2006 *Excavations at Hoddom, Dumfriesshire: an early ecclesiastical site in south-west Scotland*, Edinburgh

Lucy, S, and Reynolds, A, 2002 Burial in early medieval England and Wales: past, present and future, in S Lucy and A Reynolds (eds), *Burial in early medieval England and Wales*, London, 1-14

McCarthy, M R, 1990 *A Roman, Anglian and medieval site at Blackfriars Street, Carlisle: Excavations 1977-9*, Cumberland Westmorland Antiq Archaeol Soc, Res Ser, **4**, Kendal

McCarthy, M R, 2002 *Roman Carlisle and the lands of the Solway*, Stroud

McCarthy, M R, 2014 A post-Roman sequence at Carlisle Cathedral, *Archaeol J*, **171**, 185-257

McCarthy, M R, and Brooks, C M, 1988 *Medieval pottery in Britain AD 900-1600*, Leicester

McCarthy, M R, and Brooks, C M, 1992 The establishment of a medieval pottery sequence in Cumbria, England, in D Gaimster and M Redknap, *Everyday and exotic pottery from Europe: studies in honour of John G Hurst*, Oxford, 21-37

McCarthy, M R, and Taylor, J, 1990 Pottery of the Anglo-Saxon to post-medieval periods, in McCarthy 1990, 301-11

Mackreth, D F, 1986 Brooches, in D Gurney, *Settlement, religion and industry on the Fen-edge: three Romano-British sites in Norfolk*, E Anglian Archaeol, **31**, Gressenhall, 61-72

Mace, T, 2015 The medieval pottery, in D W Elsworth and T Mace, *Aldingham Motte, Cumbria, and its environs in the medieval period*, Cumbria Archaeol Res Rep, **5**, Kendal, 33-7

Mainman, A J, 1990 *Anglo-Scandinavian pottery from Coppergate*, Archaeology of York: the Small Finds, **16/5**, York

Mainman, A, and Rogers, N, 2000 *Craft, industry and everyday life*, Archaeology of York: the Small Finds, **17/14**, York

Maldonaldo Ramirez, A D, 2011 *Christianity and burial in late Iron Age Scotland AD 400-650*, Unpubl PhD thesis, Univ Glasgow [Online] Available at: http://theses.gla.ac.uk/2700 (accessed 12 July 2019)

Manby, T, 1986 Anglo-Saxon, the cemetery, in T Manby, Thwing 1985, *Yorkshire Archaeol Soc, Prehist Res Section Bull*, **23**, 3

Manning, W H, 1985 *Catalogue of the Romano-British iron tools, fittings and weapons in the British Museum*, London

Mannix, J, and Whellan, W, 1847 *History, gazetteer, and directory of Cumberland*, Beverley

Margary, I, 1957 *Roman roads in Britain*, 2 vols, London

Marshall, P, Bronk Ramsey, C, Dunbar, E, and Zant, J, 2019 Radiocarbon dating, in Zant and Parsons 2019, 107-15

Mathews, Canon A, 1891 The Dacre stone, *Trans Cumberland Westmorland Antiq Archaeol Soc*, 1 ser, **11**, 226-9

Matthews, C L, and Chadwick-Hawkes, S, 1985 Early Saxon settlements and burials on Puddlehill near Dunstable, Bedfordshire, in S Chadwick-Hawkes, J Campbell, and D Brown (eds), *Anglo-Saxon studies in archaeology and history*, **4**, Oxford Univ Cttee Archaeol, Oxford, 59-115

Megaw, B R S, 1937 A list of ancient beads found in Man, *J Manx Mus III*, **53**, 237

Miller, I, 2011 The post-Roman pottery from the medieval defensive ditches, in J Zant, I Miller, Q Mould, and C Howard-Davis, The northern defences of medieval Carlisle: excavations at Rickergate, 1998-9, in R M Newman (ed), *Carlisle: Excavations at Rickergate, 1998-9 and 53-55 Botchergate*, Cumbria Archaeol Res Rep, **2**, Kendal, 30-8

Miller, I, 2012 Post-Roman pottery, in Leech and Gregory 2012, 37-46

Miller, M, 1975 The commanders at Arthuret, *Trans Cumberland Westmorland Antiq Archaeol Soc*, n ser, **75**, 96-118

Moore, J W, 1966 An Anglo-Saxon settlement at Wykeham, North Yorkshire, *Yorkshire Archaeol J*, **41**, 403-44

Moore, D T, and Oakley, G E, 1979 The hones, in J H Williams, *St Peter's Street, Northampton: excavations 1973-1976*, Northampton, 280-3

Morgan, P (ed), 1978 Cheshire, in J Morris (ed), *Domesday Book*, **26**, Chichester

Mortimer, J R, 1905 *Forty years researches in British and Saxon burial mounds of East Yorkshire*, London

Murphy, T, 1959 The changing pattern of dentine exposure in human tooth attrition, *Amer J Phys Anthropol*, **17**, 167-78

Mynors, R A B, Thomson, R M, and Winterbottom, M, 1998 *William of Malmesbury:* Gesta Regum Anglorum, The History of the English Kings, **1**, Oxford

Naismith, R, 2017 *Medieval European coinage, with a catalogue of the coins in the Fitzwilliam Museum, Cambridge. 8: Britain and Ireland c. 400–1066*, Cambridge

Newman, C, and Newman, R, 2007 The medieval period research agenda, in M Brennand (ed), *The archaeology of North West England: an archaeological research framework for the North West Region, Volume 2, research agenda and strategy*, Archaeol North West, **9**, Manchester, 95-114

Newman, R M, 2006 The early medieval period resource assessment, in M Brennand (ed), *The archaeology of North West England: an archaeological research framework for North West England 1: resource assessment*, Archaeol North West, **8**, Manchester, 91-114

Newman, R M, 2007 Who was here in the Dark Ages?, in Appleby Archaeology Group, *People and the land: settlement in the Eden Valley, prehistoric until the present day. Papers presented at the one-day conference held on 6 October 2007, at Appleby Grammar School, Appleby-in-Westmorland*, Appleby, 23-32

Newman, R M, 2011 The early medieval period, in M Brennand and K Stringer (eds), *The making of Carlisle: from Romans to railways*, Cumberland Westmorland Antiq Archaeol Soc, Extra Ser, **35**, Kendal, 69-84

Nicholson, A, 1997 The iron, in Hill 1997, 404-32

Nicolson, J, and Burn, R, 1777 *The history and antiquities of the Counties of Westmorland and Cumberland*, 2 vols, London

Noel Hume, I, 1969 *A guide to artifacts of Colonial America*, New York

Northern Archaeological Associates (NAA), 2002 *Cemetery excavations at Village Farm, Spofforth, North Yorkshire*, Unpubl rep

Oakley, G E, and Hall, A D, 1979 The spindle whorls, in J H Williams, *St Peter's Street, Northampton: excavations 1973-1976*, Northampton, 286-9

Oakley, G E, and Webster, L E, 1979 The copper alloy objects, in J H Williams, *St Peter's Street, Northampton: excavations 1973-1976*, Northampton, 248-64

Oliver, T, Howard-Davis, C, and Newman, R M, 1996 A post-Roman settlement at Fremington, near Brougham, in J Lambert, *Transect through time: the archaeological landscape of the Shell North West Ethylene Pipeline*, Lancaster Imprints, **1**, Lancaster, 127-69

Oosthuizen, S, 2019 *The emergence of the English*, Leeds

O'Sullivan, D M, 1980 *A re-assessment of the Early Christian archaeology of Cumbria*, Unpubl MPhil thesis, Univ Durham

O'Sullivan, D M, 1985 Cumbria before the Vikings: a review of some 'Dark Age' problems in North-West England, in J R Baldwin and I D Whyte (eds), *The Scandinavians in Cumbria*, Edinburgh, 17-35

Oswald, A, Hildyard, R J C, and Hughes, R G, 1982 *English brown stoneware 1670-1900*, London

Ottaway, P, 1986 *Iron objects from Dacre*, Lancaster Univ Archaeol Unit, Unpubl rep

Ottaway, P, 1992a *Anglian and Anglo-Scandinavian ironwork from 16-22 Coppergate, York*, Archaeology of York: the Small Finds, **17/6**, York

Ottaway, P, 1992b Iron, in Rahtz and Meeson 1992, 80-6

Ottaway, P, 1996 The ironwork, in Hall and Whyman 1996, 99-113

Ottaway, P, 2006 *Iron objects from Village Farm, Spofforth (N Yorks): assessment report*, Northern Archaeological Associates, Unpubl rep

Ottaway, P, 2007 The coffin fittings, in C Loveluck and D Atkinson, *The early medieval settlement remains from Flixborough, Lincolnshire: the occupation sequence, c AD 600-1000*, Excavations at Flixborough, **1**, Oxford, 122-4

Ottaway, P, 2010 Iron objects, in J Nolan, The early medieval cemetery at the castle, Newcastle upon Tyne, *Archaeol Aeliana*, 5 ser, **39**, 269-75

Ottaway, P, 2014 The ironwork, in McCarthy 2014, 224-7

Ottaway, P, 2015 The ironwork from the cemetery, in P Halkon, M Millett, and H Woodhouse (eds), *Hayton, East Yorkshire: archaeological studies of the Iron Age and Roman landscapes*, Yorkshire Archaeol Rep, **7**, Leeds, 475-7

Ottaway, P, nd a *Iron objects from excavations by Martin Biddle and Birthe Kjølbye-Biddle at Repton, Derbyshire*, Unpubl rep

Ottaway, P, nd b *Iron objects from T Manby's excavations at Thwing, East Riding of Yorkshire*, Unpubl rep

Ottaway, P, nd c *The Melton iron-bound chest (excavations by Peter Halkon at Melton, East Riding of Yorkshire*, Unpubl rep

Ottaway, P, with Edwards, G, Watson, J, and Panter, I, 2009 Iron domestic fixtures, fittings and implements, in D H Evans, and C Loveluck, *Life and economy in early medieval Flixborough c AD 600-1000: the artefact evidence*, Excavations at Flixborough, **2**, Oxford, 166-87

Ottaway, P, and Rogers, N S, 2002 *Craft, industry, and everyday life: finds from medieval York*, Archaeology of York: the Small Finds, **17/15**, York

Owen-Crocker, G R, 2004 *Dress in Anglo-Saxon England*, Woodbridge

Padley, T G, 2010 *Roman and medieval Carlisle, the Lanes Volume* **1***: excavations at Old Grapes, Crown and Anchor and Lewthwaite's Lanes 1981-2. Fascicule 2: the Roman and medieval finds* [Online] Available at: http://archaeologydataservice.ac.uk/archives/view/southlanes_eh_2010/ (accessed 7 April 2021)

Pantos, A, 2003 'On the edge of things': boundaries in early medieval Britain, *Anglo-Saxon Archaeol Hist*, **12**, 38-49

Parson, W, and White, W, 1829 *A history, directory and gazetteer of Cumberland and Westmorland*, Leeds

Parsons, A J, Newman, R M, Rowland, S, and McIntyre, L, 2019 Discussion, in Zant and Parsons 2019, 119-47

Paterson, C, with Parsons, A J, and Howard-Davis, C, 2019 Early medieval finds, in Zant and Parsons 2019, 47-60

Paterson, C, Parsons, A J, Newman, R M, Johnson, N, and Howard-Davis, C, 2014 *Shadows in the sand: excavation of a Viking-age cemetery at Cumwhitton, Cumbria*, Lancaster Imprints, **22**, Lancaster

Paterson, C, and Tweddle, D, 2014 Copper-alloy, in McCarthy 2014, 211-22

Peers, C, and Radford, C A R, 1943 The Saxon monastery of Whitby, *Archaeologia*, **89**, 27-88

Pennar, M (trans), 1988 *The poems of Taliesin*, Lampeter

Périn, P, 1980 *La datation des tombes Merovingiennes*, Geneva

Pestell, T, 2009 The styli, in D H Evans and C Loveluck, *Life and economy in early medieval Flixborough c AD 600-1000: the artefact evidence*, Excavations at Flixborough, **2**, Oxford, 123-37

Pevsner, N, 1967 *The buildings of England: Cumberland and Westmorland*, Harmondsworth

Pevsner, N, 1988 *The buildings of England: North Lancashire*, rev edn, Harmondsworth

Phillips, D, 1985 *Excavations at York Minster* **2***: the cathedral of Archbishop Thomas of Bayeux*, London

Phillips, D, and Heywood, B, 1995 *Excavations at York Minster* **1***: from Roman fortress to Norman cathedral*, London

Philpott, R A, 1990 *A silver saga: Viking treasure from the North West*, Liverpool

Philpott, R (ed), 2015 *The pottery and clay tobacco pipe industries of Rainford, St Helens: new research*, The Archaeology of Rainford, **1**, Liverpool

Phythian-Adams, C, 1996 *Land of the Cumbrians*, Aldershot

Pilet, C, 1981 *Archaeologie de les necropoles de Giberville: Exposition organisée par le Musee de Normandie, Chateau de Caen, Eglise Saint George, 8/4-25/5/1981*, Caen

Pirie, E, 1996 *Coins of the Kingdom of Northumbria, c 700-867*, Llanfyllin

PAS, 2005 *Finger ring: SUR-085774* [Online] Available at: https://finds.org.uk/database/artefacts/record/id/198237 (Accessed 12 January 2021)

PAS, 2012 *Finger ring: KENT-65F288* [Online] Available at: https://finds.org.uk/database/artefacts/record/id/490515 (Accessed 12 January 2021)

PAS, 2014a *Strap fitting: DUR-738FF5* [Online] Available at: https://finds.org.uk/database/artefacts/record/id/604908 (Accessed 12 January 2021)

PAS, 2014b *Strap fitting: LVPL-1B78B7* [Online] Available at: https://finds.org.uk/database/artefacts/record/id/632653 (Accessed 12 January 2021)

PAS, 2016a *Buckles* [Online] Available at: https://finds.org.uk/counties/findsrecordingguides/buckles/ (accessed 27 January 2021)

PAS, 2016b *Pins* [Online] Available at: https://finds.org.uk/counties/findsrecordingguides/pins/ (accessed 27 January 2021)

PAS, 2016c *Mount: NARC-BD1E51* [Online] Available at: https://finds.org.uk/database/artefacts/record/id/804406 (Accessed 12 January 2021)

PAS, 2016d *Buckle: LIN-1E8803* [Online] Available at: https://finds.org.uk/database/artefacts/record/id/768205 (Accessed 12 January 2021)

PAS, 2017a *Buckle: SOM-BB843B* [Online] Available at: https://finds.org.uk/database/artefacts/record/id/822731 (accessed 27 January 2021)

PAS, 2017b *Buckle: WILT-DDE14C* [Online] Available at: https://finds.org.uk/database/artefacts/record/id/780308 (accessed 27 January 2021)

PAS, 2019 Tubular padlocks, in *Padlocks* [Online] Available at: https://finds.org.uk/counties/findsrecordingguides/padlocks/#Tubular_Padlocks (accessed 26 July 2021)

PAS, 2021 *Candle holders* [Online] Available at: https://finds.org.uk/counties/findsrecordingguides/candle-holders/ (accessed 17 September 2021)

Prehistoric Ceramics Research Group, Study Group for Roman Pottery, and Medieval Pottery Research Group, 2016 *A standard for pottery analysis in archaeology*, Draft **4** [Online] Available at: https://www.archaeologists.net/sites/default/files/Standard_for_PotteryAnalysis_Full_Draft_v4.pdf (accessed 19 June 2019)

Price, J, 1996 Fragment of a glass bangle, in Hall and Whyman 1996, 114-15

Price, J, 1997 The Roman glass, in Hill 1997, 294-6

Pritchard, F, 1991 Small finds, in A Vince (ed), *Finds and environmental evidence: aspects of Saxo-Norman London*, **2**, London Middlesex Archaeol Spec Pap, **12**, London, 120-278

Radford, C A R, 1940 Small bronzes from St Augustine's, Canterbury, *Antiq J*, **20**, 506-8

Rahtz, P A, 1969 *Excavations at King John's hunting lodge, Writtle, Essex 1955-7*, Soc Medieval Archaeol Monog Ser, **3**, London

Rahtz, P, 1974 Monasteries as settlements, *Scot Archaeol Forum*, **5**, 125-35

Rahtz, P A, 1979 *The Saxon and medieval palaces at Cheddar*, BAR, Brit Ser, **65**, Oxford

Rahtz, P, and Meeson, R, 1992 *An Anglo-Saxon watermill at Tamworth: excavations in the Bolebridge Street area of Tamworth, Staffordshire in 1971 and 1978*, CBA Res Rep, **83**, London

Railton, M, Bradley, J, Miller, I, Stoakley, M, Jackson, D, O'Meara, D, and Hall, A, 2014 Peter Gate, Cumwhinton: archaeological investigation of a medieval rural site, *Trans Cumberland Westmorland Antiq Archaeol Soc*, 3 ser, **14**, 63-102

Read, B, 2008 *Hooked clasps and eyes*, Langport

Richards, J D, 1991 *Viking Age England*, London

Roberts, B K, 1987 *The making of the English village*, London

Roberts, C, and Cox, M, 2003 *Health and disease in Britain, from prehistory to the present day*, Stroud

Roberts, I, and Whittick, C, 2013 Pontefract: a review of the evidence for the medieval town, *Yorkshire Archaeol J*, **85**, 68-96

Rodwell, W, 1981 *The archaeology of the English church*, London

Rodwell, W, and Rodwell, K, 1982 St Peter's Church, Barton-on-Humber, excavation and structural study 1978-81, *Antiq J*, **62**, 283-315

Roesdahl, E, 1977 *Fyrkat, en Jysk Vikingeborg 2: Oldsagerne og Gravpladsen*, Copenhagen

Roesdahl, E, 1991 *The Vikings*, London

Roesdahl, E, Graham-Campbell, J, Connor, P, and Pearson, K (eds), 1981 *The Vikings in England*, London

Rogers, N, 1993 *Anglian and other finds from Fishergate*, Archaeology of York, The Small Finds, **17/9**, York

Rogers, N, 2004a *Report on the iron small finds from Viewley Bridge, Ainderby Steeple*, Northern Archaeological Associates, Unpubl rep

Rogers, N, 2004b *Report of the small finds from Norton NBS03*, Northern Archaeological Associates, Unpubl rep

Rogers, N, 2009 The pins, in D H Evans and C Loveluck, *Life and economy in early medieval Flixborough, c AD 600-1000: the artefact evidence,* Excavations at Flixborough, **2**, Oxford, 32-82

Rogers, N, Hines, J, Ottaway , P, Jones, J, and Panter, I, 2009 Brooches, in D H Evans and C Loveluck, *Life and economy in early medieval Flixborough, c AD 600-1000: the artefact evidence,* Excavations at Flixborough, **2**, Oxford, 1-7

Rollason, D, 2003 *Northumbria 500-1100: creation and destruction of a kingdom,* Cambridge

Rooke, H, 1792 Druidical and other British remains in Cumberland, *Archaeologia,* **10**, 105-13

Rose, R K, 1982 Cumbrian society and the Anglo-Norman church, in S Mews (ed), *Religion and national identity: studies in church history,* **18**, Oxford, 119-35

Ross, S, 1991 *Dress pins from Anglo-Saxon England: their production and typo-chronological development,* Unpubl DPhil thesis, Univ Oxford [Online] Available at: uuid:3976b772-fccd-41fe-b8c7-f4ae08ac0295 (accessed 9 January 2019)

Rowland, S, Harrison, S, and Bradley, J, in prep Excavations in the Presbytery, Furness Abbey, Cumbria

Rynne, C, 1989 The introduction of the vertical watermill into Ireland: some recent archaeological evidence, *Medieval Archaeol,* **33**, 21-31

St Joseph, J K, 1978 Aerial reconnaissance: recent results, *Antiquity,* **52**, 236-8

Sawyer, P H, 1978 *From Roman Britain to Norman England,* London

Sayles, G O, 1964 *The medieval foundations of England,* London

Schmid, P, 1970 *Das fruhmittelalterliche graberfeld von Dunum, kreis Wittmund (Grabung 1967-8),* Neue Ausgrabungen und Forschungen in Niedersachsen, **5**, Hildersheim

Schour, I, and Massler, M, 1941 The development of the human dentition, *J American Dental Assoc,* **23**, 1946-55

Seaby, H A, and Seaby, P J, 1988 *Coins of England and the United Kingdom,* 24th edn (S Mitchell and B Read eds), London

Sharp, J E E S, and Stamp, A E, 1910 Inquisitions post mortem, Edward II, file 55, in *Calendar Inquisitions Post Mortem,* **6**, *Edward II,* British History Online [Online] Available at: http://www.british-history.ac.uk/inquis-post-mortem/vol6/pp19-35-0 (accessed 6 October 2021)

Shoesmith, R, 1980 *Excavations at Castle Green,* Hereford City Excavations, **1**, CBA Res Rep, **36**, London

Shoesmith, R, 1985 *The finds,* Hereford City Excavations, **3**, CBA Res Rep, **56**, London

Shotter, D C A, 2004 *Romans and Britons in north-west England,* 3rd edn, Lancaster

Simpson, G, 1979 Some British and Iberian penannular brooches and other early types in the Rhineland and the *Decumates Agri, Antiq J,* **59**, 319-42

Skene, W F, 1868 *The four ancient books of Wales,* 2 vols, Edinburgh

Slowikowski, A, 2011 *'Genius in a cracked pot': late medieval reduced wares, a regional synthesis,* Medieval Pottery Res Group, **4**, London

Smith, A H, 1969 *The place-names of the North Riding of Yorkshire,* Engl Place-name Soc, **5**, Cambridge

Smith, D, 1987 The stone, in Beresford 1987, 195-6

Stafford, P, 1989 *Unification and conquest: a political and social history of England in the tenth and eleventh centuries,* Oxford

Stretton, E H A, 1994 *Dacre Castle,* Penrith

Swanton, M (trans and ed), 2000 *The Anglo-Saxon chronicles,* London

Taylor, H M, and Taylor, J, 1965 *Anglo-Saxon architecture,* 3 vols, Cambridge

Taylor, J, and Webster, L, 1984 A Late Saxon strap-end mould from Carlisle, *Medieval Archaeol,* **28**, 178-81

Thomas, C, 1971a *The early Christian archaeology of North Britain,* London

Thomas, C, 1971b *Britain and Ireland in Early Christian times AD 400-800,* London

Thomas, C, 1981 *Christianity in Roman Britain to AD 500,* London

Thomas, G, 2000 *A survey of Late Anglo-Saxon and Viking-age strap-ends from Britain,* Unpubl PhD thesis, Univ London [Online] Available at: uk.bl.ethos.248475 (accessed 9 September 2021)

Thomas, G, 2009a Strap ends, in D H Evans and C Loveluck, *Life and economy in early medieval Flixborough, c AD 600-1000: the artefact evidence*, Excavations at Flixborough, **2**, Oxford, 8-16

Thomas, G, 2009b The hooked tags, in D H Evans and C Loveluck, *Life and economy in early medieval Flixborough, c AD 600-1000: the artefact evidence*, Excavations at Flixborough, **2**, Oxford, 17-22

Thompson, W N (ed), 1906 *The episcopal registers of Carlisle: the register of Bishop John de Halton*, Cumberland Westmorland Antiq Archaeol Soc Record Ser, **2**, 3 vols, Kendal

Thompson, V, 2004 *Death and dying in later Anglo-Saxon England*, Woodbridge

Trueman, M R G, 1985 *Lead fittings from Monkwearmouth and Jarrow*, Unpubl MA diss, Univ Durham

Tweddle, D, 1986 *Finds from Parliament Street and other sites in the city centre*, Archaeology of York: the Small Finds, **17/4**, London

UCLA, 2012 *Carolingian culture at Reichenau and St Gall* [Online] Available at: http://www.stgallplan.org/index.html (Accessed 10 March 2021)

University of Notre Dame, 1997 *Regal British copper coinage: introduction* [Online] Available at: https://coins.nd.edu/ColCoin/ColCoinIntros/Br-Copper.intro.html (accessed 28 September 2021)

Viner, B, and Leech, R H, 1982 Bath Gate cemetery 1969-76, in A McWhirr, L Viner, and C Wells, *Romano-British cemeteries at Cirencester*, Cirencester Excavations, **2**, Cirencester, 69-111

Wade-Martins, P, 1980 *North Elmham*, E Anglian Archaeol Rep, **9**, Gressenhall

Walton Rogers, P, 1997 *Textile production at 19-22 Coppergate*, Archaeology of York, the Small Finds, **17/11**, York

Walton Rogers, P, 2009 Textile production, in D H Evans and C Loveluck, *Life and economy in early medieval Flixborough, c AD 600-1000: the artefact evidence*, Excavations at Flixborough, **2**, Oxford, 281-316

Waterman, D M, 1959 Late Saxon, Viking and early medieval finds from York, *Archaeologia*, **97**, 59-105

Watkins, J R, 1986 A late Anglo-Saxon sword from Gilling West, N Yorkshire, *Medieval Archaeol*, **30**, 93-9

Weetch, R, 2014 *Brooches in Late Anglo-Saxon England within a North West European context: a study of social identities between the eighth and eleventh centuries*, Unpubl PhD thesis, Univ Reading [Online] Available at: uk.bl.ethos.655741 (accessed 11 January 2019)

Welch, M, 1992 *Anglo-Saxon England*, London

Whellan, W, 1850 *The history and topography of the counties of Cumberland and Westmorland*, Pontefract

White, A J, 1977 Silverdale, in P J Davey (ed), *Medieval pottery from excavations in the North West*, Liverpool, 102-3

White, A J, 2000 Pottery making at Silverdale and Arnside, *Trans Cumberland Westmorland Antiq Archaeol Soc*, n ser, **100**, 285-91

White, A, 2009 *Black Burton (Burton-in-Lonsdale); the Yorkshire pottery village*, Lancaster

White, R H, 1987 *Roman and Celtic objects from Anglo-Saxon graves: a catalogue and an interpretation of their use*, Unpubl PhD thesis, Univ Liverpool [Online] Available at: uk.bl.ethos.383363 (accessed 9 September 2021)

White, R H, 1988 *Roman and Celtic objects from Anglo-Saxon graves: a catalogue and an interpretation of their use*, BAR, Brit Ser, **191**, Oxford

Whitehead, R, 2003 *Buckles 1250-1800*, Witham

Whitehead, S, Williams, D, and Mace, T, 2013 Excavation of medieval burgage plots to the rear of 130-136 Stricklandgate, Kendal, *Trans Cumberland Westmorland Antiq Archaeol Soc*, 3 ser, **13**, 89-115

Whitelock, D, 1974 *The beginnings of English society*, Pelican History of England, **2**, Harmondsworth

Williams, G, 2008 Raiding and warfare, in S Brink (ed), *The Viking world*, London, 193-203

Willmott, H, 2002 *Early post-medieval vessel glass in England c. 1500-1670*, CBA Res Rep, **132**, York

Wilmott, T, 1997 *Birdoswald: excavations of a Roman fort on Hadrian's Wall and its successor settlements, 1987-92*, Engl Heritage Archaeol Rep, **14**, London

Wilson, A R, Cardwell, P, Cramp, R J, Evans, J, Taylor-Wilson, R H, Thompson, A, and Wacher, J R, 1996 Early Anglian Catterick and Catraeth, *Medieval Archaeol*, **40**, 1-61

Wilson, D M, 1964 *Anglo-Saxon ornamental metalwork 700-1100 in the British Museum: catalogue of the antiquities of the Later Saxon period*, London

Wilson, D M, 1976 Craft and industry, in D M Wilson (ed), *The archaeology of Anglo-Saxon England*, Cambridge, 253-81

Winchester, A J L, 1987 *Landscape and society in medieval Cumbria*, Edinburgh

Woolf, A, 2007 *From Pictland to Alba 789-1070*, Edinburgh

Yorke, B, 2006 *The conversion of Britain 600-800*, Harlow

Youngs, S M, Clark, J, and Barry, T B, 1983 Medieval Britain and Ireland in 1982, *Medieval Archaeol*, **27**, 161-229

Youngs, S M, Clark, J, and Barry, T B, 1987 Medieval Britain and Ireland in 1986, *Medieval Archaeol*, **31**, 110-91

Zant, J, and Parsons, A J, 2019 *St Michael's Church, Workington: excavation of an early medieval cemetery*, Lancaster Imprints, **26**, Lancaster

# INDEX

193

kingdom of  4, 7, 50, 137, 171  *see also* king, of
    Northumbria; kingdom of, Northumbria
    Bernicia  4, 5
    collapse of royal house  158
    Deira  4, 5
Northumbrians  4, 5, 138, 156
Norton (Teesside)  143
Norton Priory (Cheshire)  130, 157

Ogbourne St George (Wiltshire)  52
Orchard  1, 14-16, 19, 37-41, 48, 52, 72, 76, 84, 96, 112-14,
    119, 125, 132-4, 151-2  *see also* Churchyard
    demolition evidence in  112, 132-3
Ormside  10
Orphir (Orkney)  *see* Cemetery, Orphir
Osberht  *see* King, of Northumbria
Oseberg Ship  68, 71, 142
Oswald  *see* King, of Northumbria
Oswiu  *see* King, of Northumbria
Otley  13
Owain  *see* King, of the Cumbrians
Oxford  56

Padlock  123, 126, 168
    cylindrical  126
    medieval  168
    octagonal section  126
Pagan  10, 57, 71, 79, 82-3, 140  *see also* Burial, pagan
Parishes  160-2, 166, 169
Pateley Bridge (North Yorkshire)  137
Pennines  2, 4, 5, 7, 8, 143, 167
Penrith  1, 7, 11-12, 50, 133, 137, 161-3, 167, 170
Penwortham (Lancashire)  7
Pin  37, 51-2, 54-5, 71, 93, 123-5, 148
    bar  124-5
    head
        baluster-headed  54-5, 93
        biconical (rounded)  54-5
        styliform  55
    ringed  54-5, 72-3, 140
    shank  55
    stylate  93
Platform, house/structure  97-8, 107, 163
Ploughing  43, 160, 163, 165  *see also* Agricultural activity
    medieval  160
Portable Antiquities Scheme  170
Portchester (Hampshire)  78, 82
Portmahomack (Easter Ross)  *see* monasteries,
    Portmahomack
Post-medieval  58, 73, 82-3, 85-6, 94, 115-16, 123, 125,
    129-30, 132-4
    activity  87, 91, 116
Posthole  21, 24, 30-3, 37, 42, 44, 47, 58, 79, 98, 100-8,
    114, 121, 151, 163, 165
    alignment  101, 103-4
    group of  33, 98, 101, 103

isolated  37, 44, 101
Pottery  7, 16, 21, 28, 30, 42, 44, 46-8, 93-4, 96-8, 101,
    104-5, 108, 119, 121-3, 167-8
    Cistern, bung-hole  168
    Cistercian-ware  119, 168
    coarseware  37, 48, 93
    cooking pot  122
    earthenware  121, 133, 167
        brown-glazed  133
    fabric  47, 50-1, 96, 119, 121-3, 167-8
        grey  86
        medieval  121
        post-medieval  110
        thirteenth-fourteenth-century  121-2
    fine orange oxidised ware  48
    German stoneware  133
    glaze spots  122
    glazing  84
        olive glaze  122
    green-glazed ware  168
        reduced  167
    greenware, reduced  121-2
    greyware, reduced  48
    gritty redware  121
    Hambleton-type  119
    handmade  7, 21
    jugs  119, 121-2, 167-8
    Low Countries slipware  122
    medieval  16, 21, 28, 30, 37-8, 40, 46-7, 50, 93-4, 96, 98,
        108, 110, 112, 114-16, 119, 122, 166-7, 170
        decoration, combed  122
        greenware  119
    middle Saxon  50
    native pottery  7
    North Eastern wares  119
    Northern Gritty ware  119, 167
    pipkins  121-2, 168
    pitcher (handled)  50
    post-medieval  92, 94, 108, 112, 114-15, 133
        earthenware, slip-trailed black  133
        Martincamp flask  133
    prehistoric  47
    production  167
    rim  57, 82, 122-3, 132-3
        square  122
    Roman  30, 37, 48
        coarseware  37, 93
        mortarium  48
        samian ware  21, 28, 33, 48, 112
    Scarborough ware  119
    skillet  121
    Staffordshire slipware  122
    wasters  119, 122, 167
Poundbury (Dorset)  147
Pre-Conquest period  53-5, 58, 71, 82-4, 92, 126-7, 143-4
Pre-Norman period  12-13, 16, 33, 37-8, 40, 44, 50, 59,
    69, 71, 110, 117, 148, 160-2
Preston (Lancashire)  7